PRINT CULTURE and the FORMATION of the ANARCHIST MOVEMENT in SPAIN, 1890-1915

PRINT CULTURE and the FORMATION of the ANARCHIST MOVEMENT in SPAIN, 1890-1915

James Michael Yeoman

Print Culture and the Formation of the Anarchist Movement in Spain, 1890–1915
© 2022 James Michael Yeoman

This edition © 2022, AK Press (Chico and Edinburgh)
Published by arrangement with Routledge, an imprint of the Taylor & Francis Group,
an Informa Business

ISBN: 978-1-84935-458-5
Library of Congress Control Number: 2022935896

AK Press
370 Ryan Ave. #100
Chico, CA 95973
www.akpress.org
akpress@akpress.org

AK Press
33 Tower St.
Edinburgh EH6 7BN
Scotland
www.akuk.com
akuk@akpress.org

The above addresses would be delighted to provide you with the latest AK Press distribution
catalog, which features books, pamphlets, zines, and stylish apparel published and/or
distributed by AK Press. Alternatively, visit our websites for the complete catalog, latest
news, and secure ordering.

Cover artwork by Ysidro Pergamino
Printed in the United States

To Laura. To our future together.

Contents

Charts

Maps

Tables

Acknowledgments

This book began as a PhD thesis made possible by a scholarship provided by the University of Sheffield. Research was supported by the generosity of the Department of History research fund, the Royal Historical Society and the Economic History Society. Research was conducted at the Internationaal Instituut voor Sociale Geschiedenis, the Biblioteca Nacional de España, the Hemeroteca Municipal de Madrid, the Archivo Histórico Provincial de Cádiz, the Archivo Municipal de Jerez de la Frontera, Cardiff University, the London School of Economics and the British Library. My thanks to all of these institutions.

My interest in Spanish history began in 2007, when I signed up to a second-year undergraduate course led by Mary Vincent, mainly on the basis that I knew nothing about the subject. Since then, Mary has guided and encouraged my interests, through a specialist subject class, MA, several years of PhD supervision and now in my post-doctoral career. Mary continues to be a source of academic and personal support for which I am immensely grateful.

It was an excellent piece of timing to begin a PhD at the same time as Danny Evans and Matthew Kerry, both of whom have been great colleagues and friends with whom I have shared many experiences, thoughts, ambitions and frustrations. I would also like to thank Richard Cleminson, Pol Dalmau, Miriam Dobson, Carl Levy, Bob Moore, Caoimhe Nic Dháibhéid, and Gareth Stockey for their thoughts, advice and support. It has been a pleasure to work in the Department of History at Sheffield alongside so many intelligent, welcoming and fun postgraduate students. My thanks to you all, in particular Kate Davison, Liz Goodwin, Harry Mawdsley, Hannah Parker, Mark Seddon and Stephanie Wright. Since 2017 I have made many new colleagues, and more importantly, friends, at Sheffield who deserve my thanks, above all the Red Deer Writers Collective—Emily Baughan, Eliza Hartrich, Chris Millard, Simon Stevens, Danica Summerlin, Andrew Tompkins and Simon Toner—who helped immensely in revising the text (and in general are amazing people and comrades). My thanks also to James Pearson at the University of Sheffield, who designed the maps in this book.

I consider myself lucky to have many fun, supportive, interesting and interested friends in Sheffield, Liverpool, Manchester, London and beyond. I would not be at this point without my sisters Frances and Sophie, and thanks also to Rhod, Dave, Elsa, Martha, Jo and Spike for being great. There are no amount of words to express how grateful I am to my mum for her love and support. Finally, to my dad, who passed away six years to the day I am writing these words. I know he would be proud of me, as I will forever be of him.

Introduction

Between 1890 and 1915 the anarchist movement in Spain collapsed, reformed, and then expanded at an unprecedented scale and speed. Print culture was central to these developments, performing two essential functions within the movement. First, print was the site where anarchist ideas and practice came together, forming the ideological underpinning of the movement; second, print and the groups who produced it allowed anarchists to communicate between localities, providing a structure to a movement which lacked a formal organisation. In this way, print culture helped to maintain anarchism in Spain during periods of extreme pressure; it gave the movement the means to expand to new areas and develop new ideas; and it laid the foundations for a new, national confederation of anarchist-syndicates—the Confederación Nacional del Trabajo (CNT)—which underwent massive expansion from 1915 onwards, and by 1919 was the largest anarchist organisation in the world.

This investigation into anarchist print culture does not only explore what anarchism was, but also what it meant; not only *why* anarchism survived and thrived in Spain as it faded in Europe and the Americas, but also *how* it did so. It is notable how few recent studies are concerned with the transition of anarchism from the nineteenth to the twentieth century, a 'complex but fundamental period' in the construction of anarchist political culture and the future development of the movement.[1] The period 1890–1915 is more commonly treated as belonging to a wider timeframe, either as the appendage of the nineteenth-century anarchist movement, which emerged with the First International in Spain around 1870 and reached its apex in the 1880s, or as simply the prelude to the era of anarcho-syndicalism, beginning with the CNT in 1910. In contrast, this study concentrates exclusively on these twenty-five years.

Foregrounding print culture emphasises the role of networks, exchanges and collaborative development, seeking to situate Spanish anarchism within the long history of bottom-up political movements. While the size and particular manifestation of anarchism in Spain was unusual, the movement's formation and workings have much in common with smaller, contemporary anarchist movements in Europe and the Americas.

More broadly, the fact that anarchism in Spain had unique characteristics does not set it apart from other working-class mobilisations; rather it was 'as normal or as abnormal as any other labour movement' over the turn of the century, all of which had idiosyncratic features.[2] Anarchism in Spain should not, therefore, be contrasted too sharply with social democratic and communist movements in other countries, as if the latter were a homogenous, 'typical' historical development. In terms of strategy, the focus of anarchist movements on active, bottom-up engagement and loose, decentred structures is comparable to, for example, labourers' and dockers' societies in the mid-eighteenth century, European revolutionaries in 1848, progressive movements in the late nineteenth-century USA, the social movements of the 1960s and contemporary anti/alter-globalisation movements.[3] Indeed, while the latter are often held up as novel forms of grassroots activism, their 'decentred forms of political power are nothing new, but have been characteristic of many resistance and oppositionist movements throughout history'.[4] Focusing on how the many strands of anarchist ideology and practice came together in Spain, through the lens of its print culture, thus has resonances across historical eras and contexts, and allows us to see anarchism in Spain not as an historical aberration, but as one of many similar and comparable movements in history.

Anarchism in Spain, 1870–1890

Anarchist ideology was the product of two revolutionary traditions. The first was rooted in eighteenth-century liberal theories of natural rights and individual autonomy. Nineteenth-century anarchism took this position to a seemingly logical, if extreme, conclusion, regarding any interference in the free choices of the individual as anathema to their liberty. Anarchist ideology was thus hostile to the exercise of power, including within trade unions and political parties, and ultimately sought to abolish hierarchical institutions such as the state, army, police and Church. In the latter half of the nineteenth century this tradition was fused with revolutionary socialism, which articulated demands for a reordering of society along collective, egalitarian principles of distribution. The anarchist revolution was conceived with these two underlying principles in mind: it would be brought about by a revolutionary cataclysm led by the working class, who would be acting on their own, natural desire to abolish authority in the name of liberty. The result would be Anarchy: a society based on natural, egalitarian principles and free from the exercise of power.[5]

Like contemporary Marxism, anarchism saw capitalism as central to the subjugation of the working class. Yet, unlike Marxism, anarchism regarded the State and Church as additional, independent sources of oppression, which did not originate in economic processes. Together these manifestations of power formed a 'nefarious trilogy of authority':

the State (often synonymous with the military and police forces, as the embodiment of direct, physical force), the Church (which practised cultural violence against Reason and Science [*sic.*]), and Capital (which maintained a structural form of violence through wage labour).[6] Variations on these elements of 'the trilogy' or the 'triple aspect of the social question' dominated anarchist analyses in Spain, Europe and the Americas from the mid-nineteenth century onwards.

Anarchism was also distinct in the means it proposed for class struggle. Its adherents saw no legitimacy in seizing political and economic power, and instead sought the state's immediate destruction. They rejected the notion of a 'party of the workers', interpreting the founding principle of the First International—'the emancipation of the working class must be conquered by the working class themselves'—as a disavowal of parliamentary politics.[7] In place of 'politics', anarchists proposed three means of struggle: direct confrontation, which would meet the repressive violence of the state head on; education, to combat religion and liberate culture; and organisation, which would allow for resistance against capitalism. These were presented as both opposites and solutions to the trilogy of authority. In the words of one contributor to the paper of the Cádiz mariners' union: 'the master robs you, the government slaughters you, ignorance maligns you . . . unite to be strong; study to be conscious . . . make war against your enemies'.[8]

Anarchism began to draw support in Spain in the late 1860s. Unlike most of its international contemporaries, the Spanish branch of the First International (Federación Regional de España: FRE) was dominated by supporters of the Russian anarchist Mikael Bakunin, committed to principles of revolutionary, bottom-up unionism which would later define anarchist organisational practice. The first publications of the movement infused traditional working-class publishing in Spain with the new, revolutionary ideas and rhetoric of the FRE. In 1872 the FRE and its press split, reflecting the divisions between the Marxist and Bakuninist factions of the international labour movement following the repression of the Paris Commune. Bakuninism remained the dominant ideology of the FRE, represented in papers such as *El Condenado* (Madrid, 1872–1873), while a smaller, breakaway group of Marxists formed around *La Emancipación* (Madrid, 1871–1873), which included many of the founding members of the Spanish Socialist Party (Partido Socialista Obrero Español: PSOE) on its editorial board, including Pablo Iglesias, who led the PSOE from its foundation in 1879 until his death in 1925.[9]

Soon afterwards the FRE was repressed. During the brief First Republic (1873–1874) the FRE instigated a strike in Alcoy (Alicante) and briefly gained control of the town. A similar insurrection took place in Sanlúcar de Barrameda (Cádiz), alongside numerous strikes and federalist uprisings unconnected to the movement, most significantly in Cartagena.[10] As the Republic collapsed, order was restored by General Manuel Pavía, who led a fierce repression against those involved in the uprisings. In January 1874 Pavía dissolved the Cortes (Parliament) and restored the monarchy. The FRE was declared illegal and the organisation, and its press, was forced into clandestinity.[11]

The Restoration system which replaced the First Republic formed the political context in which the anarchist movement operated over the turn of the century. The Restoration settlement was designed by Antonio Cánovas del Castillo (Prime Minister 1875–1879; 1879–1881; 1884–1885; 1890–1892; 1895–1897) as a constitutional monarchy underwritten by mass suffrage, which safeguarded stability and peaceful transitions of power. Elections were rigged to ensure that the two main dynastic power blocs—Cánovas' Conservatives and the Liberals of Práxedes Mateo Sagasta (Prime Minister 1881–1883; 1885–1890; 1892–1895; 1897–1899; 1901–1902)—rotated in power, with voting returns largely determined in advance. This system guaranteed that there would be no significant electoral challenge to the political status quo until the turmoil produced by the First World War.[12] In this context, parliamentary socialism struggled to convince the working class that the pursuit of electoral victory was worthwhile. The PSOE thus remained marginal within Spanish electoral politics and only won its first seat in 1910.[13]

In contrast, the anarchist movement flourished in the early 1880s. It returned to legality in 1881, when the FRE was reformed as the Federación de Trabajadores de la Región España (FTRE). The FTRE grew rapidly; according to Anselmo Lorenzo, the organisation claimed a membership of 49,561 in 1882, primarily from Andalucía (60.63 per cent) and Cataluña (26.60 per cent), with smaller areas of support in Valencia (4.75 per cent), the two Castillas (3.13 per cent), Galicia (1.43 per cent), the Basque regions (1.43 per cent), Aragon (1.39 per cent) and Murcia (0.53 per cent).[14] The FTRE's growth was supported by a flourishing of anarchist periodicals, including its semi-official organ *La Revista Social* (Madrid, 1881–1885) whose subscription grew from 2,700 to 18,000 in its first year of publication.[15]

Like the FRE, however, the FTRE soon faced a double pressure of repression and internal divisions. In the winter of 1882–3 a series of murders in Jerez (Cádiz) were blamed on anarchist cells, in what became known as the 'Mano Negra' ('Black Hand') affair. The 'Mano Negra' was used to justify an extensive repression against the workers' movement in Andalucía, which stifled the movement in the region for almost a decade.[16] Shortly afterwards, disputes emerged within the FTRE between anarcho-collectivists and anarcho-communists over questions of organisation. The former had dominated the movement since 1870, and based their revolutionary strategy on the collective power of trade unions. In contrast, anarcho-communists were hostile to unions—which they distrusted as 'reformist'—and limited their organisation to small groups of dedicated militants. Although a minority, anarcho-communists gained prominence within the movement in the mid-1880s through papers such as *La Autonomía* (Sevilla, 1883–1884), which engaged in public attacks against the dominance of collectivists in the FTRE, leading to schism. The loose structure of the FTRE was unable to cope with the pressure caused by such disputes, and was eventually disbanded in 1888.[17] It was only in the absence of an anarchist labour federation in Spain that the socialist movement saw an opportunity to create its own national labour organisation, the Unión General de Trabajadores (UGT), which was set up in 1888 with Iglesias at its head.[18] Although the FTRE had collapsed, a number of local anarchist-orientated labour federations continued to exist into the 1890s. Anarchists also remained free to publish, and began to look to alternative strategies for revolutionary change, such as the hitherto neglected area of education, exemplified in journals such as *Acracia* (Barcelona, 1886–1888).[19] Nevertheless, there had been a tangible shift from the optimism of the early 1880s, as anarchists remained split over doctrinal questions and were distanced from the wider labour movement.

Over the following twenty-five years, anarchists in Spain sought to recapture, and, if possible, surpass their former strength. By 1915 this had been largely achieved. Anarchism was once again the ideological preference of the working class in its heartlands and had attracted tens of thousands of adherents following expansion into new areas of support. By 1919 the anarcho-syndicalist CNT claimed the support of 800,000 members, making it the largest anarchist organisation in world history.[20] This development was in complete contrast to anarchist movements elsewhere in Europe and the Americas, all of which were surpassed by their Marxist and democratic socialist counterparts in the early twentieth century. Something remarkable occurred to the anarchist movement in Spain in the years between the collapse of the FTRE and the consolidation of the CNT. Within this organisational vacuum, print became the primary mechanism by which Spanish anarchism operated on a national scale, instigating new practices, new opportunities and new challenges. At no other time in the history of the movement was print culture as central to anarchism in Spain as between 1890 and 1915, when it played a decisive role in the cultural formation of anarchism as an identity, an ideology and a movement.[21]

Approaches to Anarchism

This study is not an all-encompassing analysis of anarchist ideology, which treats anarchism as a 'general libertarian trend or sensibility in all human societies for all historical epochs'.[22] Such an approach does little to explain the experience or meaning of anarchism, and attributes historical developments to great thinkers and abstract ideas, rather than the means by which they were understood and put into practice.[23] The development of anarchism in Spain was not a linear story of success, or a neat progression from one dominant thinker to the next. There were many ideas that were adopted and then discarded, many wrong turns and failures in the history of anarchism in Spain, which were as important to the movement as its achievements. Indeed, one of the few consistent features of the anarchist movement from 1890 to 1915 was its constant experimentation. A great range of ideas became incorporated within anarchist ideology from 1890 to 1915, transforming an already diffuse set of principles and practices into a vast, nebulous entity, which permitted almost as many contradictions as convergences within its broad framework.

By far the most comprehensive analysis of anarchist ideology prior to the creation of the CNT in 1910 is Álvarez Junco's *La ideología política del anarquismo español* (1976), which gives full recognition to the multifaceted nature of the movement. Most of the ideological themes and developments discussed in this study are examined in depth in *La ideología política*, yet where Álvarez Junco is concerned with the history of ideas and ideology, here I seek to examine the related, and complementary, question of how these ideas were constructed, presented and understood.[24] Like *La ideología política*, Litvak's *Musa libertaria* (1981) remains a key text on anarchism in Spain over the turn of the century, in this case regarding anarchist culture. Litvak correctly identifies anarchist culture—its art, literature, theatre, poetry and ascetics—as a formative part of anarchist ideology, but there is little comment on the medium by which this culture was produced and transmitted, aside from one separate and rather limited section dedicated to periodicals.[25] Perhaps the closest example of this type of study is George Esenwein's *Anarchist Ideology and the Working-Class Movement in Spain*, which remains the best work in English of the nineteenth-century movement. Esenwein rarely loses sight of the process by which ideology was constructed and stresses the role of the movement's print and associational culture, given particular emphasis in his analysis of the 1880s.[26]

Following Álvarez Junco, Litvak and Esenwein, this book examines the anarchist movement in its own words. It argues that one can only confidently call activity 'anarchist' if its participants actively engaged with the movement, its ideology and its aims. As such, it rejects the methodology of studies that set out with preconceptions of what anarchism was, often equating it simply with sporadic, violent behaviour, regarded as out-of-sync with accepted narratives of historical development. Such approaches observe anything which resembles this behaviour as 'anarchist', regardless of its connection to the ideas, discourses, practice or aims of the movement.[27] This approach is flawed, not least because it follows the logic of the Spanish state during periods of repression, which greatly exaggerated the extent of anarchist support, particularly in the agrarian south of Spain where anarchism has long been conflated with rural revolt.[28] Only a cursory examination of anarchist sources would show that while militants saw it as their duty to encourage and steer peasant revolts, they were often exasperated at the disengagement of *campesinos* (fieldworkers) from the ideas of the movement. A similar, although less prevalent tendency can also be found in studies of labour activism in Spain, which again equate all violent, grassroots industrial action as anarchist in nature, even if the workers in question gave no indication of their political beliefs, or belonged to unions in direct conflict with the anarchist movement. Again, this takes a pre-defined view of what anarchism was—sporadic, confrontational, naïve—and applies this to anything that fits this behaviour. Rural rebellion and confrontational labour relations were common strategies across Spain to settle social grievances. Anarchists wanted to channel this activity into a more circumscribed and effective revolutionary movement, yet at the turn of the twentieth century they were far from achieving this goal. What these scholars are observing is thus not necessarily anarchism, or the anarchist movement.

A related tendency is to portray anarchism as a 'spunky millenarian leftover from an older era'.[29] This view of anarchism was evident in contemporary studies of the movement, such as the deeply patronising works of Bernaldo de Quirós, and the much more nuanced and rigorous *Historia de las agitaciones campesinos andaluzas* (1929) by Juan Díaz del Moral, both of which informed Gerald Brenan's analysis of anarchism in his influential *The Spanish Labyrinth* (1943). Brenan attributed the 'millenarian fervour' of anarchism to the 'Spanish temperament', which valued 'the spiritual' above the material and rejected authority as a matter of course.[30] Eric Hobsbawm, in turn, drew heavily on this interpretation for his analysis of anarchist millenarianism in *Primitive Rebels*, reframing Brenan's nationalistic, racial explanation of Spanish anarchism into one centred on Spain's stuttering industrial development.[31] In Hobsbawm's view, anarchism was akin to Anabaptism: a furious, spiritual rebellion of the dispossessed poor, who were unable (rather than unwilling) to articulate their grievances against inequality through Marxist-socialism because of the under-development of Spanish industrial capitalism.[32]

The millenarian hypothesis was widely criticised in a series of studies that emerged following the end of the Franco dictatorship in 1975, including those of Álvarez Junco, Litvak and Temma Kaplan.[33] Such works portrayed the millenarian hypothesis as mechanistic, underpinned by racial, nationalistic or economic determinism, and unable to explain the complexity of anarchist theory, the movement's internal disputes, its support amongst the urban working class or the rationality of anarchist tactics of class struggle.[34] Yet in stressing anarchism's 'modern' qualities, critics of the millenarian school maintained a distinction between modern political movements and 'pre-modern', 'primitive' religions, only now regarding anarchism more favourably as a forward-looking, 'modern' ideology. As with the millenarian hypothesis, this view is overly-schematic and limited, and rests on assertion that religious and political practice are incompatible.[35]

Like advocates of the millenarian hypothesis, those who stress anarchism's 'modern,' secular qualities also overlook anarchism as expressed and practised by anarchists, which at times did resemble a religion. Indeed, it would be surprising if anarchism were not influenced by the dominant, Catholic culture of Spain, and more generally the millenarian-revolutionary tone of most European socialist movements.[36] Anarchists had martyrs and saints, missionaries and proselytisers, baptisms, weddings and funerals, all of which resembled Spanish Catholic practice. This study does not wish to play down these comparisons, as it does not see the label of 'religion', or the claim that anarchism was highly 'emotional' as a sign that it was 'pre-modern' and therefore an insult that requires defending. At times anarchism exhibited the characteristics of a religion, while at others it resembled a more 'modern' political movement. It can as easily be compared with contemporary global justice movements as with Anabaptism. Like the former, anarchism was a decentred, transnational movement, which emphasised local action; like the latter, it required faith and passionate commitment from its adherents. The historiographical argument outlined above is thus regarded as redundant in this study, as it is based on false distinctions between religion and millenarianism on the one hand, and politics and modernity on the other. Like all religious, social and political movements, anarchism at the turn of the century was a complex mixture of emotion, thought, tradition, experience and reason, all understood within a specific economic, cultural and political context. Rather than reducing anarchism to a straightforward analytical model, we must acknowledge its complexity and attempt to understand it in its own words.

The Value of Print

Anarchist print culture operated at a time when mass media, such as the daily press, was expanding in Spain, yet had much more in common with older forms of media, such as weekly periodicals, pamphlets and broadsides.[37] This type of print culture has been examined most thoroughly in studies of seventeenth-century England, which have demonstrated how the invention of the periodical press and expansion of pamphleteering played a significant role in reflecting, creating and sustaining political communities in the fractious political climate of the English Civil War (1642–1651).[38] The study of print culture has therefore become associated with the period when it first became widely accessible, yet books, pamphlets, periodicals and broadsides never lost their significance, and remained crucial for movements such as the Quakers in England, the political factions of revolutionary France, and radical abolitionists in Antebellum USA. In all of these movements, print assisted in the formation of common identities through shared ideas and practices.[39] Books, pamphlets and periodicals served the purposes of the anarchist movement in Spain just as ably, and while it was no longer novel, this form of print culture was far from being anachronistic in the early twentieth century despite the growth of mass media.

In this study, the detailed material aspects of anarchist print culture—the paper, printing presses, binding and typographic layout—are not of particular concern. These technical aspects of anarchist printing were largely passed over to commercial printers, which meant that the production and style of the movement's periodicals and pamphlets were not particularly distinctive from those of its political and cultural rivals, such as the socialist, republican and Catholic press. What made the movement's print culture 'anarchist' was its content and those who created it, the ways in which it was distributed, the effect that it had on ideology and practice.

Print is the only means to evaluate the movement in its own words, and the only viable indicator of anarchist identity prior to the creation of the CNT. No reliable membership statistics are available for the movement from 1890 to 1915, nor was there an undisputed national voice, such as a regular daily newspaper which can be taken as a mouthpiece for the movement as a whole. Detailed sources of information on anarchist sociability and cultural practices are also sparse for many areas in Spain during this period.[40] Other sources, such as police records or those relating to labour unrest, are both limited in number and myopic in their interest in (or paranoia towards) anarchist violence and conspiracy. There is a small number of autobiographies and personal papers which focus on this period, yet most—for example Federico Urales' *Mi vida*—suffer from being written in hindsight by exceptional individuals, often with idiosyncratic experiences and agendas.[41] Such sources may add colour and detail to a history of the movement but they are not representative of the broader experience of anarchism in Spain.

In contrast, a wealth of print sources allows us to examine anarchism from the perspective of a broad range of those who engaged with the movement. Between 1890 and 1915, almost 300 anarchist periodicals and journals were launched by groups across the whole of Spain, publishing around 7,300 issues between them [see Table 0.1 and Map 0.1]. These were grassroots publications, written by ordinary members of the movement in collaboration with one another. As such, they offer access to the anarchist experience as conceived by anarchists, in a way that no other material can provide. Yet while they are valuable, anarchist papers are problematic sources. They rarely present the kind of information required in order to fully recreate an historical 'event', as the reports they give on activities such as meetings, speeches and strikes are often conflicted and hard to corroborate. What they do provide, however, is evidence of how such events were portrayed to others. While we may question the account of a particular congress, for example, the fact that it was written, published and distributed in the press allows us to examine

Table 0.1 Anarchist Titles and Issues Published in Spain by Province, 1890–1915

	No. Titles	No. Issues	Title: Issue Ratio	Surviving Issues
Spain	**298**	**7328**	**1:25**	**4930**
Andalucía	*53*	*314*	*1:6*	*211*
Almería	2	15		0
Cádiz	16	183		148
Córdoba	1	6		0
Granada	2	2		0
Huelva	6	29		24
Jaén	1	1		0
Málaga	7	10		2
Sevilla	18	68		37
Aragón	*10*	*32*	*1:3*	*13*
Huesca	1	1		0
Zaragoza	9	31		13
Asturias	*18*	*396*	*1:22*	*184*
Castilla la Nueva	*24*	*1266*	*1:53*	*1101*
Madrid	23	1246		1100
Toledo	1	20		1
Castilla la Vieja	*10*	*143*	*1:14*	*126*
Logroño	3	4		2
Santander	1	42		42
Valladolid	6	97		82
Cataluña	*107*	*3299*	*1:31*	*2448*
Barcelona	95	3149		2396
Gerona	5	52		25
Lérida	3	49		2
Tarragona	4	49		25
Extremadura	*3*	*107*	*1:36*	*10*
Badajoz	3	107		10
Galicia	*17*	*565*	*1:33*	*202*
A Coruña	14	557		196
Pontevedra	3	8		6
Islas Baleares	*4*	*516*	*1:129*	*451*
Islas Canarias	*9*	*167*	*1:19*	*21*
León	*1*	*1*	*1:1*	*0*
Salamanca	1	1		0
Murcia	*11*	*231*	*1:21*	*14*
Provincias Vascongadas	*9*	*45*	*1:5*	*34*
Guipúzcoa	2	10		7
Vizcaya	8	36		27
Valencia	*22*	*246*	*1:12*	*115*
Alicante	10	62		35
Valencia	12	184		80

Sources: Francisco Madrid Santos, 'La prensa anarquista y anarcosindicalista en España desde la I Internacional hasta el fin de la Guerra Civil,' (PhD thesis), Universidad Central de Barcelona, 1988–89), 339–642 and author's research.

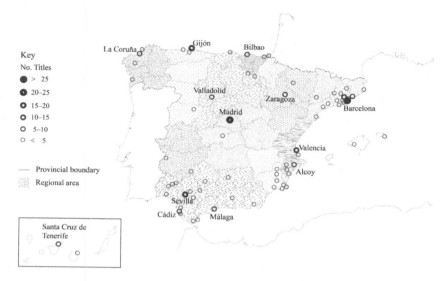

Map 0.1 Areas of Anarchist Publishing in Spain, 1890–1915.
Source: Map created by James G. Pearson.

how such activity was represented and informed the movement's collective knowledge.

This book uses print sources in three ways. First, print is used to establish how the movement represented events, ideas and discussions. As noted above, this is the most typical way in which anarchist papers have been used in works on the pre-CNT movement, from studies of ideology and culture, to discussions of the workings of the early CNT, since they are the only abundant source of information for the period 1890 to 1915.

Second, the press is used as a proxy for the movement itself. Taken collectively, the anarchist press can be used to trace the developments within Spanish anarchism on a broad scale. To illustrate this approach, we can use the press to evaluate the general state of the movement at various points in its history [see Chart 0.1]. Beginning in 1870, there was a short burst in anarchist publishing, followed by an almost total absence during the first six years of the Bourbon Restoration, when the movement was repressed and only a handful of clandestine titles were published. When anarchist practice was legalised in 1881 there was an accompanying upsurge in print. Although there were fluctuations through the 1880s, the general picture is one of a steady number of anarchist titles, as the movement operated in a climate of relative tolerance. Even the collapse of the FTRE in 1888 did not dramatically affect the general state of anarchist publishing. Looking beyond 1920, anarchist publishing

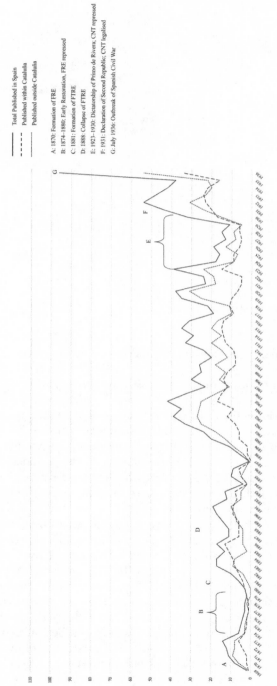

Total Published in Spain
Published within Cataluña
Published outside Cataluña

A: 1870: Formation of FRE
B: 1874–1880: Early Restoration, FRE repressed
C: 1881: Formation of FTRE
D: 1888: Collapse of FTRE
E: 1923–1930: Dictatorship of Primo de Rivera, CNT repressed
F: 1931: Declaration of Second Republic; CNT legalised
G: July 1936: Outbreak of Spanish Civil War

Chart 0.1 Number of Anarchist Publications in Print in Spain, 1869–1936

again contracted during the dictatorship of Primo de Rivera from 1923 onwards, when the CNT was repressed. This period was followed by two dramatic peaks in publishing levels, corresponding to the legalisation of the movement at the declaration of the Second Republic (1931) and the outbreak of the Civil War (1936). Although only a rough guide, there was a clear correlation between periods of high anarchist activity and high levels of anarchist publishing, which confirms Esenwein's contention that 'a thriving anarchist cultural life was manifested . . . most notably in the proliferation of libertarian newspapers, sociological journals, pamphlets, and books'.[42] Publishing activity thus represents a useful barometer for judging the general condition of the movement.[43] Also evident from the periods 1870–1890 and 1920–1936 is a link between high levels of anarchist print and the (re)formation of anarchist organisations, evident in 1870 (FRE), 1881 (FTRE) and 1931 (CNT).

With this relationship established, we can examine the period 1890 to 1920 more closely [see Chart 0.2]. This demonstrates the rapid decline of anarchist periodicals after a series of terrorist attacks of 1893, when anarchist publishing was made illegal (see Chapter 2). Following a brief respite in 1894–95, the movement's press collapsed completely in 1896 following the terrorist attack on the Corpus procession in Barcelona. At this point the movement was at its lowest ebb since the 1870s, severed from popular support and unable to function in the face of broad and heavy-handed repression. Relaxation of repression was followed by an unprecedented explosion of publishing over the turn of the century, corresponding to a general upsurge in anarchist activity across the whole of the country (see Chapter 3). Cultural initiatives flourished, and the movement extended in both size and geographic scope. From 1903 onwards, however, this expansion slowed, and by 1906 many of the gains of the previous eight years were reversed. Partial recoveries in publishing levels through subsequent years were mitigated by repression following the Tragic Week of 1909, and the outlawing of the newly-formed CNT following the general strike of 1911. It was only in the period 1911–1915 that anarchist publishing reached a comparable level to the years 1900–1905 (see Chapter 4).

The expansion of anarchist publishing in the periods 1898–1906 and 1911–1915 suggest a caveat to the link between anarchist organisations and anarchist publishing observed above. An organisation closely associated with the movement was established in 1900, known as the Federación de Sociedades de Resistencia de la Región España (FSORE), yet—as will be demonstrated in Chapter 3—this organisation achieved little of note, and was largely abandoned by the movement and its press from 1903 onwards. In 1911–1915 the CNT technically existed as a clandestine organisation, but outside Cataluña it had no tangible presence and was never discussed in the press. Thus, while in 1870–1890 and 1920–1936 high levels of publishing corresponded with the existence

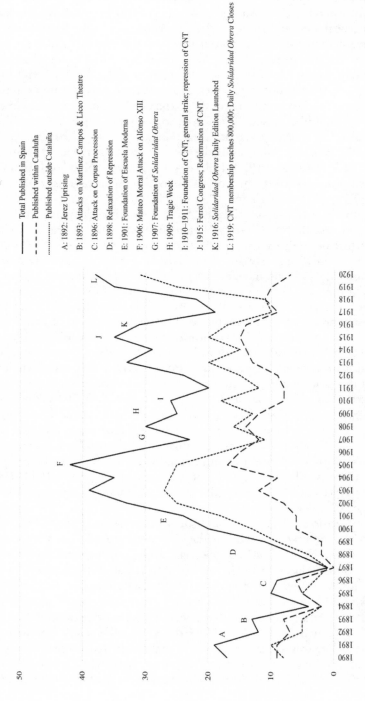

Legend:
——— Total Published in Spain
- - - Published within Cataluña
········ Published outside Cataluña

A: 1892: Jerez Uprising
B: 1893: Attacks on Martínez Campos & Liceo Theatre
C: 1896: Attack on Corpus Procession
D: 1898: Relaxation of Repression
E: 1901: Foundation of Escuela Moderna
F: 1906: Matteo Morral Attack on Alfonso XIII
G: 1907: Foundation of *Solidaridad Obrera*
H: 1909: Tragic Week
I: 1910–1911: Foundation of CNT; general strike; repression of CNT
J: 1915: Ferrol Congress; Reformation of CNT
K: 1916: *Solidaridad Obrera* Daily Edition Launched
L: 1919: CNT membership reaches 800,000; Daily *Solidaridad Obrera* Closes

Chart 0.2 Number of Anarchist Publications in Print in Spain, 1890–1920

of the FRE, FTRE and CNT, from 1890 to 1920 peaks of publishing occurred in the absence of a functioning organisation. This suggests that in this period, at least, print culture was indicative of the expansion of the wider anarchist movement and not simply a reflection of organisational strength.

Another telling development took place at the end of this period. Although there were no legal restrictions placed on anarchist publishing in 1915–19, the number of papers in print declined at a rate comparable to that seen during periods of repression. This contraction was prompted by an internal development. In 1916 the CNT organ *Solidaridad Obrera* (Barcelona) was transformed into the first successful daily publication in the movement's history. The daily *Solidaridad Obrera* contained as much content in a month as most anarchist papers published in a year, leading many publishing groups to regard their titles as redundant. Papers closed, and a number of projected publications were abandoned (see Chapter 4). This trend was reversed in 1919, when an upsurge in publishing levels followed the closure of *Solidaridad Obrera*. This study therefore has 1915 as its end point, regarding it as a seminal moment in anarchist print culture, which marked the beginning of a different relationship between the movement and its press.

As well as a representation and a proxy for the movement, this study examines print culture in its own right. Publishers, readers, correspondents and the papers themselves are regarded as having importance in and of themselves, not solely as reflections of other aspects of the movement. Given its centrality to the movement, and its importance as an historical source, it is surprising how few studies treat print culture in this way. By far the most comprehensive investigation into anarchist periodicals is the doctoral thesis of Francisco Madrid Santos, which catalogues every anarchist publication produced in Spain from 1868 to 1939, a total of around 850 titles.[44] Madrid Santos gives a detailed account of the context in which anarchist periodicals were produced: the development of print media in Spain, the finances of anarchist papers, their distribution, the legal contexts in which they operated, their language, the individuals and groups who produced them, their readers and contributors, their objectives and results. Most other studies of anarchist print have a much smaller scope, preferring to focus on a single periodical, usually the cultural journal *La Revista Blanca* or the CNT organ *Solidaridad Obrera*.[45] Some studies have also focused on the publishing activity in a local area, such as Flaquer's examination of the Madrid anarchist press during the FRE and Santullano's examination of the working-class publications of Asturias in the late nineteenth century.[46] While his scope is unparalleled, what Madrid Santos explicitly does not do is examine the content of anarchist publications in depth. He correctly states that a detailed examination of each title would be near-impossible, given the volume of material he is concerned with.[47] This study adds depth to Madrid Santos' peerless cataloguing by examining the content of the press, made manageable by limiting the timeframe to 1890–1915, when the press was the focal point of the movement's ideological development and its only recognisable structure.

Geographic Focus

Recent research on anarchism outside Spain has embraced the 'turn' to transnational studies.[48] Focusing on anarchism as a cosmopolitan, internationalist movement serves two commendable goals. First, it reflects the desires of anarchists themselves, who disregarded the legitimacy of states and actively sought to undermine their borders, dismissing nationalism as a 'fiction' which divided the international working class.[49] Second, a transnational focus also reflects a historical reality for many movements: anarchists around the world did indeed often operate 'between' nations, perhaps more so than their contemporaries. The anarchist experience was marked by movement, such as political exile and economic migration, which in turn fed into anarchist practice and ideology, and was accompanied by a movement of money, books, pamphlets and, above all, newspapers, which flowed between movements in different nations and continents. Kenyon Zimmer, in his discussion of Jewish and Italian anarchist migrants in the USA, clearly stresses the significance of these networks:

> It would be difficult to overstate the functional importance of newspapers in the anarchist movement. The printed word created a transnational community of anarchists and transmitted the movement's ideology across space while sustaining collective identities across time. Affiliation with the movement and with particular factions within it often rested on attachments to specific periodicals rather than formal organizations.[50]

A transnational lens is therefore the only means to fully understand anarchism in its local and national articulations, not least because most movements had a negligible, or fleeting, 'national' presence, while anarchist individuals and ideas had a substantial global influence for over seventy years.

In many ways Spain was no different. The movement was linked to a wider transnational network of ideas, activists and materials, which had profound influence on the development of anarchism in Spain. Indeed, many accounts of the 'origins' of anarchism in Spain begin with the arrival of Bakunin's Italian emissary, Giuseppe Fanelli, who travelled to Barcelona and Madrid in 1868 and convinced audiences of workers to join the First International.[51] Despite the breakdown of the International in 1872, the Spanish movement never lost its transnational connections, and remained in constant contact with internationally-based groups and individuals in Europe and the Americas. Many of these links were sustained by anarchists exiled from Spain. During periods of repression many of the key figures in the movement's print culture spent time outside Spain, either in enforced exile—as with Teresa Mañe [Soledad Gustavo] and Juan Montseny [Federico Urales] (UK and France, 1896–7), Teresa Claramunt (UK and France 1896–8), Anselmo Lorenzo (France 1896–7), Francisco Ferrer (France and Belgium 1907–9) and Antonio Loredo (Argentina and Uruguay 1902–1909; Argentina and France 1910)—or as a pre-emptive move to avoid arrest, as with Pedro Esteve (USA, Mexico, Argentina 1892+) and José Prat (Argentina 1897–8).[52] Some remained in exile and became key foreign correspondents to the movement's press, including Fernando Tárrida del Marmól (born in Havana, moved to Spain as a teenager, exiled in France, Belgium and the UK 1896–1915) and Vicente García (UK and France 1901–1930).[53] Many exiles who remained abroad engaged in the anarchist press of their new location, including Esteve, who joined the editorial group of *El Despertar*, an influential Spanish-language periodical based in New York.[54] Most, however, returned to Spain after a fairly short period of time, bringing with them their transnational experiences and inspirations for new ideas and initiatives. During their exile in Paris, Mañe and Montseny, for example, were deeply impressed by both Jean Grave's anarchist periodical *Les Temps Nouveaux* and the literary journal *La Revue Blanche*, and upon their return to Spain launched the journal *La Revista Blanca* as a synthesis of these two publications.[55]

Beyond these high-profile figures, transnational links and networks between Spain and international movements were sustained by migrants. Around three million Spaniards emigrated over the turn of the century, the vast majority of whom settled in Argentina (~52 per cent), Cuba (~26 per cent) and Brazil (~10 per cent).[56] Significant pockets of Spanish migration could also be found in cities such as London, Paris, Bordeaux, Toulouse, New York, and Tampa, and in sites of major industrial projects, including the Panama Canal and South Wales.[57] While it is near-impossible to gauge the exact number of anarchists within migration figures, it is clear that a significant proportion identified with the movement when they left Spain, and others took up anarchist ideas in their new environment. Indeed, because of the high proportion of working-class men in migration figures, the likelihood is that the anarchist presence in such communities was stronger than in many areas of Spain.[58] As has been established in a number of studies, these migrants formed a substantial part of international anarchist and syndicalist movements, particularly in Argentina and Cuba.[59] Several key figures in international anarchist print culture left Spain for economic reasons, including the typesetter Antonio Pellicer Paraire, who worked across Mexico, Cuba and the United States in the 1870s before returning to Spain, where he edited *Acracia* from

1886–1887. Pellicer Paraire then left again for Argentina in 1891, where he became an important figure in anarchist publishing and organising, until his withdrawal from the movement in 1902.[60] Another migrant who encapsulated the relationship between transnational movement and print activity was Julio Camba, who was 16 when he left Galicia for Buenos Aires in 1898. Camba became a regular contributor to *La Protesta Humana* before being deported in 1902, as part of a series of crackdowns on Spanish anarchist migrants by the Argentine government in the early twentieth century. Upon his return, Camba joined the editorial team behind *Tierra y Libertad* (Madrid) and later founded *El Rebelde* (Madrid), two of the most important Spanish anarchist papers in print in the early twentieth century.[61]

Spanish communities abroad made a significant contribution to the anarchist press in Spain. International correspondences formed a substantial part of most periodicals, keeping the movement informed of the developments, success and failures of anarchism around the world. Reports on state repression were particularly common, maintaining a sense that the enemy faced by anarchists was essentially interchangeable—indeed, many such reports would be titled *siempre lo mismo* [always the same]— in whatever context they found themselves. Migrants also provided material support to the movement's print culture. International groups were often amongst the first to request new periodicals, books and pamphlets, and were generally seen as more reliable and dedicated subscribers than many of their comrades in Spain. Many periodicals owed their existence to donations and remittances from international communities, collected at workplaces and communal events, from the anarchist centres of Paris to the workcamps of the Panamá Canal, the bakeries of Buenos Aires to the ironworks of South Wales. Migrant and exile communities also sent their own publications to Spain. Spanish-language periodicals from the Americas, including *¡Tierra!* (Havana), *La Protesta Humana* (Buenos Aires), *Regeneración* (Mexico City; later Los Angeles) and *El Despertar* (New York) were distributed widely amongst the movement. International publications were particularly significant when anarchist print culture was repressed in Spain, as they became both a rare source of news and an outlet for Spanish activists and correspondents whose usual channels of communication had been severed.[62]

International press networks also linked the Spanish movement to groups and individuals beyond the Hispanic world: to writers, theorists, groups and organisations that did not have their origins in Spain, and who had little or no direct physical contact with the movement. Many of the key ideological developments within the movement had their origins outside Spain, including the three discussed in depth in this study: propaganda by the deed, anarchist educational theory, and syndicalism. The French movement, and French theorists and writers had a particularly strong influence in the Spanish anarchist press—a fact that is often overlooked in transnational studies that focus on links between Spain and the Americas—as did major international figures in turn-of-the-century anarchism, such as Pyotr Kropotkin, Emma Goldman and Errico Malatesta.[63] As will be shown throughout this book, these ideas were picked up and translated to the Spanish context through the exchange of newspapers, pamphlets and books maintained between publishers in every country with an anarchist presence, forging 'common interests and concerns that were not unique to one nation but formed a part of a transnational anarchist ideology'.[64]

Taken together, the international dimensions of the Spanish movement and its press reveal that it is perhaps wrong to speak of 'Spanish anarchism', but rather an anarchist movement based in Spain, which was shaped in large part by international theories, events and activism from inception. This study does not, however, take a wholly transnational approach. As I and Danny Evans have noted elsewhere, the movement in Spain fits uneasily into the transnational paradigm, which may explain why few studies discuss the transnational influences of and upon the Spanish movement.[65] While anarchists themselves would like to see no distinction between the contexts in which they operated, there were differences between the experience of anarchism in Spain and elsewhere, not least in terms of the scale and significance of their movements. Unlike the movements of Italy, Germany, Eastern Europe, and France—all of which had great influence upon the development of a global, or at least Atlantic, anarchist network—the movement in Spain attracted a genuine mass following for several decades. While some Spanish militants were highly influential in international contexts, many others did not leave Spain, were not exiles or migrants, and did not—or could not—engage in international activism directly. This did not prevent them from contributing to the development of anarchism within the borders of Spain: to adapt Carl Levy's depiction of Errico Malatesta, many of these 'cosmopolitans' remained 'rooted' in their country of birth, where they helped to develop the largest anarchist movement in world history.[66] Likewise because of the links established by anarchist print culture, anarchists did not necessarily have to move to participate in the international movement. Ricardo Mella, for example, was read across both sides of the Atlantic and was regarded as one of the most important thinkers of his generation yet spent his entire life in Galicia and Asturias in northern Spain.[67]

The size of the movement in Spain also invites areas of research which do not apply to most of their contemporaries. Those working on the movement in Spain can engage with similar questions to those of a transnational focus, such as the experiences of local militancy, sociability, repression, and fleeting explosions of activity; but they are also studying a movement which claimed the support of around 5 per cent of the national population in 1917 (dwarfing most comparable movements), and twenty years later carried out the only anarchist revolution in world history. This is not to say that the relative success of anarchism in Spain *could* only happen in Spain, but that it *did* only happen in Spain; anarchists may have 'sought revolution everywhere' but it was only in Spain that this came close to a reality.[68] The 'transnational turn' can thus help in adding to our understanding the international influences upon the Spanish movement, and vice versa, but cannot remove the question of national context altogether. Thus, rather than prioritising international influences upon the Spanish movement, this study seeks to incorporate them into a wider discussion alongside developments that took place within Spain.

Transnational approaches also raise methodological concerns when applied to Spain. When discussing anarchist migrants and exiles, based in 'nodal' cities on both sides of the Atlantic (such as London, Paris, New York, Havana and Buenos Aires) it is appropriate to see provincial and rural contexts as largely irrelevant and bereft of anarchist support.[69] Transnationalism in these contexts thus signifies largely inter-urban interactions, where the state's geographic reach over territory was ignored, or hardly challenged by non-state actors. Concentrating on this manner of activity does not always follow the anarchist premise of undermining borders but rather can serve to maintain them, viewing the world as 'formed and ordered by a static framework of clearly distinguishable nation states' across which anarchist actors (begrudgingly) operated: in short, the transnationalism under investigation is one of movement across fixed borders and overlooked national interiors.[70]

As I have noted elsewhere, this does not mean that the premises of transnational history should be discarded, nor that historians of anarchism should return to solely national studies.[71] Rather, this critique asks scholars to disrupt the fixed image of the state, regarding international exchanges and networks as part of a process which extended beyond frontiers and cosmopolitan centres, and into provinces and localities.[72] Anarchists faced borders at these junctures as well: borders of language, culture, history, class, gender and race, as well as between urban and rural contexts and areas of differing political and economic significance. In the process of building a mass movement in Spain, anarchists were constantly attempting to cross these borders, engaging in negotiations between individuals and communities, and developing flows of information and exchange. Those interested in these processes—in the 'exploration of exchanges, crossings, transfer, influences and counter-influences, the movement of people, products, technology and ideas'—commonly identified as the hallmark of transnational histories, should thus recognise that they took place within nations as well as between them.[73]

The term I believe best encapsulates this activity is translocalism. This concept aims to explain the process by which individuals and groups prioritise action in their immediate environment, while at the same time aspiring to transcend boundaries both within and between nations. The premises of translocalism have a great deal to offer historians of bottom-up political movements by drawing attention to the 'material flows . . . the movement of styles, ideas, images and symbols' which form a collective imagination and instigate collective action across localities, without the need for formal political structures.[74] In order to foster this translocalism, anarchists in Spain needed a mechanism through which local experiences could be expressed, shared and framed within a broader understanding of the universal struggle against authority. Since centralised structures and channels were unavailable, they constructed an alternative: a grassroots network of periodicals, which maintained a flow of information across and beyond Spain, and in the process bound individuals and groups together in a collaborative development of the movement and its ideology.

Anarchist efforts to bridge divides between rural and urban contexts, and the centres and peripheries of power had mixed results in turn-of-the-century Spain. The spread of anarchism across Spain was not uniform: it had numerous directions, rhythms and tempos, which responded to both national and local conditions. Studying anarchist print helps to recreate a sense of this fluid geography. From 1890–1915 engagement in anarchist periodicals waxed and waned across the whole of the country. Some areas, such as Cádiz, were deeply engaged in anarchist print culture in the nineteenth century, yet gradually diminished in significance after 1906. In contrast, the anarchist press had a negligible presence in the Asturian port of Gijón until 1898, yet after this point the city was home to a string of significant anarchist publications, reflecting and contributing to the city's increasing prominence in the wider movement. A reading of anarchist print which encompasses a broad geographic scope helps to recognise this fluidity and look beyond it, with the aim of reconstructing a sense of the general direction of the movement between 1890 and 1915.

A translocal focus also helps to bring scholarship on the Spanish movement into discussion with the prevailing transnational focus of anarchist studies, with its emphasis on movement and exchanges. Unlike most recent Spanish works on the movement, this study is not bound to a particular locality. It is a study of anarchism across the whole of Spain, albeit with one major exception: it does not discuss the Catalan movement or periodicals produced in the region, except in reference to their influence elsewhere.[75] Its scope thus encompasses around half of the movement in Spain, spread in clusters in south-west Andalucía (Cádiz, Sevilla and to a lesser extent, Huelva), the Islas Canarias, the Levante (Valencia and Murcia), the Islas Baleares, cities on the northern coast (La Coruña, Gijón and Bilbao) and Madrid [see Map 0.1]. This geographic scope addresses an imbalance in the historiography of this period, itself a result of the imbalanced geography of the movement.

Barcelona was the centre of anarchism in Spain. From the mid-nineteenth century onwards the city expanded massively, drawing in migrants from surrounding Cataluña, neighbouring Aragon and Valencia, and the rural south, who arrived in a city which had developed a distinct economy, politics and culture.[76] Anarchism became the dominant ideology of the city's working class—both 'local' and 'migrant'—which became a highly concentrated body of support for the movement. Barcelona was also the location of many of the major developments in the history of Spanish anarchism. From 1890 to 1915 the city was the site of all but one of the major anarchist terrorist attacks in Spain, the home of Francisco Ferrer's Escuela Moderna, and the headquarters of the CNT. Clearly, nowhere else in Spain was as significant to the movement as Barcelona.

The experience of anarchism in Barcelona was, however, unique. Anarchists in Barcelona could count themselves as among thousands of like-minded people, spending their lives in predominantly anarchist *barrios* (districts) and anarchist workplaces.[77] They were also far more likely to suffer from repression, which frequently swept through Barcelona following anarchist outrages and labour unrest. The city thus exemplified the highs and lows of the anarchist experience in Spain, which helped to form a distinct collective identity built upon cycles of success, defeat and resistance. Because of its significance, Barcelona weighs heavily on the history of anarchism in Spain, making it difficult to discuss the movement without an imbalance towards the north-east of the country. Many studies which purport to cover all of Spain are in fact studies of Barcelona, with only passing references to the movement outside the city. As such, Barcelona is plotted as a 'nodal' city like many others in the international anarchist network, while the rest of Spain appears only as a rather passive reservoir of support.[78] Other studies have made clear their intention to study the region separately. These include some of the best scholarship on the movement, covering many of the most significant features of the development of anarchism over the turn of the twentieth century.[79]

A sense of Catalan chauvinism also makes occasional appearances in the historiography, often as an off-shoot of the millenarian hypothesis discussed earlier. For writers such as de Quirós, Brenan and Hobsbawm— and those who continue to rely on their interpretations—'millenarian', violent, communistic forms of anarchism were evident primarily in the rural south of Spain, while the more 'modern', unionist, collectivist and syndicalist aspects of the movement developed in the industrialised north-east.[80] This characterisation infantilises the southern movement, drawing on the persistent stereotyping of Andalusians as poor, passionate and temperamental, in contrast to their industrious, sober compatriots in the north. Going one step further in his influential 1919 study, de Quirós paints the relationship between the main regions of anarchist support in Spain as one of a 'marriage', in which 'Cataluña has always been the male, the director and protector; and Andalucía the passive female . . . the earth is, after all, femininity, and Andalucía is only earth . . . [w]ork is virility, and this is the role of Cataluña'.[81]

Few subsequent works employ such overtly gendered and racist language, yet all of the above studies rely in some part on an assumed difference between Spaniards of different regions, which can be used to explain the various tendencies within the movement. Such assumptions are demonstrably wrong. While syndicalism did develop first in Cataluña, this had more to do with its proximity to France and the nature of industry in the region, than the innate work ethic and sobriety of Catalans. Collectivism—the ideological predecessor of syndicalism— was strong across the whole of Spain, particularly in Andalucía, whose societies made up the majority (~61 per cent) of the collectivist FTRE (1881–1888), while Catalan societies made up around 26 per cent of this organisation.[82] Likewise, over the turn of the century several collectivist and syndicalist publications were based in the south of Spain—such as *La Solidaridad* (Sevilla), *La Protesta* (La Línea de la Concepción), *El 4º de Febrero* (Huelva) and *La Voz del Obrero del Mar* (Cádiz)—as were important collectivist and syndicalist thinkers, such as José Sánchez Rosa.

It is true that spontaneous, rural violence took place in Andalucía over the turn of the century, in which some anarchists were involved, yet there is little evidence to suggest this came from an innate communism of this region. Indeed, in police reports from the repression of the 1892 Jerez uprising, the two papers cited as being the most widely circulated amongst the fieldworkers were *El Productor* (Barcelona) and *La Anarquía* (Madrid), both of which were of a collectivist orientation. As will be discussed in Chapter 2, rural uprisings were a complex mixture of material grievances and political instigation, over which anarchists had some influence but cannot be said to have fully controlled. On the other hand, of the four major incidents of propaganda by the deed (terrorist violence) in Spain—commonly identified as the main anarcho-communist tactic during the 1890s—three took place in Barcelona, two were committed by Catalans, another by an Italian and the forth by an unknown assailant. Anarcho-communist papers were published in Andalucía during the 1880s and 1890s, including *El Socialismo* (Cádiz), *El Oprimido* (Algeciras), and *La Tribuna Libre* (Seville), but they were also launched in Valencia (*La Controversia*), Zaragoza (*El Rebelde, El Eco del Rebelde, El Invencible,* and *El Comunista*) and, above all, Barcelona (*La Revolución Social, El Revolucionario, El Porvenir Anarquista, Ravachol, El Eco de Ravachol* and *Ariete Anarquista*).

In short, geography does little to help explain the different tendencies within Spanish anarchism. Rather, activists interpreted anarchism in different ways across all regions of Spain, including Cataluña. What can be discerned, however, is a difference in the anarchist experience between Cataluña and other regions in Spain. Many areas of anarchist support outside Cataluña had similar economic and social profiles. Many were ports, or other centres of trade. While industrialisation was increasing across Spain, the economies of these cities were based largely on casual, artisan and agrarian labour. Aside from Madrid, Valencia and, to a lesser extent Sevilla, most had modest urban populations surrounded by larger rural hinterlands. Some of these rural areas were also sites of support for the movement, as in Cádiz province, although many, for example rural Galicia, were not. Anarchists in provincial cities generally came from comparable working backgrounds, including construction and dec-oration (bricklayers, labourers and painters); woodwork and furniture making (carpenters, cabinetmakers and turners); clothing (tailors, boot-makers and hatters); agriculture; metalwork; and other artisans, such as locksmiths and glaziers.[83] Although smaller in number, some teachers and other professionals—such as the railway surveyor Ricardo Mella— also played an important role in the movement's print culture.

Unlike the mass support of the urban proletariat of Barcelona and its surrounding towns, anarchism in other regions of Spain consisted of smaller pockets of activists, often within cities separated by vast dis-tances. Here, anarchist activity was often a struggle against local authori-ties, rival political movements and prevailing working-class attitudes. It was also more piecemeal, fragmented, and less prone to dramatic mani-festations of anarchist practice. This disparity was acknowledged by anarchists based outside Cataluña, some of whom wrote enviously of the development of the movement in Barcelona while the rest of Spain lan-guished in inactivity and 'ignorance'.[84] At the same time, many activists expressed a desire to prevent the movement from centralising around its Barcelona core, and there was a feeling that the strength of anarchism in Cataluña had created a sense of superiority amongst the city's workers and publishers, who were accused of ignoring or belittling their provin-cial comrades.[85]

Local studies elsewhere in Spain have attempted to address the his-toriographical imbalance towards Cataluña. Andalucía, as the second 'heartland' of anarchism in Spain, has been particularly well served, above all in the excellent works of Jacques Maurice.[86] Cádiz province has received particular attention in studies of the turn-of-the-century move-ment, many of which focus the rich anarchist culture which developed in the area, while others concentrate on the rural violence seen as endemic to the region.[87] The early twentieth-century movement in Sevilla has also been investigated, most notably in the opening chapters of González Fernández' excellent *Utopía y realidad*, and Velasco Mesa's comparative analyses of revolutionary discourses in the general strikes of Liège (1886) and Sevilla (1901).[88] Less attention has been given to the other provinces within Andalucía.[89] In other regions the period 1890–1915 is often placed as a starting point in studies of a longer timeframe, as in Barrio Alonso's work on anarchism in Asturias (1890–1936) and Radcliff's examination of political polarisation in Gijón (1900–1937).[90] A handful of accounts exist for Galicia and the Islas Canarias, while the minority anarchist pres-ence in the Basque regions and Logroño has also been the subject of studies of a longer time-frame.[91] Anarchism in the Islas Baleares has been the subject of only one short monograph, which only briefly covers the pre-CNT movement.[92] Little investigation of this period has focused on Valencia and Aragon, both of which had a strong CNT presence in later years.[93] Perhaps surprisingly, Madrid has been almost entirely neglected by scholarship of anarchism in Spain. The capital was the site of a number of anarchist unions, national congresses and, as will be shown in this work, challenged Barcelona as the centre of anarchist publishing in Spain in the early twentieth century, yet it remains understudied.

The geographic divergence in studies of the movement reflects the prevailing trend in Spanish historiography towards local and regional history. This approach is particularly suited to the anarchist movement, which placed a heavy emphasis on local, autonomous activity. Detailed studies of local areas add much to our understanding of the day-to-day realities of anarchism, and how the ideas of the movement were interpreted in relation to specific, local conditions. The best of these works—for example, those of González Fernández and Barrio Alonso—successfully situate anarchism in its local or regional arena, without sealing it off from the wider developments of the movement. Nevertheless, the proliferation of local studies has not fully addressed the geographic imbalance in the historiography of the movement. Taken individually, none of these areas can compete with the size and significance of Barcelona. Taken collectively, however, as in this study, the movement outside Cataluña was as large, as important and as representative of anarchism in Spain.

Book Outline

The first chapter of this book outlines the general features and trends in anarchist publishing over the period 1890–1915, providing a contextual foundation for subsequent chapters. This study then follows the development of three strategies adopted within the movement between 1890 and 1915, through three thematic and chronological sections. Chapter 2 focuses on the theme of violence. Between 1890 and 1898 anarchism in Spain became entangled with violence, particularly after 1893 and the advent of 'propaganda by the deed' (terrorism, which was designed to shock the working class into revolutionary action). This development was extremely damaging for the movement, which was targeted with severe, violent repression from the state. The violence of these years is the most commonly studied aspect of the pre-CNT anarchist movement in Spain. Such works are drawn to exceptional, unrepresentative figures, whose actions were largely confined to Barcelona, yet the effect of violence upon the wider movement remains understudied. Chapter 2 seeks to re-examine the role of violence within the anarchist movement, exploring how anarchists constructed different meanings of popular, individual and state violence. These debates took place primarily in print, and reveal the movement's heterogeneous response to violence as a revolutionary strategy. Examination of the press also reveals how publishing groups attempted —and ultimately failed—to respond effectively to repression, through the construction of a martyr culture, and by providing the practical means to foster solidarity with their comrades across Spain.

Chapter 3 addresses the revival of the movement and its adoption of education as a revolutionary strategy. From 1899 to 1906 anarchist cultural practices flourished, driven in large part by a dramatic expansion of the movement's periodical press. This study treats the press as the site of common ground between the numerous works on anarchist culture and education, which have proliferated in the historiography of the movement since the early 1980s.[94] Studies of education in this period have long focused almost exclusively on Cataluña, above all on the pioneering anarchist educator Francisco Ferrer and his Escuela Moderna in Barcelona. The weight of Ferrer's legacy is such that it finds its way into almost every discussion of anarchist educational projects at this time.[95] Chapter 3 seeks to situate Ferrer and anarchist educational theory within the broader movement. In doing so it touches upon ideas of anarchist spaces and sociability, which have hitherto focused largely on Cataluña—above all in the numerous works of Pére Solà—or later periods.[96] Outside Cataluña, the history of anarchist cultural and spatial practice in the early twentieth century has largely been absorbed into wider studies of working-class culture, and the focus has often rested on specific regions—particularly Asturias—and the socialist movement.[97] Chapter 3 also engages with the early development of anarchist-feminism, which has previously been mentioned only as a prelude to studies of the 'Mujeres Libres' feminist group of the 1930s. The periodical press was the site where all the many strands of anarchist cultural development came together, allowing for an examination of how these aspects of the anarchist cultural programme integrated and interacted with the movement. Print carried anarchism into new areas, and helped in the establishment of cultural spaces and schools which, in turn, formed the foundations of the movement in localities across the whole of Spain. At the same time, periodicals maintained communications between these areas, providing a structure to the movement as it re-established its presence as a national entity.

Chapter 4 analyses the developments in anarchist organisational strategy and the creation of the CNT, from 1907 to 1915. Perhaps surprisingly, the adoption of syndicalism within Spanish anarchism and the formation of the CNT—particularly on a national level—has drawn little attention since the seminal studies of Xavier Cuadrat and Antonio Bar. Once again, these scholars (and the few which have followed them) have focused on the movement's epicentre in Barcelona, and the internal politics of the early CNT leadership.[98] Very few studies have focused on how syndicalism was regarded elsewhere, how it was presented in relation to previous organisational theories, the contingencies in the development of the CNT, or the early resistance to the organisation. Examination of the periodicals of this period provides a sense of the cultural formation of syndicalism within the anarchist movement outside Cataluña. The anarchist press was vital in the process of promoting —and, in some cases, resisting—the spread of syndicalism and in bringing disparate groups together to assist in the creation of the CNT, firstly in its inaugural congresses in 1910 and 1911, and again during the early years of the First World War. Chapter 4 ends with a symbolic milestone for the movement and its press, when the CNT's official organ, *Solidaridad Obrera*, was transformed into the movement's first stable daily publication in 1916, leading to a contraction and centralisation of the hitherto pluralised and fragmented anarchist print culture.

Notes

1. Óscar Freán Hernández, 'El anarquismo español: Luces y sombres en la historiografía reciente sobre el movimiento libertario,' *Ayer* 84, 4 (2011): 222.
2. Bert Altena, 'Analysing Revolutionary Syndicalism: The Importance of Community,' in *New Perspectives on Anarchism, Labour and Syndicalism: The Individual, the National and the Transnational*, ed. David Berry and Constance Bantman (Newcastle-upon-Tyne: Cambridge Scholars Publishing, 2010), 182.
3. David Featherstone, *Resistance, Space and Political Identities: The Making of Counter-Global Networks* (Oxford: Wiley-Blackwell, 2008), 59–78; Sidney G. Tarrow, *Power in Movement: Social Movements and Contentious Politics* (Cambridge: Cambridge University Press, 2011), 37–56; Samuel Cohn, 'The "Modernity" of Medieval Popular Revolt,' *History Compass* 10, 10 (2012): 731–741.
4. Andy Cumbers, Paul Routledge and Corinne Nativel, 'The Entangled Geographies of Global Justice Networks,' *Progress in Human Geography* 32, 2 (2008): 190.
5. José Álvarez Junco, *La ideología política del anarquismo español (1868–1910)* (Madrid: Siglo XXI, 1991), 17–42; Carl Levy, 'Social Histories of Anarchism,' *Journal for the Study of Radicalism* 4, 2 (2010): 4–5.
6. Lily Litvak, *Musa libertaria: Arte, literatura y vida cultural del anarquismo español (1890–1913)* (Madrid: Fundación de Estudios Libertarios Anselmo Lorenzo, 2001), 69–99; Martha A. Ackelsberg, *Free Women of Spain: Anarchism and the Struggle for the Emancipation of Women* (Edinburgh: AK Press, 2005), 37–38.
7. William Smaldone, *European Socialism: A Concise History with Documents* (Lanham: Rowman and Littlefield, 2014), 81–82.
8. *La Voz del Obrero del Mar* (Cádiz, II), 13 October, 1907, 3.
9. Josep Termes, *Anarquismo y sindicalismo en España: La Primera Internacional (1864–1881)* (Barcelona: Crítica, 1977), 11–170. See also Rafael Flaquer Montequi, *La clase obrera madrileña y la Primera Internacional, (1868–1874): Un análisis de prensa* (Madrid: Editorial Cuadernos Para el Dialogo, 1977), 96–99 and 141–180; George Esenwein, *Anarchist Ideology and the Working-Class Movement in Spain, 1868–1898* (Berkeley: University of California Press, 1989), 11–38.
10. Temma Kaplan, *Anarchists of Andalusia, 1868–1903* (Princeton: Princeton University Press, 1977), 105–110.

11. Termes, *Anarquismo y sindicalismo*, 197–276.
12. José Valera Ortega, *Los amigos políticos: Partidos, elecciones y caciquismo en la Restauración (1875–1900)* (Madrid: Alianza, 1977), 135–203.
13. Paul Heywood, *Marxism and the Failure of Organised Socialism in Spain: 1879–1936* (Cambridge: Cambridge University Press, 1990), 1–28.
14. Anselmo Lorenzo, *El proletariado militante: Memorias de un internacionalista* (Madrid: Alianza, 1974), 425. A larger figure of 57,934 is given in Esenwein, *Anarchist Ideology*, 83 with explanatory notes on 229–330, n.9.
15. Francisco Madrid Santos, 'La prensa anarquista y anarcosindicalista en España desde la I Internacional hasta el fin de la Guerra Civil,' (PhD thesis, Barcelona: Universidad Central de Barcelona, 1988–89), 94–111.
16. Kaplan, *Anarchists of Andalusia*, 126–134.
17. The FTRE split into two organisations: The Federación de Resistencia de Capital (known as the Pacto de Unión y Solidaridad) and the Organización Anarquista de la Región Española. Both did very little of note, see Esenwein, *Anarchist Ideology*, 98–133.
18. Santiago Castillo, *Historia de la UGT: Un sindicalismo consciente, 1873–1914* (Madrid: Siglo XXI, 2008), 90–96.
19. Carlos Serrano Lacarra, '*Acracia*, los anarquistas y la cultura,' in *El anarquismo español y sus tradiciones culturales*, ed. Bert Hofmann, Pere Joan i Tous and Manfred Tietze (Frankfurt/Madrid: Vervuert/Iberoamericana, 1995), 347–360.
20. CNT membership figures in 1915 and 1919 given in Antonio Bar, *La CNT en los años rojos: Del sindicalismo revolucionario al anarcosindicalismo (1910–1926)* (Madrid: Akal, 1981), 338–339 and 490–492.
21. See Manuel Pérez Ledesma, 'La formación de la clase obrera: Una creación cultural,' in *Cultura y movilización en la España contemporánea*, ed. Rafael Cruz and Manuel Pérez Ledesma (Madrid: Alianza, 1997), 201–233.
22. Levy, 'Social Histories of Anarchism,' 24.
23. The most obvious example of such a study is Peter Marshall, *Demanding the Impossible: A History of Anarchism* (London: Fontana, 1993), which traces anarchist ideology to ancient China.
24. See Gary Rivett, 'English Newsbooks, Storytelling and Political Criticism,' *Media History* 19, 1 (2013): 3–4.
25. Litvak, *Musa libertaria*, 211–238. See also Lily Litvak, 'La prensa anarquista (1880–1913),' in Hofmann, Tous and Tietze, *El anarquismo español*, 215–235 and 'La buena nueva: Cultura y prensa anarquista (1880–1913),' *Revista de Occidente* 304 (2006): 5–18.
26. Esenwein, *Anarchist Ideology*, 124–133.
27. See Jason Garner, *Goals and Means: Anarchism, Syndicalism, and Internationalism in the Origins of the Federación Anarquista Ibérica* (Edinburgh: AK Press, 2016), 4.
28. See Chapter 2.
29. Levy, 'Social Histories of Anarchism,' 8.
30. See comments in Kaplan, *Anarchists of Andalusia*, 207–209. Constancio Bernaldo de Quirós, 'El espartaquismo agrario andaluz,' *Revista general de legislación y jurisprudencia*, 134 (1919): 307–319, 396–413 and 491–502; Juan Díaz del Moral, *Historia de las agitaciones campesinas andaluzas-Córdoba: Antecedentes para una reforma agraria* (Madrid: Alianza, 1967); Gerald Brenan, *The Spanish Labyrinth: An Account of the Social and Political Background of the Civil War* (Cambridge: Cambridge University Press, 2014), 214–268.
31. Eric Hobsbawm, *Primitive Rebels: Studies in Archaic Forms of Social Movement in the 19th and 20th Centuries* (New York: W.W. Norton, 1965), 74, n.1.

32. A similar tone is evident in Hobsbawm's treatment of the English peasantry in Eric Hobsbawm and George Rudé, *Captain Swing* (London: Lawrence and Wishart, 1969), for example 72–93.

33. Pere Gabriel, 'Historiografía reciente sobre el anarquismo y el sindicalismo en España, 1870–1923,' *Historia Social* 1 (1988): 46–48. Other critiques include: James Casey, 'The Spanish Anarchist Peasant: How Primitive a Rebel?,' *Journal of European Studies* 8, 34 (1978): 34–43; John R. Corbin, 'The Myth of Primitive Spain,' *Anthropology Today* 5, 4 (1989): 15–17.

34. Kaplan, *Anarchists of Andalusia*, 210–212. See also Pérez Ledesma, 'La formación de la clase obrera,' 203–205.

35. Jonathan C.D. Clark, 'Secularization and Modernization: The Failure of a "Grand Narrative",' *The Historical Journal* 55, 1 (2012): 161–194.

36. Martha Grace Duncan, 'Spanish Anarchism Refracted: Theme and Image in the Millenarian and Revisionist Literature,' *Journal of Contemporary History* 23, 3 (1988): 323–346; Esenwein, *Anarchist Ideology*, 1–4; Levy, 'Social Histories of Anarchism,' 8–10.

37. For an excellent study of a mainstream title in this era see Pol Dalmau, *Press, Politics and National Identities in Catalonia: The Transformation of La Vanguardia, 1881–1931* (Brighton: Sussex Academic Press, 2017).

38. On the first English newsbooks and historiographical debate surrounding this moment see the work of Joad Raymond, including *The Invention of the Newspaper: English Newsbooks, 1641–1649* (Oxford: Clarendon, 1996), 80–126.

39. See for example Jeremy D. Popkin, *Revolutionary News: The Press in France, 1789–1799* (Durham: Duke University Press, 1990), 106–123; Augusta Rohrbach, '"Truth Stronger and Stranger than Fiction": Reexamining William Lloyd Garrison's *Liberator*,' *American Literature* 73, 4 (2001): 727–755; Kate Peters, *Print Culture and the Early Quakers* (Cambridge: Cambridge University Press, 2005). For an overview of the role of print in modern political mobilisation, see Tarrow, *Power in Movement*, 57–70.

40. Carolyn P. Boyd, 'The Anarchists and Education in Spain, 1868–1909,' *The Journal of Modern History* 48, 4 (1976): 138–139; Michel Ralle, 'La sociabilidad obrera en la sociedad de la Restauración (1875–1910),' *Estudios de Historia Social* 3, 50–51 (1989): 163.

41. For a catalogue of anarchist autobiographies produced during the twentieth century see Joël Delhom, 'Inventario provisorio de las memorias anarquistas y anarcosindicalistas españolas,' *Cahiers de civilisation espagnole contemporaine* 4 (2009), accessed 15 September, 2013, https://journals.openedition.org/ccec/2677.

    Delhom's data shows that only 70 of the nearly 400 autobiographies written from 1900 onwards could conceivably cover the turn-of-the-century (i.e. their authors were born prior to 1915). Detailed discussion of this period in these sources occurs in far fewer (approximately 15).

42. Esenwein, *Anarchist Ideology*, 9.

43. A similar approach is taken in Kenyon Zimmer, *Immigrants against the State: Yiddish and Italian Anarchism in America* (Chicago: University of Illinois Press, 2015), 4–5. Zimmer uses circulation figures for his assessment of the strength of anarchism in the USA, which are unavailable for most Spanish publications.

44. The much shorter monograph version of this thesis, Francisco Madrid Santos, *Solidaridad Obrera y el periodismo de raíz ácrata* (Badalona: Ediciones Solidaridad Obrera, 2007), concentrates on a single periodical and is, understandably, far less comprehensive than the 2 volume thesis. Madrid Santos builds on the work of Víctor Manuel Arbeloa, 'La prensa obrera en España,

(1869–1899),' *Revista de Trabajo* 30 (1970): 117–195 and Susanna Tavera i García, 'La premsa anarco-sindicalista, (1868–1931),' *Recerques* 8 (1978): 85–102.

45. Amongst the many works on *La Revista Blanca* see Susanna Tavera i García, '*La Revista Blanca*: Análisis de una publicación anarquista,' (PhD thesis, Barcelona: Universidad de Barcelona, 1973); Antonio Prado, *Escritoras anarco-feministas en La Revista Blanca (1898–1936): Matrimonio, familia y estado* (Madrid: Fundación de Estudios Libertarios Anselmo Lorenzo, 2011); Richard Cleminson, 'The Construction of Masculinity in the Spanish Labour Movement: A Study of the *Revista Blanca*,' *International Journal of Iberian Studies* 24, 3 (2011): 201–217. On *Solidaridad Obrera* see, amongst others, Susana Tavera i García, *Solidaridad Obrera: Fer-se i desfer-se d'un diari anarcosindicalista (1915–1939)* (Barcelona: Col·legi de Periodistes de Catalunya, 1992).

46. Gabriel Santullano, 'Algunas notas sobre la prensa obrera en Asturias en el siglo XIX (1868–1899),' *Boletín del Instituto de Estudios Asturianos* 88–89 (1976): 509–534; Flaquer Montequi, *La clase obrera.* See also Miguel Íniguez, *La prensa anarquista en el País Vasco, La Rioja y Navarra* (Vitoria: Albor, 1996).

47. Madrid Santos, 'La prensa anarquista,' 18.

48. On these trends see Levy, 'Social Histories of Anarchism,' 18–23; David Berry and Constance Bantman, 'Introduction: New Perspectives on Anarchism, Labour and Syndicalism: The Individual, the National and the Transnational,' in Berry and Bantman, *New Perspectives on Anarchism*, 1–13; Constance Bantman and Bert Altena, 'Introduction: Problematizing Scales of Analysis in Network-Based Social Movements,' in *Reassessing the Transnational Turn: Scales of Analysis in Anarchist and Syndicalist Studies*, ed. Constance Bantman and Bert Altena (London: Routledge, 2015), 3–22.

49. Carl Levy, 'Anarchism and Cosmopolitanism,' in *The Palgrave Handbook of Anarchism*, ed. Carl Levy and Matthew Adams (Cham: Palgrave Macmillan, 2018), 125–148.

50. Zimmer, *Immigrants against the State*, 4. Other works which stress the role of print in transnational anarchist networks include: Constance Bantman, 'Internationalism without an International? Cross-Channel Anarchist Networks, 1890–1914,' *Revue belge de philology et d'histoire* 84, 4 (2006): 961–981; Davide Turcato, 'Italian Anarchism as a Transnational Movement, 1885–1915,' *International Review of Social History* 52, 3 (2007): 407–444; Kirwin R. Shaffer, 'Havana Hub: Cuban Anarchism, Radical Media and the Trans-Caribbean Anarchist Network, 1902–1915,' *Caribbean Studies* 37, 2 (2009): 45–81; Ilham Khuri-Makdisi, *The Eastern Mediterranean and the Making of Global Radicalism: 1860–1914* (Berkeley: University of California Press, 2010).

51. One of the most questionable versions of this story can be found in Marshall, *Demanding the Impossible*, 453–454. Fanelli's importance was popularised in English by Brenan in *The Spanish Labyrinth*, 225–229, which cites Lorenzo's, *El proletariado militante*, 38–44, as the basis for this account. Esenwein gives his own, better, version of the story in *Anarchist Ideology*, 14–17. The implausibility of this story, given that Fanelli spoke no Spanish yet apparently 'captivated his audiences through "expressive mimicry"' (citing Lorenzo) is highlighted by Paul Heywood, 'The Labour Movement in Spain before 1914,' in *Labour and Socialist Movements in Europe before 1914*, ed. Dick Geary (Oxford: Berg, 1989), 233, although the oft-overlooked role of Rafael Farga Pellicer (who may have helped translate Fanelli's French) is stressed in James A. Baer, *Anarchist Immigrants in Spain and Argentina* (Chicago: University of Illinois Press, 2015), 17.

52. Baer, *Anarchist Immigrants*, 32–37.
53. Benedict Anderson, *Under Three Flags: Anarchism and the Anti-Colonial Imagination* (London: Verso, 2005), 169–173; James Michael Yeoman, 'Salud y anarquía desde Dowlais: The Translocal Experience of Spanish Anarchists in South Wales, 1900–1915,' *International Journal of Iberian Studies* 29, 3 (2016): 279–282.
54. Zimmer, *Immigrants against the State*, 54–55.
55. See Chapter 3.
56. Blanca Sánchez Alonso, 'Those Who Left and Those Who Stayed Behind: Explaining Emigration from the Regions of Spain, 1880–1914,' *The Journal of Economic History* 60, 3 (2000): 730–735.
57. Kirwin R. Shaffer, 'Panama Red: Anarchist Politics and Transnational Networks in the Panama Canal Zone, 1904–1913,' in *In Defiance of Boundaries: Anarchism in Latin American History*, ed. Geoffroy de Laforcade and Kirwin R. Shaffer (Gainesville: University Press of Florida, 2015), 57–80; Yeoman, 'Salud y anarquía.'
58. My own cautious estimates of anarchist support in South Wales is of 10% of the migrant community, which would swell or shrink according to local conditions, see Yeoman, 'Salud y anarquía,' 275–278. At its peak in 1911, the anarchist community in Panamá could have numbered as high as 1,000, of a workforce of around 10,000, although this high-point was not maintained for long: see Julie Greene, *The Canal Builders: Making America's Empire at the Panama Canal* (New York: Penguin, 2009), 175. On Argentina see Baer, *Anarchist Immigrants*, 38–50, and on Cuba see Amparo Sánchez Cobos, *Sembrando ideales: Anarquistas españoles en Cuba: 1902–1925* (Seville: Consejo Superior de Investigaciones Científicas, 2008), 47–98.
59. Martha A. Ackelsberg, 'It Takes More Than a Village! Transnational Travels of Spanish Anarchism in Argentina and Cuba,' *International Journal of Iberian Studies* 29, 3 (2016): 205–223.
60. Baer, *Anarchist Immigrants*, 21–22, 30–31 and 51–52. The claim made by Baer that Pellicer Paraire left Spain in 1891 to escape the repression of Montjuich (based on a report in *Tierra y Libertad* in 1916) does not fit the chronology of repression in Spain: the 'clutches' of the 'tigers of Montjuich' intensified later in the decade, after the advent of propaganda by the deed in 1893. See Chapter 2 of this book.
61. Baer, *Anarchist Immigrants*, 52–54.
62. Díaz del Moral, *Historia de las agitaciones*, 179–181. See also Ackelsberg, 'Transatlantic Travels,' 207 and Yeoman, 'Salud y anarquía,' 280.
63. One of the few works on the French influences on the Spanish movement is Teresa Abelló Güell, *Les relacions internacionals de l'anarquisme català (1881–1914)* (Barcelona: Edicions 62, 1987).
64. Baer, *Anarchist Immigrants*, 6; Khuri-Makdisi, *The Eastern Mediterranean*, 30–31.
65. Danny Evans and James Michael Yeoman, 'Introduction: New Approaches to Spanish Anarchism,' *International Journal of Iberian Studies* 29, 3 (2015): 199–204.
66. Carl Levy, 'The Rooted Cosmopolitan: Errico Malatesta: Syndicalism, Transnationalism and the International Labour Movement,' in Berry and Bantman, *New Perspectives on Anarchism*, 71–77.
67. See thoughts on the value of 'grounded' actors in transnational movements in Katherine Brickell and Ayona Datta, 'Introduction: Translocal Geographies,' in *Translocal Geographies: Spaces, Places, Connections*, ed. Katherine Brickell and Ayona Datta (Farnham: Ashgate, 2011), 3–4 and Clemens Greiner and Patrick Sakdapolrak, 'Translocality: Concepts, Applications and

Emerging Research Perspectives,' *Geography Compass* 7, 5 (2013): 376–377. On Mella's influence in Argentina see Baer, *Anarchist Immigrants*, 48.

68. Baer, *Anarchist Immigrants*, 6.
69. Zimmer, *Immigrants against the State*, 2–3.
70. Greiner and Sakdapolrak, 'Translocality,' 374.
71. Yeoman, '*Salud y anarquía*,' 274–275.
72. Michael Werner and Bénédicte Zimmerman, 'Beyond Comparison: *Histoire Croisée* and the Challenge of Reflexivity,' *History and Theory* 45, 1 (2006): 30–50.
73. Richard Croucher and John McIlroy, 'Introduction: Beyond National History,' *Labor History* 54, 5 (2013): 485–486.
74. Greiner and Sakdapolrak, 'Translocality,' 376–379.
75. In this book the term 'Catalan' will be used to define those papers published in this region, however this should not be taken that they used the Catalan language or were regionalist in outlook, see Madrid Santos, 'La prensa anarquista,' 31–35 and 96–99.
76. Chris Ealham, *Anarchism and the City: Revolution and Counter-Revolution in Barcelona, 1898–1937* (Edinburgh: AK Press, 2010), 1–10.
77. Ealham, *Anarchism and the City*, 22–53.
78. For example, Bar, *La CNT*.
79. A small selection of works centred on Cataluña and Barcelona over the turn of the century: Joaquín Romero Maura, *La rosa de fuego: Republicanos y anarquistas: La política de los obreros barceloneses entre el desastre colonial y la Semana Trágica* (Barcelona: Ediciones Grijalbo, 1975); Xavier Cuadrat, *Socialismo y anarquismo en Cataluña (1899–1911): Los orígenes de la CNT* (Madrid: Ediciones de la Revista de Trabajo, 1976); and more recently Angel Smith, *Anarchism, Revolution and Reaction: Catalan Labour and the Crisis of the Spanish State, 1898–1923* (New York: Berghahn, 2007).
80. Baer, *Anarchist Immigrants*, 32–33 is one example of a recent study which conforms to this position.
81. Bernaldo de Quirós, 'El espartaquismo agrario andaluz,' 410.
82. Lorenzo, *El proletariado militante*, 425.
83. See Chapter 3.
84. See letter from isolated anarchist in Bilbao in *La Protesta* (Valladolid), 23 March, 1900, 2.
85. *El Libertario* (Gijón), 16 November, 1912, 4 and 23 November, 1912, 3. For example see attacks on *El Productor* (Barcelona), in *La Cuestión Social* (Valencia), 4 June, 1892, 2 and *La Controversia* (Valencia), 3 June, 1893, 2–3.
86. Jacques Maurice, *El anarquismo andaluz: Campesinos y sindicalistas, 1868–1936* (Barcelona: Crítica, 1990) and *El anarquismo andaluz: Una vez más* (Granada: Editorial Universidad de Granada, 2007). See also Antonio López Estudillo, *Republicanismo y anarquismo en Andalucía: Conflictividad social agraria y crisis finisecular (1868–1900)* (Córdoba: Ediciones de La Posada, 2001); José Luis Gutiérrez Molina, 'Andalucía y el anarquismo (1868–1936),' *Ayer* 45, 1 (2002): 171–195.
87. For example: Kaplan, *Anarchists of Andalusia*; José Luis Gutiérrez Molina, *La tiza, la tinta y la palabra: José Sánchez Rosa: Maestro y anarquista andaluz (1864–1936)* (Ubrique: Tréveris, 2005); Antonio López Estudillo, *Insurrección y provocación policial: Los sucesos de Jerez de 1892* (La Laguna: Tierra de Fuego, 2008).
88. Ángeles González Fernández, *Utopía y realidad: Anarquismo, anarcosindicalismo y organizaciones obreras: Sevilla, 1900–1936* (Sevilla: Diputación Provincial de Sevilla, 1996); Custodio Velasco Mesa, *Los nombres de la cuestión social: Discurso y agitaciones obreras: Lieja y Sevilla en el tránsito de los siglos XIX y XX* (Sevilla: Diputación de Sevilla, 2003).

89. Exceptions include Antonio María Calero Amor, *Historia del movimiento obrero en Granada (1909–1923)* (Madrid: Editorial Tecnos, 1973).
90. Ángeles Barrio Alonso, *Anarquismo y anarcosindicalismo en Asturias, 1890–1936* (Madrid: Siglo XXI, 1988); Pamela Beth Radcliff, *From Mobilization to Civil War: The Politics of Polarization in the Spanish City of Gijón, 1900–1937* (Cambridge: Cambridge University Press, 1996).
91. Gérard Brey, 'Economie et mouvement syndical en Galice (1840–1911)' (PhD thesis, Pau: Université de Pau et des Pays de l'Adour, 1989); Óscar Freán Hernández, *El movimiento libertario en Galicia, 1910–1936* (Sada: Ediciós do Castro, 2006); Oswaldo Brito González, *Historia del movimiento obrero canario* (Madrid: Editorial Popular, 1980); Raquel Pérez Brito, *El anarquismo y los orígenes del movimiento obrero canario, 1900–1910* (La Laguna: Asociación Beecham, 2005); Carlos Gil Andrés, *Protesta popular y movilización en la Rioja de fin de siglo, 1890–1906* (Logroño: Instituto de Estudios Riojanos, 1995); Alfredo Velasco Núñez, *El hilo negro vasco: Anarquismo y anarcosindicalismo en el País Vasco (1870–1936)* (Bilbao: Martxoak, 2009).
92. Ignacio Martín Jiménez, *Conflicto social y pensamiento anarquista en Menorca (1897–1936)* (Palma de Mallorca: Plaguetes del Raval, 2007).
93. Laura Vicente Villanueva, *Sindicalismo y conflictividad social en Zaragoza (1916–1923)* (Zaragoza: Institución Fernando el Católico, 1993), 36–59. Both regions are better served in recent historiography focused on the Second Republic and Civil War.
94. See José Álvarez Junco and Manuel Pérez Ledesma, 'Historia del movimiento obrero: ¿Una segunda ruptura?,' *Revista de Occidente* 12 (1982): 19–41.
95. Pére Solà i Gussinyer, 'El honor de los estados y los juicios paralelos en el Caso Ferrer Guardia: Un cuarto de siglo de historiografía sobre la "Escuela Moderna" de Barcelona,' *Cuadernos de Historia Contemporánea* 26 (2004): 49–75.
96. For example see Pére Solà i Gussinyer, *Historia de l'associacionisme català contemporani: Barcelona i comarques de la seva demarcació: 1874–1966* (Barcelona: Generalitat de Catalunya, 1993).
97. Xavier Motilla Salas, 'Bases bibliográficas para una historia de la sociabilidad, el asociacionismo y la educación en la España contemporánea,' *Historia de la educación: Revista interuniversitaria* 31 (2012): 339–358.
98. For example, Garner, *Goals and Means* and Carles Sanz, *La CNT en pie: Fundación y consolidación anarcosindicalista, 1910–1931* (Barcelona: Anomia, 2011).

Bibliography

Archives

BPC: Biblioteca Provincial de Cádiz. Cádiz.
BVA: Biblioteca Virtual de Andalucía. Online.
HMM: Hemeroteca Municipal de Madrid. Madrid.
IISG: Internationaal Instituut voor Sociale Geschiedenis. Amsterdam.

Primary Sources

Anarchist Press

El Libertario. Gijón, 1912–1913. HMM and IISG.
La Controversia. Valencia, 1893. IISG.

La Cuestión Social. Valencia, 1892. IISG.
La Protesta. Valladolid/Sabadell/La Línea de la Concepción, 1899–1902. BVA and IISG.
La Voz del Obrero del Mar. Cádiz, II Epoch, 1907–1908. BPC and IISG.

Memoirs, Books and Pamphlets by Contemporary Authors

Lorenzo, Anselmo. *El proletariado militante: Memorias de un internacionalista.* Madrid: Alianza, 1974. IISG.

Secondary Sources

Abelló Güell, Teresa. *Les relacions internacionals de l'anarquisme català (1881–1914).* Barcelona: Edicions 62, 1987.
Ackelsberg, Martha A. *Free Women of Spain: Anarchism and the Struggle for the Emancipation of Women.* Edinburgh: AK Press, 2005.
Ackelsberg, Martha A. 'It Takes More Than a Village!: Transnational Travels of Spanish Anarchism in Argentina and Cuba.' *International Journal of Iberian Studies* 29, 3 (2016): 205–223.
Altena, Bert. 'Analysing Revolutionary Syndicalism: The Importance of Community.' In Berry and Bantman, *New Perspectives on Anarchism,* 180–220.
Álvarez Junco, José. *La ideología política del anarquismo español (1868–1910).* Madrid: Siglo XXI, 1991.
Álvarez Junco, José, and Manuel Pérez Ledesma. 'Historia del movimiento obrero: ¿Una segunda ruptura?.' *Revista de Occidente* 12 (1982): 19–41.
Anderson, Benedict. *Under Three Flags: Anarchism and the Anti-Colonial Imagination.* London: Verso, 2005.
Arbeloa, Víctor Manuel. 'La prensa obrera en España, (1869–1899).' *Revista de Trabajo* 30 (1970): 117–195.
Bantman, Constance. 'Internationalism without an International? Cross-Channel Anarchist Networks, 1890–1914.' *Revue belge de philology et d'histoire* 84, 4 (2006): 961–981.
Bantman, Constance, and Bert Altena. 'Introduction: Problematizing Scales of Analysis in Network-Based Social Movements.' In *Reassessing the Transnational Turn: Scales of Analysis in Anarchist and Syndicalist Studies,* edited by Constance Bantman and Bert Altena, 3–22. London: Routledge, 2015.
Bar, Antonio. *La CNT en los años rojos: Del sindicalismo revolucionario al anarcosindicalismo (1910–1926).* Madrid: Akal, 1981.
Barrio Alonso, Ángeles. *Anarquismo y anarcosindicalismo en Asturias, 1890–1936.* Madrid: Siglo XXI, 1988.
Baer, James A. *Anarchist Immigrants in Spain and Argentina.* Chicago: University of Illinois Press, 2015.
Bernaldo de Quirós, Constancio. 'El espartaquismo agrario andaluz.' *Revista general de legislación y jurisprudencia* 134 (1919): 307–319, 396–413 and 491–502.
Berry, David, and Constance Bantman, eds. *New Perspectives on Anarchism, Labour and Syndicalism: The Individual, the National and the Transnational.* Newcastle-upon-Tyne: Cambridge Scholars Publishing, 2010.

Berry, David, and Constance Bantman. 'Introduction: New Perspectives on Anarchism, Labour and Syndicalism: The Individual, the National and the Transnational.' In Berry and Bantman, *New Perspectives on Anarchism*, 1–13.

Boyd, Carolyn P. 'The Anarchists and Education in Spain, 1868–1909.' *The Journal of Modern History* 48, 4 (1976): 125–170.

Brenan, Gerald. *The Spanish Labyrinth: An Account of the Social and Political Background of the Civil War*. Cambridge: Cambridge University Press, 2014.

Brey, Gérard. 'Economie et mouvement syndical en Galice (1840–1911).' PhD thesis, Pau: Université de Pau et des Pays de l'Adour, 1989.

Brickell, Katherine, and Ayona Datta. 'Introduction: Translocal Geographies.' In *Translocal Geographies: Spaces, Places, Connections*, edited by Katherine Brickell and Ayona Datta, 3–20. Farnham: Ashgate, 2011.

Brito Gonález, Oswaldo. *Historia del movimiento obrero canario*. Madrid: Editorial Popular, 1980.

Calero Amor, Antonio María. *Historia del movimiento obrero en Granada (1909–1923)*. Madrid: Editorial Tecnos, 1973.

Casey, James. 'The Spanish Anarchist Peasant: How Primitive a Rebel?' *Journal of European Studie* 8, 34 (1978): 34–43.

Castillo, Santiago. *Historia de la UGT: Un sindicalismo consciente, 1873–1914*. Madrid: Siglo XXI, 2008.

Clark, Jonathan C.D. 'Secularization and Modernization: The Failure of a "Grand Narrative".' *The Historical Journal* 55, 1 (2012): 161–194.

Cleminson, Richard. 'The Construction of Masculinity in the Spanish Labour Movement: A Study of the *Revista Blanca*.' *International Journal of Iberian Studies* 24, 3 (2011): 201–217.

Cohn, Samuel. 'The "Modernity" of Medieval Popular Revolt.' *History Compass* 10, 10 (2012): 731–741.

Corbin, John R. 'The Myth of Primitive Spain.' *Anthropology Today* 5, 4 (1989): 15–17.

Croucher, Richard, and John McIlroy. 'Introduction: Beyond National History.' *Labor History* 54, 5 (2013): 485–490.

Cuadrat, Xavier. *Socialismo y anarquismo en Cataluña (1899–1911): Los orígenes de la CNT*. Madrid: Ediciones de la Revista de Trabajo, 1976.

Cumbers, Andy, Paul Routledge, and Corinne Nativel. 'The Entangled Geographies of Global Justice Networks.' *Progress in Human Geography* 32, 2 (2008): 183–201.

Dalmau, Pol. *Press, Politics and National Identities in Catalonia: The Transformation of La Vanguardia, 1881–1931*. Brighton: Sussex Academic Press, 2017.

Delhom, Joël. 'Inventario provisorio de las memorias anarquistas y anarcosindicalistas españolas.' *Cahiers de civilisation espagnole contemporaine* 4 (2009). Published online, accessed 15 September, 2013. https://journals.openedition.org/ccec/2677.

Díaz del Moral, Juan. *Historia de las agitaciones campesinas andaluzas-Córdoba: Antecedentes para una reforma agraria*. Madrid: Alianza, 1967.

Duncan, Martha Grace. 'Spanish Anarchism Refracted: Theme and Image in the Millenarian and Revisionist Literature.' *Journal of Contemporary History* 23, 3 (1988): 323–346.

Ealham, Chris. *Anarchism and the City: Revolution and Counter-Revolution in Barcelona, 1898–1937*. Edinburgh: AK Press, 2010.

Esenwein, George. *Anarchist Ideology and the Working-Class Movement in Spain, 1868–1898*. Berkeley, CA: University of California Press, 1989.

Evans, Danny, and James Michael Yeoman. 'Introduction: New Approaches to Spanish Anarchism.' *International Journal of Iberian Studies* 29, 3 (2015): 199–204.

Featherstone, David. *Resistance, Space and Political Identities: The Making of Counter-Global Networks*. Oxford: Wiley-Blackwell, 2008.

Flaquer Montequi, Rafael. *La clase obrera madrileña y la Primera Internacional, (1868–1874): Un análisis de prensa*. Madrid: Editorial Cuadernos Para el Dialogo, 1977.

Freán Hernández, Óscar. *El movimiento libertario en Galicia, 1910–1936*. Sada: Ediciós do Castro, 2006.

Freán Hernández, Oscar. 'El anarquismo español: Luces y sombras en la historiografía reciente sobre el movimiento libertario.' *Ayer* 84, 4 (2011): 209–223.

Gabriel, Pere. 'Historiografía reciente sobre el anarquismo y el sindicalismo en España, 1870–1923.' *Historia Social* 1 (1988): 45–54.

Garner, Jason. *Goals and Means: Anarchism, Syndicalism, and Internationalism in the Origins of the Federación Anarquista Ibérica*. Edinburgh: AK Press, 2016.

Gil Andrés, Carlos. *Protesta popular y movilización en la Rioja de fin de siglo, 1890–1906*. Logroño: Instituto de Estudios Riojanos, 1995.

González Fernández, Ángeles. *Utopía y realidad: Anarquismo, anarcosindicalismo y organizaciones obreras: Sevilla, 1900–1936*. Sevilla: Diputación Provincial de Sevilla, 1996.

Greene, Julie. *The Canal Builders: Making America's Empire at the Panama Canal*. New York, NY: Penguin, 2009.

Greiner, Clemens, and Patrick Sakdapolrak. 'Translocality: Concepts, Applications and Emerging Research Perspectives.' *Geography Compass* 7, 5 (2013): 376–377.

Gutiérrez Molina, José Luis. 'Andalucía y el anarquismo (1868–1936).' *Ayer* 45, 1 (2002): 171–195.

Gutiérrez Molina, José Luis. *La tiza, la tinta y la palabra: José Sánchez Rosa: Maestro y anarquista andaluz (1864–1936)*. Ubrique: Tréveris, 2005.

Heywood, Paul. 'The Labour Movement in Spain before 1914.' In *Labour and Socialist Movements in Europe Before 1914*, edited by Dick Geary, 231–265. Oxford: Berg, 1989.

Heywood, Paul. *Marxism and the Failure of Organised Socialism in Spain: 1879–1936*. Cambridge: Cambridge University Press, 1990.

Hobsbawm, Eric. *Primitive Rebels: Studies in Archaic Forms of Social Movement in the 19th and 20th Centuries*. New York, NY: W.W. Norton, 1965.

Hobsbawm, Eric, and George Rudé. *Captain Swing*. London: Lawrence and Wishart, 1969.

Hofmann, Bert, Pere Joan i Tous, and Manfred Tietze, eds. *El anarquismo español y sus tradiciones culturales*. Frankfurt/Madrid: Vervuert/Iberoamericana, 1995.

Íniguez, Miguel. *La prensa anarquista en el País Vasco, La Rioja y Navarra*. Vitoria: Albor, 1996.

Kaplan, Temma. *Anarchists of Andalusia, 1868–1903*. Princeton: Princeton University Press, 1977.

Khuri-Makdisi, Ilham. *The Eastern Mediterranean and the Making of Global Radicalism: 1860–1914*. Berkeley: University of California Press, 2010.

Levy, Carl. 'Social Histories of Anarchism.' *Journal for the Study of Radicalism* 4, 2 (2010): 1–44.

Levy, Carl. 'The Rooted Cosmopolitan: Errico Malatesta: Syndicalism, Transnationalism and the International Labour Movement.' In Berry and Bantman, *New Perspectives on Anarchism*, 61–79.

Levy, Carl. 'Anarchism and Cosmopolitanism.' In *The Palgrave Handbook of Anarchism*, edited by Carl Levy and Matthew Adams, 125–148. Cham: Palgrave Macmillan, 2018.

Litvak, Lily. 'La prensa anarquista (1880–1913).' In Hofmann, Tous and Tietze, *El anarquismo español*, 215–235.

Litvak, Lily. *Musa libertaria: Arte, literatura y vida cultural del anarquismo español (1890–1913)*. Madrid: Fundación de Estudios Libertarios Anselmo Lorenzo, 2001.

Litvak, Lily. 'La buena nueva: Cultura y prensa anarquista (1880–1913).' *Revista de Occidente* 304 (2006): 5–18.

López Estudillo, Antonio. *Republicanismo y anarquismo en Andalucía: Conflictividad social agraria y crisis finisecular (1868–1900)*. Córdoba: Ediciones de La Posada, 2001.

López Estudillo, Antonio. *Insurrección y provocación policial: Los sucesos de Jerez de 1892*. La Laguna: Tierra de Fuego, 2008.

Madrid Santos, Francisco. 'La prensa anarquista y anarcosindicalista en España desde la I Internacional hasta el fin de la Guerra Civil.' PhD thesis, Barcelona: Universidad Central de Barcelona, 1988–1989. Published online, accessed 12 May, 2012. http://cedall.org/Documentacio/Castella/cedall203410101.htm.

Madrid Santos, Francisco. *Solidaridad Obrera y el periodismo de raíz ácrata*. Badalona: Ediciones Solidaridad Obrera, 2007.

Martín Jiménez, Ignacio. *Conflicto social y pensamiento anarquista en Menorca (1897–1936)*. Palma de Mallorca: Plaguetes del Raval, 2007.

Marshall, Peter. *Demanding the Impossible: A History of Anarchism*. London: Fontana, 1993.

Maurice, Jacques. *El anarquismo andaluz: Campesinos y sindicalistas, 1868–1936*. Barcelona: Crítica, 1990.

Maurice, Jacques. *El anarquismo andaluz: Una vez más*. Granada: Editorial Universidad de Granada, 2007.

Motilla Salas, Xavier. 'Bases bibliográficas para una historia de la sociabilidad, el asociacionismo y la educación en la España contemporánea.' *Historia de la educación: Revista interuniversitaria* 31 (2012): 339–358.

Pérez Brito, Raquel. *El anarquismo y los orígenes del movimiento obrero canario, 1900–1910*. La Laguna: Asociación Beecham, 2005.

Pérez Ledesma, Manuel. 'La formación de la clase obrera: Una creación cultural.' In *Cultura y movilización en la España contemporánea*, edited by Rafael Cruz and Manuel Pérez Ledesma, 201–233. Madrid: Alianza, 1997.

Peters, Kate. *Print Culture and the Early Quakers*. Cambridge: Cambridge University Press, 2005.

Popkin, Jeremy D. *Revolutionary News: The Press in France, 1789–1799*. Durham: Duke University Press, 1990.

Prado, Antonio. *Escritoras anarco-feministas en La Revista Blanca (1898–1936): Matrimonio, familia y estado*. Madrid: Fundación de Estudios Libertarios Anselmo Lorenzo, 2011.

Radcliff, Pamela Beth. *From Mobilization to Civil War: The Politics of Polarization in the Spanish City of Gijón, 1900–1937*. Cambridge: Cambridge University Press, 1996.

Ralle, Michel. 'La sociabilidad obrera en la sociedad de la Restauración (1875–1910).' *Estudios de Historia Social* 3, 50–51 (1989): 161–199.

Raymond, Joad. *The Invention of the Newspaper: English Newsbooks, 1641–1649*. Oxford: Clarendon, 1996.

Rivett, Gary. 'English Newsbooks, Storytelling and Political Criticism.' *Media History* 19, 1 (2013): 3–16.

Rohrbach, Augusta. '"Truth Stronger and Stranger than Fiction": Reexamining William Lloyd Garrison's *Liberator*.' *American Literature* 73, 4 (2001): 727–755.

Romero Maura, Joaquín. *La rosa de fuego: Republicanos y anarquistas: La política de los obreros barceloneses entre el desastre colonial y la Semana Trágica*. Barcelona: Ediciones Grijalbo, 1975.

Sánchez Alonso, Blanca. 'Those Who Left and Those Who Stayed Behind: Explaining Emigration from the Regions of Spain, 1880–1914.' *The Journal of Economic History* 60, 3 (2000): 730–755.

Sánchez Cobos, Amparo. *Sembrando ideales: Anarquistas españoles en Cuba: 1902–1925*. Sevilla: Consejo Superior de Investigaciones Científicas, 2008.

Santullano, Gabriel. 'Algunas notas sobre la prensa obrera en Asturias en el siglo XIX (1868–1899).' *Boletín del Instituto de Estudios Asturianos* 88–89 (1976): 509–534.

Sanz, Carles. *La CNT en pie: Fundación y consolidación anarcosindicalista, 1910–1931*. Barcelona: Anomia, 2011.

Serrano Lacarra, Carlos. '*Acracia*, los anarquistas y la cultura.' In Hofmann, Tous and Tietze, *El anarquismo español*, 347–360.

Shaffer, Kirwin R. 'Panama Red: Anarchist Politics and Transnational Networks in the Panama Canal Zone, 1904–1913.' In *In Defiance of Boundaries: Anarchism in Latin American History*, edited by Geoffroy de Laforcade and Kirwin R. Shaffer, 57–80. Gainesville: University Press of Florida, 2015.

Smaldone, William. *European Socialism: A Concise History with Documents*. Lanham: Rowman and Littlefield, 2014.

Smith, Angel. *Anarchism, Revolution and Reaction: Catalan Labour and the Crisis of the Spanish State, 1898–1923*. New York: Berghahn, 2007.

Solà i Gussinyer, Pére. *Historia de l'associacionisme català contemporani: Barcelona i comarques de la seva demarcació: 1874–1966*. Barcelona: Generalitat de Catalunya, 1993.

Solà i Gussinyer, Pére. 'El honor de los estados y los juicios paralelos en el Caso Ferrer Guardia: Un cuarto de siglo de historiografía sobre la "Escuela Moderna" de Barcelona.' *Cuadernos de Historia Contemporánea* 26 (2004): 49–75.

Tarrow, Sidney G. *Power in Movement: Social Movements and Contentious Politics*. Cambridge: Cambridge University Press, 2011.

Tavera i García, Susanna. '*La Revista Blanca*: Análisis de una publicación anarquista.' PhD thesis, Barcelona: Universidad de Barcelona, 1973.

Tavera i García, Susanna. 'La premsa anarco-sindicalista, (1868–1931).' *Recerques* 8 (1978): 85–102.

Tavera i García, Susana. *Solidaridad Obrera: Fer-se i desfer-se d'un diari anarco-sindicalista (1915–1939)*. Barcelona: Col·legi de Periodistes de Catalunya, 1992.

Termes, Josep. *Anarquismo y sindicalismo en España: La Primera Internacional (1864–1881)*. Barcelona: Crítica, 1977.

Turcato, Davide. 'Italian Anarchism as a Transnational Movement, 1885–1915.' *International Review of Social History* 52, 3 (2007): 407–444.

Valera Ortega, José. *Los amigos políticos: Partidos, elecciones y caciquismo en la Restauración (1875–1900)*. Madrid: Alianza, 1977.

Velasco Mesa, Custodio. *Los nombres de la cuestión social: Discurso y agitaciones obreras: Lieja y Sevilla en el tránsito de los siglos XIX y XX*. Sevilla: Diputación de Sevilla, 2003.

Velasco Núñez, Alfredo. *El hilo negro vasco: Anarquismo y anarcosindicalismo en el País Vasco (1870–1936)*. Bilbao: Martxoak, 2009.

Vicente Villanueva, Laura. *Sindicalismo y conflictividad social en Zaragoza (1916–1923)*. Zaragoza: Institución Fernando el Católico, 1993.

Werner, Michael, and Bénédicte Zimmerman. 'Beyond Comparison: *Histoire Croisée* and the Challenge of Reflexivity.' *History and Theory* 45, 1 (2006): 30–50.

Yeoman, James Michael. '*Salud y anarquía desde Dowlais*: The Translocal Experience of Spanish Anarchists in South Wales, 1900–1915.' *International Journal of Iberian Studies* 29, 3 (2016): 273–289.

Zimmer, Kenyon. *Immigrants against the State: Yiddish and Italian Anarchism in America*. Chicago: University of Illinois Press, 2015.

1 With Words, With Writings and With Deeds
Anarchist Print Culture, 1890–1915

Over the turn of the twentieth century, the experience of anarchism in Spain was expressed and shaped by the producers, distributors and consumers of the movement's print. Printed sources were not a simply a repository of information, but the symbolic and material site where numerous, dynamic elements of anarchism converged.[1] They were crucial in the formation of anarchist discourse, which 'configured experiences' and gave meaning to abstract ideas.[2] Print was particularly important for an ideology that loathed 'inertia'.[3] Rather than a series of static ideas—or, in the words of anarchist commentators, 'dogma'—anarchism required constant, active engagement from its followers in order to have meaning.[4] At times, a minority within the movement demanded 'action' in contrast to the 'theoretical' work of propaganda.[5] Much more common, however, were those who regarded 'intellectual labour' as a vital component of anarchist practice, which shaped revolutionary action and made it possible.[6] The value of print was 'immense,' as it rid workers of 'political lethargy,' turning the active working class into 'proselytisers for the cause of liberty'.[7] Propaganda was a means of struggle, a way to introduce new comrades to the ideas of anarchism, to 'educate and direct opinion, exposing the most just ideas' and 'to conquer the sympathies of all people'.[8] Thus the argument of Marcel van der Linden that 'what counts is what [a] movement does in practice, and not how it justifies what it does' is based on a false distinction between words and deeds. To construct ideology and culture through print inspired practice, and was practice in itself.[9] To engage in print—to write, edit, print, receive, distribute, read, hear and respond to periodicals—was to engage in the movement. This did not come at the expense of activity, but rather fostered and reinforced other forms of participation. 'We the anarchists'—wrote the most respected theorist in the movement, Ricardo Mella, in 1902—'work for the coming revolution with words, with writings and with deeds . . . the press, the book, the private and public meeting are today, as ever, abundant terrain for all initiatives'.[10]

Anarchist publications were generally one of five types: books, pamphlets, journals, periodicals and *hojas* (broadsides). In the words of the most respected figure in the movement, Anselmo Lorenzo (1841–1914), longer forms of writing, such as books and pamphlets, were a means to 'store in perfect classification all the knowledge' needed to produce the revolution.[11] Over 700 anarchist books and pamphlets were published between 1890 and 1915, covering an enormous range of subjects, such as geography, history, political theory, biology and birth control, sociology, current affairs, the law, art and literature.[12] Some books were extremely popular, particularly those of Pyotr Kropotkin, whose *Mutual Aid* sold 20,000 in three years, while *The Conquest of Bread*—which went through eleven editions over the turn of the century—had sold approximately 28,000 copies by 1909. Marx's *Capital* sold around 9,000 copies in the same period.[13] Although they were popular, most groups could not afford to publish books. Their production was thus limited to handful of larger publishers, such as the 'Escuela Moderna' and 'Salud y Fuerza' groups of Barcelona. In contrast, pamphlet publishing flourished across the movement from 1890 to 1915. As well as prose, pamphlets were used to publish plays, poetry, songs and transcripts from conferences. These shorter publications provided an inexpensive, one-off contribution to print culture. Despite their cheap paper and flimsy binding, these items were treasured by their readers. Popular pamphlets would be reprinted numerous times by groups across the country. Errico Malatesta's dialogue *Entre campesinos*, for example, was published in 15 different editions from 1889–1915.[14] At the other extreme to longer forms of print were *hojas*, or broadsides: one-sheet publications designed for specific, immediate calls to action such as notices for upcoming demonstrations and strikes. They were also used to reach out to individuals outside the movement, handed out in a local area or affixed as posters in public spaces. *Hojas* were particularly popular during elections, as in 1896 and 1913, when they carried calls to abstain from voting.[15] While few *hojas* from the period have survived, books and pamphlets are abundant in the archives, to the point that a systematic analysis of their role within print culture merits study in itself. Therefore, despite their importance to anarchist print culture, books, pamphlets and *hojas* have been used sparingly in this study, which instead focuses on the other 'blade' in the 'double-edged sword' of anarchist print: the weekly and monthly press.[16]

Of the 298 anarchist periodicals and journals launched between 1890 and 1915, roughly two-thirds were based outside Cataluña (191, 64 per cent; to 107, 36 per cent from Cataluña), accounting for just over half the total number of issues (c.4,029 issues, 55 per cent; to c.3,299 issues, 45 per cent from Cataluña). Of these, 2,482 issues from non-Catalan papers have survived in various archives in Spain, the Netherlands and Britain. These publications form the main source base for this study.[17]

Periodicals were a middle ground between the theoretical depth provided by books and pamphlets and the immediacy of *hojas*. In periodicals, anarchist theory was presented in short, easily-digestible articles, deployed as a means to articulate the 'daily struggle for truth'.[18] Rather than the singular voice of a pamphlet or book, periodicals were the product of numerous editors, authors, correspondents and readers, engaged in dialogue with one another. Periodicals were sites of discussion and dispute, and their content was constantly modified and updated, giving them a sense of development lacking in other forms of print. They were thus more representative of how the movement constructed and interpreted—rather than simply transmitted—theory in relation to practice, and vice versa. The press was also used to distribute other aspects of print culture. Extracts from a pamphlet were often printed on the third and fourth pages of a paper, designed to be torn out, folded and assembled with serialised extracts from subsequent issues. After several weeks or months, the subscriber to the paper would be able to bind a complete pamphlet together with string, which is how many remain in the archives. A similar, although less common, practice was to print a *hoja* on the last page, which again would be ripped out of the paper and used as independent material.[19]

The vast majority of anarchist periodicals consisted of one sheet of paper, which would be folded to create four pages. This was a common size for many papers in Spain, including the PSOE's weekly *El Socialista* (Madrid) and much larger national newspapers, such as the Republican daily *El País* (Madrid).[20] The only exception to this format in anarchist publishing were journal-style publications, such as *La Revista Blanca* (Madrid), which consisted of longer pieces over eight, sixteen or thirty-two pages. Journals of this type have been included in this study, although since they were much less common than four-page periodicals they form only a minor part of the analysis.

Four-page papers would usually open with theoretical pieces and commentaries on current affairs, followed by sections devoted to letters from correspondents and smaller news sections. On the final page most papers would publish administrative information, including summaries of collections and solidarity campaigns. Other regular sections included poetry, short stories and plays; digests and refutations the of 'bourgeois,' Catholic, Republican and socialist press; columns containing brief sardonic remarks on local and national news; international news; and 'bibliographies,' which contained information on other publications of the movement. In contrast to most other publications in Spain (although not *El Socialista*), only a handful of anarchist papers contained adverts.[21] Pictures were also rare, and usually only appeared in special or commemorative issues, such as those published on the anniversaries of executions of martyrs.[22] These were drawn from a relatively small pool of images, often repeating pictures used in previous years and/or other publications.[23] Drawings and photographs were clearly popular with readers, and many publishing groups made larger orders to their printers for issues containing images to cope with the expected increased demand.[24]

Although several attempts to establish an anarchist daily were made between 1890 and 1915, all proved too costly to maintain. Most anarchist periodicals aspired to a regular weekly, fortnightly or monthly output.[25] In practice, most were much more erratic, which meant that they were often published days, weeks or months after the events they reported on took place. 'Breaking news' was occasionally crammed on to the back page of publications, usually in verbatim copies of telegraph wires from official sources, but by and large papers relied upon the postal system for news.[26] This lack of immediacy meant that these publications were much more akin to media such as newsbooks and parish newsletters than mass readership daily 'newspapers'.

Publishing groups considered themselves as engaged in a totally different activity to the 'bourgeois,' 'salaried' press. The mainstream press in Spain had expanded dramatically during the Restoration period, offering a form of public expression which was largely denied by the political system.[27] Anarchists saw these papers as 'vile . . . intellectual cretinism', consisting of nothing more than political intrigues, sensationalism, bull fights, adverts and slander against their movement.[28] Yet while they advised their readers against reading these papers, labelling it 'moral suicide,' they were aware that their readers were likely to receive at least one daily mainstream paper alongside their weekly anarchist periodical.[29] Rather than a substitute for the mainstream press, anarchist papers provided an alternative, parallel source of news and discussion.[30] Some papers devoted a huge amount of space to attacks on other papers, not only national dailies, but also local papers, religious publications, republican periodicals and *El Socialista*. In contrast, other anarchist papers were generally seen as comrades. Established papers advised their readers to subscribe to 'all of the anarchist press' and gave as much support as they could to aspiring publishing groups and new titles.

Rather than journalists or intellectuals, anarchist publishers generally saw themselves as 'workers'. This included the few print professionals who worked within anarchist periodicals—Ernesto Álvarez, for example, edited *La Anarquía* (Madrid) while he worked as a proof-reader for *El Globo* (Madrid), and the typographers of Barcelona were an important part of the early CNT—whose work for the movement was separate from their occupation.[31] Thus the people who managed anarchist papers were largely the same as those who made up the bulk of the movement: they were coopers, bootmakers, locksmiths, seamen, dockers, and construction workers. None received payment for their services to the anarchist press. Establishing and running a periodical was regarded as a crucial part of the struggle against authority, rather than an opportunity for professional or financial gain.[32] Most conducted their work for the anarchist press after the working day.[33] Some papers were set up as the organ of a workers' society or federation, such as *El Obrero del Río Tinto* (Río Tinto), founded by the anarchist copper miners' society 'Los

Manumitidos,' and *Solidaridad Obrera*, (Gijón), which acted as the organ of the Gijón anarchist labour federation. Other papers were founded by loosely structured 'propaganda' groups, who were united only by their shared desire to spread anarchist ideas.

Launching a periodical was a difficult task. A group would often publicise its intentions in other papers of the movement, asking for donations to help cover start-up costs.[34] Another method of raising funds was to arrange a raffle, for which the prizes were usually books, either of anarchist literature or other useful materials, such as dictionaries and atlases. The whole movement would be invited to participate, linking anarchists together across localities in a simple and popular activity.[35] Raffles were also used to sustain existing papers, to help with the publication of pamphlets, to cover the cost of propaganda tours and, in one case, to raise money to send a comrade from Tenerife to Madrid for surgery.[36]

The majority of periodicals were produced by commercial printers, which was a potential source of difficulty. Local authorities frequently persuaded or coerced printers into rejecting existing orders and rethinking their relationship with the anarchist movement.[37] Relationships with printers could also be strained for more mundane reasons, such as delays or mistakes in the printing, which could lead to public attacks on printing houses by the very papers they produced.[38] Many groups aspired to set up their own printing press as a means to secure their independence. One of the few groups to succeed in this aim was the El Corsario group in La Coruña, who established the 'El Progreso' printers in late 1895. Within a few months the printing house was thousands of pesetas in debt and under police surveillance, and less than a year after it had been founded 'El Progreso' was forced to close.[39] In the following years a few, slightly more successful publishers were established and staffed by anarchists, but in general anarchist publishers continued to rely upon printers external to the movement until after 1915.[40]

The content of papers came from a variety of sources. Locally-focused stories and theoretical pieces were often written by the publishing group themselves, particularly if they were experienced writers.[41] Other content was copied from articles from other papers, or from texts by theorists in the international movement, such as Pyotr Kropotkin and Errico Malatesta. The remainder of the paper would be made up from original material from correspondents and contributors based across Spain. As soon as a newspaper was established it would be inundated with letters containing theoretical reflections, stories, poetry, calls for solidarity, news of union activities, meetings and collections, and reports of scandalous behaviour by employers and police. Editorial decisions were difficult for many publishing groups, as this could be interpreted as an exercise of authority. Many editors apologised to correspondents whose work they did not print, blaming lack of space in the paper, though this hardly explained why some articles made it to print ahead of others.[42] Established authors appeared to be preferred over others, as were those that kept their articles brief, did not need corrections, and paid for their own postage (letters were often sent without stamps, passing the cost of postage onto the receiver).[43] Correspondents often became irate with editorial decisions, and were asked to show 'patience' and 'understanding' when their works were not published. Nevertheless, there remained no shortage of individuals willing to send in material.

Most correspondents were workers and activists, who acted as spokespersons for the movement in their locality.[44] In areas which did not sustain a periodical, the link between the correspondent and a publishing group was the prime means through which local anarchists communicated with the wider movement. Aware of their geographically diverse readership, anarchist periodicals sought to publish content from a range of local correspondents, which was regarded as relevant to anarchists everywhere. They also aspired to forge links across the whole of Spain, and in many cases across Europe and the Americas. Papers would regularly travel hundreds of miles to reach their readership; for example, *La Protesta*, based in La Línea de la Concepción —a town on the southern coast of Andalucía, on the border with Gibraltar—was sent to over 80 different villages, towns and cities in the space of a year, travelling as far as Bilbao (506 miles), Mahón (582 miles), Dowlais (South Wales; 1,081 miles), New York (3,636 miles) and Buenos Aires (5,971 miles) [see Map 1.1].[45]

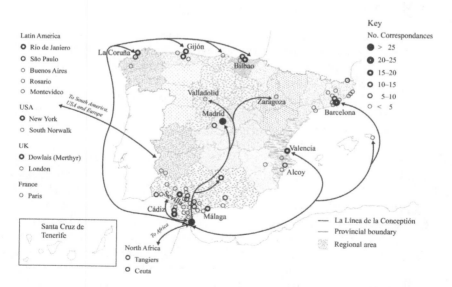

Map 1.1 Distribution of *La Protesta* (La Línea de la Concepción), 1901–1902.

Source: Map created by James G. Pearson.

The flow of information between publishers and correspondents ran both ways. As well as acting as stringers, correspondents (also known as *paqueteros*) received and distributed papers in their local area. This could be done by hand, or through a workers' centre or kiosk. These sites were important focal points for anarchist communities, acting as information hubs and places of socialisation.[46] Distribution could also involve reading papers to others. In 1900, an average of 63.8 per cent of Spanish adults were illiterate, a figure which was more acute amongst women, and amongst the working-class constituencies that anarchists sought to reach.[47] Yet this was not as serious a barrier to anarchist publishers as might be assumed. Reading newspapers aloud was a popular communal practice in Spain throughout the nineteenth century, which gave all papers a wider audience than would be expected from their modest print runs and the limited literacy of their audience.[48] With this in mind, it is assumed—although near impossible to prove—that the audience for anarchist papers was 5–15 times larger than the number they printed.[49] Reading periodicals, books and pamphlets aloud fostered sociability and gave illiterate and semi-literate workers the chance to engage with the ideas of the movement, inviting their 'commentary, criticism and debate,' which was welcomed by anarchist authors and editors.[50] The task of reading anarchist papers to others would be undertaken by literate individuals, known as *lectors* (readers), who were often also the local correspondent.[51] The readings often took place at public meetings and smaller gatherings in centres, as observed by the reformist commentator Ramiro de Maeztu in 1901:

> These books, pamphlets and periodicals are not read in the manner of others . . . the reader of anarchist works—generally a worker—does not have a library, nor buys books for himself. [I have] witnessed the reading of [Kropotkin's] *The Conquest of Bread* in a workers' centre. In a room dimly lit by a candle, up to fourteen workers met every night of the winter. One of them reads laboriously, the others listen . . . I have also witnessed the reading of the Bible in a puritan household. The impression was identical.[52]

Papers could also be read during working hours, where 'teams of workers would divide labour so that one of them would be free to read anarchist literature'.[53] Through these practices the printed word became the spoken word. This process was assisted by the language and structure of many articles in the press. The page-long paragraphs, repetition and rhetorical devices within anarchist writing can make them trying for a solitary reader, yet when spoken aloud they come to life.[54] This is particularly noticeable when articles ended with capitalised phrases such as 'VIVA LA ANARQUIA! VIVA LA REVOLUCION SOCIAL!,' designed to elicit a call-and-response style climax to a reading. The texts of the anarchist press were thus not reserved for an elite, literature readership, but rather 'lived' through repeated communal readings, which ensured that anarchist papers could reach a much greater audience than the poor levels of literacy in Spain would suggest was possible.[55]

Correspondents were also responsible for collecting money for publishing groups. The most common price for a single issue was 5 céntimos, a small but significant sum for unemployed and badly-paid individuals with little or no disposable income.[56] The only exception were anarcho-communist publications, which were funded solely by voluntary donations. The anarcho-communist view was that periodicals should be as accessible as possible, even at the risk of increased ephemerality. 'When will those comrades [other anarchist papers] . . . understand' —asked the anarcho-communist *La Controversia*—'that no pamphlet nor periodical, being edited by anarchists, should be sold nor bought, but that each one, *according to their forces*, should assist in propaganda?'[57] For the majority of papers which did charge, correspondents would receive a discount for making bulk orders, which would often be sent by the publishing group prior to receiving payment. Correspondents were also responsible for collecting money for the solidarity funds managed by anarchist papers, set up to provide assistance for anarchist strikers, prisoners and widows of former comrades. These collections would be made at workplaces and during social events, such as meetings, plays, marriages and funerals, in the manner of a Catholic offertory.[58]

The numerous roles entrusted to correspondents made them crucial in maintaining the networks of anarchist print culture.[59] They were the 'nodes' through which the anarchist press was channelled into localities, and the thoughts, experiences and money from localities were channelled out to publishers. Their literacy and connections gave them a position of authority and influence within the movement at large, making them focal points and 'informal elites' at the local level.[60] On a national level, publishing groups gave the movement a semblance of coherence which was lacking in its fissiparous ideology. Just as correspondents controlled the flow of information and finances in their locality, publishing groups acted as the 'supernodes,' directing the workings of the movement across Spain.[61] Publishing houses also established strong links with one another. When a new paper was launched it would be sent to all other anarchist papers in Spain, often until the paper went out of print. These bonds were particularly important for smaller papers, which relied upon well-established titles for exposure and distribution. Since larger papers were relatively stable and published regularly, they could maintain a flow of information between more erratic titles and their readership, for example by informing publishers of changes to orders from correspondents. Relations between papers were underpinned by a sense of duty to support one another, which was, in theory, seen as more important than potential ideological or personal disagreements between editors. Some

papers also maintained exchanges with publishers in different movements, above all *El Socialista*, despite regular and public criticism of the
socialist movement and its paper from almost all of its anarchist contemporaries. Such links usually only became apparent when they broke
down, as in 1902, when ties between *La Protesta* and *El Socialista* were
severed after 'many years' of exchange, which had hitherto endured in
spite of the deep antagonism between the editors Ernesto Álvarez and
Pablo Iglesias.[62]

Bonds between papers also extended beyond Spain, connecting publishing houses to the larger anarchist papers in Europe and the Americas,
and were one of the key constitutive elements of anarchist transnationalism. As well as generating and distributing print around the world,
publishing houses operated as archives of the international movement's
press. Indeed, the extensive collection of the movement's press in the
International Institute of Social History in Amsterdam is largely based
on papers sent from Spain to titles such as *Freedom* (London) and *Les
Temps Nouveaux* (Paris) and subsequently archived, and not from the
generally poorly-conserved collections within Spain itself.

Anarchist print culture had a hierarchy, based on the standing of publishers and the papers they produced. Despite the exchange system within
the press, smaller papers, managed by relatively unknown anarchists were
often largely ignored. In contrast, larger, well-established papers drew
respect, as did those associated with the elites of anarchist print culture,
such as Federico Urales, Soledad Gustavo, Anselmo Lorenzo, Fermín Salvochea, Ricardo Mella and José Prat. Many of these papers were based
in Barcelona, for example *El Productor*, *Tierra y Libertad* (post-1906)
and *Solidaridad Obrera*. Yet from 1890–1915 papers such as *La Anarquía* (Madrid), *La Idea Libre*, (Madrid), *El Corsario* (La Coruña), *La
Protesta* (Valladolid-Sabadell-La Línea de la Concepción), *Acción Libertaria* (Gijón), and, in particular, *La Revista Blanca* and *Suplemento a
la Revista Blanca* (Madrid) all claimed a readership and influence which
matched that of their contemporaries in Barcelona. These elite publishing
groups had links with hundreds of localities in Spain and drew contributions from leading figures in international anarchist circles. Larger papers
connected anarchists in Spain, Europe and the Americas and were the
first to bring new works and ideas to the movement. They were also the
central points of national solidarity campaigns, which often raised thousands of pesetas for the cause. When such papers offered interpretations
of theory and suggested new directions for the movement, it was as close
to an 'official' statement as was possible. Yet this elite position was also
fragile. The anti-hierarchical premise of anarchism ensured that no single
voice could legitimately claim to be the undisputed mouthpiece of the
movement. Disputes regularly erupted within and between publishing
groups, leading to splits and the creation of rival papers. Even the most
prominent individuals in the movement could be ostracised and lose their

links to the wider movement, as happened with the 'Urales family' publishing group in 1904.[63]

The links between readers, correspondents and publishers added horizontal linkages to the movement, uniting it in a shared engagement in print culture. For most of the period 1890–1915 the press system was the closest thing to a national structure within Spanish anarchism. The nature of this organising system—with its bottom-up collaboration, anti-hierarchical premise, and basis on solidarity and mutual aid, rather than formal procedures—was both product of anarchist ideology and practice, and shaped anarchist ideology and practice. This symbiotic relationship between movement and press was noted by contemporary observers such as Juan Díaz del Moral:

> th[e] great spread of the libertarian press gives [the movement], without doubt, its peculiar structure. The anarchist periodical serves as an organ of communication between all followers and workers [. . .] To subscribe to a periodical and pay for a subscription, to buy or sell books, to announce the creation and address of groups, to discover the whereabouts or the situation of a friend or relative, to notify of a change of address, to broadcast the names and addresses of police confidents, the worker uses the periodical, which fulfils these functions admirably.[64]

The role of periodicals in shaping ideological developments was demonstrated most clearly in their encouragement of open debate between theorists, activists and ordinary members of the movement. Many maintained a *tribuna libre* ('open forum') section, to which anyone could contribute their thoughts on current affairs or ideological discussions. Such sections often developed into full-blown public arguments. As will be shown through the following chapters, many papers published a plurality of positions on the most contentious issues faced by the movement over the turn of the century, including of the legitimacy of terrorism, the difference between of 'free' education and indoctrination, the value or dangers of adopting syndicalist organisation, and the movement's position on the First World War. These open forums rarely resolved debates, and largely consisted of back-and-forths between individuals with settled opinions, yet in some cases they did guide the eventual editorial line of the publications they appeared in. In contrast, publishers with a more defined stance would avoid such forums, or used their editorial discretion to publish only those positions they agreed with.[65]

As well as ad-hoc debates, publishing groups occasionally launched or hosted more formal debates and literary competitions, known as *certámenes*. Such initiatives had developed in the 1880s as important vehicles for disseminating anarchist ideas.[66] Themes for discussion would be circulated through the anarchist press, inviting authors from across the country to send in their entries. Smaller *certámenes* (also known as *concursos*) would often be conducted solely through print, with high-profile activists and theorists across Spain appointed as judges, who received and evaluated texts which related to their assigned theme, and winners being informed by the organising committee through an assigned periodical. Winners would sometimes receive a monetary prize, and—more significantly to many—have their pieces published as a pamphlet.[67]

Because they did not require participants to meet face-to-face, these smaller *certámenes* were seen as an affordable means of stimulating public, intellectual exchange across the movement, and could involve writers based outside Spain. Indeed, one of the most prominent *concursos* of the period was the initiative of an activist based in Panamá, M.D. Rodríguez, who in 1911 called for a debate on the direction of the movement, to be managed by the largest periodical of the time, the Barcelona-based *Tierra y Libertad*.[68] Reponses were to be judged by leading theorists and publishers, with the best in each category receiving 50 pesetas. Dozens of entries were sent to *Tierra y Libertad* over the following year, most of which were published on its front page. Contributions came from across Spain—from San Sebastián, Madrid, Sevilla, Valencia, Barcelona and Huelva—as well as Paris, New York and Argentina.[69] Selecting winners for the three themes of the competition proved difficult. The pedagogue Federico Forcada, tasked with judging a question on educational methods, was disappointed with the entries and refused to pick a winner.[70] Likewise, the publisher Leopoldo Bonafulla neglected his role as judge of a question on the organisation of the future society, much to the annoyance of Rodríguez. For the winner of the final theme, on the validity of syndicalist tactics, the editors of *Tierra y Libertad* selected M. Sánchez Romanista, whose piece struck a balance between ardent support for syndicalism and criticism of its limitations. Romanista wrote in to express his profound gratitude for the recognition he received, and split his winnings into two donations, 25 pesetas to support anarchist prisoners, and 25 to support *Tierra y Libertad*.[71] Despite its rather limp conclusion, this competition and others like it demonstrated the reciprocal, bottom-up nature of ideological exchange which was sustained between anarchists within Spain and beyond.

Occasionally, larger literary competitions could conclude with a conference, where publishers, judges and participants in the *certámen* would meet, discuss entries and distribute awards and prizes. The most notable of these events were the two *Certámenes Socialistas* held in Reus (1885) and Barcelona (1889), both of which had a long afterlife in the cultural and intellectual development of the movement.[72] These events were an opportunity for number of young writers to gain prominence in the movement and gain entry into the 'informal elite' of anarchist publishing, including Ricardo Mella, who, aged 24, entered a celebrated essay on the problems caused by emigration from Galicia to the *Primer Certámen*, and four years later at the *Segunda* won an award for his utopian fiction *La Nueva Utopia*. The proceedings of both *Certámenes Socialistas* were published as books, both of which were reprinted several times over the following decades, as were pamphlets of individual entries.[73] Nothing of the scale of the *Certámenes Socialistas* was repeated in the period 1890–1915, yet they remained a model for publishers and activists aiming to undertake smaller, comparable projects.

The 'loose groups, informal networks and fluctuating associations' sustained by anarchist print culture was a fitting structure for a movement that distained formal hierarchies, and brought with it a number of advantages, such as flexibility and a high degree of grassroots participation.[74] At the same time, however, fragilities ran throughout this structure, which often buckled under internal and external pressures. Papers of all sizes frequently collapsed, with few lasting beyond a handful of issues. The average lifespan of a paper outside Cataluña was roughly 21 issues per title (compared to 31 in Cataluña) [see Table 0.1]. Even this small ratio is skewed by a few exceptional titles such as *El Porvenir del Obrero* (Mahón), which produced 413 issues over two epochs from 1899–1915. In contrast, papers in Andalucía collapsed far more readily. 53 periodicals were produced in the region in this period—the highest number outside Cataluña—yet these publications managed an average of only six issues per title.

Financial difficulties were endemic to anarchist papers and the most common cause of their collapse. In order to break even, papers usually had to secure a print run of around 4,000 copies per issue.[75] Although the majority of papers in Spain did not publish their sales, it can be assumed that most did not reach this figure. Those that did publish their balances reveal a common theme, with printing costs outstripping income from sale for every issue, resulting in a steadily growing deficit.[76] Some were able to mitigate these financial difficulties by external sources of income, such as a wealthy backer (which was very rare), or membership fees from a local workers' society. Papers with international links to migrant communities often benefitted from the better pay and generosity of their international comrades, most notably the *Acción Libertaria* group—which published *Acción Libertaria* (Gijón-Vigo), *El Libertario* (Gijón) and *Acción Libertaria* (Madrid)—whose publications were supported primarily by remittances from Panamá from 1910 to 1913.[77] Migrant groups in Argentina, the USA, France and UK were also significant donors to the movement's press, often choosing to send money to publications based in their home town, or to publishing groups which aligned with their factional preferences. If a publishing group did not reach sufficient sales or were not linked to some form of external funding, they were constantly in debt. Many papers tried to plug this gap by opening donation funds for the periodical, which rarely worked.

While the goal of a print run of 4,000 was beyond most papers, a few did manage to reach and/or surpass this figure over the turn of the century, most notably the *Suplemento a la Revista Blanca*, which at its peak in 1900–1902 claimed to distribute 15,000 copies. In periods of high publishing activity, such as 1900–1906 and 1911–1915 several papers comfortably exceeded the minimum level of distribution needed to remain financially viable. Those that did so had a much larger distribution than anarchist papers in other countries. According to delegates at the 1907 International Anarchist Congress, *Freiheit* (New York) published around 3,000 copies, *Der Anarchist* (Berlin) around 1,800 and *Freedom* (London) around 1,500.[78] Distribution alone, however, could not ensure the survival of an anarchist paper. Internal fragilities were rife in the print system, most notably the reliance of publications on their correspondents. One of the most common notices across all papers were calls for correspondents to pay for the papers they had received.[79] If these calls went unheeded, subscriptions were cancelled and threats were made to publish the names of non-paying correspondents.[80] These threats were occasionally carried out, publicly branding such correspondents as untrustworthy 'crooks' in an attempt to blacklist them from their colleagues and other papers.[81] Non-paying correspondents were 'bad comrades', seen as 'the principal cause of the disappearance of [the anarchist press]' and 'vampires,' who preyed upon the goodwill of publishers in order to make money.[82] Larger papers were not immune from this problem; indeed, the combination of high distribution and unpaid subscriptions often caused major papers to collapse more readily than for those of a smaller print run, which found it easier to scrape by on donations. For example, *El Rebelde* (Madrid), claimed a healthy readership of around 8,000, yet in 1905 collapsed as a result of correspondents failing to wire over money from sales.[83] A similar problem affected *Acción Libertaria* (Madrid), which at the time of closure was distributing 6,000 copies of each issue.[84]

Anarchist papers were also exposed to a range of external pressures. Their reliance on the official postal system (*Correos*) was the source of many frustrations. Although postal workers (*carteros*) were occasionally seen as fellow workers, they were more commonly seen as untrustworthy agents of the state. A common accusation against *carteros* was that they stole from letters, and many papers advised correspondents to wire over money rather than risk it in the post.[85] Ernesto Álvarez—editor of *La Anarquía*, *La Idea Libre* and *La Protesta*—was particularly critical of the *carteros*, labelling them slow, careless and dishonest. At one point he sardonically wondered if 'Jerez were in the Congo' after a package of papers arrived there from Madrid four weeks late, and a decade later he claimed that a donkey would be quicker than Spanish mail trains.[86] More serious problems also resulted from the *Correos*. All post directed to anarchist papers was subject to interception by authorities. Papers were often aware that their post was being read, as many letters arrived showing clear signs of having been opened.[87] This would suggest that interception was as much about intimidating anarchist publishers as gaining information on the movement, which in some cases appears to have worked. The editors of the Madrid-based *El Libertario*, for example, decided to write a handwritten note on its final issue to one correspondent, advising against using the paper's title in correspondence as they knew their post was being read.[88]

In theory, anarchist papers operated within a relatively tolerant legal context. The 1883 Press Law established freedom of expression in print, relaxing the restrictive publishing climate of the early Restoration.[89] In practice, however, the anarchist press was persecuted with 'rigour and severity'.[90] Publishers were denounced to local authorities on a regular basis, particularly if they celebrated violent activity or criticised members of the Church, military, and politicians. If successfully prosecuted, papers were not censored, but rather the entire issue would be stalled, or, preferably (for the authorities), the paper would be forced to close. At times papers appeared to revel in hostile attention. *El Rebelde*, for example, printed a regular section named 'Our Denouncements' (which reached number 35 within 50 issues), signing off each one with a glib 'until next time'.[91] While being reported to the authorities and put on trial may have demonstrated that a paper was being combative and subversive—as an anarchist publication should be—more often than not they drained the already limited funds of publishing groups, and hastened, if not directly caused, the collapse of a paper.

While papers could survive the attentions of hostile authorities in normal circumstances, very few managed to weather periods when constitutional guarantees—including press freedoms—were suspended. The most prolonged period of this kind came in the mid-1890s, when the public practice of anarchism was prohibited. By late 1896 every anarchist paper in Spain had closed. Similar, although briefer and less intense periods of repression followed in 1906, 1909 and 1911. Some of these were direct closures: editors were imprisoned, offices searched and materials were seized. Correspondence lists were often confiscated and used to identify prominent activists across the country. Almost as problematic were the indirect results of repression, which severed the networks binding publishing groups to the wider movement, starving their papers of funds and readers. International groups and publications could help to mitigate these problems, but could not fully fill the void created by severe nationwide repression.

All of these problems ensured that the majority of anarchist periodicals were acutely ephemeral. Yet they were not disposable, transitory, or insignificant. Anarchist papers were treasured by their readers, preserved in complete collections in homes, centres and workplaces, to be returned to for multiple readings.[92] The presence of printed material ascribed local anarchist centres with an anarchist significance and meaning, transforming rooms and other spaces into 'libraries'.[93] Requests frequently came in to newspapers for back issues so that a group constructing a library had a complete collection on offer to those visiting.[94] Again, Ramiro de Maeztu gives a good sense of the way in which anarchist print was treated by its readers:

> One reads an infinitely larger number of 'bourgeois' periodicals, but in these it is the present which occupies everything, and that which happens today is followed by that of tomorrow . . . the interest is entirely fleeting. This is not the case with anarchist periodicals . . . the influence of these publications outlives their death . . . I know of many men who conserve a complete collection of issues. How many [bourgeois] weeklies could you say that about?[95]

Anarchist print thus had significance and longevity which marked it out from the more disposable, mainstream press. It provided the movement with an 'institutional memory': a body of texts containing ideas, events and narratives, which provided a reference point in future years.[96] Print collections thus served to militate against the problems experienced by anarchist publishers in maintaining long-running publications, ensuring a lasting significance for each paper published.

From 1890 to 1915, nothing was as central to or as representative of anarchism in Spain as the periodical press. These were the 'revealed words' of the movement; the carriers of the ideas which gave meaning to the anarchist experience and guided almost every significant development of this period.[97] Those who created, distributed and contributed to this print culture sustained the movement for a quarter of a century, forming a flexible and surprisingly durable structure, upon which the anarchist movement in Spain formed as a mass movement.

Notes

1. See approach of Roger Chartier, 'Texts, Printing, Readings,' in *The New Cultural History*, ed. Lynn Hunt (Berkeley: University of California Press, 1989), 154–175 and Matthew Lenoe, *Closer to the Masses: Stalinist Culture, Social Revolution, and Soviet Newspapers* (Cambridge: Harvard University Press, 2004), 1–8.
2. Manuel Pérez Ledesma, 'La formación de la clase obrera: Una creación cultural,' in *Cultura y movilización en la España contemporánea*, ed. Rafael Cruz and Manuel Pérez Ledesma (Madrid: Alianza, 1997), 206.
3. *Acción Libertaria* (Vigo), 6 September, 1911, 2 and *Solidaridad Obrera* (Gijón), 15 January, 1910, 1.
4. *Tribuna Libre* (Gijón), 22 May, 1909, 1.
5. *La Protesta* (La Línea de la Concepción), 22 February, 1902, 1–2.
6. *El Proletario* (Cádiz), 1 May, 1902, 4.
7. *La Acción* (La Coruña), 11 November, 1909, 1; *Al Paso* (Sevilla, II), 18 November, 1910, 4.
8. *El Corsario* (La Coruña), 27 December, 1891, 1.
9. Marcel van der Linden, 'Second Thoughts on Revolutionary Syndicalism,' *Labour History Review* 63, 2 (1998): 183.

10. *La Protesta* (La Línea de la Concepción), 7 June, 1902, 1.
11. Cited in Francisco Madrid Santos, 'La prensa anarquista y anarcosindicalista en España desde la I Internacional hasta el fin de la Guerra Civil,' (PhD thesis, Barcelona: Universidad Central de Barcelona, 1988–89), 63.
12. Figure compiled from Ignacio Soriano and Francisco Madrid Santos, 'Antología documental del anarquismo español VI.I: Bibliografía del anarquismo en España, 1868–1939, Enriquecida con notas y comentarios,' (5th edition, 2012), 67–448. Published online, accessed 12 December, 2012, http://cedall.org/Documentacio/Castella/cedall203410103.htm.
13. Lily Litvak, *Musa libertaria: Arte, literatura y vida cultural del anarquismo español (1890–1913)* (Madrid: Fundación de Estudios Libertarios Anselmo Lorenzo, 2001), 282 gives the sales of *The Conquest of Bread* at 50,000, however 22,000 of these copies were sent to the Americas, see Soriano and Madrid Santos, 'Antología documental,' 16–17, 212–213 and 216.
14. Soriano and Madrid Santos, 'Antología documental,' 237–238.
15. See *La Idea Libre* (Madrid), 28 March, 1896, 1 and 4 April, 1896, 4; *Acción Libertaria* (Madrid), 14 November, 1913, 1.
16. Anselmo Lorenzo, cited in Madrid Santos, 'La prensa anarquista,' 63.
17. See Table 0.1 in the Introduction.
18. Madrid Santos, 'La prensa anarquista,' 63.
19. For example, see *hoja* 'Justicia y libertad,' published in *El Productor* (Barcelona, II), 1 August, 1903, 4.
20. David Ortiz, Jr., *Paper Liberals: Press and Politics in Regency Era Spain* (Westport: Greenwood Press, 2000), 58.
21. The only exceptions to this rule are the few daily publications of this period, such as *La Organización* (Gijón), *La Defensa del Obrero* (Gijón); the earliest issues of *El Productor* (Barcelona), when the paper was published as a daily [1 February, 1887–8 March, 1887] and *Solidaridad Obrera* (Barcelona), III, after it transformed into a daily publication in March 1916.
22. Exceptions to this rule include *La Anarquía* (Madrid), *Tierra y Libertad* (Madrid), and most journal-style publications, all of which published a relatively large number of images. See María Antonia Fernández, 'La revolución social en imágenes: Iconografía de la prensa socialista y anarquista Española (1872–1920),' *Spagna Contemporanea* 28 (2005): 88–92 and 100–105.
23. See picture of storming of Bastille which appeared in both *La Anarquía* (Madrid), 17 July, 1891, 1 and *La Idea Libre* (Madrid), 13 July, 1895, 1. Also in José Álvarez Junco, *La ideología política del anarquismo español (1868–1910)* (Madrid: Siglo XXI, 1991), 604.
24. For example see *Suplemento a la Revista Blanca* (Madrid), 20 April, 1901, 4; *La Protesta* (Valladolid), 27 October, 1899, 4. The same was true of larger daily papers, see María Cruz Seoane Couceiro, *Oratoria y periodismo en la España del siglo XIX* (Madrid: Castalia, 1977), 419–420.
25. Exceptions included anarcho-communist papers such as *El Comunista* (Zaragoza), which stated it would appear 'when able'.
26. Madrid Santos, 'La prensa anarquista,' 23–30.
27. Ortiz, Jr., *Paper Liberals*, 1–7.
28. *La Protesta* (Valladolid), 12 August, 1899, 2; *Juventud* (Valencia), 4 January, 1903, 1.
29. *La Razón Obrera* (Cádiz), 28 December, 1901, 3.
30. For example see *El Corsario* (La Coruña), 1 October, 1893, 1–2.
31. Angel Smith, 'Los tipógrafos de Barcelona (1899–1914): Relaciones laborales, desarrollo sindical y praxis política,' in *El trabajo a través de la historia*, ed. Santiago Castillo (Madrid: Asociación de Historia Social, 1996), 437–445. On Álvarez see Madrid Santos, 'La prensa anarquista,' 135, n.685.

32. Seoane, *Oratoria y periodismo*, 409–410.
33. See for example, masthead of *El Corsario*: 'Office Hours, From Seven to Nine in the Evening'.
34. Example of start-up costs for a small paper (c.400 issues): *La Razón Obrera* (Cádiz), 23 September, 1901, 4.
35. See raffle of Castilian dictionary to assist launch of *Acción Libertaria* (Gijón), won by a comrade in Vigo: *Acción Libertaria* (Gijón), 25 November, 1910, 4 and 9 December, 1910, 4.
36. *Liberación* (Elche), 1 September, 1912, 4; *El Rebelde* (Madrid), 12 May, 1904, 4; *Suplemento a la Revista Blanca* (Madrid), 23 March, 1901, 1; *Tribuna Libre* (Gijón), 17 July, 1909, 4.
37. *El Rebelde* (Madrid), 14 July, 1904, 1.
38. For example see *La Protesta* (La Línea de la Concepción), 11 July, 1901, 1 and 16 January, 1902, 4.
39. *El Corsario* (La Coruña), 16 January, 1896, 1; *El Productor: Extracto del estado de cuentas de El Progreso*, 11 November, 1896, 1.
40. Soriano and Madrid Santos, 'Antología documental,' 23–28.
41. For example the 'Germinal' group in Gijón which produced *Acción Libertaria*, which included Mella, Eleuterio Quintanilla and Pedro Sierra Alvarez.
42. *El Corsario* (La Coruña), 17 January, 1895, 4; notice in *La Voz del Obrero del Mar* (Cádiz), II, 4 April, 1908, 1.
43. See apology that a number of articles had not been published to make space for an article by Mella in *La Protesta* (Valladolid), 25 May, 1900, 4.
44. See call for correspondents in *Suplemento a la Revista Blanca* (Madrid), 2 June, 1900, 3.
45. On the link between *La Protesta* and Dowlais see James Michael Yeoman, '*Salud y anarquía desde Dowlais*: The Translocal Experience of Spanish Anarchists in South Wales, 1900–1915,' *International Journal of Iberian Studies* 29, 3 (2016): 278–282.
46. For example, the kiosk 'El Sol' in La Coruña run by local correspondent Enrique Taboada: *Suplemento a la Revista Blanca* (Madrid), 30 November, 1901, 4; *El Rebelde* (Madrid), 9 January, 1904, 3; see also *Germinal* (La Coruña), 24 December, 1904, 4, in which comrades in Pontevedra (Galicia) were told to write to the kiosk if they had any information on a local comrade's father who had gone missing.
47. David Ortiz, Jr., 'Redefining Public Education: Contestation, the Press and Education in Regency Spain, 1885–1902,' *Journal of Social History* 35, 1 (2001): 76.
48. Seoane, *Oratoria y periodismo*, 7–18; María Ángeles García Maroto, *La mujer en la prensa anarquista: España, 1900–1936* (Madrid: Fundación de Estudios Libertarios Anselmo Lorenzo, 1996), 234.
49. Marie Laffranque, 'Juan Montseny y los intelectuales: 1899–1905,' *Anthropos* 78 (1987): 42.
50. Roger Chartier, 'Leisure and Sociability: Reading Aloud in Modern Europe,' in *Urban Life in the Renaissance*, ed. Susan Zimmerman and Ronald F.E. Weissman (Newark: University of Delaware Press, 1989), 107.
51. Juan Díaz del Moral, *Historia de las agitaciones campesinas andaluzas-Córdoba: Antecedentes para una reforma agraria* (Madrid: Alianza, 1967), 190–191. See also reports of groups in Sevilla reading *La Protesta* (Valladolid), 26 January, 1900, 3 and 9 February, 1900, 4.
52. *El Imparcial* (Madrid), 28 November, 1901, 3.
53. Ángel Herrerín López, 'Anarchist Sociability in Spain: In Times of Violence and Clandestinity,' *Bulletin for Spanish and Portuguese Historical Studies* 38, 1 (2013): 163.

54. Ilham Khuri-Makdisi, *The Eastern Mediterranean and the Making of Global Radicalism: 1860–1914* (Berkeley: University of California Press, 2010), 20.
55. See Chartier, 'Texts, Printing, Readings,' 161 and Herrerín López, 'Leisure and Sociability,' 104.
56. See Susanna Tavera i García, 'La premsa anarco-sindicalista, (1868–1931),' *Recerques* 8 (1978): 101, n.77 which cites a Barcelona worker who sacrificed his daily coffee to buy *Solidaridad Obrera*. Journal-style papers were usually a little more expensive, and a few four-page periodicals were priced at 10 céntimos.
57. *La Controversia: Suplemento al núm. 3 de 'La Controversia'* (Valencia), 1 July, 1893, 1; *La Controversia* (Valencia), 19 August, 1893, 6–7.
58. Herrerín López, 'Anarchist Sociability,' 166.
59. Compare with discussion of 'imagineers' in contemporary translocal movements and networks in Andy Cumbers, Paul Routledge and Corinne Nativel, 'The Entangled Geographies of Global Justice Networks,' *Progress in Human Geography* 32, 2 (2008): 196.
60. Constance Bantman, 'Internationalism without an International? Cross-Channel Anarchist Networks, 1890–1914,' *Revue belge de philology et d'histoire* 84, 4 (2006): 969–970; Cumbers, Routledge and Nativel, 'The Entangled Geographies,' 189. See also William A. Gamson and Gadi Wolfsfeld, 'Movements and Media as Interacting Systems,' *Annals of the American Academy of Political and Social Science* 528 (1993): 114–125.
61. Cumbers, Routledge and Nativel, 'The Entangled Geographies,' 190.
62. *La Protesta* (La Línea de la Concepción), 15 February, 1902, 4. See Jose Álvarez Junco, *The Emergence of Mass Politics in Spain: Populist Demagoguery and Republican Culture, 1890–1910* (Brighton: Sussex Academic Press, 2002), 15 on the dispute between these editors.
63. See Chapter 3.
64. Díaz del Moral, *Historia de las agitaciones*, 181.
65. For example, the position of *Tierra y Libertad* (Barcelona) during the First World War, which refused to publish anything sent in by pro-Entente correspondents, and—in a move uncommon to most papers—refused right of reply to individuals they critiqued. Contrast this stance with that of *El Porvenir del Obrero* (Mahón), which despite having a clear pro-Entente position, gave a lot of space to 'neutralist' contributors such as Vicente García. See Chapter 4.
66. Manuel Morales Muñoz, 'La subcultura anarquista en España: el primer certámen socialista (1885),' *Mélanges de la Casa Velázquez* 27, 3 (1991): 47–60.
67. For example, Juan Serrano y Oteyza's, *El pecado de Cain*, was published in *Revista Social* in 1882 and as a stand-alone pamphlet in 1887. See Soriano and Madrid Santos, 'Antología documental,' 339.
68. *Tierra y Libertad* (Barcelona, IV), 22 February, 1911, 4; *Acción Libertaria* (Gijón), 17 March, 1911, 4.
69. Entries run in *Tierra y Libertad* (Barcelona, IV), 22 February, 1911–7 February, 1912.
70. *Tierra y Libertad* (Barcelona, IV), 16 August, 1911, 3.
71. *Tierra y Libertad* (Barcelona, IV), 20 December, 1911, 3.
72. See Manuel Morales Muñoz, *Cultura e ideología en el anarquismo español (1870–1910)* (Málaga: Centro de Ediciones de la Diputación de Málaga, 2002), 66–73 and 117–138.
73. See Soriano and Madrid Santos, 'Antología documental,' 44, 60, 67, 118–119, 122, 145, 249, 254, 256, 307, 349.
74. Bantman, 'Internationalism,' 969.
75. Madrid Santos, 'La prensa anarquista,' 36–38.
76. For example *Fraternidad* (Gijón, II), 3 February, 1900, 4 and 17 February, 1900, 4; *El Látigo* (Baracaldo), 14 December, 1912, 3–4 and 16 January, 1914, 4.

77. Kirwin R. Shaffer, 'Panama Red: Anarchist Politics and Transnational Networks in the Panama Canal Zone, 1904–1913,' in *In Defiance of Boundaries: Anarchism in Latin American History*, ed. Geoffroy de Laforcade and Kirwin R. Shaffer (Gainesville: University Press of Florida, 2015), 64–67. See also Chapter 4.
78. *The International Anarchist Congress Held at the Plancius Hall, Amsterdam on August 26th–31st, 1907* (London: Freedom, 1907), 3–7. These figures also demonstrate the wider spread of anarchist publications in Spain compared to other countries, as in most cases the papers cited were the only anarchist publication in print, whereas in Spain there were usually at least 15. The USA was an exception to this rule, being the site of a plurality of anarchist papers in a range of languages in the early twentieth century, which together claimed a circulation in the tens of thousands over the turn of the century, peaking in 1910 at over 100,000. See Kenyon Zimmer, *Immigrants against the State: Yiddish and Italian Anarchism in America* (Chicago: University of Illinois Press, 2015), 4–5.
79. See repeated calls for debts to be settled in *Suplemento a la Revista Blanca* (Madrid), 4 August, 1900, 3; 11 August, 1900, 4; 18 August, 1900, 2.
80. *Solidaridad Obrera* (Gijón), 25 June, 1910, 4.
81. *El Libertario* (Gijón), 7 December, 1912, 4; *Acción Libertaria* (Gijón), 27 November, 1911, 4.
82. *Acción Libertaria* (Gijón), 16 December, 1910, 4; *Tierra y Libertad* (Madrid), 14 May, 1903, 3.
83. *El Rebelde* (Madrid), 12 January, 1905, 1. See also *El Porvenir del Obrero* (Mahón), 22 February, 1907, 4 on the collapse of *Via Libre* (Zaragoza).
84. *Acción Libertaria* (Madrid), 19 December, 1913, 4.
85. *La Idea Libre* (Madrid), 5 January, 1895, 2; *Suplemento a la Revista Blanca* (Madrid), 8 July, 1899, 4; *Fraternidad* (Gijón, II), 11 March, 1900, 4; *El Rebelde* (Madrid), 9 January, 1904, 3.
86. *La Idea Libre* (Madrid), 25 August, 1894, 4; *La Protesta* (La Línea de la Concepción), 22 June, 1901, 4.
87. *Suplemento a la Revista Blanca* (Madrid), 14 September, 1901, 4.
88. *El Libertario* (Madrid), 20 February, 1910, 3: note written on copy in the International Institute of Social History (IISG), Amsterdam.
89. Carlos Soria, 'La ley española de policía de imprenta de 1883,' *Documentación de las Ciencias de la Información* 6 (1982): 21–23. See also Seoane, *Oratoria y periodismo*, 398–399 and Ortiz, Jr., *Paper Liberals*, 5.
90. Madrid Santos, 'La prensa anarquista,' 44–50.
91. *El Rebelde* (Madrid), 1 December, 1904, 3.
92. Madrid Santos, 'La prensa anarquista,' 50–51.
93. Tom Goyens, 'Social Space and the Practice of Anarchist History,' *Rethinking History* 13, 4 (2009): 451–452; Herrerín López, 'Anarchist Sociability,' 164.
94. For one example of such a request see *La Protesta* (Valladolid), 12 April, 1901, 4.
95. *El Imparcial* (Madrid), 28 November, 1901, 3.
96. Charlotte Linde, 'The Transformation of Narrative Syntax into Institutional Memory,' *Narrative Inquiry* 9, 1 (1999): 139–174.
97. Morales Muñoz, *Cultura e ideología*, 123.

Bibliography

Archives

AFPI: Archivo Fundación Pablo Iglesias. Online.
BNE: Biblioteca Nacional de España. Madrid.
BPC: Biblioteca Provincial de Cádiz. Cádiz.
BVA: Biblioteca Virtual de Andalucía. Online.

CED: cedall.org. Online.
HMM: Hemeroteca Municipal de Madrid. Madrid.
IISG: Internationaal Instituut voor Sociale Geschiedenis. Amsterdam.
LOC: Library of Congress: Digital Collections. Online.
LSE: London School of Economics. London.

Primary Sources

Anarchist Press

Acción Libertaria. Gijón/Vigo, 1910–1911. HMM and IISG.
Acción Libertaria. Madrid, 1913. IISG.
Al Paso. Sevilla, II, Epoch, 1909–1910. IISG.
El Comunista. Zaragoza, 1895. IISG.
El Corsario. La Coruña, 1890–1896. IISG.
El Libertario. Madrid, 1909–1910. IISG.
El Libertario. Gijón, 1912–1913. HMM and IISG.
El Porvenir del Obrero. Mahón, 1898–1907. BNE, HMM and IISG.
El Productor. Barcelona, 1887–1893. IISG.
El Productor. Barcelona, II Epoch, 1901–1902. IISG.
El Proletario. Cádiz, 1902–1903. IISG.
El Rebelde. Madrid, 1903–1905. HMM and IISG.
Fraternidad. Gijón, II Epoch, 1899–1900. IISG.
Germinal. La Coruña, 1904–1905. IISG.
Juventud. Valencia, 1903. IISG.
La Acción. La Coruña, 1908. IISG.
La Anarquía. Madrid, 1890–1893. IISG and LSE.
La Controversia. Valencia, 1893. IISG.
La Defensa del Obrero. Gijón, 1901. IISG.
La Idea Libre. Madrid, 1894–1899. HMM and IISG.
La Organización. Gijón, 1902. IISG.
La Protesta. Valladolid/Sabadell/La Línea de la Concepción, 1899–1902. BVA
   and IISG.
La Protesta. Madrid, 1901. IISG.
La Razón Obrera. Cádiz, 1901–1902. HMM.
La Voz del Obrero del Mar. Cádiz, II Epoch, 1907–1908. BPC and IISG.
Liberación. Elche, 1912. IISG.
Nueva Aurora. Málaga, 1909. IISG.
Solidaridad Obrera. Gijón, 1909–1910. IISG.
Solidaridad Obrera. Barcelona, III–IV Epoch, 1913–1919. CED.
Suplemento a la Revista Blanca. Madrid, 1899–1902. IISG.
Tierra y Libertad. Madrid, 1902–1904. IISG.
Tierra y Libertad. Barcelona, IV Epoch, 1910–1919. CED.
Tribuna Libre. Gijón, 1909. IISG.

Supplements and Almanacs to Periodicals

El Productor: Extracto del estado de cuentas de El Progreso. La Coruña, 11 November, 1896. IISG.
La Controversia: Suplemento al núm. 3 de 'La Controversia'. Valencia, 1 July, 1893. IISG.

Other Press

El Imparcial. Madrid, 1867–1933. BNE.
El Socialista. Madrid, 1886–1939. AFPI.

Memoirs, Books and Pamphlets by Contemporary Authors

The International Anarchist Congress Held at the Plancius Hall, Amsterdam on August 26th–31st, 1907. London: Freedom, 1907. LOC.

Secondary Sources

Álvarez Junco, José. *La ideología política del anarquismo español (1868–1910).* Madrid: Siglo XXI, 1991.
Álvarez Junco, Jose. *The Emergence of Mass Politics in Spain: Populist Demagoguery and Republican Culture, 1890–1910.* Brighton: Sussex Academic Press, 2002.
Bantman, Constance. 'Internationalism without an International? Cross-Channel Anarchist Networks, 1890–1914.' *Revue belge de philology et d'histoire* 84, 4 (2006): 961–981.
Chartier, Roger. 'Leisure and Sociability: Reading Aloud in Modern Europe.' In *Urban Life in the Renaissance*, edited by Susan Zimmerman and Ronald F.E. Weissman, 103–120. Newark: University of Delaware Press, 1989.
Chartier, Roger. 'Texts, Printing, Readings.' In *The New Cultural History*, edited by Lynn Hunt, 154–175. Berkeley: University of California Press, 1989.
Díaz del Moral, Juan. *Historia de las agitaciones campesinas andaluzas-Córdoba: Antecedentes para una reforma agraria.* Madrid: Alianza, 1967.
Fernández, María Antonia. 'La revolución social en imágenes: Iconografía de la prensa socialista y anarquista Española (1872–1920).' *Spagna Contemporanea* 28 (2005): 81–105.
Gamson, William A., and Gadi Wolfsfeld. 'Movements and Media as Interacting Systems.' *Annals of the American Academy of Political and Social Science* 528 (1993): 114–125.
García Maroto, María Ángeles. *La mujer en la prensa anarquista: España, 1900–1936.* Madrid: Fundación de Estudios Libertarios Anselmo Lorenzo, 1996.
Goyens, Tom. 'Social Space and the Practice of Anarchist History.' *Rethinking History* 13, 4 (2009): 439–457.
Herrerín López, Ángel. 'Anarchist Sociability in Spain: In Times of Violence and Clandestinity.' *Bulletin for Spanish and Portuguese Historical Studies* 38, 1 (2013): 155–174.
Khuri-Makdisi, Ilham. *The Eastern Mediterranean and the Making of Global Radicalism: 1860–1914.* Berkeley: University of California Press, 2010.
Laffranque, Marie. 'Juan Montseny y los intelectuales: 1899–1905.' *Anthropos* 78 (1987): 42–46.
Lenoe, Matthew. *Closer to the Masses: Stalinist Culture, Social Revolution, and Soviet Newspapers.* Cambridge: Harvard University Press, 2004.
Linde, Charlotte. 'The Transformation of Narrative Syntax Into Institutional Memory.' *Narrative Inquiry* 9, 1 (1999): 139–174.
Linden, Marcel van der. 'Second Thoughts on Revolutionary Syndicalism.' *Labour History Review* 63, 2 (1998): 182–196.

Litvak, Lily. *Musa libertaria: Arte, literatura y vida cultural del anarquismo español (1890–1913)*. Madrid: Fundación de Estudios Libertarios Anselmo Lorenzo, 2001.

Madrid Santos, Francisco. 'La prensa anarquista y anarcosindicalista en España desde la I Internacional hasta el fin de la Guerra Civil.' PhD thesis, Barcelona: Universidad Central de Barcelona, 1988–1989. Published online, accessed 12 May, 2012. http://cedall.org/Documentacio/Castella/cedall203410101.htm.

Morales Muñoz, Manuel. 'La subcultura anarquista en España: el primer certámen socialista (1885).' *Mélanges de la Casa Velázquez* 27, 3 (1991): 47–60.

Morales Muñoz, Manuel. *Cultura e ideología en el anarquismo español (1870–1910)*. Málaga: Centro de Ediciones de la Diputación de Málaga, 2002.

Ortiz, David, Jr. 'Redefining Public Education: Contestation, the Press and Education in Regency Spain, 1885–1902.' *Journal of Social History* 35, 1 (2001): 73–94.

Ortiz, David, Jr. *Paper Liberals: Press and Politics in Regency Era Spain*. Westport: Greenwood Press, 2000.

Pérez Ledesma, Manuel. 'La formación de la clase obrera: Una creación cultural.' In *Cultura y movilización en la España contemporánea*, edited by Rafael Cruz and Manuel Pérez Ledesma, 201–233. Madrid: Alianza, 1997.

Seoane Couceiro, María Cruz. *Oratoria y periodismo en la España del siglo XIX*. Madrid: Castalia, 1977.

Smith, Angel. 'Los tipógrafos de Barcelona (1899–1914): Relaciones laborales, desarrollo sindical y praxis política.' In *El trabajo a través de la historia*, edited by Santiago Castillo, 437–445. Madrid: Asociación de Historia Social, 1996.

Shaffer, Kirwin R. 'Panama Red: Anarchist Politics and Transnational Networks in the Panama Canal Zone, 1904–1913.' In *In Defiance of Boundaries: Anarchism in Latin American History*, edited by Geoffroy de Laforcade and Kirwin R. Shaffer, 57–80. Gainesville: University Press of Florida, 2015.

Soria, Carlos. 'La ley española de policía de imprenta de 1883.' *Documentación de las Ciencias de la Información* 6 (1982): 11–40.

Soriano, Ignacio, and Francisco Madrid Santos. 'Antología documental del anarquismo español VI.I: Bibliografía del anarquismo en España, 1868–1939, Enriquecida con notas y comentarios.' 5th edition, 2012. Published online, accessed 12 December, 2012. http://cedall.org/Documentacio/Castella/cedall203410103.htm.

Tavera i García, Susanna. 'La premsa anarco-sindicalista, (1868–1931).' *Recerques* 8 (1978): 85–102.

Yeoman, James Michael. '*Salud y anarquía desde Dowlais*: The Translocal Experience of Spanish Anarchists in South Wales, 1900–1915.' *International Journal of Iberian Studies* 29, 3 (2016): 273–289.

Zimmer, Kenyon. *Immigrants against the State: Yiddish and Italian Anarchism in America*. Chicago: University of Illinois Press, 2015.

2 More Workers' Blood!

Anarchism and Violence, 1890–1898

From 1890 to 1898 anarchism in Spain was defined by violence. Popular uprisings and acts of terrorism undertaken in the name of anarchism proliferated in these years, followed by an intensification of state repression against the movement. Violence also dominated the anarchist press. Periodicals became saturated with the rhetoric of violence and discussions of the legitimacy of violent methods. A varied, yet patterned response to violence emerged within anarchist print culture through the decade, reflecting a plurality of positions on the subject from within a fractured movement.

Studies of anarchist violence have tended to focus on the perpetrators of terrorism, with only a secondary interest in the effects of violence upon the broader movement and its press.[1] Focusing on the minority of anarchists who committed or supported violent acts can lead to some questionable conclusions about the wider movement. For example, the works of Ángel Herrerín López and Juan Avilés Farré portray the violence of the 1890s as an indirect cause of the longevity of anarchism in Spain.[2] To these scholars, violence helped to cement the movement in Spain, while similar movements in Europe and the Americas faded away. This is not because anarchist violence was successful in inspiring others to the cause—as was the terrorists' intention—but rather because the repression of the Spanish state was so broad and ruthless that it provoked sympathy for anarchists from the Spanish public, while providing the movement with a cultural repertoire of martyrs and a collective memory of struggle.[3] In France and Italy— so the argument goes—the state reacted to similar acts of terrorism in a limited manner, persecuting only the perpetrators of crimes.[4] At the same time, these states began to address the social factors behind anarchist support, which undermined anarchist critiques and led its supporters towards more social democratic channels, which Spanish governments were either unwilling or unable to turn to.[5]

The Spanish state's failure to accommodate demands for reform undoubtedly contributed to a climate in which some anarchists saw violence as a viable strategy. Rather than attempting to militate against social grievances through politics, the Restoration state turned to 'indiscriminate, illegal and extremely harsh repression,' often through a military police force named the Civil Guard.[6] Created in the 1840s to police the Spanish countryside, from the mid-nineteenth century the Civil Guard was frequently employed in urban contexts during disturbances, gaining deep resentment for its brutal conduct.[7] In periods of acute unrest local authorities could declare a state of war (*estado de guerra*), in which constitutional guarantees were suspended, and all administrative, judicial, political and civil powers were passed over to the military.[8] Mass arrests, imprisonment without charge and torture were common occurrences during such periods, particularly in Barcelona and Andalucía. In this context, a violent response to the state's actions appealed to sections of the anarchist movement. Yet this was never supported by a majority, nor was violence the exclusive domain of anarchists. The Spanish state's frequent resort to violence can thus help explain why some individuals took it upon themselves to conduct terrorism, but it does little to explain the general attitude of the movement.

Nor does repression help to explain the longevity of anarchism in Spain. Repression demonstrably worked, and the 1890s were a disaster for the anarchist movement in Spain, which required 'at least a modicum of official tolerance' to exist.[9] Had the suffocation of the anarchist movement continued much longer than 1898 the movement might have been irreversibly crushed. This was recognised by anarchists who engaged in the movement's print culture, who began to adopt a rather forlorn, introspective tone from 1893 onwards, which was distinct from the revolutionary grandstanding that characterised anarchist periodicals in both the 1880s and 1900s. In the early years of the decade the anarchist press provided the movement with a forum through which it could engage with the question of violence and its effects. As the climate of violence intensified, however, the movement's print culture became increasingly difficult to maintain. By 1896 the Spanish anarchist press had completely disappeared, for the first time since the 1870s.[10] As anarchist publishing collapsed, the collective responses to repression—for example the creation of martyrs and a repeated invocation of past experiences of hardship—may have helped to maintain the few anarchist groups still able to publish. The hundreds of anarchists directly affected by repression may also have forged a sense of communion during imprisonment and exile. However, these responses were the signs of an 'impotent and desperate' movement on its knees, rather than a movement building strength for future decades.[11] Martyrs may have been necessary for the movement in the 1890s, but they were largely forgotten when the movement returned to legality. As the years of violence subsided, the anarchist press looked to the future, towards different methods for revolutionary change such as education and organisation, which helped the movement attract mass support in a context of relative stability and legality.

In contrast to studies which focus on terrorism and repression, some scholars have diminished the centrality of violence to the anarchist movement. Madrid Santos, for example, claims that to frame this decade around violent events is 'tendentious'.[12] Similarly, Litvak is keen to stress the 'fundamentally peaceful' nature of anarchist ideology and downplay the role of violence within the movement.[13] This desire to shift focus away from anarchist violence is understandable, given that terrorism was supported by a minority and carried out by only a handful of militants based in Barcelona. Likewise, compared to the size of the movement, relatively few recognised anarchist militants took part in rural uprisings and urban insurrections, and the movement generally denied claims of anarchist instigation in these events. Yet, the broader implications of these episodes were undeniably enormous, and cannot be written out of the anarchist experience of the 1890s, simply because it was conducted by a minority, or because it had a negative effect on the movement. Outside Cataluña, newspapers and associations were closed and prominent local anarchists were arrested, severing the movement's mechanisms of exchange and its networks of communication and, in the process, threatening the existence of anarchism in Spain.

The sections which follow examine the various forms of violence within the anarchist press of this period, examining how the movement portrayed uprisings, terrorism, repression and war through the lens of anarchist ideology. In doing so this chapter will explore how anarchist print culture gave meaning to the violence which surrounded Spanish anarchism in the 1890s, and how the press networks sought—and failed—to maintain the movement at this juncture. Violence became the prime concern for the movement's press, producing a heterogeneous, often conflicted response, which neither foregrounded the perpetrators of violence nor ignored their actions. The reaction to state violence—repression, and, later in the decade, war—was also far from uniform. There was no consensus on violence from within the movement; no single, definable position. Thus, violence both defined and divided the movement in the 1890s, accentuating factionalism and hastening its collapse.

The Legitimacy of Violence

Anarchist ideology was based upon a critique of violence. To anarchists, society was based on the domination of authority, which systematised violence as a means to control and exploit the working class.[14] This violence was manifest in various forms: through culture, as the enforced ignorance of the masses by religion and the institutions of the Church; through the structural oppression of capitalism, which enslaved the working class to work for the profit of the bourgeoisie; and through the state, which articulated violence in its most stark and direct form through the repressive mechanisms of the army and police. This latter form of violence—violence as direct, physical force—formed the basis of the anarchist experience of the 1890s.

Anarchists sought an end to violence through the destruction of authority. The result of the revolution—Anarchy—was synonymous with peace and harmony: a new order in which the rule of violence would be abolished.[15] This did not necessarily mean that anarchists were peaceful. While some pacifist sections within the movement regarded any use of force as illegitimate, others advocated revolutionary violence as means to establish peace, or as a means of self-defence against the violence of authority.[16] The legitimacy of violence was thus subject to interpretations based on its origin and purpose. State violence, as war (external state violence) and repression (internal state violence), was illegitimate by its nature. In contrast, collective violence undertaken by 'the people' was frequently portrayed as a legitimate response to oppression. Nevertheless, popular violence was rarely glorified in its own right, rather, it was seen as a necessary, regrettable likelihood. This was the position of Ricardo Mella, the most celebrated anarchist theorist and writer of the period. In *La Nueva Utopia* (1890)—one of the most widely-read pieces of anarchist fiction of the late nineteenth century—Mella suggested that the revolution would be heralded by 'the noise of arms, the roar of cannons, the impressive clamour of battle, [and] torrents of blood necessarily spilt,' all of which would bring forth a bloody 'prologue of . . . immense transformation'. However, Mella situated this violence far away from the new society he described, 'in distant lands' between unspecific actors. For Mella, revolutionary violence was vaguely defined, and not the conscious product of individuals, nor a planned mass uprising or insurrection.[17] In this and similar imaginings of the revolution, violence appeared only as a brief interlude between the oppressive contemporary world and the peace of an anarchist future.[18]

In the 1880s, discussions of violence within the anarchist movement had been largely theoretical. The only major violent incident of the decade was the 'Mano Negra' affair of 1883, when the Andalucían authorities blamed a series of murders on a clandestine revolutionary network of anarchists, based in the countryside around Jerez de la Frontera, a city twenty miles north of Cádiz known primarily as the home of sherry production. The existence of the 'Mano Negra' was disputed by the anarchist movement, and has since been the subject of lengthy historiographical debate.[19] Whether it existed or not, the 'Mano Negra' was used to justify an extensive repression against the workers' movement in Andalucía: newspapers and workers' societies were closed and around 5,000 workers in Cádiz province were imprisoned. Of the seventeen that stood trial for the murders in June 1883, two were absolved, seven were given long prison sentences and eight were executed by public garrotting.[20] Those who remained in prison were intermittently the subjects of amnesty campaigns within the anarchist press until their release (into exile) twenty years later.[21] While it was clearly a significant moment for the movement, the 'Mano Negra' affair did not challenge the model of violence within anarchist ideology. To anarchists, the incident was always seen as an invention of the state, which remained ultimate source of violence. The violence of 'the people' was thus denied, rather than brought into question.

Around the same time, a new revolutionary strategy developed within the anarchist movement. 'Propaganda by the deed' originated in the international anarchist movement during the 1870s as a method to shock the working class into revolutionary action.[22] Originally, the term applied to insurrectionary violence, conducted by groups of anarchists engaged in guerrilla-like struggles against the state. By the 1880s 'propaganda by the deed' also incorporated individual action and a range of direct, violent deeds, including robbery and protest.[23] At times the phrase was also used to signify any activity not confined to print, for example acts of solidarity towards fellow workers.[24] By 1890, however, 'propaganda by the deed' was primarily used to refer to acts of individual violence, such as assassinations of symbolic figures and indiscriminate public bombings. Although anarchists largely rejected the term 'terrorism', this is how 'propaganda by the deed' has been understood since this point.[25]

It is difficult to consider terrorism as part of a broader tactic of class struggle—as suggested by Herrerín López—which included labour protests and uprisings.[26] 'Propaganda by the deed' was far more controversial than popular forms of violence, and subject to debates linked to doctrinal splits between the movement's anarcho-collectivist and anarcho-communist factions. These groups had different interpretations of legitimate revolutionary activity. Anarcho-collectivists saw working-class mobilisation through trade unions as the best means to bring forth revolutionary change. This position had dominated the anarchist movement in its early years, and was the guiding principle of the FTRE in the 1880s. Yet collectivists had been challenged mid-way through this decade by the relatively new position of anarcho-communism. Rather than a source of revolutionary potential, anarcho-communists saw unions as inherently reformist, and advocated only small group organisation and direct agitation. The disputes between these two groups hamstrung the FTRE from 1895 onwards, as collectivists and communists coalesced into antagonistic groups, and attacked one another through the anarchist press. In 1888 the organisation was disbanded, yet this did not deter the warring factions within the movement, who continued to polemicize against one another in the following years.

Divisions between these groups were reflected in contrasting attitudes to anarchist violence. Anarcho-communists saw confrontation with the state as a necessary step towards the establishment of a peaceful anarchist future. Direct action, committed by individuals or small groups, appealed to anarcho-communists, as it gave them a sense of immediacy and individual power. Spectacular acts of terrorism would awaken the working class from their stupor; violence would lead the people to revolution, without recourse to unions, legalism or intellectualism.[27] Anarcho-communists were thus the main advocates of propaganda by the deed in Spain from the mid-1880s onwards, as the tactic appealed to their conception of legitimate revolutionary activity. Yet as support for 'propaganda by the deed' grew in anarchist circles, so too did its critics. Although the majority of the movement conceded that violence might be necessary in the ultimate revolution, and accepted collective violence—such as civil disobedience, strikes and sabotage—most anarchists regarded individual violence and terrorism as morally unacceptable. This was particularly true of anarcho-collectivists, who correctly predicted that propaganda by the deed would invite repression and alienate working-class support, rather than inspire it.[28] Likewise, not all anarcho-communists were supportive, most notably Pyotr Kropotkin, who published a clear rejection of the legitimacy and effectiveness of terrorist tactics in the French anarchist periodical *La Révolté* (Paris), shortly before the wave of anarchist terrorism began across Europe.[29] Nevertheless, in Spain the supporters and critics of propaganda by the deed aligned closely to the doctrinal splits within anarchism. Anarcho-collectivists tended to reject terrorism as a legitimate strategy, and although not all anarcho-communists were terrorists, all terrorists were anarcho-communists, or were portrayed as such in anarcho-communist papers.

These divisions over organisation and the validity of terrorism remained in place for the first years of the 1890s. There seemed little that could bring the movement together on these fundamental questions of strategy. Indeed, in the event, nothing did. The dispute was settled only by repression later in the decade, which made both positions irrelevant. Anarcho-communist groups and publications were repressed because of their advocacy of violent tactics, while anarcho-collectivism became meaningless when the wider movement was made illegal, making union organising impossible.

Popular Violence: 1890–1892

The 1890s are usually depicted as the decade when anarchism became synonymous with terrorism. While this is an apt depiction of the movement after 1893, the first episodes of violence during the 1890s were not novel, and do not fit easily into the category of propaganda by the deed. Rather, they were part of a broader manifestation of popular violence, in which anarchist figures and anarchist ideology were a factor, but were not the sole cause. Popular violence was commonly associated with labour unrest. In nineteenth-century Spain strikes and protests were often accompanied by attacks on individuals and property and small explosions, almost as a matter of course. Often the identity of those involved in these incidents was unclear; however from the 1870s onwards they were normally attributed to anarchist militants acting within the wider labour movement.[30]

In 1890–92 anarchists joined the socialist movement in staging mass demonstrations and strikes during May Day celebrations.[31] Aside from larger strikes in Barcelona and Bilbao, most May Day events across Spain were 'relatively tranquil' in 1890.[32] In Cádiz, however, the anarchist paper *El Socialismo* attempted to escalate May Day demonstrations into city-wide disturbances, as a means of demonstrating the strength of the city's working class.[33] This paper was edited by Fermín Salvochea (1842–1907), a prolific contributor to the anarchist press and instigator of numerous educational 'missions' to the Andalucían countryside.[34] Salvochea believed that collective agitation during labour unrest could be transformed into revolutionary activity. Following disturbances in 1890, the local authorities in Cádiz closed *El Socialismo* prior to May Day 1891, and arrested Salvochea and two other members of the paper's publishing group.[35] Over the following days thousands marched in protests in Cádiz, accompanied by explosions across the city which killed five bystanders. Again, Salvochea and *El Socialismo* were blamed, after the police claimed to have discovered explosives at the paper's offices.[36] These claims were vehemently denied by those involved, who claimed the 'discovery' of explosives was a police set-up.[37]

The cause of *El Socialismo* was taken up by the anarchist press across Spain, in particular *La Anarquía*, edited by the veteran anarcho-collectivist Ernesto Álvarez.[38] As well as declaring the prisoners' innocence, *La Anarquía* organised a relief fund for their families, which raised around 1,500 pesetas in six months.[39] A similar fund was opened by *El Corsario*, a much smaller paper which served as the mouthpiece of the La Coruña anarchist labour federation.[40] The cause of the May Day prisoners briefly captured the attention of the national movement: meetings were held in Barcelona, Madrid and Valencia to publically denounce the Cádiz authorities, and the names of the prisoners were adopted within anarchist naming practice, for example the newly-founded 'Salvochea' group of Trebujena (Cádiz).[41] When the editors of *El Socialismo* were absolved at the end of 1891 the anarchist press was jubilant, printing reports of Salvochea's exemplary performance in court and claiming that thousands of workers thronged the streets of Cádiz in celebration, despite the fact that Salvochea remained in prison.[42]

The events in Cádiz marked the first anarchist press campaign against repression during the 1890s. Elements of the response to the arrest of Salvochea—publishing letters sent from prison, opening subscriptions for prisoners and their families, and eulogising the victims of state violence—became regular features of anarchist papers over the next eight years. The response played into a wider narrative which attacked the groundless claim that anarchists were responsible for every public disturbance.[43]

Anarchist papers denied any guilt on behalf of those imprisoned; the state remained the source of violence, while the random, anonymised violence accompanying labour unrest was passed off as a justifiable reaction of 'the people' to their oppression. For anarchist commentators, nothing within their ideology explained this violence, thus to blame the movement for such incidents was simply an excuse to arrest its figureheads and close its papers.[44]

The Jerez Uprising

On the night of 8 January 1892 an uprising took place in Jerez de la Frontera (Cádiz). Five to six hundred *campesinos* (fieldworkers) marched into the city armed with agricultural tools, hoping to rouse a revolt from the local population. Neither the *jerezanos* nor the local soldiers backed the rebellion, leaving the *campesinos* isolated, and the uprising was put down within hours. In total three people were killed: Antonio Núñez Montenegro, a soldier in the Cuban army who was shot from the local barracks by mistake, and two young men—Manuel Castro Palomino, a local tax official and José Soto, a travelling wine salesman—who were labelled as 'bourgeois' and targeted by mob violence.[45]

No singular motivating factor can be used to explain the events in Jerez. Rural rebellions were nothing new in Spain, particularly in Andalucía.[46] Similar incidents had taken place in previous decades, including attacks on Utrera and El Arahal (Sevilla) in 1857 by local fieldworkers, and a revolt in Loja (Granada) led by Rafael Pérez del Álamo, known as the 'Spartacus of Andalucía', in 1861.[47] Similar incidents were associated with the anarchist movement from 1870 onwards. During the First Spanish Republic, uprisings took place in Sanlúcar de Barrameda (Cádiz) and Alcoy (Alicante), inspired by the FRE.[48] After 1892 uprisings continued to take place in the south, as in 1903, when a similar incident erupted in Alcalá del Valle (Cádiz).[49] Thus the Jerez uprising belongs within a wider context of rural violence in modern Spain, which is often attributed to anarchist support in Andalucía. Yet the causal connection between rural uprising and anarchist ideology is questionable, and, in the case of Jerez in 1892, has been a source of historiographical debate for over a century.[50] Although local anarchists were undeniably involved, by no means were all the *campesinos* of Jerez dedicated members of the movement, nor were they gripped by a 'collective madness' or a 'bestial' urge for violence, as claimed by one contemporary commentator.[51] Rather, the *campesinos* had concrete, realisable demands, including the release of local prisoners, and a desire to protest against the appalling economic situation of the region.[52] In the words of Ricardo Mella, in Jerez 'one did necessarily have to be an anarchist to be pushed towards rebellion'.[53] These material objectives were probably of more pressing concern than the desire to land a 'definitive' blow to the prevailing social order.[54]

A desire for an anarchist revolution may have spurred many *campesinos* to action; yet just as many were put off from joining the uprising because it was raining.[55] Thus on the night of 8 January 1892 ideological and material motivations collided with immediate and long-term grievances, to produce an act of popular violence, which can be associated with the ideology and practice of anarchism, but is not entirely explained by it.

Severe repression had begun in Andalucía before any anarchist paper could comment on the uprising. Without access to their own correspondents in Cádiz, anarchist commentators begrudgingly relied upon official reports from the government and mainstream media for information.[56] Some papers agreed with the official depiction of the uprising as an act of revolutionary violence. The anarcho-communist paper *La Tribuna Libre* (Sevilla), for example, had been warning that the Andalucían workers were on the brink of revolution since the end of 1891.[57] When the uprising took place, the paper saw it as a spontaneous, rational and inevitable response to the crippling poverty in Jerez. Violence was wholly justified as a means to end 'tyranny' and enable the workers to 'feed themselves,' and the paper's only regret was that the uprising had not been successful.[58] In keeping with anarcho-communist perspectives on violence, the paper advised its readers that a failure to meet 'force with force' would leave them cursed by future generations.[59] After publishing its support for the failed uprising, *La Tribuna Libre* was immediately forced to close.

A more common response was to refuse to condemn the uprising, while denying its connection to anarchism. A fortnight after the events, *El Corsario* stated that there was good reason for popular violence in Jerez. The scandalous aftermath of the Mano Negra affair and the 'atrocious' exploitation of the Andalucían fieldworkers gave the *campesinos* of the region the right to take matters into their own hands. Yet, within the same issue, the paper attacked the coverage of the incident in the 'bourgeois press', which (it claimed) had spuriously used the uprising to slander the anarchist movement, despite the fact that anarchists had 'demonstrated a thousand times that we never have to use such means' and that the movement preferred the 'honourable' tactics of written propaganda, education and trade unionism.[60] Thus, this paper neither condemned the uprising nor sanctioned it as legitimate anarchist behaviour. These mixed messages on violence became a common feature of *El Corsario* over the following years, particularly in the paper's coverage of anarchist terrorism.

The most thorough discussions of the Jerez uprising were provided by *La Anarquía*, by far the largest paper of the movement outside Cataluña, and second only in reputation to *El Productor* (Barcelona). The paper repeatedly denied that the uprising was a 'political' revolution—which 'are only possible in barracks'—or a 'social' revolution, which the paper stated could only take place 'in great cities such as London, Paris, New York or Berlin'.[61] The fact that lines of communication and transport had not been attacked was also regarded as evidence that the uprising had not been intended as a revolution. While the paper did admit that some of those who took part were anarchists, it suggested that they had been misguided and had placed too much faith in the revolutionary potential of the Jerez fieldworkers.[62]

For *La Tribuna Libre* the Jerez uprising was anarchist in nature, whereas for *El Corsario* and *La Anarquía* it was not. Despite their differences, all of the papers denied that the Jerez uprising had been deliberately instigated by anarchists. This was a direct refutation of claims made in the mainstream press and *El Socialista*, which declared that the uprising was the result of the political immaturity of the Andalucían working class and their support for anarchist 'fantasies' and 'gibberish'.[63] Hesitance to accept responsibility for the uprising may be seen as an attempt by anarchist papers to avoid censorship. It also reflected the fact that anarchist commentators denied that revolution required leadership.[64] Variations of this perspective appeared regularly in the anarchist press in following years, for example during discussions of anarchist education, in which claims of indoctrination provoked arguments within the movement, and in the early congresses of the CNT, where the question of leadership within the workers movement was the subject of lengthy debate. In all of these instances, as in Jerez, 'manipulation' of the working class was seen as anathema. Anarchist militancy and propaganda was therefore not seen as leadership, but direction, or instruction, which helped the working class realise their natural, reasoned desires for autonomy. Whether they supported the uprising or not, the movement's press was thus united in claiming that the incident could not be attributed to anarchist instigation.

The First Martyrs

In contrast to anarchist commentators, the local authorities in Jerez never questioned the assumption that the uprising was a direct result of anarchist instigation. Responsibility for restoring order in the region was given over to the army, who treated the event as a military insurrection. The resulting repression was both fierce and wide-ranging. The Civil Guard spent months scouring the Jerez countryside, rounding up labour organisers and known anarchists. The anarchist press and its networks were singled out as 'the key means by which the rebellion was organised' and the bedrock of working-class activity in the region. During searches, anarchist papers became incriminating evidence—defendants were asked at trial if they 'recognised' packages of *El Productor* and *La Anarquía*, as one would be asked to identify a weapon—and known correspondents and distributors were amongst the first to be arrested. In total 315 suspects were detained, three quarters of them fieldworkers, most of whom identified as anarchists. The movement in Cádiz province was flattened: its labour organisations were closed, its publishing activity was halted and its most active militants were imprisoned.[65]

The first trial related to the uprising was held one month later, focusing on the most serious accusations of sedition and murder. Two military tribunals sat in judgement on the accused, drawing on evidence provided by an informant, Félix Grávalo, and confessions extracted under torture.[66] Eight were brought to trial, four of whom were executed: two self-declared anarchists, Antonio Zarzuela and Jesús Fernández Lamela, who were blamed for instigating the uprising, and Manuel Fernández Reina [*Busiqui*] and Manuel Silva Leal [*el Lebrijano*], who were convicted for the murder of Manuel Castro Palomino. All four were garrotted on 10 February 1892.[67] Manuel Caro Clavo (given a life sentence for his alleged role in the murder of Palomino) died in his cell on the same day as the executions.[68] The informant Grávalo was given life imprisonment for rebellion, as were José Romero Loma and Antonio González Macías, both of whom denied that they were anarchists.[69] Later in the year a further forty-six stood trial for their alleged role in the uprising, including José Sánchez Rosa and Manuel Díaz Caballero, who were accused of visiting Fermín Salvochea in prison with Lamela and Grávalo to plan the uprising. They and eight others received life sentences, while a further seven received terms of between eight and twenty years. Salvochea—who had not directly participated in the uprising as he was in prison—received a twelve-year sentence.[70]

Although the uprising itself was unexceptional, its repression was remarkably severe. The disproportionate response of the authorities was criticised in many independent and liberal papers, such as *El Heraldo* (Madrid), which saw the uprising as a product of hunger and misery, which was 'not something you kill with bullets but rather requires prudent measures and knowledge'.[71] The republican paper *La Justicia* (Madrid) did not deny the culpability of the Jerez 'anarchists,' but it considered the heavy-handed response as an 'abominable crime' and a 'political blunder,' which was the result of pressure put on the tribunals by the government and the mainstream press.[72]

The anarchist press responded to the executions in a more outraged and ominous manner. *La Anarquía* was quick to label the repression as the 'error of errors,' stating that the state's 'perverse' and 'bloodthirsty' response to the uprising would 'brew eternal hatred' and provoke 'bloody massacres'.[73] The violence of contemporary society had provoked the uprising, which in turn had led to the shedding of 'more workers' blood'.[74] Similarly, *El Corsario* was keen to point out to 'the bourgeoisie' that they had achieved 'absolutely nothing': 'perhaps you have done something in benefit of your cause? No. . . . Have you frightened those to whom we spread and defend [our] ideas? Even less . . . how much you are going to suffer if you do not try to amend yourself! See well what you have done; think and reflect while there is time'.[75] For these papers, unless this cycle of violence ended and anarchism and peace were established, there would be further violent responses. This was not necessarily desired by anarchist commentators, but it was expected nevertheless.

The initial anger of the anarchist press following the executions reflected the mood of the movement in Spain and abroad. After 10 February Spanish consulates across Europe saw protests against the executions, punctuated by explosions and violent confrontations with police. Demonstrations took place across Spain, most notably in Barcelona, where an explosion in the Plaza Real killed one bystander and wounded several others.[76] Similar attacks continued through the year, including an attempt to plant explosives in the entrance to the Cortes (Parliament) in Madrid which was blamed on the *La Anarquía* publishing group. Ernesto Álvarez and the typographer Francisco Ruiz were arrested and held in custody for a fortnight before being released.[77] Catalan anarcho-communist papers had called for such responses and celebrated them when they took place.[78] In contrast, the handful anarcho-communist published outside Cataluña at this time were less confrontational. In a discussion of the 'feudal' repression of Jerez, *El Oprimido*, a short-lived anarcho-communist paper published in Algeciras (Cádiz), insisted that 'anarchists are not supporters of the right of force . . . because despair does not drive anyone to violate the laws of nature'.[79] Similarly, *La Controversia* (Valencia) adopted a far more conciliatory tone than its anarcho-communist contemporaries in Cataluña.[80] Most other non-Catalan papers also distanced the movement from these attacks and instead blamed them on the police. One of the three convicted for the attempted attack on the Cortes—Francisco Muñoz—was widely believed to be an *agent provocateur*, and the incident was seen as an excuse to quell forthcoming May Day unrest in the capital.[81] *La Cuestión Social* declared that anarchists 'do not need to place explosives in public plazas, since this would not resolve any problem, and we are not terrorists . . . only tyranny and despotism make use of the means of terror; the lovers of the liberty of the human race do not appeal to such trivial and ridiculous methods'.[82] It was not anarchists who planted bombs but 'the enemies of the worker'.[83]

The executions of Jerez marked the beginning of a sustained anarchist martyrology in Spain, which would come to dominate the movement's press for the following decade.[84] Valorising those who had been persecuted was a well-established response by anarchists, who sought to 'turn the state's most drastic punishment—death—against it by denying the state's ability to terrify or defeat them,' establishing a 'reservoir of cultural images that [anarchists] continued to utilise for propaganda'.[85] Martyrs existed in Spanish anarchist culture prior to 1890s, but these had primarily been either historical figures, reimagined as martyrs to progressive ideas—for example Galileo Galilei, Giordano Bruno and Michael Servetus—or contemporary revolutionaries persecuted abroad.[86] The memory of the Paris Commune of 1871 was strong in Spanish anarchist culture; for example, in 1886 anarchist groups in Barcelona commemorated the fifteenth anniversary of the Commune with musical pieces, poetry, short plays and lectures in honour of the 'martyrs' of French repression.[87] The most prominent foreign martyrs, however, were the five anarchists blamed for the Haymarket 'Affair' of May 1886, when a protest in favour of the eight-hour day in Chicago had turned into a riot, and a bomb had been thrown at the police, killing seven officers and wounding several others. In response, the anarchists Albert Parsons, George Engel, Adolph Fischer and August Spies were hanged on 11 November 1887, while Luis Lingg committed suicide in his cell the previous evening.[88] All five were immediately made into martyrs by anarchist movements in the Americas and Europe, including Spain, where the anarchist press unanimously declared their outrage at the executions.[89] The 'Chicago Martyrs' were the subject of numerous special editions of papers and standalone pamphlets, including *¡¡Siete setencías de muerte!!* (1887), in which Ernesto Álvarez used the executions as evidence that all political systems, monarchical and republican, were sustained by violent oppression.[90] These foreign martyrs became central to anarchist commemorative culture in Spain, surpassing even those executed following the 'Mano Negra' affair five years previously. Their international notoriety and assumed innocence captured the imagination of the movement, which made them an unquestioned symbol of the violent nature of the state. 11 November became a date of remembrance, replacing the anniversary of the Commune as the prime date in the anarchist calendar, marked by special editions of periodicals and new publications.[91]

After 10 February 1892 Spanish anarchism had martyrs of its own. *El Corsario* reified all five of those who had died in the aftermath of the uprising, dedicating its whole front page to the names of Zarzuela, Lamela, Fernandez Reina, Silvo Leal and Caro Clavo, followed by the statement: 'redemptive ideas invigorate themselves with the blood of its martyrs'.[92] The paper made no distinction between the executed, and downplayed the significance of the declaration against anarchism signed by Silvo Leal in the hours before his death, stating that he was illiterate and did not know what he was doing.[93] Over the turn of the year 1892–3, the La Coruña workers' federation which published *El Corsario* experienced severe economic difficulties. The paper was saved from collapse by the propaganda group 'Ni Dios Ni Amo' (Neither God Nor Master).[94] Its comrades at *El Productor* (Barcelona)—who had previously largely ignored the paper—celebrated *El Corsario*'s new-found 'independence and liberty' from the workers' organisation, which had prevented it from fully embracing anarchist ideas.[95] One of the first acts of the new editors was to publish a special edition dedicated to the Jerez martyrs. Every article was full of praise for the honourable qualities of the executed—'Loyalty, Valour, Suffering, Abnegation and Heroism'—and cries of 'Glory to the martyrs of Jerez!' and 'Hurrah for Anarchy!'[96] 'Ni Dios Ni

Amo' also organised an event on the evening of the 10 February 1893 at the local workers' centre.[97] Precisely what the paper's readers should do to venerate these martyrs was unclear. Commentators occasionally suggested that anarchists should seek 'vengeance' when 'a new occurrence such as that of Jerez recurs,' yet generally readers were encouraged to simply remember the names of the executed and continue their work for anarchism.[98]

La Anarquía, was more selective in its portrayal of the martyrs of Jerez. For this paper, martyr status was based upon two principles: innocence and a commitment to anarchism. These criteria were not met by all of those who died on 10 February. While lauding Zarzuela and Lamela, who were executed for 'being anarchists,' the paper made no mention of Fernández Reina, Silva Leal, who had been convicted of murder, or Caro Clavo, convicted as an accomplice to murder.[99] These three were widely believed to be guilty, even within anarchist circles, and none of them were recognised as being committed members of the anarchist movement.[100] Thus they were excluded from the martyr-narrative of *La Anarquía*, which venerated only the innocent, anarchist 'comrades Zarzuela and Lamela'.[101] *La Anarquía* was also selective in its practical responses to the repression. The paper initially set up a relief fund for all four families of those executed in Jerez, yet after just one week the paper removed its support for the families of Fernández Reina and Silva Leal, since they were already receiving money from the 'high classes,' having repented for their actions and denied involvement with movement.[102] They were replaced with the family of Caro Clavo, who—the paper reported, although it could not possibly have known—had died with a cry of 'Viva la Anarquía!' The subscription was closed in the following July, by which time it had raised 170 pesetas.[103]

This stance drew criticism from other papers. *La Controversia* (Valencia), for example, attacked *La Anarquía*, stating that in a society founded on violence it was impossible to judge between guilty and innocent, thus all of those who died in Jerez deserved reverence.[104] Nevertheless, *La Anarquía* was not entirely alone in its selective interpretation of the Jerez martyrs. One year after the executions, Ricardo Mella published a detailed study of the uprising, stressing that the two men convicted of murder (Fernández Reina and Silva Leal) were not anarchists; a fact which had been overlooked by both the mainstream press and the military tribunals.[105] While this 'was of little importance' to Mella—who considered all those involved to be 'victims of bourgeois exploitation'—he did see it as evidence of a deliberate blurring of the facts by the government, which sought to link anarchism to all violent activity.[106] For Mella, there was nothing within anarchism itself which either explained the uprising or justified the movement's repression.

On the first anniversary of the executions *La Anarquía* returned to its praise for the executed, in particular for Lamela, whose portrait was printed on the paper's front page alongside a eulogy which claimed that 'the death of one Lamela has caused the resurrection of new Lamelas . . . fervent anarchist[s], dedicated revolutionar[ies]'. Once again the paper stressed the innocence of Lamela and Zarzuela (and to a lesser extent Caro Clavo), while the names of Fernández Reina and Silva Leal were entirely absent.[107] Selective remembrance was also evident during a memorial service in Jerez in 1893, where the graves of Lamela, Zarzuela and Caro Clavo were the site of a public demonstration of around 4,000 people. No mention was made of the graves of Fernández Reina or Silva Leal in a report of the demonstration sent to *La Anarquía* from Lamela's brother Juan.[108]

Other non-Catalan papers gave scant attention to the Jerez 'martyrs'. The uprising was mentioned only twice in the four issues of *La Cuestión Social* (Valencia), in which the repression was written into a narrative alongside the Paris Commune and Chicago, as an example of how 'the anarchist idea was put into the hands of the executioner'. The paper made no mention of martyrs, and repeatedly stated that individual violence was not an appropriate response to repression.[109] Instead, it stressed that education and organisation were the only viable routes to an anarchist future.[110]

The Jerez uprising and its repression did not have a dramatic impact on conceptions of violence as portrayed by the anarchist press. Depictions of popular violence during the uprising were largely uniform: the violence was understandable and to some extent inevitable, given the misery of the Jerez fieldworkers. Only a few, smaller papers portrayed the uprising as a legitimate revolutionary moment, and no anarchist publication outside Cataluña suggested that it had been the product of anarchist instigation. Differences did emerge, however, in the interpretation of the state violence that followed. The movement was united in its critique of the excessive and bloody repression, yet its papers differed in their interpretation of who deserved commemoration as martyrs. *El Corsario* was the main advocate of a broad interpretation of legitimate popular violence and the illegitimacy of the state's repression. In contrast, *La Anarquía* and figures such as Mella were keen to stress the nuance between anarchist activity—which, they claimed, was not responsible for the violence in Jerez—and that of 'the people', with the latter being understandable but not deserving the same veneration. Although relatively slight at this point, these distinctions developed during the remainder of the decade, when a wave of terrorist attacks forced the movement to accept the reality of violence committed in the name of anarchism.

Individual Violence: Terrorism in Barcelona: 1893–1896

1892 was a turning point for the international anarchist movement. Although anarchism had long been associated with uprisings, labour unrest, and to a lesser extent murder and robbery, from this year onwards anarchist violence became associated primarily with terrorism.[111] The first high-profile anarchist terrorist attacks occurred in France. In March 1892 a series of explosives were planted across Paris by a group of anarchists led by François Koenigstein, known by his maternal surname, 'Ravachol'.[112] Shortly afterwards the group was apprehended and all of its members sentenced to life imprisonment. Ravachol gained international notoriety from the moment of his arrest. He became a symbol of the depravity of anarchism in the popular press; a model type of the 'mad bomber' who threatened the general public with revolutionary ideas and violent tactics. The eminent criminologist Cesare Lombroso—who usually opposed the death penalty—stated that he 'would not hesitate' to execute a terrorist such as Ravachol.[113] In France, Ravachol's actions were the cause of controversy and debate in anarchist circles. While some saw him as an inspiration and admired his staunch defence of anarchism during his trial, others regarded his actions as detrimental to the cause and labelled him 'an assassin and not an anarchist'.[114] Following a separate investigation, Ravachol was found guilty of several murders—including that of a 93-year-old hermit, which took place the previous year—and was guillotined.[115]

Ravachol briefly attracted a great deal of attention in the Spanish anarchist press. Many papers praised the defence given by 'comrade Ravachol' in the courtroom and sold copies of his portrait.[116] Numerous groups and individuals took up his name in veneration, such as the 'Ravachol' group of Sevilla and the moniker 'Hurrah for Ravachol!' which appeared in one subscription list.[117] One correspondent to *El Corsario* went as far as to name one of his twins Ravachol (the other was named Spartacus).[118] Yet in Spain, as in France, anarchist opinion on Ravachol's actions was mixed. *El Corsario* found itself torn between not wishing to 'make common cause with those who commit crimes' while maintaining that Ravachol was an 'energetic and dedicated . . . revolutionary' whose actions were the fault of 'this corrupt society'.[119] Álvarez's *La Anarquía* had a much clearer position, labelling Ravachol as one 'obsessed by maleficent influence,' and claimed that he should not have been tried as a criminal, but as a 'therapeutic case,' deserving neither praise nor condemnation, but compassion and 'education'.[120] In contrast, anarcho-communist groups deemed Ravachol as being 'logical in his acts' and attacked *La Anarquía* and other papers which had 'injured, libelled and dragged [his name] through the mud'.[121] In Cataluña, the short-lived anarcho-communist publication *Ravachol* (Sabadell, 1892, 2 issues) revelled in the actions of its namesake, while its successor *El Eco de Ravachol* (Sabadell, 1892–1893, 3 issues) provided its readers with two pages of information on the production of dynamite, ostensibly to help comrades in the explosives industry avoid accidents.[122]

The Spanish movement soon had terrorists of its own, although the first was nothing like as celebrated as Ravachol. In June 1893, for the second time in a year, the editorship of *La Anarquía* was held responsible for an attempted attack on the government. The paper's typographer Francisco Ruiz was killed while planting a bomb at the house of the prime minister, Cánovas del Castillo, after the explosive detonated prematurely (reportedly because Ruiz was smoking a cigarette). His remains were scattered across the nearby street, including a card bearing the name of Ernesto Álvarez. *La Anarquía* was immediately closed and Álvarez was arrested, along with the paper's printers and numerous well-known anarchists in Madrid.[123] Ruiz's actions were amateurish and embarrassing to his colleagues in *La Anarquía*, who had constantly denied the legitimacy of using terrorism to further the anarchist cause. The attack did not capture the movement's attention, nor was it portrayed as a true act of terrorism. *La Controversia* depicted his death as tragic, rather than heroic, and suggested that Ruiz was more of a republican federalist than an anarchist.[124] *El Corsario* stressed that Ruiz had 'killed no-one, nor injured, nor caused any damage; he was the only victim,' and suggested that the arrests which had followed were simply the product of government's 'blind' hatred of anarchism.[125] Later in the year this paper publicised a fund for Ruiz's widow instigated by an anarchist group in Sestao (Vizcaya), although this received little support from the paper's readership.[126] Scant attention was paid to Ruiz in future years, even by his former colleagues in *La Anarquía*.

The Attack on Martínez Campos

The first true act of anarchist terrorism in Spain took place two months later. On 24 September 1893 Paulino Pallás Latorre, an unemployed printer from Cambrils (Tarragona), threw 2 Orsini bombs at General Martínez Campos during the Fiesta de la Merced in Barcelona.[127] Martínez Campos was virtually untouched by the attack, but one Civil Guard and one civilian were killed, and several bystanders were wounded. Pallás remained at the scene, shouting 'Viva la Anarquía!' as he was apprehended. Pallás's attack was the first clear incident of 'propaganda by the deed' in Spain: a spectacular act of individual violence, of clear authorship, with a specific and symbolic target, designed to provoke a response which would benefit the anarchist movement.[128]

The attack forced the anarchist press to relocate away from Cataluña. Aside from *La Anarquía*, in the early 1890s all of the well-established papers of the movement were based in Barcelona. The most important, *El Productor*, had emerged in 1887 as an attempt to reconcile the doctrinal differences between anarcho-communists and anarcho-collectivists.[129] With a print run of up to 7,000 issues, and an extensive national and international distribution network, the paper was acknowledged as 'the most important workers' publication of its time' and 'the voice of Spanish anarchism,' not only by anarchists but also by the authorities who sought to curb its influence.[130] Under pressure from the city's authorities after the attack on Martínez Campos, *El Productor*'s printers refused to take any further orders from the paper. All of the other printers in the city did the same.[131] As their paper was being suffocated out of existence, the editors of *El Productor* decided to pass their affairs over to a publishing group outside the city. With *La Anarquía* closed following Ruiz's attack, the only remaining candidate was *El Corsario*, the only non-communist paper outside Cataluña still in print.[132] Following this move, anarchist publishing in Barcelona ceased, and did not regain its pre-eminence in the movement until 1901.[133]

The shift from Cataluña to Galicia as the centre of the anarchist press network was unexpected. Although rural Galicia had long been regarded as a cultural backwater, Galician cities had been home to a mixture of progressive political movements, and maintained a strong tradition of republican federalism. The FRE had held outposts La Coruña and Ferrol since the 1870s, and was particularly strong amongst artisans and construction workers.[134] A number of anarchist-worker papers were published in Galicia prior to the 1890s, however as the 'worst conserved' of all local anarchist newspapers, little is known about them other than their extremely short existence.[135] Like these papers, *El Corsario* was relatively marginal to anarchist print culture until 1893. The handover from *El Productor* dramatically increased the scope of the paper, and made it responsible for the movement's national campaign funds.[136] This wholesale transfer of concerns from one anarchist paper to another was repeated twenty years later, when *El Libertario* (Gijón) became *Acción Libertaria* (Madrid) in 1913.[137] Both were dramatic and unprecedented measures to sustain the movement through a period of repression, revealing a sense of common purpose across publishers and a belief that their activities provided anarchism in Spain with a structure which should be maintained.

As in its reaction to the Jerez uprising, *El Corsario* presented a conflicted interpretation of the attack on Martínez Campos. The paper appeared to sympathise with Pallás, who was portrayed as an 'honourable man and worker' whose unemployment had brought misery to his family, and admired his 'spirit of rebellion,' but did not agree with his violent tactics, which had not been undertaken for collective aims in the name of the anarchist movement.[138] *El Corsario* also rejected the claim of the bourgeois press that Pallás was motivated by the 'mere fact of being an anarchist' and denied that the anarchist books and papers owned by Pallás had 'confused his intelligence' (which was suggested by his own defence council).[139] Rather than celebrate Pallás's terrorist act, *El Corsario* sought to explain it through an anarchist analysis—society is corrupt, change is necessary, and individuals, driven by despair will inevitably commit violent acts such as this—while avoiding stating that terrorism was acceptable.

Key

No. Titles

● > 25

◐ 20–25

◑ 15–20

○ 10–15

○ 5–10

○ < 5

—— Provincial boundary

▨ Regional area

Map 2.1 Areas of Anarchist Publishing in Spain, 1890–1898.
Source: Map created by James G. Pearson.

Pallás was executed by firing squad on 6 October in Montjuich Castle in Barcelona. In its coverage of the execution, *El Corsario* again stressed the desperation of Pallás and his family's plight: 'Pallás has been shot—for what crime?—because [he was] tired of traversing the world in search of bread to feed his children . . . and rather than dying like a coward he believed it best to protest'.[140] The fact that Pallás had thrown a bomb into a crowded public space with the aim of killing a symbolic military figure—his 'deed'—was barely mentioned.[141] Nor did *El Corsario* publish Pallás's own explanation for the attack, which he had outlined in a letter sent from his cell in Montjuich to the Republican paper *El País* (Madrid), in which he made little mention of his hardship, but rather stressed that he had been motivated by a desire to 'regenerate' Spain's 'gangrenous' society through a great 'bath of blood'.[142] These comments were not repeated by *El Corsario*, which appeared unwilling to accept that such ideas belonged to a self-identified anarchist.

In contrast, anarcho-communist papers reprinted Pallás's letter with enthusiasm.[143] At the time of Pallás's attack there were three anarcho-communist papers published outside Cataluña: *El Rebelde* (Zaragoza), *La Controversia* (Valencia) and *El Oprimido* (Algeciras). All of these papers depicted Pallás as an anarcho-communist, which they saw as a means to attack their rivals in the wider movement. In the days following the attack on Martínez Campos, prominent anarcho-collectivists in

Barcelona had suggested to the mainstream press that the repression of the movement was unreasonable, since Pallás had not been involved in the city's anarchist unions.[144] Anarcho-communist papers such as *El Oprimido* saw this as evidence that he was 'a *communist* anarchist,' never to be 'seen in "meetings" . . . nor demonstrations of any kind . . . like Ravachol . . . [he] lived intensely, reflecting in solitude on the means to put his ideas into practice'.[145] *La Controversia* was likewise incensed by claims from the Barcelona movement that Pallás was 'not an anarchist' as he was unknown to the Barcelona police, and sarcastically advised its readers to 'register yourselves!' with their local Civil Guard, if they wanted to be accepted by anarcho-collectivists.[146] This paper also attacked the anarchist periodical *La Tratamontana* (Barcelona), which had declared that those who used dynamite were 'not anarchists,' in response to Pallás's terrorism.[147] *La Controversia* pointed out that there had been no vote on the subject, nor should there be, as true anarchists acted upon their own volition.[148]

Anarcho-communist papers saw Pallás's act as a legitimate response to the ills of contemporary society. It was not an individual act of a desperate man—as portrayed in *El Corsario*—but a symbolic and calculated blow against society. They praised the propaganda aspect of his attack, which was 'an immense protest against the crimes, the infamies and the social torments' of contemporary society.[149] They also praised the honourable way in which he had conducted himself, by remaining at the scene, accepting arrest and holding to his anarchist beliefs in court. For *La Controversia*, 'true men'—like Pallás— did not shy away from such deeds; they were not '*mujerzuelas* [tarts]' who regretted their actions.[150] This use of misogynistic rhetoric was uncommon in the wider anarchist press. Framing violence in a gendered manner emphasised Pallás's violence as one of a strong, independent individual, fully immersed in the ideals of anarcho-communism. He was virile and prepared to act, in contrast to the weak, effeminate passivity which marked the opponents of terrorism, including those within the anarchist movement.

If Pallás intended his terrorism to act as an effective means of propaganda, he might have expected more robust support from the movement's press. Only a small number of papers had given unconditional support for his actions, and even these did not necessarily suggest that his terrorism should be repeated. The situation of the anarchist press deteriorated after Pallás's attack and subsequent execution. *El Rebelde* was denounced to the local authorities, and *La Controversia* and *El Oprimido* closed at the end of October 1893, as did the Catalan publications *La Revancha* (Reus) and *La Conquista del Pan* (Barcelona), while *La Tramontana* was suspended until 1895.[151] The only paper which survived this wave of closures was *El Corsario*, which was left as the sole anarchist commentator on the next incident of anarchist violence.

The Líceo Bombing

On 7 November 1893, a month after Pallás's execution, two Orsini bombs were thrown into the stalls of the Líceo Opera Theatre in Barcelona during a performance of Rossini's *William Tell*. Fourteen people were killed immediately and a further six succumbed to their injuries in the following weeks.[152] Investigations into the attack began immediately. Unlike Pallás, the author of the Líceo attack had not remained at the scene and proclaimed the values of anarchism, yet it was widely assumed that this was another incident of anarchist terrorism, prompting clamours for a specific law against the movement across the mainstream Spanish press.[153] A state of war was declared in Barcelona, which remained in place for over a year, accompanied by a huge wave of arrests targeting anarchists and 'ringleaders' in the labour movement, who were taken to the military fortress of Montjuich for questioning.[154] Suspects were tortured and documents from newspapers and workers' associations were seized, but it was not until January 1894 that a culprit was established. Santiago Salvador Franch, a former bartender and alcohol smuggler, was arrested in Zaragoza, where he confessed to the police after unsuccessfully attempting to commit suicide.[155] In the following months Salvador attempted to repent his actions, publicly renouncing anarchism and begging for forgiveness from the Catholic Church.[156] When salvation was unforthcoming, he changed position again and publically mocked the Church prior to his execution, which he met, like Pallás, with the cry of 'Viva la Anarquía!' on 21 November 1894.[157]

The Líceo bombing was different to Pallás's attack on Martínez Campos. It was not an attempted assassination, but an indiscriminate attack upon the general public. This, added to Salvador's muddled attempts at escaping and constant backtracking made him a more ambiguous author of 'propaganda by the deed' than his predecessors Ravachol and Pallás. This confusion was reflected in the pages of *El Corsario*, the sole anarchist publication in print at the time. The paper's first response was to condemn the 'salaried' press for its myopic depiction of current events in Spain: 'Hypocrites! . . . you cry for the victims of the *Líceo* and yet you are not even shaken when 200 miners are left buried between the rubble'.[158] Without a distinct author or motive for the attack, the paper focused on the repression in Barcelona, calling for solidarity across the country for those comrades arrested and warning the authorities to 'bear in mind not to give further motive for reprisals' since the movement 'already has enough'.[159] Yet as with the attack on Martínez Campos, *El Corsario* displayed no ecstasy in the violence of the Líceo bombing, and denied the revolutionary potential of terrorism, declaring that 'we know that Anarchism [*sic*] cannot succeed through terrorising, but through convincing; we do not want . . . to implant our ideas by imposition, but by freedom'.[160]

El Corsario was still adjusting to its role as the main publication of the movement and much of its print space was dedicated to administrative affairs. Its editors felt responsible for maintaining the movement's national and international networks, which were threatened by the bombing of the Líceo, particularly as no one had accepted responsibility for the attack. Repression was inevitable, given the paper's standing as the sole anarchist paper left in print. Seemingly aware of its imminent closure, the paper informed its readers of the immense difficulty it was having in December 1893—a month before Salvador's arrest—and closed shortly afterwards.[161]

The Lull, 1894–1896

Anarchist outrages continued to take place outside Spain in the following years, above all in France. Between November 1893 and June 1894 a string of attacks took place in Paris, including an assault on a Serbian diplomat by Léon Leauthier; the bombing of the National Assembly by August Vaillant; the bombing of the café Terminus by Émile Henry; and the assassination of President Carnot by Sante Caserio.[162] Most of these figures cited revenge as one of their key motivations: Vaillant referenced the execution of Ravachol at trial; Henry's attack took place one week after Vaillant's execution, which had infuriated him; while Caserio claimed he was motivated for vengeance for all of his predecessors, and sent a photograph of Ravachol to Carnot's widow-to-be, which arrived on the same day that he murdered her husband.[163]

In contrast to the spiralling violence in France, there was lull in anarchist terrorism in Spain after the Líceo bombing. This allowed for a partial reconstruction of anarchist print culture. A handful of titles emerged in Barcelona, including *Ciencia Social* (Barcelona), a journal of 'sociology, arts and writing' launched in October 1895. Yet the largest papers of the movement continued to be based outside the city. Unlike their colleagues at *El Productor*, the administration of *El Corsario* was not completely incapacitated by repression, and the paper returned to print in September 1894. Although this second epoch was not marked by any new anarchist attacks in Spain, the paper did comment on the continuing violence in France. Vaillant, Henry and Caserio were commemorated as martyrs by the paper, which was far more prepared to celebrate anarchist terrorism abroad than it was in Spain.[164] Nevertheless, the paper retained its general tone of negativity towards violence, for example in the piece 'I do not conform', which declared the throwing of bombs to be 'unwanted' and its perpetrators 'not good anarchists'.[165]

As anarchist outrages ceased in Spain, a series of short-lived anarcho-communist papers were launched in Zaragoza: *El Eco del Rebelde*, (1894), *El Invencible*, (1895) and *El Comunista*, (1895), which between them published only nine issues. These papers followed the publishing line of *El Rebelde*, and retained their predecessors' celebratory attitude to terrorism.[166] Vicente García [pseud. Palmiro] the former editor of *El Combate* (Bilbao) and a frequent contributor to the anarchist press, suggested to the readers of *El Eco del Rebelde* that 'the violence of society' should be 'combatted with another force,' before stating that 'the anarchists know perfectly well that by getting rid of one bourgeois, two or twenty, one general, marques, prince, king, emperor etc. we do not end evil' but if an anarchist was to 'possess enough phosphorus' and 'considered it more honourable . . . to give a harsh lesson to the society of banditry than to die as a coward' then he was not to blame.[167] The contributor 'Yllenatnom' [J. Montanelli] was equally convinced of the need for action, stating in *El Invencible* that the only route to a peaceful society was 'violent revolution' and an acceptance that 'blood must be spilt'.[168] Both papers stressed the martyrdom of Ravachol, Pallás, Salvador, Vaillant, Henry and Caserio, and were convinced that their example would be followed: 'prepare the scaffolds, sharpen the guillotines . . . the anarchist knows how to die'.[169] Both papers were denounced in quick succession and their editor, Nicaso Domingo, was imprisoned, but this did not prevent the publication of *El Comunista* three months later.[170] This paper continued largely in the same style as its predecessors: immediate revolution was the only solution to the injustices of modern society, while peaceful revolutionary strategies such as education were futile, since they would not 'produce the great social cataclysm' and would serve only to 'reinforce the phalanxes of the privileged'.[171] *El Comunista* was forced to close after just four issues, marking the end of nineteenth-century anarcho-communist publishing in Spain.[172]

Despite the violent rhetoric of these anarcho-communist papers, they were not entirely untroubled by terrorism. Even for these groups, anarchists were not 'supporters of force' out of choice, rather they were obliged to adopt these tactics in order to remove the yoke of oppression from the masses they sought to liberate. Terrorism was thus only justified because they were locked in a 'life-and-death contest' with the ruling classes.[173] This distinguishes the anarcho-communists of the early 1890s from the Nietzchean-influenced sections of the movement a decade later, whose espousal of violence was much more concerned with 'sculpting' a new humanity, rather than as a means towards a peaceful future.[174] Nevertheless, the anarcho-communist heyday of the late 1880s and early 1890s was brought to an end by its support for terrorism, which became increasingly untenable after 1893. Although few anarcho-communists had actually carried out terrorist attacks, they and their press had become victims of their own hubris in a context of repression, placing themselves outside the law and distancing themselves from support within the wider movement.

It was not only anarcho-communism that suffered in this period. Anarcho-collectivism had ceased to be used as a term by most anarchist papers in the early 1890s. Those who supported collectivism's preference for unionism, such as Ricardo Mella, began to refer to themselves simply as supporters of *anarquismo sin adjetivos* ['anarchism without adjectives'].[175] This was also the stated position of papers such as *El Productor* and *El Corsario*, which sought to present a unity of purpose within the movement by avoiding disputes with anarcho-communist papers. Despite these attempts at reconciliation, anarcho-communist groups continued to refer to all non-communist papers by the term 'collectivists'. This was intended as an insult, which presented communism as the only true form of anarchism and collectivism as quasi-parliamentarism.[176]

Collectivism ceased to have much relevance as the movement lost support from large swathes of the working class. Rather than anarchism 'without adjectives,' anarcho-collectivism had been reduced to anarchism without support, epitomised in the last collectivist publication of the 1890s, *La Idea Libre* (Madrid). After Francisco Ruiz's botched attack on Cánovas and the closure of *La Anarquía*, Ernesto Álvarez and the remainder of his publishing group set about the reconstruction of their paper. The result, *La Idea Libre*, was another example of the group's preference for discussions of ideology, world events and cultural projects such as 'revolutionary' theatre.[177] The first issue of the paper was published in April 1894, at almost exactly the same time that legislation criminalising the provocation of 'violence committed by explosives'—in effect a law against anarchism—was passed through the Cortes.[178] In this context, *La Idea Libre* initially struggled to get off the ground.[179] Its early subscription lists were small, and the paper constantly railed against the 'scandalous abuses' of the postal service, which reportedly 'lost,' tampered with and delayed packages of the paper.[180] Nevertheless, by mid-1895 the paper had become the most respected publication of the movement, and received contributions from the leading figures in Spanish anarchism, such as Anselmo Lorenzo (often simply 'L'.), José Prat ('J.P'. and 'Urania') and above all Mella (going by his various titles of 'R', 'R.M'. and 'Raúl'), alongside 'Tracio' ('Thracian') who it can be assumed was Álvarez.[181]

La Idea Libre did not discuss individual terrorists. The name of Santiago Salvador did not appear a single time in the paper, nor did those of the French anarchist terrorists, although it did make one short reference to the assassination of President Carnot.[182] Pallás was mentioned only in passing, when the paper briefly explained that it would not be printing his portrait as it had previously announced, since no picture of him existed.[183] This was not true, as at least three portraits of Pallás had been published in the mainstream press between September and October 1893, as well as in the anarchist paper *La Controversia*. It is hard to believe that Álvarez was unaware of these images.[184] The paper was, however, prepared to discuss the uprising in Jerez, which it portrayed as a product of economic grievances rather than 'invented' revolutionary agitation.[185]

As in *La Anarquía*, the paper was only concerned with Lamela, Zarzuela and Caro Clavo, whom it saw as the victims rather than the perpetrators of violence.[186]

Instead of discussing terrorists, the paper clung to the ever-diminishing prospects of cementing anarchism within the workers' movement.[187] The 1894 legislation permitted local authorities to suppress any working-class organisation which could be said to facilitate 'criminal' intent, including unions, publications, meetings and 'discussions in general'. Although similar laws were drawn up across Europe following terror-ist outrages, their application in Spain was more indiscriminate, and successfully suppressed the wider workers' movement until 1898.[188] Former collectivists despaired of this situation in the pages of *La Idea Libre*, blaming 'individual acts' which had brought about 'confusion' and an indelible stain on the name of anarchism.[189] They rejected the 'fanaticism' of 'idiots,' whose 'anachronistic' programme for destruc-tion had changed nothing and had instead brought immense harm upon the movement.[190]

La Idea Libre represented the last publication of nineteenth-century anarcho-collectivism. Discussions of union organisation were largely absent from the paper, not because its contributors no longer valued this strategy, but because it was futile to even imagine the reconstruction of a popular anarchist movement at this time. A telling feature of *La Idea Libre*, which set it apart from its predecessor *La Anarquía* and its suc-cessor *La Protesta* (1899–1902), was its frequent evocation of the past. Historical pieces praised past glories such as the French Revolutions of 1789 and 1848, the Paris Commune and the Spanish First Republic as evidence of mass, spontaneous revolutionary action, moments of glory which contrasted with the seemingly endless repression of the 1890s. The paper also differed from earlier anarchist papers (including Álvarez's *Bandera Social*, *Bandera Roja* and *La Anarquía*) in its criticism of May Day celebrations. Previously a sign of worker strength, the date had been hijacked and 'disfigured' by parliamentary socialists and transformed into a 'humdrum *fiesta* . . . of slavery' which was 'losing character and importance every year,' to the point that it was now 'a wasted symbol'.[191] The content and rhetoric of *La Idea Libre* was indicative of its inability to speak to the wider workers' movement and the precarious state of Spanish anarchism in general. Such resignation, introspection and lament had been uncommon in the anarchist press up to this point.

The debate between anarcho-collectivists and anarcho-communists had torn the movement apart in the late 1880s, making the FTRE unwork-able and leaving deep resentments between the conflicting parties. By 1895 the argument had been settled, but neither had emerged victori-ous. The antagonism of communism and the irrelevance of collectivism ensured that both of these sectors of anarchist thought waned when con-fronted with the realities of violence and repression.

The Corpus Cristi Bombing

The lull in anarchist violence was shattered in the summer of 1896. On 7 June a bomb exploded during the Corpus Cristi procession at the junction of Cambios Nuevos and Arenas de Cambio in Barcelona, leaving 12 dead and more than 70 hospitalised.[192] As with the Líceo bombing, the author of this act was initially unknown; indeed, a definite identity for the bomber was never established.[193] Nevertheless, once again the culprit was assumed to be an anarchist. Vengeance was the order of the day in both the mainstream press and the Cortes. Repression targeted specifically against anarchism intensified, exceeding that which followed the attacks of 1893 in both severity and scale. Hundreds of anarchists were arrested in Barcelona, alongside republicans, socialists, unionists, masons, free-thinkers, secular educators and anyone who 'resisted the status quo'. The rest of Spain was not exempt from this spirit of retribution. Legislation passed in September 1896 made the expression of anarchism illegal, in an attempt to outlaw the ideology. Any group, centre or periodical bearing the name 'anarchist' was banned, as were those which 'disguised their [anarchist] ends,' and crimes of the press were placed under military jurisdiction.[194]

Following this attack anarchist publishing became near-impossible. *La Idea Libre* was able to publish only a single issue in the wake of the Corpus Cristi bombing, which opened its front page with an unambiguous condemnation of the attack:

> Whoever the authors of the attack of Barcelona may be, we object to the brutal act carried out last Sunday in the Condal City [Barcelona], and we solemnly declare that, if the success of our ideas were founded upon the bodies of defenceless women and innocent children, we would renounce them. Our long-standing opinions in respect to this point in particular are well-known; this new protest of ours arises from honourable impulses of conscience, which do not allow us to associate ourselves, nor to have any kind of relation with, those who intend to command by terror as opposed to by reason and conviction.[195]

The paper's position was clear: not only was the terrorist attack on the Corpus unacceptable, so too were those of Pallás and Salvador. *La Idea Libre* did not consider individual violence as a by-product of the potential revolution, but as anathema which inhibited it. The paper was suspended shortly afterwards, its offices were closed, and its editors and contributors were brought in for questioning in Barcelona.[196]

Only one paper remained in print beyond this point. The second epoch of *El Corsario* had ended in April 1895. In a manner similar to the demise of *El Productor*, the printers of La Coruña refused to print the paper and forced it into closure, despite no illegal activity on its part.[197] This did not deter the paper's publishing group, which spent the latter half of 1895 securing funds to purchase their own printing-house, named 'El Progreso'. This was a rare achievement in anarchist print culture, and in the context of the 1890s it was seen as a moment of transcendental importance, which bucked the recent downward trajectory of the movement by placing the means of propaganda in the hands of anarchist publishers themselves.[198] Buoyed by this success, *El Corsario* resumed print in January 1896, making it one of the few papers in print when the Corpus bombing took place six months later. As with the two attacks of 1893 the paper neither defended nor condemned the bombing, and suggested a number of times that it could have had been a plot devised by the 'Black International' of Jesuits to justify extreme reactionary measures.[199] Once again *El Corsario* was unwilling to embrace, justify or even fully acknowledge the existence of anarchist violence, despite the overwhelming popular belief that the author of the attack was indeed an anarchist.[200] As repression spread across the country, *El Corsario* attempted to bypass closure by launching a new title, named *El Productor*. This manoeuvre failed: each of the five issues of *El Productor* was denounced, the paper was closed and 'El Progreso' went bankrupt.[201]

Unlike any other paper, *El Corsario* had been in print during the Jerez uprising and all of the terrorist attacks in Barcelona. During all of these incidents the paper had been unwilling to acknowledge that violence had been committed in the name of the movement. When it did engage in discussion on violence, it was presented as potentially justifiable but far from essential to anarchist practice, claiming to understand the cause of anarchist terrorism yet refusing to unequivocally support it.[202] The end result was one of mixed messages, which makes *El Corsario* an apt symbol of the movement's attitude to violence in general. There was no consensus on the legitimacy of anarchist violence from within the movement, indeed, even within individual papers opinions were divided and ambiguous on this subject. Thus, to claim that the movement uniformly supported or rejected terrorism is to ignore the movement's plurality, as manifest in its press. After the Corpus bombing there could be no further comment on the subject. Following the closure of *El Productor* (La Coruña) no anarchist periodical remained in print in Spain, leaving the movement repressed, voiceless, and desperate.

State Violence: 1893–1898

The final act of propaganda by the deed of the 1890s took place one year later. Michele Angiolillo was an Italian typographer, who was working in Spain when the Corpus Cristi bombing took place. Suspecting that he would be arrested for being an anarchist, he left the country and spent months travelling around Europe, making acquaintances with high-profile anarchists and notable figures in the Cuban and Philippine independence movements. He returned to Spain in the summer of 1897, while the repression of the anarchist movement was still ongoing. On 8 August, he located and shot dead Prime Minister Canóvas del Castillo at the Basque spa town of Santa Águeda. Like Pallás, Angiolillo remained at the scene of his attack and attempted to use his trial as a platform to advocate anarchist ideals. He was found guilty, and on 20 August he was garrotted.[203]

The attack on Canóvas was hardly a surprise. He was seen as the architect of repression and responsible for the excesses of the Spanish authorities in Barcelona. He was loathed within and beyond anarchist circles across Europe, where the repression in Spain provoked widespread condemnation and prompted a revival of the image of 'Black Spain' analogous to the fifteenth-century Inquisition, in which Canóvas played the role of the Grand Inquisitor Tomás de Torquemada. His assassination was, in the words of Herrerín López, 'a death foreseen a thousand times' by both anarchists and the Spanish police since 1896, and prompted widespread celebration in anarchist communities across the world.[204]

The murder of Canóvas brought an end to the blanket repression of the 1890s, which was now regarded as having encouraged further terrorist attacks. Instead of widespread retribution, the state restricted persecution to those guilty of obviously criminal acts.[205] Thus the response from the Spanish authorities to Canóvas' assassination was muted in comparison to that which had followed previous acts of terrorism. Although legislation against anarchism remained in effect until 1901, local authorities began to scale down repression, allowing for a de facto legalisation of the movement in most areas (although not Cataluña) and a re-emergence of the anarchist press.

At first, the return to anarchist publishing in Spain after almost a year of silence was inauspicious. The first paper to emerge was *La Idea Libre*, which returned to print in the same month as Canóvas's assassination.[206] *La Idea Libre* initially printed a modest print-run of 2,000 copies, yet it became clear that only a fraction of its former network was capable of resuming engagement with the movement's press. The paper soon scaled back dramatically, subsequently printing only 157 copies for those who had explicitly requested them.[207] Although this figure steadily grew, as did donations to help cover the paper's deficit, from August 1897 to July 1898 anarchist publishing remained limited to this one paper. As in its former epoch, *La Idea Libre* did not celebrate those who had committed terrorism. Its views on anarchist violence had not changed: terrorism was a 'microbe', fermented by the state, and it had no place in the struggle for ideas. The paper wanted the spiral of terrorism and repression to end, and for anarchists to be allowed to conduct their legitimate work as educators, through 'books, newspapers [and] the noble struggle of contradiction and debate'.[208]

The Blood of 'True' Martyrs

Since *La Idea Libre* was the only anarchist paper in print in 1897, there was no contemporary discussion of Angiolillo in the movement's press. Nevertheless he, Pallás and Salvador, have been cited as examples of anarchist martyrs who were universally celebrated by the anarchist movement.[209] For Avilés and Herrerín López, repression and martyrdom were central to the anarchist experience of this period, as they created a culture of resistance and a shared experience of struggle. Thus, anarchist violence was in some ways a success, as it provoked the state into exposing its violent nature, giving credence to the anarchist critique of society and sustaining support for the movement.[210] Herrerín López's definition of 'true martyrs' were those who committed acts of violence, stayed at the scene, defended the ideals of anarchism while on trial, and met their inevitable 'immolation' at the hands of the state with calmness and pride. By this definition, Pallás and Angiolillo were the only true martyrs of this period. Salvador's flight, attempted suicide and apparent conversion to Christianity after the bombing of the Líceo muddied his martyr status, and since no author was identified for the attack on the Corpus Cristi the movement had no martyr to venerate following this attack.[211]

An examination of martyrdom within the anarchist press reveals a different picture. Pallás and Angiolillo were martyrs to some papers, as was Salvador; while for others none of these figures were deserving of veneration. There was no consensus on the meaning of martyrdom, but rather a plurality, which mirrored the heterogeneous reaction to anarchist terrorism. This was despite the fact that the execution of a terrorist was an act of state violence, rather than the individual violence for which they were punished. Internal state violence, such as arrest, imprisonment, exile and execution, had hitherto been universally condemned in anarchist theory.[212] The fact that the movement's reaction to the punishment of terrorists was mixed suggests that individual violence had altered this long-standing belief. Little analysis of this opinion within the anarchist movement has taken place, nor has the construction of martyrdom within anarchist papers. Instead these processes are assumed to have been straightforward, and are referred to with only passing reference to the words of the movement itself.

Unsurprisingly, papers which valorised terrorism were clear that those executed for carrying out attacks were martyrs. Pallás's execution was particularly significant for anarcho-communist papers. While *La Controversia* claimed that it had no emotional reaction to the event—stating that 'his death does not move us'—the paper wrote Pallás into a lineage of martyrs, who demonstrated the state's violence and legitimated further acts of terrorism.[213] Pallás remained a martyr in anarcho-communist papers through the following years, although he was rarely discussed as deserving of special worth. Instead he was generalised, written into a pantheon of martyrs who had collectively shed blood and sacrificed themselves in order to 'fortify the new land,' germinating thousands of new anarchists and assuring the victory of the idea.[214] Although no anarcho-communist papers were in print to commemorate Salvador's execution, when they returned in 1894–5 he too appeared on the pantheon alongside Pallás.[215] These papers were the most willing to invoke martyrdom to validate a violent response from anarchists, and are often used in studies of anarchist terrorism as evidence of a widespread use violent rhetoric within the movement.[216] This is despite the fact that all of these papers were acutely ephemeral, and much smaller than their contemporaries *El Corsario* and *La Idea Libre*.

A far more enduring martyrology was constructed by *El Corsario*. While this paper had held back from celebrating the violence of Pallás and Salvador, both men were immediately made into martyrs at the time of their execution, and continued to feature regularly in the paper until its final closure in 1896. Pallás was referred to as a 'martyr' in *El Corsario* from the moment he was executed. The paper frequently made references to Christian martyrdom in discussions of his death, subverting traditional religious rhetoric into a form more acceptable to an anarchist audience. Pallás's death was sacrificial and redemptive, but to a cause with very different values to the Catholic Church: 'What did Tertullian say at the start of Christianity? "The blood of the martyrs is the seed of Christians": [ours] will be much greater since we are accompanied by Reason [*sic*] and Justice [*sic*]'.[217] The issue dedicated to Pallás's death was so popular that the paper sold its entire print run, and apologised for being unable to meet requests for extra copies of the issue in following weeks.[218]

The memory of Pallás was invoked in other forms of print. Within days of Pallás's execution, Juan Montseny i Carret—a former cooper and teacher, and a growing presence in anarchist publishing—wrote to *El Corsario* to announce the publication of a pamphlet titled *Consideraciónes sobre el hecho y muerte de Pallás*, [*Considerations on the Deed and Death of Pallás*], which would be used to raise funds for Pallás's widow and their three children, one of whom Montseny would later briefly adopt.[219] The responsibility for the fund, which by December had reached 565 pesetas, fell upon Montseny himself, while the pamphlet was published by the La Coruña printers 'El Gutenberg' which also printed *El Corsario*.[220] This pamphlet was the only extended writing on Pallás published in the period. Rather than a glorification of terrorism or martyrdom, the pamphlet gave a rather general discussion of anarchist ideology, while Pallás and his attack on Martínez Campos was referred to only in passing.[221]

As 1893 progressed, contributors to *El Corsario* demonstrated their allegiance to Pallás's memory, as with the group named 'Bomba Pallás' created in Buenos Aires with the aim of collecting money for the martyr's family. Pallás's name also lived on in the pseudonyms of contributors, such as 'one who desires to avenge the death of Pallás' (0.25 pesetas), 'one who has 1000 *duros* (a coin of 5 pesetas) for bombs and to support the act of Pallás' (0.25 pesetas)' and 'the head of Martínez Campos' (0.25 pesetas)'.[222] A year on from his execution, Pallás was memorialised on the front page of *El Corsario*, where he was explicitly compared to Christ.[223] The paper maintained the name of the 'unforgettable' Pallás through an open subscription for his family, which caused controversy in 1895 when it was claimed that Pallás's widow, Ángela Vallés, had enrolled their children in a Catholic school.[224] Vallés—who was herself arrested following the attack on the Corpus procession—denied any wrongdoing, and was vouched for by Montseny in an open letter to the paper.[225] The fund set up upon Pallás's execution was closed in July 1895 with the final figure in excess of 660 pesetas, slightly less than the 820 pesetas had been collected through sales of Montseny's pamphlet.[226] Pallás also continued to feature heavily in correspondence to the paper, where he was depicted as a timeless, ever-present symbol, as in one letter from a correspondent who claimed that Pallás had appeared to him in a dream on the anniversary of his death, calling for revenge in his name.[227]

The treatment of Pallás by *El Corsario* fits the description of a 'true' anarchist martyr. His death was eulogised, the date of his execution was commemorated and his memory was sustained. Pallás also served as a point of coalescence, his execution providing the basis for nation-wide demonstrations of solidarity and exchange. A similar construction was evident in the paper's portrayal of Santiago Salvador, who is a more problematic figure for Herrerín López's definition of martyrdom. When Salvador was executed, *El Corsario* printed a eulogy about his sacrifice at the hands of the violent Spanish state, praising his death for the 'most noble of causes, the most beautiful of ideas: ANARCHISM!'[228] Salvador was 'one more' martyr, taking his place alongside Pallás, Ravachol, Vaillant, Henry and Caserio.[229] As in the wake of Pallás's execution, spontaneous collections began to appear in the paper for Salvador's family.[230] He was evidently just as much a martyr as Pallás to the writers and contributors of *El Corsario*, despite his less than committed approach to his arrest, capture and sentence.

Unlike anarcho-communist papers, *El Corsario* made Pallás and Salvador martyrs without discussing their violence or advocating violent responses. Instead, the paper employed the symbolism of martyrdom to call for acts of solidarity and unity across the movement. Together with its discussions of anarchist violence, this paper continually straddled a boundary between what was acceptable (being the subject of violence) and what was left unspoken (being the author of violence). For *El Corsario* anarchism was certainly a cause worth dying for, but whether it was a cause worth killing for was unclear.

In contrast, *La Idea Libre* made no attempt to portray terrorists as martyrs. The paper had no interest in discussing acts of terrorism, nor did it devote any space to the execution or memory of Pallás and Salvador. Even Angiolillo, whose act was seemingly the most justifiable of all the anarchist violence of the 1890s, received no attention in the paper when it returned in 1897. For *La Idea Libre*, the blood of terrorists did not germinate new anarchists, it 'sterilised' the soil. What was needed was 'work and intelligence,' which were the only legitimate means of action in 'the vast and infinite struggle for existence'.[231] Angiolillo was thus denied of martyr status in the immediate aftermath of his attack. In future years Angiolillo's name appeared sparsely, and he was not held up as a martyr to be revered and remembered as Pallás and Salvador had been.[232] Most post-1898 papers made no reference to Angiolillo, and only a handful of correspondences suggested that his name was maintained in the wider culture of the movement.[233] The same was true of Pallás and Salvador, who lost their martyr status and appeared only fleetingly after 1898. Thus these 'true' martyrs—the self-immolating advocates of propaganda by the deed, proud of being found guilty by a society they loathed—were a contested and transitory feature of the anarchist press, questioning the premise that their example helped to sustain the movement into the twentieth century.

Anarchist terrorism did not end in 1897. In the following decades anarchists were responsible for an attempt on Prime Minister Antonio Maura (Barcelona, 1904), several attempts on King Alfonso XIII (Madrid, 1902; Paris 1905; Madrid 1906; Madrid 1913) and the successful assassination of Prime Minister José Canalejas (Madrid, 1912). Those responsible for these attacks briefly attracted the attention of the anarchist press, however none of them gained the notoriety of their predecessors of the 1890s, nor were they martyred.[234] After 1898 the anarchist press usually distanced itself from terrorism and denied its causal connection to anarchist ideology. Rather than celebrating or denouncing anarchist terrorists and martyrs who had killed for the cause, after 1898 the anarchist press simply stated that terrorism had nothing to do with them. During the 1890s, terrorists had been used by a few papers as examples of 'men of action' engaged in direct struggle against authority. In the climate of repression this was one of the few ways in which anarchist papers could hope to forge a sense of unity across the movement. Yet marking dates and proclaiming glories to the dead did nothing to prevent the movement from collapse, and any potential benefit the example of terrorists may have provided was massively outweighed by the damage their actions brought upon their comrades in the movement.

The Blood of the Innocent

Although the term 'martyr' proliferated in the anarchist press of the 1890s, it was not reserved exclusively for executed terrorists. Instead, the term was applied liberally, to include the victims of repression, participants in strikes and uprisings, such as that of Jerez, as well as the victims of industrial accidents. According to Herrerín López, all of these individuals had a lesser martyr status than Pallás and Angiolillo, or 'were not martyrs' at all, since their victimhood was passive.[235] This claim is not born out in examination of the movement's press. These figures attracted a more unified, consistent and practical response from the anarchist press than the authors of propaganda by the deed, suggesting that innocence was a more significant factor in the creation of anarchist martyrs than a deliberate desire for immolation.

After 1893 repression defined the anarchist experience in Barcelona, where anyone with connection to the anarchist movement fell under suspicion. Over 260 individuals were detained following the attack on the Líceo, many of whom remained in prison without charge for over a year. Many were subject to torture, two of whom (Miguel Nacher and Juan Bernich) died in their cells, and one, Martín Borrás, committed suicide in prison. Another six anarchists—Mariano Cerezuela Subías, José Codina Juncá (both of whom were initially been blamed for the Líceo attack), Jaime Sogas Martí, Manuel Archs Solanelles, José Sabat Ollé and José Bernat Cirerol—were found guilty of conspiracy with Pallás in the attack on Martínez Campos. They were executed on 21 May 1894, the same day that Emile Henry was guillotined in France.[236] Of those on trial for the Líceo attack, 16 were absolved, including the prominent publisher José Prat, and two were declared in contempt of court. The remaining seven adjudged guilty for the Líceo attack (Nacher, Cerezuela, Codina, Sogas, Archs, Sabat and Bernat) were already dead.[237] Unlike Pallás and Salvador, all of these individuals were presumed to be innocent by the anarchist press.

El Corsario denied that a wider conspiracy within the anarchist movement had prompted the attacks in 1893. Instead, the paper asserted that both Pallás and Salvador had acted alone, and claimed that the authorities in Barcelona were using the attacks as a pretext to destroy the wider, essentially peaceful anarchist movement in the city. *El Corsario* was particularly aggrieved when it became unwillingly culpable in this repression. In early 1894 its subscription lists were seized and used as a 'guide for the vampires' of the state in tracking down suspects.[238] Later that year, Montseny began to work on another pamphlet, this time to raise funds for the families of Nacher, Bernich and Borrás. This would become *El proceso de un gran crimen* (1895), a diatribe against the arbitrary arrests and torture that had become synonymous with the anarchist experience in Barcelona.[239] As with the subscription lists of *El Corsario*, the police used the distribution of this pamphlet to locate suspects. The authorities made it known that 2,000 copies of the pamphlet were available at the home of an accomplice named Joaquín Llagostera y Sabaté and arrested all those who showed up. Llagostera y Sabaté was declared an 'infamous traitor' by *El Corsario*, which also published his description and encouraged comrades to give him his 'reward'.[240] Actions such as these by the Spanish authorities reveal both the value and fragility of the movement's reliance on print. When the movement could operate legally, the links maintained by papers created a fluid structure, which could expand and converge without recourse to a central organisation. During times of repression these same connections became incriminating evidence and were used to smash the movement apart.

The assumed innocence of the victims of repression did not prevent them from being portrayed as martyrs. In November 1894 *El Corsario*'s ever-growing list of martyrs included those executed following the Paris Commune, the Mano Negra affair and the Haymarket, Lamela, Zarzuela and Pallás, the nine 'innocent' suspects of the Martínez Campos attack, as well as those who had been condemned to life imprisonment, such as Domingo Mir and Rafael Miralles. All were 'martyrs of Anarchy,' regardless of either their deeds or their punishment. What was important is that they were anarchists who had been subject to the violence of the state.

As well as a rhetorical device, *El Corsario* invoked martyrdom as a means of provoking practical, material solidarity from its readership, in the form of open subscriptions to support the families of the executed and imprisoned. The readership of the paper did not consider authors of the violence to be more deserving than their innocent counterparts. The paper ran three funds: one for the family of Pallás, one for all anarchist prisoners in Spain, and one for the families of those who had been 'murdered' in early 1894 (Nacher, Borrás and Bernich). Between April 1895 and August 1896 the general solidarity fund had grown five times as much (+171.04 pesetas) as that of the fund specifically for Pallás's family (+33.95 pesetas), and both were dwarfed by the growth in the fund for Nacher, Borrás and Bernich (+1,670.80 pesetas).[241]

Innocent martyrdom was also a common theme in anarcho-communist papers. As with *El Corsario*, these papers extended their portrayal of martyrs to include the victims of repression.[242] *El Rebelde* also extended its conception of martyrdom to include the victims of industrial accidents, including four workers who had died during the construction of a road in Zaragoza.[243] This proliferation of 'martyrs' indicates that rather than having a specific function within anarchist culture, martyrdom could be bestowed upon anyone who had suffered at the hands of the state, whether they had committed acts of violence or not.

For *La Idea Libre*, innocence was an essential component of what constituted a martyr, which emphasised the moral worth of the victims of state violence. This condition included a range of individuals, but pointedly excluded terrorists. By far the most prominent martyrs in the paper were those of Chicago, who were memorialised in special editions and a series of biographies and portraits.[244] As in *La Anarquía*, the paper also emphasised innocence in its portrayals of the repression which followed the Jerez uprising.[245] This was an inversion of Herrerín López's

formulation of anarchist martyrdom: instead of violence and immolation, *La Idea Libre* made innocence a defining feature of a 'true' martyr.
Yet the paper made few references to the repression of the 1890s, aside
from one brief reference in May 1895, when it published the portraits
of Archs, Bernat, Codina, Sabat and Cerezuela at the behest of 'various friends,' who were hoping to raise money to ease the misery of an
'unnamed' family.[246]

Repression intensified following the attack on the Corpus procession
in 1896. In Barcelona, anyone who was known to hold beliefs or engage
in practices deemed 'different' was suspect. In total 424 individuals were
arrested, including many figures active in the anarchist press, such as
Montseny (imprisoned and exiled for 13 months), Anselmo Lorenzo
(imprisoned for 17 months) and Teresa Claramunt.[247] Montjuich Castle became the symbol of repression. Its cells were filled with prisoners,
many of whom were subject to brutal torture: suspects were deprived of
food, drink and sleep; they were gagged and manacled by hand and foot
for days; they were beaten, forced to sit on hot irons and were sexually
abused.[248] Others, such as Francisca Saperas, the widow of Martín Borrás, were forced to convert to Catholicism to avoid having their children
being sent to a religious orphanage. The infamous 'Proceso de Montjuich'
[Montjuich trial] began in December 1896. Of the 87 brought to trial,
five—Tomás Ascheri, Antonio Nogués, José Molas, Luis Mas and Joan
Alsina—received death sentences, which were carried out on 4 May
1897. Few, even amongst the Barcelona authorities, genuinely believed
that these figures were responsible for the bombing. Around 50 others
were exiled to France and a further 20 were given prison sentences of
between 10 and 20 years.[249]

No anarchist papers were in print to comment on this wave of repression, however a 200-page exposé on the Proceso was compiled by
Ricardo Mella and José Prat, and published by *El Corsario* as *La barbarie gubermantal en España*. This 'devastating critique of the Spanish
government' outlined the brutality of the repression in Barcelona, and the
feeble evidence used to imprison, exile and execute hundreds of workers
and intellectuals.[250] Prat left Spain for Buenos Aires following the assassination of Cánovas del Castillo (presumably pre-empting arrest) where
he joined the editorial board of the newly-founded *La Protesta Humana*,
which went on to become one of the most important anarchist periodicals in the world.[251] Repression in Spain was a major topic in the early
years of *La Protesta Humana*. The first issue of the paper contained a
lengthy letter from Prat (at this point still in Spain), which gave details on
the sentences, last moments and execution of the anarchists condemned
for their adjudged involvement in the Cambios Nuevos bombing.[252]
Over the following year, the paper maintained regular columns denouncing the actions of the Spanish government from Spanish contributors in
Buenos Aires, as well as reproducing works from Spanish and European

papers.[253] Thus, while anarchist publishing in Spain was curtailed, news and contributions from the Spanish movement continued to hold a presence in the international anarchist press, which was distributed widely across Spain, helping to maintain a limited version of the print networks that were essential to the movement's existence.[254]

There was also a strong reaction to the repression from the mainstream press across Europe, and protests against the Spanish government regularly took place in France and Britain, often accompanied by Spanish exiles, as in Liverpool when 28 exiles, including Montseny, arrived in the city in July 1897.[255] Yet the on-going repression in 'Black Spain' itself hampered any sustained critique of the government until early 1898.[256]

When *La Idea Libre* returned to print it devoted more space to the victims of repression than in its previous epoch. The paper was particularly supportive of Francisco Callís Calderón, who had been tortured and 'unjustly condemned' to life imprisonment, and opened a subscription for his 70-year-old mother.[257] As before, the paper was only concerned with the innocent, such as those who had been unjustly shot in Montjuich, and those who continued to 'vegetate in the prisons of Africa and the Peninsula'.[258] The paper was adamant that the sentences should not be pardoned, but overturned, thus affirming the accused's innocence.[259] Many of its contributors supported this stance, and reported that public opinion was also in favour of a revision of the trials.[260] In early 1898 a campaign for a revision of the trials was launched by the Republican daily *Progreso*, which drew support from a broad section of Spanish public opinion and inspired meetings in La Coruña, Zaragoza, Gijón and Barcelona.[261] *Progreso*'s campaign included contributions from numerous high-profile anarchist writers, including Montseny—now going by the pseudonym Federico Urales—who returned to Madrid in November 1897 with his wife Soledad Gustavo (pseud. Teresa Mañé Miravet), a prominent anarchist-feminist author and teacher.[262] Montjuich remained a primary concern in the publications of the 'Urales family', particularly *La Revista Blanca* (launched July 1898) and its *Suplemento* (launched May 1899).[263] These publications kept the cause of the remaining victims of repression alive in anarchist print culture until 1900, when the remaining 23 prisoners had their sentences reduced to exile.[264] Following this partial success, the paper immediately turned its attentions to the five remaining prisoners of the Jerez uprising of 1892, organising a protest tour through Andalucía in May 1900, led by Gustavo.[265] The campaign attracted support from a number of mainstream papers and was supported in protest meetings in Galicia and Cataluña. On 8 February 1901 the government of Marcelona Azcárraga approved a royal pardon for the prisoners of Jerez, and the last 'martyrs' of the 1890s were released.

Martyrdom was evoked with regularity in the following years, above all in 1909 following the execution of Francisco Ferrer.[266] Yet the martyrs of the 1890s were almost entirely absent from these future discussions.

Zarzuela, Lamela, Pallás and Salvador were not remembered into the twentieth century, nor were their dates of execution commemorated. The innocent martyrs of Jerez and Montjuich also disappeared from anarchist print culture after their release. Only the Chicago martyrs retained their position as the exemplary examples of state violence, albeit with a more diminished presence than in previous years.[267] Thus the claim that the movement was sustained by its creation of martyrs is not borne out in the central mechanism of anarchist culture: its press. While martyrdom was invoked with regularity in this period, it was not a stable, nor a singular concept which promoted a unified response from the movement. Some aspects of the anarchist press' response to repression—for example sub-scription funds—did help to maintain a sense of cohesion in the 1890s, however it is clear that the anarchist press at this time was not operat-ing from a position of strength. Repression was neither invited nor wel-comed by anarchist papers, which were the movement's clearest targets outside Cataluña. Periodicals tried, and ultimately failed, to employ vari-ous forms of martyrdom as a unifying cause in the face of difficulties, but rather than a symbol of the movement's survival, the evocation of mar-tyrdom was no more than evidence of the dismal situation that it faced.

The Cuban War and the 'Disaster' of 1898

One of the most consistent elements of anarchist ideology was its hostil-ity to war and militarism. Both were constantly derided in the anarchist press as the ultimate expression of the violence inherent in the state, which forced men to kill one another in the name of the 'nation' or 'Empire,' misleading 'the people' away from their genuine goals of emancipation and liberty.[268] A particular hatred was reserved for conscription, which demonstrated the state's exploitation of the working class, while allow-ing the bourgeoisie to pay to be excused from service.[269] Yet many anar-chists preferred to see themselves as anti-militarists, rather than pacifists, which legitimised popular violence if it was directed against the state and could therefore be seen as revolutionary or an act of self-defence. Nevertheless, there was little discussion within the Spanish movement on what constituted a legitimate response to war, which left the movement's ideological position on the matter unclear.

This ambiguity was exposed at the outbreak of the Cuban War of Independence in February 1895, which in theory should have provided a common point for the anarchist movement to focus its long-standing antagonism to state violence.[270] From the outbreak of the war, the move-ment's press was united in its condemnation of conscription, which was portrayed as a means of sending hundreds of thousands of working-class Spaniards to fight in the appalling conditions of rural Cuba—depicted as a 'swamp' brimming with 'plagues'—for the sake of the state's capitalist interests.[271] In the summer of 1896 *El Corsario* developed this critique into a national campaign which dominated its final issues. The paper was inspired by women's protest meetings across Spain, regarding them as the first manifestation of a popular, revolutionary anti-war sentiment. The paper called upon its readers to join with these 'mothers of Spain,' who shared anarchism's 'love' and 'humanitarianism'.[272]

Yet despite their shared stance on Spain's militarism, anarchist papers differed in their portrayal of the Cuban insurrection. *El Corsario* was supportive of the independence movement, most evidently in the column 'The Week in Cuba' from correspondent 'Pantin' in Havana, which ran throughout its third and final epoch.[273] This section reflected the mood of most Cuban anarchists towards the conflict, who saw the cause for a 'Free Cuba' as the first step towards wider social emancipation on the island.[274] The insurrection was considered a revolutionary war between 'the people and the Spanish oligarchy', and therefore legitimate.[275] The strong and regular connection between *El Corsario* and the island reflected a shared sense of purpose between Cuban nationalists and Spanish anarchists in La Coruña, a link which was underwritten by the high levels of migration between Galicia and Cuba in the nineteenth century.[276]

The handful of anarcho-communist papers published during the war also lent their support to the insurrection. Writing in *El Eco del Rebelde*, Vicente García portrayed the Cuban cause as the same as that of anarchists in Spain, both of whom legitimately used violence against the bourgeois state.[277] Towards the end of 1895 *El Comunista* published an extract from the pamphlet *Cuba libre* by the black insurgent leader General Antonio Maceo, portraying him as the 'soul of the revolution,' and agreeing with his depiction of the black Cuban cause as the same as that of 'anarchists in Europe; slaves of Africa . . . Jews, exiles, émigrés everywhere'. The paper was also supportive of Maceo's call to 'Destroy! Destroy! Destroy all the time and at all hours' as the best means to secure 'autonomy'.[278] *El Comunista*'s identification with the cause for racial equality within Cuban independence contrasted sharply with the mainstream Spanish press, which caricatured the black Cuban revolutionaries as wild, bloodthirsty savages.[279]

Sympathy towards the Cuban independence movement was also common in international anarchist circles. Numerous personal connections existed between Cuban and anarchist revolutionaries, often made in exile in cities such as Paris and London. The two causes were united in figures such as Fernando Tárrida del Mármol, a Cuban anarchist who had been arrested in Barcelona following the Corpus bombing. Following his release, Tárrida moved to Paris and then on to London, where he published accounts of the brutal repression of the anarchist movement in Barcelona. Tárrida explicitly linked the repression of anarchism to Spanish colonial rule of Cuba, underlined by a common cause against the Spanish state, which was attracting increasing international criticism for its heavy-handed reaction to domestic and colonial revolutionaries.[280]

La Idea Libre maintained a different perspective on the Cuban war to its contemporaries. It recognised the war as a capitalist adventure to prevent the secession of the island, yet it did not hold much faith that the workers of Cuba would benefit from a new republican state.[281] This paper saw a basic contradiction between nationalism and anarchism, seeing independence as a means to bring about a change in authority, rather than its abolition.[282] *La Idea Libre*'s Cuban correspondents emphasised the need to organise workers and 'persuade them towards their complete economic and social emancipation' above the mere 'political' freedoms being fought for at the time.[283] They ignored the bulk of the fighting, and never once mentioned the leaders of the independence movement, such as José Martí. Instead they focused on vague reports that a 'true' social revolution was imminent and claimed that the majority of workers who supported the revolution did so because of hunger, rather than Cuban nationalism.[284] This was a view shared by the publisher Pedro Esteve, who had fled Spain in 1892 to avoid arrest. From his new location in New York, Esteve spent the war arguing in the city's Spanish-language anarchist periodical, *El Despertar*, that 'Cuban independence alone would not benefit the Cuban people,' and refused to support the movement for a Republic. His position led to a split within *El Despertar*'s publishing group, which resulted in Esteve moving with the paper to Paterson (New Jersey).[285]

The differing conceptions on the war in Cuba paralleled similar divisions over anarchist violence within Spain. Some sections of the press supported the revolutionary struggle of the Cuban people, seeing it as analogous to the popular and individual violence directed against the Spanish state. *La Idea Libre* saw the war differently, as simply a struggle between two ills, mirroring its negative attitude towards terrorism. Where these papers could agree, however, was in their condemnation of Spain's role in the war. Imperialism and war remained anathema, as expressions of externalised state violence which was illegitimate by its nature.

In contrast to the Cuban insurrection, anarchist papers paid little attention to the growing Philippine independence movement and gave only a limited response to the revolution which broke out in the colony in August 1896. In the final few issues of *El Corsario* and its short-lived successor *El Productor*, the Philippine cause was celebrated as part of an international struggle against the 'yoke of oppression,' yet there was no sense of the common cause that the paper had made with the Cuban independence movement.[286] With the collapse of the anarchist press in October 1896, no further attention to the Philippines could be provided by the anarchist press in Spain. Likewise, coverage of the war in Cuba ceased as repression made anarchist publishing impossible.

By the time the anarchist press returned, both conflicts were drawing to a close. Despite desperate attempts from Spanish diplomats to keep the US out of the wars in Cuba and the Philippines, three years of stalemate persuaded President McKinley that intervention was necessary. The US declared war on Spain on 25 April 1898, and by 13 August, the US navy had crushed the Spanish forces in both the Philippines and Cuba, signalling an end to both wars of independence and the end of the Spanish Empire. In Spain, this 'disaster' had a profound impact on public political discourse, prompting a prolonged period of introspection in which 'Spain's political system, its national character, and Spanish nationhood itself . . . began to be widely questioned'.[287] In contrast, *La Idea Libre* welcomed US intervention in the war, and saw the defeat of Spain as a moment of 'atonement' for the Spanish bourgeoisie.[288] Nevertheless, the paper remained pessimistic about the prospects of the new Cuban Republic, claiming that the nationalists had simply swapped an imperial master for the domination of US capitalism.[289] By the time that other anarchist papers emerged later in the year the war was over, and had largely disappeared as a subject of discussion.

With the end of the war in Cuba and the relaxation of repression, the anarchist press began to look to the future. As the movement's press returned, it called for new methods towards the revolution and new responses to the challenge of authority. In the following years the movement would no longer be defined by violence, but by its drive for cultural and organisational expansion, both of which were spearheaded by its press. In *La Idea Libre*, pieces such as 'Faith in the Future' by José Prat— who returned to Barcelona from Buenos Aires in 1898—demonstrated the paper's shift from the introspective, nostalgic tone of 1894–6. Rather than dwelling on past glories and tragedies, Prat employed history as an example of the inevitable march of progress, which could not be quelled by periods of repression.[290] Likewise, the recently-launched *La Revista Blanca* saw the movement's return to legality as a new dawn for anarchism in Spain. The journal's emphasis on education and culture, and a general sense of optimism, represented a sharp change in tone from the press of previous years.

The violence of the 1890s had brought anarchism in Spain to its knees. It divided anarchist opinion and prompted the creation of competing cultural symbols. Only three anarchists in Spain threw bombs in Barcelona, killing a total of 34 people. Another killed a prime minister, and around hundred anarchists were held responsible for a rural uprising in which three people died. Many within the movement supported these actions and just as many condemned them. Individuals, groups and newspapers changed their attitude through the decade, some hardening in their support for violence, some refuting their former positions to condemn it outright. This heterogeneous, fluid situation was created and mediated by the anarchist press, which also attempted to sustain the movement through the symbolism of martyrdom and practical activity, such as solidarity funds. The efforts of the press were ultimately futile, as repression wiped out its fragile infrastructure, severing the networks of communication which the movement relied upon. When the press returned, the symbols provided by the perpetrators and victims of violence of the 1890s did not resonate past the turn of the century. Violence remained a salient feature of anarchism in Spain: strikes and protests continued to be marked by violence, violent uprisings continued to take place, anarchists continued to commit violent acts, and were routinely subject to the violence of the state. Yet violence ceased to define the movement and dominate its print culture. Instead, anarchists in Spain moved on from this decade, and put this disastrous period behind them.

Notes

1. Notable exceptions include José Álvarez Junco, *La ideología política del anarquismo español (1868–1910)* (Madrid: Siglo XXI, 1991), 494–510; George Esenwein, *Anarchist Ideology and the Working-Class Movement in Spain, 1868–1898* (Berkeley: University of California Press, 1989), 166–188.
2. Juan Avilés Farré and Ángel Herrerín López, 'Propaganda por el hecho y propaganda por la represión: Anarquismo y violencia en España a fines del siglo XIX,' *Ayer* 80, 4 (2010): 165–192. See also Ángel Herrerín López, 'España: La propaganda por la represión, 1892–1900,' in *El nacimiento del terrorismo en occidente: Anarquía, nihilismo y violencia revolucionaria*, ed. Juan Avilés Farré and Ángel Herrerín López (Madrid: Siglo XXI, 2008), 103–139 and *Anarquía, dinamita y revolución social: Violencia y represión en la España entre siglos (1868–1909)* (Madrid: Catarata, 2011), 172–180.
3. Avilés Farré and Herrerín López, 'Propaganda por el hecho,' 167 and 189–190. See also Richard Bach Jensen, 'The International Campaign against Anarchist Terrorism, 1880–1930s,' *Terrorism and Political Violence* 21, 1 (2009): 100–101.
4. Juan Avilés Farré, 'El terrorismo anarquista como propaganda por el hecho: de la formulación teórica a los atentados de Paris, 1877–1894,' *Historia y Política* 21 (2009): 188; Jensen, 'The International Campaign,' 106–107.
5. Richard Bach Jensen, 'The International Anti-Anarchist Conference of 1898 and the Origins of Interpol,' *Journal of Contemporary History* 16, 2 (1981): 340 and 'Daggers, Rifles and Dynamite: Anarchist Terrorism in Nineteenth-Century Europe,' *Terrorism and Political Violence* 16, 1 (2004): 142–143.
6. Ángel Herrerín López, 'Anarchist Sociability in Spain: In Times of Violence and Clandestinity,' *Bulletin for Spanish and Portuguese Historical Studies* 38, 1 (2013): 157.
7. Eduardo González Calleja, *La razón de la fuerza: Orden público, subversión y violencia política en la España de la Restauración (1875–1917)* (Madrid: Editorial CSIC, 1998), 32–64.
8. Mary Vincent, *Spain, 1833–2002: People and State* (Oxford: Oxford University Press, 2007), 32–33.
9. A comparison with the Russian anarchist movement emphasises this point, see Jensen, 'Daggers, Rifles and Dynamite,' 121.
10. On the 1870s see Francisco Madrid Santos, 'La prensa anarquista y anarcosindicalista en España desde la I Internacional hasta el fin de la Guerra Civil,' (PhD thesis, Barcelona: Universidad Central de Barcelona, 1988–89), 86–93.
11. Rafael Núñez Florencio, *El terrorismo anarquista (1888–1909)* (Madrid: Siglo XXI, 1983), 185.

12. Francisco Madrid Santos, *Solidaridad Obrera y el periodismo de raíz ácrata* (Badalona: Ediciones Solidaridad Obrera, 2007), 42.

13. Lily Litvak, *Musa libertaria: Arte, literatura y vida cultural del anarquismo español (1890–1913)* (Madrid: Fundación de Estudios Libertarios Anselmo Lorenzo, 2001), 194–210, at 195.

14. *La Controversia* (Valencia), 7 October, 1893, 3–4; *El Eco del Rebelde* (Zaragoza), 6 June, 1895, 1–2.

15. Álvarez Junco, *La ideología política*, 311–322.

16. *El Porvenir del Obrero* (Mahón, II), 29 April, 1915, 3–4.

17. Ricardo Mella, *La Nueva Utopía*, in *El Cuento Anarquista (1880–1911): Antología*, ed. Lily Litvak (Madrid: Fundación de Estudios Libertarios Anselmo Lorenzo, 2003), 219. See also José Luis Ramos-Gorostiza, 'Socio-Economic Utopianism in Spain at the End of the Nineteenth Century: *La Nueva Utopia* by Ricardo Mella,' *Utopian Studies* 20, 1 (2009): 5–39 and Esenwein, *Anarchist Ideology*, 147–152.

18. For example see *La Anarquía* (Madrid), 5 June, 1892, 1–2.

19. The central text which claims to prove the existence of the 'Mano Negra' remains Clara Lida, 'Agrarian Anarchism in Andalusia: Documents on the Mano Negra,' *International Review of Social History* 14, 3 (1969): 315–352. Lida's position is supported in Herrerín López, *Anarquía, dinamita*, 58–59. Critics of Lida's 'proof' of the Mano Negra include Temma Kaplan, *Anarchists of Andalusia, 1868–1903* (Princeton: Princeton University Press, 1977), 126–134; Esenwein, *Anarchist Ideology*, 84–92.

20. Herrerín López, *Anarquía, dinamita*, 57–58.

21. The final (and ultimately successful) amnesty campaign for the 'Mano Negra' prisoners began in *Tierra y Libertad* (Madrid), 25 January, 1902, 1.

22. Álvarez Junco, *La ideología política*, 493–494; Bach Jensen, 'Daggers, Rifles and Dynamite,' 121–126.

23. Esenwein, *Anarchist Ideology*, 61–63.

24. *El Socialismo* (Cádiz), 12 January, 1890, 4.

25. An excellent overview of this subject is provided by Constance Bantman, 'The Era of Propaganda by the Deed,' *The Palgrave Handbook of Anarchism*, ed. Carl Levy and Matthew Adams (London: Palgrave Macmillan, 2018), 371–387.

26. Herrerín López, 'Anarchist Sociability,' 161.

27. Esenwein, *Anarchist Ideology*, 166–172.

28. Álvarez Junco, *La ideología política*, 508–510.

29. Bach Jensen, 'Daggers, Rifles and Dynamite,' 126. Explanatory note from Bach Jensen.

30. Esenwein, *Anarchist Ideology*, 172–174; Herrerín López, *Anarquía, dinamita*, 60–64.

31. *La Victima del Trabajo* (Valencia), 26 June, 1890, 1; *El Combate* (Bilbao), 11 November, 1891, 2–3.

32. Angel Smith, *Anarchism, Revolution and Reaction: Catalan Labour and the Crisis of the Spanish State, 1898–1923* (New York: Berghahn, 2007), 107–108.

33. Kaplan, *Anarchists of Andalusia*, 169.

34. Jacques Maurice, *El anarquismo andaluz: Campesinos y sindicalistas, 1868–1936* (Barcelona: Crítica, 1990), 219–220.

35. *La Anarquía* (Madrid), 24 December, 1891, 2–3. See also the case against Salvochea, Juan José García and José Ponce in Archivo Histórico Provincial de Cádiz (AHPC): Libro de Sentencias de Tribunal de Juzgados: 1892: I: Sentencia número 1, 9 March, 1892.

36. *La Anarquía* (Madrid), 3 September, 1891, 2 and 11 September, 1891, 2. See also Kaplan, *Anarchists of Andalusia*, 169.

37. *La Anarquía* (Madrid), 18 September, 1891, 1–2 and 6 November, 1891, 2.
38. *La Anarquía* (Madrid), 26 June, 1891, 4. On Álvarez see Federico Urales, *Mi vida*, Vol. 1 (Barcelona: La Revista Blanca, 1930), 142–144 and Madrid Santos, 'La prensa anarquista,' 118–119, 128.
39. *La Anarquía* (Madrid), 11 September, 1891–98; March, 1892.
40. *El Corsario* (La Coruña), 27 September, 1891–25; October, 1891. Last published balance: 40,40 pesetas.
41. *La Anarquía* (Madrid), 7 August, 1891, 4; 25 September, 1891, 2–3; 1 October, 1891, 1–2; 9 October, 1891, 2–3.
42. *La Anarquía* (Madrid), 11 December, 1891, 2. See also Ricardo Mella, *Los sucesos de Jerez: 8 Enero 1892–10 Febrero 1892* (Barcelona: Tipografía Calle San Rafael, 1893), 9–10. Manuel Díaz y Martel, from Puerto Real (Cádiz) shouted 'death to the bourgeoisie!' at the celebrations and was arrested. He was sentenced to two months and one day imprisonment for sedition, see Archivo Histórico Provincial de Cádiz (AHPC): Libro de Sentencias de Cádiz: 1892: I: Sentencia número 249, 12 May, 1892 and *La Anarquía* (Madrid), 24 December, 1891, 2–3.
43. *El Corsario* (La Coruña), 24 January, 1892, 4.
44. For example *La Anarquía* (Madrid), 2 July, 1891, 2; *La Cuestión Social* (Valencia), 30 April, 1892, 1–2.
45. Kaplan, *Anarchists of Andalusia*, 173–176; Herrerín López, *Anarquía, dinamita*, 76–77. Jerez civil records detailing deaths: Archivo Municipal de Jerez de la Frontera (AMJF): C.24 [Previously 3302: this earlier record is given by Kaplan and subsequent studies, but has since been relabelled]: Proceso contra anarquistas: Ejecución de los anarquistas: Protocolo No.302: Año 1891–2: Certificación gratuitas 28 (Palomino); 29 (Soto); 30 (Núñez Montenegro).
46. Victor V. Magagna, *Communities of Grain: Rural Rebellion in Comparative Perspective* (Ithaca: Cornell University Press, 1991), 180.
47. Josep Termes, *Anarquismo y sindicalismo en España: La Primera Internacional (1864–1881)* (Barcelona: Crítica, 1977), 22–23; Constancio Bernaldo de Quirós, 'El espartaquismo agrario andaluz,' *Revista general de legislación y jurisprudencia*, 134 (1919): 312.
48. Kaplan, *Anarchists of Andalusia*, 104–110.
49. Herrerín López, *Anarquía, dinamita*, 208–214.
50. Antonio López Estudillo, *Insurrección y provocación policial: Los sucesos de Jerez de 1892* (La Laguna: Tierra de Fuego, 2008), 3–6.
51. Bernaldo de Quirós, 'El espartaquismo agrario andaluz,' 402, critiqued in Maurice, *El anarquismo andaluz*, 124–125.
52. Gerard Brey, 'Crisis económica, anarquismo y sucesos de Jerez, 1886–1892,' in *Seis estudios sobre el proletariado andaluz (1868–1939)*, ed. Ramón Rodríguez Aguilera (Córdoba: Ayuntamiento de Córdoba, 1984), 75–127; Maurice, *El anarquismo andaluz*, 124–125.
53. Mella, *Los sucesos de Jerez*, 11.
54. Esenwein, *Anarchist Ideology*, 183–184.
55. Kaplan, *Anarchists of Andalusia*, 174–175.
56. *El Corsario* (La Coruña), 24 January, 1892, 2–3.
57. *La Tribuna Libre* (Sevilla), 23 December, 1891, 4. See also Madrid Santos, 'La prensa anarquista,' 138.
58. *La Tribuna Libre* (Sevilla), 23 January, 1892, 1.
59. *La Tribuna Libre* (Sevilla), 23 December, 1891, 3–4.
60. *El Corsario* (La Coruña), 24 January, 1892, 2–3 and 4.
61. *La Anarquía* (Madrid), 22 January, 1892, 2.
62. *La Anarquía* (Madrid), 15 January, 1892, 1.

63. *El Socialista* (Madrid), 15 January, 1892, 1.
64. See *La Cuestión Social* (Valencia), 21 May, 1892, 2.
65. Esenwein, *Anarchist Ideology*, 179–184; López Estudillo, *Insurrección y provocación policial*, 27–28; Herrerín López, *Anarquía, dinamita*, 76–80.
66. Kaplan, *Anarchists of Andalusia*, 176–181. Kaplan's excellent reconstruction of the repression in Jerez is mainly based on records at AMJF: C.24: Proceso contra anarquistas: Caja 4, which contains hundreds of telegrams from Civil Guardsmen. Futher primary information is available in Cajas 5–8bis.
67. Records of executions: AMJF: C.24: Proceso contra anarquistas: Ejecución de los anarquistas: Protocolo No.302: Año 1891–2: Certificación gratuitas: 111 (Lamela); 112 (Zarzuela); 113 (Fernández Reina); 114 (Silva Leal).
68. The cause of Caro Clavo's death is unclear. Kaplan, *Anarchists of Andalusia*, 180 claims that it was possibly suicide, while Salvochea claimed that it was a result of an untreated stomach infection, see Herrerín López, *Anarquía, dinamita*, 77–80. Caro Clavo's death record simply states that he died suddenly: AMJF: C.24: Ejecución de los anarquistas: Protocolo No.302: Año 1891–2: Certificación gratuita 115.
69. José Aguilar Villagrán, *El asalto campesino a Jerez de la Frontera en 1892* (Jerez de la Frontera: Centro de Estudios Históricos Jerezanos, 1984), 85–88.
70. Coverage of sentences in *El Corsario* (La Coruña), 15 January, 1893, 3.
71. Cited in Esenwein, *Anarchist Ideology*, 182.
72. Article cited in *La Anarquía* (Madrid), 11 February, 1892, 2.
73. *La Anarquía* (Madrid), 11 February, 1892, 2.
74. *La Anarquía* (Madrid), 3 March, 1892, 1.
75. *El Corsario* (La Coruña), 14 February, 1892, 2–3.
76. Herrerín López, *Anarquía, dinamita*, 82. This incident was blamed on a group of anarcho-communists based in Gracia (Barcelona), whose publication *El Porvenir Anarquista* was closed and its editorial group arrested, see Madrid Santos, 'La prensa anarquista,' 41–42.
77. *La Correspondencia de España* (Madrid), 5 April, 1892, 3; *La Anarquía* (Madrid), 21 April, 1892, 2–3 and 29 April, 1892, 3 and 4. While in prison Álvarez was accused of having instigated the Jerez uprising, a charge which his paper strongly denied, see *La Anarquía* (Madrid), 13 May, 1892, 2.
78. *Ravachol* (Sabadell), 11 November, 1892, 1–2 and 3–4.
79. *El Oprimido* (Algeciras), 11 October, 1893, 2.
80. The closest *La Controversia* came to justifying violence was in was in the article 'Otra táctica,' published in the issue of 1 June, 1893, 2. Even this article was mild compared to the tone of the Catalan anarcho-communist publications.
81. *La Anarquía* (Madrid), 21 April, 1892, 2–3 and 6 May, 1892, 1; *El Corsario* (La Coruña), 1 May, 1892, 1–2. See also López Estudillo, *Insurrección y provocación policial*, 34.
82. *La Cuestión Social* (Valencia), 30 April, 1892, 2.
83. *El Corsario* (La Coruña), 30 July, 1893, 2.
84. Litvak, *Musa libertaria*, 197–200; Avilés Farré and Herrerín López, 'Propaganda por el hecho,' 173–174.
85. Elun Gabriel, 'Performing Persecution: Witnessing and Martyrdom in the Anarchist Tradition,' *Radical History Review* 98 (2007): 46.
86. References to Galileo, Bruno and Juan Huss in *La Cuestión Social* (Valencia), 21 May, 1892, 2; anarchist educational society named 'Miguel Servet' in *El Corsario* (La Coruña), 24 July, 1892, 4 and 31 July, 1892, 3.
87. *Acracia: Suplemento al número 5 de Acracia: 18 de marzo 1871–1886: Velada socialista artístico-literaria en conmemoración del XV aniversario de*

la proclamación de la Commune de París (Barcelona), May 1886, i–xx. See also celebrations organised by *La Anarquía* to celebrate the Commune in 1892: *La Anarquía* (Madrid), 25 March, 1892, 4. On the immediate impact of the Commune in Spain see Clara Lida, 'La comuna de París y sus repercusiones: El caso Español,' in *El poder y la sangre: Guerra, estado y nación en la década de 1860*, ed. Guillermo Palacios and Erika Pani (México, DF: El Colegio de México, 2014), 183–195.

88. See the contrasting interpretations of this event in Paul Avrich, *The Haymarket Tragedy* (Princeton: Princeton University Press, 1984) and Timothy Messer-Kruse, *The Haymarket Conspiracy: Transatlantic Anarchist Networks* (Urbana: University of Illinois Press, 2012).

89. *El Socialismo* (Cádiz), 12 December, 1887, 3; frontispiece of *Acracia* (Barcelona), November, 1887, 1. See also Susana Sueiro Seoane, 'Prensa y redes anarquistas transnacionales: El olvidado papel de J.C. Campos y sus crónicas sobre los mártires de Chicago en el anarquismo de lengua hispana,' *Cuadernos de Historia Contemporánea* 36 (2014): 266–274.

90. Ernesto Álvarez, *¡¡Siete sentencias de muerte!! Proceso de los anarquistas en Chicago* (Madrid: Tarjetería de Primitivo Fernández, 1887), 3–7.

91. Anna Ribera and Alejandro de la Torre, 'Memoria libertaria: Usos del calendario militante del anarquismo hispanoamericano,' *Historias* 75 (2010): 109–110 and 119–122. For example see *El Corsario: Suplemento a "El Corsario" Numero 78: Honor a las Mártires de Chicago: 11 de noviembre de 1887* (La Coruña), November, 1891, 1. On the broader cultural legacy of the Chicago martyrs in Spain see Esenwein, *Anarchist Ideology*, 159–160; Litvak, *Musa libertaria*, 197–198.

92. *El Corsario* (La Coruña), 14 February, 1892, 1.

93. *El Corsario* (La Coruña), 21 February, 1892, 4.

94. *El Corsario: A Sus Lectores* (La Coruña), 1 January, 1893, 1.

95. *El Productor* (Barcelona), 12 January, 1893, 3. On *El Productor* previously ignoring the paper see *El Corsario* (La Coruña), 3 January, 1892, 4.

96. *El Corsario* (La Coruña), 10 February, 1893, 2–3.

97. *El Corsario* (La Coruña), 10 February, 1893, 1.

98. *El Corsario* (La Coruña), 10 February, 1893, 1.

99. *La Anarquía* (Madrid), 11 October, 1892, 1.

100. *La Anarquía* (Madrid), 25 February, 1892, 2.

101. *La Anarquía* (Madrid), 18 February, 1892, 1 and 4.

102. *La Anarquía* (Madrid), 18 February, 1892, 4 and 25 February, 1892, 2 and 4.

103. *La Anarquía* (Madrid), 15 July, 1892, 4.

104. *La Controversia* (Valencia), 7 October, 1893, 4.

105. Mella, *Los sucesos de Jerez*, 18–19.

106. Mella, *Los sucesos de Jerez*, 13; Esenwein, *Anarchist Ideology*, 181.

107. *La Anarquía* (Madrid), 10 February, 1893, 1–4.

108. *La Anarquía* (Madrid), 17 February, 1893, 2–3. See also Kaplan, *Anarchists of Andalusia*, 184.

109. *La Cuestión Social* (Valencia), 30 April, 1892, 1–2; 21 May, 1892, 1–2 and 4 June, 1892, 1.

110. This paper was denounced to both civil and military authorities for its activities prior to 1 May 1892, see *La Anarquía* (Madrid), 27 May, 1892, 4.

111. Bach Jensen, 'Daggers, Rifles and Dynamite,' 133–134.

112. John Merriman, *The Dynamite Club: How a Bombing in Fin-de-Siècle Paris Ignited the Age of Modern Terror* (Boston and New York: Houghton Mifflin Harcourt, 2009), 69–80.

113. Cited in Edward J. Erickson, 'Punishing the Mad Bomber: Questions of Moral Responsibility in the Trials of French Anarchist Terrorists,' *French History* 22, 1 (2008): 61.

114. Avilés Farré, 'Los atentados de Paris,' 179–183, at 180.
115. Merriman, *The Dynamite Club*, 82.
116. *La Cuestión Social* (Valencia), 28 May, 1892, 4; *La Anarquía* (Madrid), 27 April, 1893, 4 and 5 May, 1893, 4; *El Corsario* (La Coruña), 21 May, 1893, 4.
117. *El Corsario* (La Coruña), 22 January, 1893, 4 and 19 March, 1893, 4.
118. *El Corsario* (La Coruña), 8 October, 1893, 3.
119. *El Corsario* (La Coruña), 17 July, 1892, 3–4.
120. *La Anarquía* (Madrid), 21 April, 1892, 2 and 15 July, 1892, 1–2.
121. *La Controversia* (Valencia), 3 June, 1893, 1.
122. *El Eco de Ravachol* (Sabadell), 21 January, 1893, 1. On the denouncement of *Ravachol*, see *El Productor* (Barcelona), 15 December, 1892, 2 and 6 July, 1893, 1. See also Madrid Santos, 'La prensa anarquista,' 139.
123. *El Imparcial* (Madrid), 21 June, 1893, 2; *El Corsario* (La Coruña), 29 June, 1893, 3. See also Herrerín López, *Anarquía, dinamita*, 90–91.
124. *La Controversia* (Valencia), 1 July, 1893, 6.
125. *El Corsario* (La Coruña), 29 June, 1893, 3.
126. *El Corsario* (La Coruña), 15 October, 1894, 3. Two months later the fund for Ruiz's widow was only 20 pesetas, compared to the 170 pesetas raised for the widow of Paulino Pallás, see *El Corsario* (La Coruña), 3 December, 1894, 4. This discrepancy in the two funds remained constant in the following months, see *El Corsario: A los habituales lectores de El Corsario y á todos los anarquistas* (La Coruña), June 1894. See also sales of Ruiz's portrait for the benefit of his family in *El Corsario* (La Coruña), 27 December, 1894, 4.
127. On the development of the Orsini bomb—named after an Italian nationalist, who tested his device in Sheffield—see Benedict Anderson, *Under Three Flags: Anarchism and the Anti-Colonial Imagination* (London: Verso, 2005), 115, n.89.
128. Herrerín López, *Anarquía, dinamita*, 93–96.
129. *El Productor* (Barcelona), 8 June, 1888, 1. See also Esenwein, *Anarchist Ideology*, 126–127.
130. Víctor Manuel Arbeloa, 'La prensa obrera en España, (1869–1899),' *Revista de Trabajo* 30 (1970): 163–165. The paper was singled out following the Jerez uprising as the prime motivator for the unrest of the *campesinos*; see Kaplan, *Anarchists of Andalusia*, 177–178 and Avilés Farré and Herrerín Lopez, 'Propaganda por el hecho,' 173–174.
131. Madrid Santos, 'La prensa anarquista,' 134. The suspension of the paper was commented on in *El Corsario* (La Coruña), 8 October, 1893, 3.
132. *El Corsario* (La Coruña), 5 November, 1893, 4.
133. Joaquín Romero Maura, *La rosa de fuego: Republicanos y anarquistas: La política de los obreros barceloneses entre el desastre colonial y la Semana Trágica* (Barcelona: Ediciones Grijalbo, 1975), 204.
134. Óscar Freán Hernández, *El movimiento libertario en Galicia, 1910–1936* (Sada: Ediciós do Castro, 2006), 11–12.
135. Madrid Santos, 'La prensa anarquista,' 137, n.697. The problem of conservation also applies to the earliest issues of *El Corsario*, as even the most complete collection of this title begins in March 1891, almost a year after the paper began publishing.
136. *El Corsario* (La Coruña), 5 October, 1893, 3–4 and 12 November, 1893, 4.
137. See Chapter 4.
138. Compare with French anarchist response to Émile Henry in Avilés Farré, 'Los atentados de Paris,' 185.
139. *El Corsario* (La Coruña), 1 October, 1893, 1–2 and 8 October, 1893, 3 and 4.
140. *El Corsario* (La Coruña), 15 October, 1893, 1.
141. *El Corsario* (La Coruña), 1 October, 1893, 1–2.

142. Letter sent by Paulino Pallás to Alexandro Lerroux, then editor of *El Pais*, dated 3 October, 1893, published in *El País* (Madrid), 8 October, 1893, 1. See also José Álvarez Junco, *El emperador del Paralelo: Lerroux y la demagogia populista* (Madrid: Alianza Editorial, 1990), 147–150 and Herrerín López, *Anarquía, dinamita*, 94–96.
143. *El Rebelde* (Zaragoza), 11 November, 1893, 3–4.
144. *El Liberal* (Madrid), 27 September, 1893, 1; *La Controversia* (Valencia), 7 October, 1893, 4.
145. *El Oprimido* (Algeciras), 11 October, 1893, 2–3. Emphasis added.
146. *La Controversia* (Valencia), 7 October, 1893, 4, emphasis in original.
147. On *La Tramontana* see Madrid Santos, 'La prensa anarquista,' 31–35 and 96–99.
148. *La Controversia* (Valencia), 7 October, 1893, 4.
149. *La Controversia* (Valencia), 7 October, 1893, 1.
150. *La Controversia* (Valencia), 7 October, 1893, 1.
151. Notice of suspensión of *El Rebelde* in *El Corsario* (La Coruña), 3 December, 1893, 4. See also *El Eco del Rebelde* (Zaragoza), 6 June, 1895, 1 and Madrid Santos, 'La prensa anarquista,' 363 and 413–415.
152. Herrerín López, *Anarquía, dinamita*, 98–99.
153. See *El Imparcial* (Madrid), 9 November, 1893, 1–2 and 12 November, 1893, 1 and 2. The bombing made news across the continent, for example in the famous front-page depiction of the event in *Le Petit Journal: Supplément Illustré* (Paris), 25 November, 1893, 1. See also Jensen, 'Daggers, Rifles and Dynamite,' 141–142.
154. Herrerín López, *Anarquía, dinamita*, 100. Figures on the total number of arrests vary, Nuñéz Florencio puts the number at 124 in *El terrorismo anarquista*, 193, whilst the contemporary French anarchist paper *La Révolte* (Paris), 6 January, 1894 claimed that 500 had been arrested since Pallás attack.
155. *El Imparcial* (Madrid), 2 January, 1894, 2.
156. Esenwein, *Anarchist Ideology*, 187.
157. Álvarez Junco, *La ideología política*, 496. An account of Salvador's apparent conversion, confession and desire to enter the Dominican order can be found in *La Época* (Madrid), 27 August, 1894, 2; and his final moments in *La Época* (Madrid), 21 November, 1894, 1.
158. *El Corsario* (La Coruña), 19 November, 1893, 3. The article does not specify which mining disaster it refers to.
159. *El Corsario* (La Coruña), 19 November, 1893, 4.
160. *El Corsario* (La Coruña), 3 December, 1893, 1.
161. *El Corsario* (La Coruña), 3 December, 1893, 3.
162. Avilés Farré, 'Los atentados de Paris,' 183–186.
163. Lucía Rivas Lara, 'El terrorismo anarquista en Francia,' in Avilés and Herrerín López, *El nacimiento del terrorismo*, 63–74; Herrerín López, *Anarquía, dinamita*, 159–160.
164. *El Corsario* (La Coruña), 3 January, 1895, 2 and 7 February, 1895, 1.
165. *El Corsario* (La Coruña), 7 March, 1895, 2.
166. *El Eco del Rebelde* (Zaragoza), 6 June, 1895, 1; *El Invencible* (Zaragoza), 27 August, 1895, 1.
167. *El Eco del Rebelde* (Zaragoza), 6 June, 1895, 1–2.
168. *El Invencible* (Zaragoza), 27 August, 1895, 1–2.
169. *El Eco del Rebelde* (Zaragoza), 6 June, 1895, 2; *El Invencible* (Zaragoza), 27 August, 1895, 1 and 2. See also *El Eco del Rebelde: Suplemento al Num.3 de El Eco del Rebelde*, (Zaragoza), 16 June, 1895, 2.
170. *El Invencible* (Zaragoza), 27 August, 1895, 1.
171. *El Comunista* (Zaragoza), 30 November, 1895, 4.

172. *El Corsario* (La Coruña), 4 June, 1896, 4.
173. Esenwein, *Anarchist Ideology*, 168.
174. *Anticristo* (La Línea de la Concepción), 31 March, 1906, 1.
175. Esenwein, *Anarchist Ideology*, 134–154.
176. *El Eco del Rebelde* (Zaragoza), 6 June, 1895, 2–3.
177. Discussion of the theatre was given a great deal of space in *La Idea Libre*, particularly towards the end of the first epoch, when a regular common 'Teatro Moderno' appeared (for example see, 29 February, 1896, 2–3; 14 March, 1896, 3–4 and 25 April, 1896) alongside adverts for Teresa Claramunt's 'Teatro Circo Barcelonés,' (for example in 7 March, 1896, 4) and front-page portraits and biographies of the 'revolutionary' Norwegian playwrights Bjørnstjerne Bjørnson and Henrick Ibsen, see 22 May, 1896, 1 and 15 December, 1896, 1 respectively.
178. Gonzalo Rojas Sánchez, 'Legislación sobre asociaciones anarquistas en España: 1890–1910,' *Revista Chilena de Derecho* 8 (1981): 76–77.
179. *La Idea Libre* (Madrid), 16 February, 1895, 2.
180. Examples of public complaints about the Correros in *La Idea Libre*, (Madrid), 13 August, 1894, 3; 25 August, 1894, 4; 29 December, 1894, 1–2, n.1; 5 January, 1895, 2; 11 May, 1895, 4; 1 November, 1895, 4 and throughout its administrative correspondence section.
181. The claim that Álvarez was probably 'Traico' is supported by the fact that this name does not appear in any issue in a period when he was ill in 1896, see *La Idea Libre* (Madrid), 8 February, 1896–15 February, 1896. Tracio is presumably a reference to the legendary Thracian slave-leader Spartacus, the subject of Álvarez's few pamphlet *Espartaco (bosquejo histórico)* (Madrid: La Idea Libre, 1895). Álvarez also named his son Spartacus, see *La Protesta* (La Línea de la Concepción), 31 July, 1901, 4.
182. *La Idea Libre* (Madrid), 11 January, 1896, 2.
183. *La Idea Libre* (Madrid), 15 June, 1895, 4.
184. Portraits of Pallás published in *El Liberal* (Madrid), 28 September, 1893, 1; *La Época* (Madrid), 3 October, 1893, 2; *La Ilustración Ibérica* (Barcelona), 7 October, 1893, 2 and *La Controversia* (Valencia), 7 October, 1893, 1.
185. *La Idea Libre* (Madrid), 8 February, 1896, 1–2.
186. *La Idea Libre* (Madrid), 8 February, 1896, 2.
187. *La Idea Libre* (Madrid), 20 October, 1894, 4.
188. Herrerín López, *Anarquía, dinamita*, 107–110.
189. *La Idea Libre* (Madrid), 23 March, 1895, 1.
190. *La Idea Libre* (Madrid), 10 November, 1894, 3–4. See also Antón Fernández Álvarez, *Ricardo Mella o el anarquismo humanista* (Barcelona: Anthropos, 1990), 44.
191. *La Idea Libre* (Madrid), 9 May, 1894, 2; 11 April, 1895, 3; 11 May, 1895, 1; 7 March, 1896, 1; 1 May, 1896, 2.
192. An artist's impression of this attack can be found in *El País* (Madrid), 11 June, 1896; reproduced in Álvarez Junco, *El emperador*, n.page (in pictures section between pages 160 and 161).
193. Debates over the responsibility for the attack began immediately within anarchist circles which have continued into the historiography of the period. See Herrerín López, *Anarquía, dinamita*, 147–152.
194. Rojas Sánchez, 'Legislación,' 77–78; Herrerín López, *Anarquía, dinamita*, 130–137.
195. *La Idea Libre* (Madrid), 12 June, 1896, 1.
196. Herrerín López, *Anarquía, dinamita*, 141.
197. See *El Corsario: Suplemento al no.212 de El Corsario* (La Coruña), 16 May, 1895, 1.

110   *More Workers' Blood!*

198. *El Corsario* (La Coruña), 9 January, 1896, 1; *La Idea Libre* (Madrid), 18 January, 1896, 3. See also Madrid Santos, 'La prensa anarquista,' 137.
199. *El Corsario* (La Coruña), 25 June, 1896, 4. See also Herrerín López, *Anarquía dinamita*, 150.
200. Every mainstream paper, as well as the socialist and republican press blamed not only the adjudged anarchist perpetrator for the attack but also the ideas of anarchism in general. For *El Corsario*'s indignant response to the attacks of the socialists see *El Corsario* (La Coruña), 25 June, 1896, 1–2. The only exception was the Pi i Margall's federalist paper, *El Nuevo Regimen*, see Herrerín López, *Anarquía dinamita*, 130–131.
201. *El Productor* (La Coruña), 1 October, 1896, 4 and *El Productor: Extracto del estado de cuentas de El Progreso*, La Coruña, 11 November, 1896, 2.
202. *El Corsario* (La Coruña), 3 December, 1893, 1.
203. Frank Fernández, *La sangre de Santa Águeda: Angiolillo, Betances y Cánovas: Análisis de un magnicidio y sus consecuencias históricas* (Miami: Ediciones Universal, 1994), 50–63; Anderson, *Under Three Flags*, 193.
204. Kenyon Zimmer, *Immigrants against the State: Yiddish and Italian Anarchism in America* (Chicago: University of Illinois Press, 2015), 122–123.
205. Rojas Sánchez, 'Legislación,' 79; Herrerín López, *Anarquía, dinamita*, 161.
206. The exact date of the first issue of this epoch is unknown, but is suggested as being August 1897 in *La Idea Libre* (Madrid), 136, 6 August, 1898, 4. See also Madrid Santos, 'La prensa anarquista,' 136–137.
207. *La Idea Libre* (Madrid), 6 August, 1898, 4.
208. *La Idea Libre* (Madrid), 2 January, 1898, 2.
209. Herrerín López, *Anarquía, dinamita*, 176.
210. Áviles Farré and Herrerín López, 'Propaganda por el hecho,' 192.
211. Herrerín López, *Anarquía, dinamita*, 176–178.
212. Álvarez Junco, *La ideología política*, 266–271.
213. *La Controversia* (Valencia), 7 October, 1893, 1.
214. *El Eco del Rebelde* (Zaragoza), 6 June, 1895, 2; *El Invencible* (Zaragoza), 27 August, 1895, 1–2.
215. *El Eco del Rebelde* (Zaragoza), 6 June, 1895, 2.
216. See for example Núñez Florencio, *El terrorismo anarquista*, 169–185.
217. *El Corsario* (La Coruña), 15 October, 1893, 1 and 2–3.
218. *El Corsario* (La Coruña), 29 October, 1893, 4.
219. *El Corsario* (La Coruña), 15 October, 1893, 2. See also Antoni Dalmau, *El procés de Montjuïc: Barcelona al final del segle XIX* (Barcelona: Editorial Base, 2010), 73–74.
220. *El Corsario* (La Coruña), 3 December, 1893, 3.
221. Juan Montseny i Carret, *Consideraciones sobre el hecho y muerte de Pallás* (La Coruña: El Corsario, 1893).
222. *El Corsario* (La Coruña), 3 December, 1893, 4.
223. *El Corsario* (La Coruña), 4 October, 1894, 1.
224. Letter sent to *El Corsario* from Barcelona (27 February, 1895), printed in *El Corsario* (La Coruña), 3 March, 1895, 4.
225. *El Corsario* (La Coruña), 28 March, 1895, 4; 4 April, 1895, 1–2. See also Dalmau, *El procés de Montjuïc*, 73–74 and Herrerín López, *Anarquía, dinamita*, 146–147.
226. *El Corsario* (La Coruña), 9 January, 1896, 4 and 6 August, 1896, 4.
227. *El Corsario* (La Coruña), 18 October, 1894, 1.
228. *El Corsario* (La Coruña), 11 October, 1894, 4 and 29 November, 1894, 1–2.
229. *El Corsario* (La Coruña), 6 December, 1894, 1–2 and 3 January, 1895, 2.

230. Collections from 'Humanity' Group in Havana, in *El Corsario* (La Coruña), 14 March, 1895, 4 and 4 April, 1895, 4.
231. *La Idea Libre* (Madrid), 25 June, 1898, 2–3.
232. Only seven references to Angiolillo were made in 119 issues of *La Revista Blanca*, the most prominent publication of the post-1898 period. For example *La Revista Blanca* (Madrid), 15 November, 1905, 297. The date of Angiolillo's execution was also marked in the 'anarchist calendar' published in *La Revista Blanca: Almanaque de la Revista Blanca para 1900* (Madrid: La Revista Blanca, 1899), 10.
233. An official report published in 1905 claimed that there was a group in La Coruña named 'Angiolillo': Gustavo La Iglesia y García, *Caracteres del anarquismo en la actualidad* (Barcelona: Gustavo Gil, 1907), 293, n.1. Aside from this one example, such usage of Angiolillo's name was scant.
234. Herrerín López, *Anarquía, dinamita*, 214–231.
235. Herrerín López, *Anarquía, dinamita*, 177.
236. *El Corsario* (La Coruña), 8 November, 1894, 1.
237. Herrerín López, *Anarquía, dinamita*, 102–103 and 111–113.
238. *El Corsario: A los habituales lectores de 'El Corsario' y a todos los anarquistas* (La Coruña), June, 1894, 1.
239. The pamphlet was also published in Argentina by the group 'La Lucha,' and was serialised in the paper *El Obrero Panadero* (Buenos Aires). See Gonzalo Zaragoza, *Anarquismo argentino (1876–1902)* (Madrid: Ediciones de la Torre, 1996), 161 and 169 n.63.
240. *El Corsario* (La Coruña), 25 April, 1895, 4.
241. Comparison from point where subscriptions appear simultaneously: *El Corsario: Suplemento al no.212 de El Corsario* (La Coruña), 16 May, 1895, 2, to *El Corsario* (La Coruña), 6 August, 1896, 4.
242. *El Eco del Rebelde* (Zaragoza), 6 June, 1895, 2.
243. *El Rebelde* (Zaragoza), 21 October, 1893, 4.
244. Special editions to the Chicago martyrs of *La Idea Libre* (Madrid), 10 November, 1894 and 16 November, 1895. The portrait series in early 1896 was muddled at the pre-printing stage because of a mistake by Álvarez, explanation given in *La Idea Libre* (Madrid), 15 February, 1896, 3–4. The series ran Lingg (correct portrait-biography), 18 January, 1896, 1–2; Spies biography/Parsons portrait: 25 January, 1896), 1–2; Parsons biography/Engel portrait: 1 February, 1896, 1. The portraits are identical to those published in *Frank Leslie's Illustrated Newspaper* (New York), 12 November, 1887, the day after the executions took place.
245. *La Idea Libre* (Madrid), 8 February, 1896, 1–2.
246. *La Idea Libre* (Madrid), Archs: 11 May, 1895, 3; Bernat: 18 May, 1895, 3; Codina: 26 May, 1895, 3; Cerezuela: 8 June, 1895, 3.
247. Montseny gives an account of his experience of his arrest, imprisonment and exile in Urales, *Mi vida*, Vol. 1, 78–253.
248. On Montjuich Castle see Álvarez Junco, *El emperador*, 133–134.
249. Herrerín López, *Anarquía, dinamita*, 140–152. Documents from the trial in Dalmau, *El procés de Montjuïc*, 401–447.
250. R.M [Ricardo Mella] and J.P. [José Prat], *La barbarie gubernamental en España: Documentos sobre las torturas de Montjuich* (Brooklyn: El Despertar, 1897), 38–42. This publication stated it was published in New York through the anarchist publishers 'El Despertar,' however it was actually published clandestinely in La Coruña, see Ignacio Soriano and Francisco Madrid Santos, 'Antología documental del anarquismo español VI.I: Bibliografía del anarquismo en España, 1868–1939, Enriquecida con notas y

comentarios,' (5th edition, 2012), 94. Published online, accessed 12 December, 2012, http://cedall.org/Documentacio/Castella/cedall203410103.htm.

251. James A. Baer, *Anarchist Immigrants in Spain and Argentina* (Chicago: University of Illinois Press, 2015), 37.

252. *La Protesta Humana* (Buenos Aires), 13 June, 1897, 3.

253. See for example: *La Protesta Humana* (Buenos Aires), 19 August, 1897, 1; 2 September, 1897, 1; 2 January, 1898, 2; 18 March, 1898, 1.

254. Juan Díaz del Moral, *Historia de las agitaciones campesinas andaluzas-Córdoba: Antecedentes para una reforma agraria* (Madrid: Alianza, 1967), 181.

255. *Campaña de 'El Progreso' a favor de las víctimas del proceso de Montjuich* (Barcelona: Tarascó, Viladot y Cuesta Impresores, 1898), 562–568; Urales, *Mi vida*, Vol. 1, 215–221. See also Teresa Abelló Güell, 'El proceso de Montjuich ante la opinión pública europea,' *Estudios de Historia Social* 40 (1987): 275–289.

256. Herrerín López, *Anarquía, dinamita*, 152–157.

257. *La Idea Libre* (Madrid), 2 January, 1898, 2 and 26 February, 1898, 4.

258. *La Idea Libre* (Madrid), 12 February, 1898, 1 and 25 June, 1898, 2.

259. *La Idea Libre* (Madrid), 2 January, 1898, 2.

260. *La Idea Libre* (Madrid), 26 February, 1898, 3; 12 March, 1898, 3; 26 March, 1898, 4.

261. Álvarez Junco, *El emperador*, 158–169.

262. On Montseny's decision to change his publishing name, see Urales, *Mi vida*, Vol. 1, 141–143.

263. See for example *Suplemento a la Revista Blanca* (Madrid), 24 June, 1899, 1; reproduced in Álvarez Junco, *El emperador*, n.page (in pictures section between pages 160 and161).

264. A full revision of the 'proceso' only came thirty years later, when Pere Corominas (who had been arrested in 1896) annulled the trials in his capacity as Minister for Justice in the Catalan Generalitat during the Second Republic. See Álvarez Junco, *El emperador*, 173, n.101 and Dalmau, *El procés de Montjuïc*, 450–534.

265. *Suplemento a la Revista Blanca* (Madrid), 19 May, 1900, 3.

266. See Chapter 4.

267. *El Rebelde* (Madrid), 10 November, 1904, 1.

268. Álvarez Junco, *La ideología política*, 272–277; Rafael Núñez Florencio, 'Patria y ejercito desde la ideología anarquista,' *Hispania: Revista Española de Historia* 178 (1991): 589–643.

269. The most celebrated publication on this subject was Fermín Salvochea's *La contribución de sangre: Al esclavo* (Madrid: La Revista Blanca, 1900), which also includes one of the few post-1898 references to Pallás in print on page 20.

270. A summary of the war is given in Sebastian Balfour, *The End of the Spanish Empire, 1898–1923* (Oxford: Clarendon, 1997), 1–63.

271. *La Idea Libre* (Madrid), 18 January, 1896, 2; *El Corsaio* (La Coruña), 30 January, 1896, 1. The Spanish Minister of War put the total figure of Spanish troops sent to island at 214, 333, see Balfour, *The End of the Spanish Empire*, 11, n.2.

272. *El Corsario*, (La Coruña), 30 July, 1896, 1–2; 6 August, 1896, 1; 20 August, 1896, 1 and *El Corsario: Suplemento al Número 245 de El Corsario*, (La Coruña), 22 August, 1896, 1. Reports on protest meetings in *El Corsario*, (La Coruña), 6 August, 1896, 2; 20 August, 1896, 3.

273. *El Corsario* (La Coruña), 9 January, 1896–20; August, 1896. See also Álvarez Junco, *La ideología política*, 263–265, especially n.63.

274. Amparo Sánchez Cobos, *Sembrando ideales: Anarquistas españoles en Cuba: 1902–1925* (Sevilla: Consejo Superior de Investigaciones Científicas, 2008).
275. Rafael Núñez Florencio, 'Los anarquistas españoles y americanos ante la Guerra de Cuba,' *Hispania: Revista Española de Historia* 179 (1991): 1077–1092, at 1092.
276. See Sánchez Cobos, *Sembrando ideales*, 90.
277. *El Eco del Rebelde* (Zaragoza), 6 June, 1895, 1–2.
278. *El Comunista* (Zaragoza), 31 December, 1895, 2–3. See Ada Ferrer, *Insurgent Cuba: Race, Nation, and Revolution, 1868–1898* (Chapel Hill: University of North Carolina Press, 1999), 144–145.
279. Antonio Elorza, 'Con la marcha de Cádiz (imágenes españolas de guerra de independencia cubana, 1895–1898),' *Estudios de Historia Social* 44–47 (1988): 327–386.
280. Anderson, *Under Three Flags*, 170–173 and 183–184.
281. *La Idea Libre* (Madrid), 29 February, 1896, 1; 9 March, 1895, 3; 14 March, 1896, 3.
282. Gerald E. Poyo, 'The Anarchist Challenge to the Cuban Independence Movement, 1885–1890,' *Cuban Studies* 15, 1 (1985), 33–35.
283. Letter from 'Grupo Número 1: Federación de Cuba,' printed in *La Idea Libre* (Madrid), 11 April, 1896, 3.
284. *La Idea Libre* (Madrid), 15 June, 1895, 3 and 25 January, 1896, 4. This attitude was similar to that of the PSOE, see Carlos Serrano, 'El PSOE y la Guerra de Cuba (1895–1898),' *Estudios de Historia Social* 8–9 (1979): 289.
285. Zimmer, *Anarchist Immigrants*, 122.
286. *El Corsario* (La Coruña), 27 August, 1896, 4; *El Productor* (La Coruña), 8 October, 1896, 2–3.
287. Balfour, *The End of the Spanish Empire*, 21–49. On the public reaction to the loss of Cuba, see Carlos Serrano, 'Guerra y crisis social: Los motines de mayo del 98,' *Estudios de Historia de España* 1 (1981): 439–450; Sebastian Balfour, 'Riot, Regeneration and Reaction: Spain in the Aftermath of the 1898 Disaster,' *The Historical Journal* 38, 2 (1995): 405–423.
288. *La Idea Libre* (Madrid), 26 March, 1898, 4.
289. *La Idea Libre* (Madrid), 20 August, 1898, 3. On post-war Cuban anarchism see Kirwin R. Shaffer, 'Cuba Para Todos: Anarchist Internationalism and the Cultural Politics of Cuban Independence, 1898–1925,' *Cuban Studies* 31 (2000): 45–75.
290. *La Idea Libre* (Madrid), 16 September, 1898, 1–2 and 24 September, 1898, 1–2.

Bibliography

Archives

AA: archivesautonomies.org. Online.
AFPI: Archivo Fundación Pablo Iglesias. Online.
AHPC: Archivo Histórico Provincial de Cádiz. Cádiz.
AMJF: Archivo Municipal de Jerez de la Frontera. Jerez de la Frontera.
BL: British Library. London.
BNE: Biblioteca Nacional de España. Madrid.
BVA: Biblioteca Virtual de Andalucía. Online.
CED: cedall.org. Online.

HMM: Hemeroteca Municipal de Madrid. Madrid. '
IISG: Internationaal Instituut voor Sociale Geschiedenis. Amsterdam.
LSE: London School of Economics. London.
UCLA: University of California Los Angeles Library: Digital Collections. Online.

Primary Sources

Anarchist Press

Acracia. Barcelona, 1886–1888. HMM.
Anticristo. La Línea de la Concepción, 1906. IISG.
El Combate. Bilbao, 1891. IISG.
El Comunista. Zaragoza, 1895. IISG.
El Corsario. La Coruña, 1890–1896. IISG.
El Eco de Ravachol. Sabadell, 1893. IISG.
El Eco del Rebelde. Zaragoza, 1895. IISG.
El Invencible. Zaragoza, 1895. IISG.
El Oprimido. Algeciras, 1893. IISG.
El Porvenir del Obrero. Mahón, II Epoch, 1912–1915. BNE, HMM and IISG.
El Productor. Barcelona, 1887–1893. IISG.
El Productor. La Coruña, 1896. IISG.
El Rebelde. Zaragoza, 1893. IISG.
El Rebelde. Madrid, 1903–1905. HMM and IISG.
El Socialismo. Cádiz, 1886–1891. BL and IISG.
La Anarquía. Madrid, 1890–1893. IISG and LSE.
La Controversia. Valencia, 1893. IISG.
La Cuestión Social. Valencia, 1892. IISG.
La Protesta. Valladolid/Sabadell/La Línea de la Concepción, 1899–1902. BVA
    and IISG.
La Protesta Humana. Buenos Aires, 1897–1904. UCLA.
La Revancha. Reus, 1893. IISG.
La Revista Blanca. Madrid, 1898–1905. BNE, HMM and IISG.
La Révolte. Paris, 1887–1895. AA.
La Tribuna Libre. Sevilla, 1891–1892. IISG.
La Victima del Trabajo. Valencia, 1889–1891. IISG.
Ravachol. Sabadell, 1892. IISG.
Suplemento a la Revista Blanca. Madrid, 1899–1902. HMM and IISG.
Tierra y Libertad. Madrid, 1902–1904. IISG.
Tierra y Libertad. Barcelona, 1904–1905. CED.

Supplements and Almanacs to Periodicals

*Acracia: Suplemento al número 5 de Acracia: 18 de marzo 1871–1886: Velada
    socialista artístico-literaria en conmemoración del XV aniversario de la proc-
    lamación de la Commune de París.* Barcelona, May, 1886. HMM.
*El Corsario: Suplemento a 'El Corsario' Numero 78: Honor a las Mártires de
    Chicago: 11 de noviembre de 1887.* La Coruña, November, 1891. IISG.
El Corsario: A Sus Lectores. La Coruña, 1 January, 1893. IISG.

El Corsario: A los habituales lectores de El Corsario y á todos los anarquistas. La Coruña, June, 1894. IISG.

El Corsario: Suplemento al no.212 de El Corsario. La Coruña, 16 May, 1895. IISG.

El Corsario: Suplemento al Número 245 de El Corsario. La Coruña, 22 August, 1896. IISG.

El Eco del Rebelde: Suplemento al Num.3 de El Eco del Rebelde. Zaragoza, 16 June, 1895. IISG.

El Productor: Extracto del estado de cuentas de El Progreso. La Coruña, 11 November, 1896. IISG.

La Revista Blanca: Almanaque de la Revista Blanca para 1900. Madrid: La Revista Blanca, 1899. IISG.

Other Press

El Imparcial. Madrid, 1867–1933. BNE.
El Liberal. Madrid, 1879–1936. BNE.
El País. Madrid, 1887–1921. BNE.
El Socialista. Madrid, 1886–1939. AFPI.
Frank Leslie's Illustrated Newspaper. New York, 1855–1922. BL.
La Correspondencia de España. Madrid, 1859–1925. BNE.
La Época. Madrid, 1849–1936. BNE.
La Ilustración Ibérica. Barcelona, 1883–1898. BNE.
Le Petit Journal: Supplément Illustré. Paris, 1884–1944. BL.

Memoirs, Books and Pamphlets by Contemporary Authors

Álvarez, Ernesto. *¡¡Siete sentencias de muerte!! Proceso de los anarquistas en Chicago.* Madrid: Tarjetería de Primitivo Fernández, 1887. IISG.
Álvarez, Ernesto. *Espartaco (bosquejo histórico).* Madrid: La Idea Libre, 1895. Serialised in *La Idea Libre* (Madrid), 23 November, 1895–15 May, 1896.
Campaña de 'El Progreso' a favor de las víctimas del proceso de Montjuich. Barcelona: Tarascó, Viladot y Cuesta Impresores, 1898. IISG.
La Iglesia y García, Gustavo. *Caracteres del anarquismo en la actualidad.* Barcelona: Gustavo Gil, 1907. BL.
Mella, Ricardo. *Los sucesos de Jerez: 8 Enero 1892–10 Febrero 1892.* Barcelona: Tipografía Calle San Rafael, 1893. IISG.
Mella, Ricardo. *La Nueva Utopía.* In *El Cuento Anarquista (1880–1911): Antología,* edited by Lily Litvak, 217–259. Madrid: Fundación de Estudios Libertarios Anselmo Lorenzo, 2003.
Mella, Ricardo, and José Prat. *La barbarie gubernamental en España: Documentos sobre las torturas de Montjuich.* Brooklyn: El Despertar, 1897. IISG.
Montseny i Carret, Juan. *Consideraciones sobre el hecho y muerte de Pallás.* La Coruña: El Corsario, 1893. IISG.
Salvochea, Fermín. *La contribución de sangre: Al esclavo.* Madrid: La Revista Blanca, 1900. BNE.
Urales, Federico. *Mi vida,* 3 Volumes. Barcelona: La Revista Blanca, 1930. IISG.

Secondary Sources

Abelló Güell, Teresa. 'El proceso de Montjuich ante la opinión pública europea.' *Estudios de Historia Social* 40 (1987): 275–289.

Aguilar Villagrán, José. *El asalto campesino a Jerez de la Frontera en 1892*. Jerez de la Frontera: Centro de Estudios Históricos Jerezanos, 1984.

Álvarez Junco, José. *El emperador del Paralelo: Lerroux y la demagogia populista*. Madrid: Alianza Editorial, 1990.

Álvarez Junco, José. *La ideología política del anarquismo español (1868–1910)*. Madrid: Siglo XXI, 1991.

Anderson, Benedict. *Under Three Flags: Anarchism and the Anti-Colonial Imagination*. London: Verso, 2005.

Arbeloa, Víctor Manuel. 'La prensa obrera en España, (1869–1899).' *Revista de Trabajo* 30 (1970): 117–195.

Avilés Farré, Juan. 'El terrorismo anarquista como propaganda por el hecho: de la formulación teórica a los atentados de Paris, 1877–1894.' *Historia y Política* 21 (2009): 169–190.

Avilés Farré, Juan and Ángel Herrerín López, eds. *El nacimiento del terrorismo en occidente: Anarquía, nihilismo y violencia revolucionaria*. Madrid: Siglo XXI, 2008.

Avilés Farré, Juan and Ángel Herrerín López. 'Propaganda por el hecho y propaganda por la represión: Anarquismo y violencia en España a fines del siglo XIX.' *Ayer* 80, 4 (2010): 165–192.

Avrich, Paul. *The Haymarket Tragedy*. Princeton: Princeton University Press, 1984.

Baer, James A. *Anarchist Immigrants in Spain and Argentina*. Chicago: University of Illinois Press, 2015.

Balfour, Sebastian. 'Riot, Regeneration and Reaction: Spain in the Aftermath of the 1898 Disaster.' *The Historical Journal* 38, 2 (1995): 405–423.

Balfour, Sebastian. *The End of the Spanish Empire, 1898–1923*. Oxford: Clarendon, 1997.

Bantman, Constance. 'The Era of Propaganda by the Deed.' In *The Palgrave Handbook of Anarchism*, edited by Carl Levy and Matthew Adams, 371–387. London: Palgrave Macmillan, 2018.

Bernaldo de Quirós, Constancio. 'El espartaquismo agrario andaluz.' *Revista general de legislación y jurisprudencia* 134 (1919): 307–319, 396–413 and 491–502.

Brey, Gerard. 'Crisis económica, anarquismo y sucesos de Jerez, 1886–1892.' In *Seis estudios sobre el proletariado andaluz (1868–1939)*, edited by Ramón Rodríguez Aguilera, 75–127. Córdoba: Ayuntamiento de Córdoba, 1984.

Dalmau, Antoni. *El procés de Montjuïc: Barcelona al final del segle XIX*. Barcelona: Editorial Base, 2010.

Díaz del Moral, Juan. *Historia de las agitaciones campesinas andaluzas-Córdoba: Antecedentes para una reforma agraria*. Madrid: Alianza, 1967.

Elorza, Antonio. 'Con la marcha de Cádiz (imágenes españolas de guerra de independencia cubana, 1895–1898).' *Estudios de Historia Social* 44–47 (1988): 327–386.

Erickson, Edward J. 'Punishing the Mad Bomber: Questions of Moral Responsibility in the Trials of French Anarchist Terrorists.' *French History* 22, 1 (2008): 51–73.

Esenwein, George. *Anarchist Ideology and the Working-Class Movement in Spain, 1868–1898*. Berkeley, CA: University of California Press, 1989.

Fernández, Frank. *La sangre de Santa Águeda: Angiolillo, Betances y Cánovas: Análisis de un magnicidio y sus consecuencias históricas*. Miami: Ediciones Universal, 1994.

Fernández Álvarez, Antón. *Ricardo Mella o el anarquismo humanista*. Barcelona: Anthropos, 1990.

Ferrer, Ada. *Insurgent Cuba: Race, Nation, and Revolution, 1868–1898*. Chapel Hill: University of North Carolina Press, 1999.

Freán Hernández, Óscar. *El movimiento libertario en Galicia, 1910–1936*. Sada: Ediciós do Castro, 2006.

Gabriel, Elun. 'Performing Persecution: Witnessing and Martyrdom in the Anarchist Tradition.' *Radical History Review* 98 (2007): 34–62.

González Calleja, Eduardo. *La razón de la fuerza: Orden público, subversión y violencia política en la España de la Restauración (1875–1917)*. Madrid: Editorial CSIC, 1998.

Herrerín López, Ángel. 'España: La propaganda por la represión, 1892–1900.' In Avilés and Herrerín López, *El nacimiento del terrorismo*, 103–139.

Herrerín López, Ángel. *Anarquía, dinamita y revolución social: Violencia y represión en la España entre siglos (1868–1909)*. Madrid: Catarata, 2011.

Herrerín López, Ángel. 'Anarchist Sociability in Spain: In Times of Violence and Clandestinity.' *Bulletin for Spanish and Portuguese Historical Studies* 38, 1 (2013): 155–174.

Jensen, Richard Bach. 'The International Anti-Anarchist Conference of 1898 and the Origins of Interpol.' *Journal of Contemporary History* 16, 2 (1981): 323–347.

Jensen, Richard Bach. 'Daggers, Rifles and Dynamite: Anarchist Terrorism in Nineteenth-Century Europe.' *Terrorism and Political Violence* 16, 1 (2004): 116–153.

Jensen, Richard Bach. 'The International Campaign against Anarchist Terrorism, 1880–1930s.' *Terrorism and Political Violence* 21, 1 (2009): 89–109.

Kaplan, Temma. *Anarchists of Andalusia, 1868–1903*. Princeton: Princeton University Press, 1977.

Lida, Clara. 'Agrarian Anarchism in Andalusia: Documents on the Mano Negra.' *International Review of Social History* 14, 3 (1969): 315–352.

Lida, Clara. 'La comuna de París y sus repercusiones: El caso Español.' In *El poder y la sangre: Guerra, estado y nación en la década de 1860*, edited by Guillermo Palacios and Erika Pani, 183–195. México, DF: El Colegio de México, 2014.

Litvak, Lily. *Musa libertaria: Arte, literatura y vida cultural del anarquismo español (1890–1913)*. Madrid: Fundación de Estudios Libertarios Anselmo Lorenzo, 2001.

López Estudillo, Antonio. *Insurrección y provocación policial: Los sucesos de Jerez de 1892*. La Laguna: Tierra de Fuego, 2008.

Madrid Santos, Francisco. 'La prensa anarquista y anarcosindicalista en España desde la I Internacional hasta el fin de la Guerra Civil.' PhD thesis, Barcelona: Universidad Central de Barcelona, 1988–1989. Published online, accessed 12 May, 2012. http://cedall.org/Documentacio/Castella/cedall203410101.htm.

Madrid Santos, Francisco. *Solidaridad Obrera y el periodismo de raíz ácrata*. Badalona: Ediciones Solidaridad Obrera, 2007.

Magagna, Victor V. *Communities of Grain: Rural Rebellion in Comparative Perspective*. Ithaca: Cornell University Press, 1991.

Maurice, Jacques. *El anarquismo andaluz: Campesinos y sindicalistas, 1868–1936*. Barcelona: Crítica, 1990.

Merriman, John. *The Dynamite Club: How a Bombing in Fin-de-Siècle Paris Ignited the Age of Modern Terror*. Boston and New York: Houghton Mifflin Harcourt, 2009.

Messer-Kruse, Timothy. *The Haymarket Conspiracy: Transatlantic Anarchist Networks*. Urbana: University of Illinois Press, 2012.

Núñez Florencio, Rafael. *El terrorismo anarquista (1888–1909)*. Madrid: Siglo XXI, 1983.

Núñez Florencio, Rafael. 'Los anarquistas españoles y americanos ante la Guerra de Cuba.' *Hispania: Revista Española de Historia* 179 (1991): 1077–1092.

Núñez Florencio, Rafael. 'Patria y ejercito desde la ideología anarquista.' *Hispania: Revista Española de Historia* 178 (1991): 589–643.

Poyo, Gerald E. 'The Anarchist Challenge to the Cuban Independence Movement, 1885–1890.' *Cuban Studies* 15, 1 (1985): 29–42.

Puelles, Fernando de. *Fermín Salvochea: Republica y anarquismo*. Sevilla: Galán, 1984.

Ramos-Gorostiza, José Luis. 'Socio-Economic Utopianism in Spain at the End of the Nineteenth Century: *La Nueva Utopia* by Ricardo Mella.' *Utopian Studies* 20, 1 (2009): 5–39.

Ribera, Anna, and Alejandro de la Torre. 'Memoria libertaria: Usos del calendario militante del anarquismo hispanoamericano.' *Historias* 75 (2010): 105–124.

Rivas Lara, Lucía. 'El terrorismo anarquista en Francia.' In Avilés and Herrerín López, *El nacimiento del terrorismo*, 53–77.

Rojas Sánchez, Gonzalo. 'Legislación sobre asociaciones anarquistas en España: 1890–1910.' *Revista Chilena de Derecho* 8 (1981): 71–86.

Romero Maura, Joaquín. *La rosa de fuego: Republicanos y anarquistas: La política de los obreros barceloneses entre el desastre colonial y la Semana Trágica*. Barcelona: Ediciones Grijalbo, 1975.

Sánchez Cobos, Amparo. *Sembrando ideales: Anarquistas españoles en Cuba: 1902–1925*. Sevilla: Consejo Superior de Investigaciones Científicas, 2008.

Serrano, Carlos. 'El PSOE y la Guerra de Cuba (1895–1898).' *Estudios de Historia Social* 8–9 (1979): 287–310.

Serrano, Carlos. 'Guerra y crisis social: Los motines de mayo del 98.' *Estudios de Historia de España* 1 (1981): 439–450.

Shaffer, Kirwin. 'Cuba Para Todos: Anarchist Internationalism and the Cultural Politics of Cuban Independence, 1898–1925.' *Cuban Studies* 31 (2000): 45–75.

Smith, Angel. *Anarchism, Revolution and Reaction: Catalan Labour and the Crisis of the Spanish State, 1898–1923*. New York, NY: Berghahn, 2007.

Soriano, Ignacio, and Francisco Madrid Santos. 'Antología documental del anarquismo español VI.I: Bibliografía del anarquismo en España, 1868–1939, Enriquecida con notas y comentarios.' 5th edition, 2012. Published online, accessed 12 December, 2012. http://cedall.org/Documentacio/Castella/cedall203410103.htm.

Sueiro Seoane, Susana. 'Prensa y redes anarquistas transnacionales: El olvidado papel de J.C. Campos y sus crónicas sobre los mártires de Chicago en el anarquismo de lengua hispana.' *Cuadernos de Historia Contemporánea* 36 (2014): 259–295.

Termes, Josep. *Anarquismo y sindicalismo en España: La Primera Internacional (1864–1881)*. Barcelona: Crítica, 1977.

Vincent, Mary. *Spain, 1833–2002: People and State*. Oxford: Oxford University Press, 2007.

Zaragoza, Gonzalo. *Anarquismo argentino (1876–1902)*. Madrid: Ediciones de la Torre, 1996.

Zimmer, Kenyon. *Immigrants against the State: Yiddish and Italian Anarchism in America*. Chicago: University of Illinois Press, 2015.

3 The Cult of Reason
Anarchism and Education, 1899–1906

The assassination of Cánovas del Castillo and the 'Disaster of 1898' brought a change in the political climate in Spain, which permitted a regrouping of the anarchist movement. Although legislation against anarchism remained in effect until 1901, after 1898 it was rarely implemented, bringing about a de facto legalisation of anarchist practice in every area outside Cataluña.[1] What followed was a remarkable expansion of anarchism across the whole of Spain, which soon dwarfed the nineteenth-century movement in term of size, spread, level of activity and cultural development. In the words of Juan from Cádiz, repression 'had not stopped the march of progress' and the movement was springing back to life 'with more fervour' than ever before.[2] Invigorated by its newly-found support, the movement began to realise objectives that had previously been solely theoretical, particularly those associated with the broad revolutionary strategy of education. The accompanying expansion of 1899–1906 reshaped anarchism in Spain, laying a cultural foundation for the movement which would last until 1939.

Anarchist periodicals flourished in this period, not only re-emerging in areas where they had previously existed—such as Madrid, Cádiz, La Coruña and, after 1901, Barcelona—but also launching in new localities, for example Valladolid, Huelva, Santander, La Línea de la Concepción, Gijón and the Islas Canarias. By the end of this period there were more anarchist periodicals in print than at any other point in the history of the movement.[3] Papers provided an ideological structure to anarchist activity and experience, united disparate groups of activists, and framed the discourse and meaning of the movement. When the press prospered, so did the movement. The significance of this period is frequently overlooked, often either left out of studies, or incorporated into wider discussions of the nineteenth-century movement.[4] But this ignores the shift which took place within anarchism in these years, which was a consequence of the failure of violent revolutionary tactics and the experience of repression in the previous decade. Many of the ideas invoked after 1898 were not particularly 'new,' but they were put into effect in new areas and with markedly more success than ever before. Likewise, these years were not simply a prelude to twentieth-century movement, studies of which often only begin with the origins of the CNT in 1907.[5] The turn of the century was neither the same as the periods which surrounded it nor totally distinct, but was rather a crossroads, where neither violence nor labour organisation was regarded as the best tactic to advance the anarchist cause. Instead, the movement looked to 'education': an ambiguous revolutionary strategy, which represented a broad range of ideas, aspirations and activities, and was symbolised above all by an explosion of print culture.

In anarchist ideology, power and authority did not reside solely in the state or capitalism, but were also manifest in cultural violence, namely religion.[6] The Church, regarded as an 'enemy of Reason' [sic], fed the working-class fantasies of God and redemption that aimed to pacify protest and maintain ignorance in order to assure servility.[7] Education would combat this manifestation of authority. Reason, science and progress were sacrosanct, and regarded as being locked in a constant struggle with superstition and faith. There could be no compromise between these forces: more education meant less religion, science would 'destroy the palace of God,' its light would 'invad[e] dark chambers inhabited by mysticism until at last no darkness should be left'.[8] The term 'education' had been ubiquitous in Spanish anarchist discourse since the 1860s, signifying a large range of ideas and methods, at the root of which were mutually-reinforcing aims: a raising of 'culture' amongst the working-class and a revolutionary overhaul of schooling.[9] Together these ambitions formed a revolutionary tactic, which sought individual improvement for collective ends, bringing about a 'transformation of reality' through self-enlightenment.

Anarchism's focus on 'cultural ascendency' as revolutionary strategy marked it out from its contemporaries.[10] While many of its cultural aspirations were similar to those of Spanish liberals and republicans, anarchists differed from middle-class educators in their emphasis on the lower strata of society and their view that education would bring forth a destruction of the status quo. The socialist movement was far less concerned with education and culture than their anarchist contemporaries, and its central periodical, *El Socialista*, gave 'little . . . literary, scientific and cultural . . . nourishment' to its readers.[11] In contrast, anarchists used print as the prime means of realising their educational ambitions. Pamphlets, books, journals and newspapers transmitted ideas, and provided a system by which anarchists could structure grassroots educational initiatives.[12] Engagement with print culture required education, in the form of literacy and comprehension of anarchist theory; it imparted education, through the practice of skills such as reading; and it transmitted education, through the constant exchange of anarchist ideas.[13]

During the 1870s, anarchist educational aspirations remained secondary to organisational concerns. In the early years of the movement the revolution was seen as imminent, thus the most important task for

anarchists was to ensure that it was carried out correctly. Cultural emancipation could wait until Anarchy had arrived.[14] Similarly, in the early 1880s
the movement was primarily concerned with strengthening its influence in
the labour movement, and gave little attention to educational ideas. This
changed in 1886 with the arrival of *Acracia* (Barcelona, 1886–1888), the first
anarchist publication to give prominence to theory and culture over 'politics and agitation'.[15] *Acracia* focused on enlightenment as a revolutionary
tactic, hoping to bypass doctrinal arguments between anarcho-collectivists
and communists that split the movement in the late 1880s.[16] The journal
situated anarchist ideology within the rhetoric of late nineteenth-century
social science, stressing that anarchism was 'scientific' and 'sociological,' a
product of reason rather than *a priori* belief. This language was employed
in direct opposition to religion, framing science and sociology as weapons
against the 'imbecilic superstition' of Catholicism.[17] This discourse spread
from *Acracia* into almost every anarchist publication of the late 1880s,
and was exemplified by nation-wide conferences and literary competitions, most notably the two *Certámenes Socialistas* held in Reus (1895)
and Barcelona (1899).[18] Education remained an abstract idea, however,
confined to the pages of the anarchist press and the intellectual elite of the
movement, and any prospects for enacting educational ideas were soon
quelled by the repression of the 1890s.

La Revista Blanca: Defining the Movement Through Print

The educational discourse reappeared within the movement as soon as
repression relaxed in 1898. This was symbolised by the arrival of *La
Revista Blanca* (*The White Journal*), the most significant anarchist cultural publication since *Acracia*, launched in July 1898 as a fortnightly
publication of 'sociology, science and the arts' under the editorship Soledad Gustavo (pseud. Teresa Mañé) and Federico Urales (pseud. Juan
Montseny). Gustavo and Urales modelled their new publication on the
French literary journal *La Revue Blanche*, whose editors they had met
during their exile from Spain in 1897–98.[19]

La Revista Blanca was one of the longest-lasting and most influential
publications in the history of Spanish anarchism. It was also one of the
most well-read anarchist publications prior to the creation of the CNT,
with an estimated print-run of between 6,000 and 8,000.[20] Gustavo and
Urales used this platform to encourage the development of anarchism
through education. The very first article in *La Revista Blanca* demonstrated Urales's belief that greater attention to theory would foster revolutionary action: 'changes in ideas turn themselves into changes in facts . . .
elements which transmit to the people reforming ideas; [they] serve as
communication between the past and the future, between that which
reigns and that which should reign . . . this is the mission that *La Revista*

Blanca proposes'.[21] Urales believed that workers would assist in their own 'transformation of spirits' by reading the journal.[22] Until January 1901, it maintained an open 'Workers' Section,' which promoted cultural exchange between the journal and its readers. One letter to this section aptly represents this process. Its author, Hermenegildo Guilafre, expressed 'immense satisfaction' that Urales had 'placed a section of this journal to the disposition of workers, with the object of assisting their literary interests and to encourage them towards the study of contemporary problems'. Guilafre had been frustrated with both the mainstream press and *El Socialista*, which had refused to print the 'poor writings' of an ordinary worker. In contrast, *La Revista Blanca*'s openness demonstrated the true mission of the workers' press: 'to educate and dignify the class with the aim of preparing it for the material and intellectual battles to come'.[23]

The publication's emphasis on workers' concerns led it to launch a separate weekly publication, the *Suplemento a la Revista Blanca* (hereafter *Suplemento*) in May 1899.[24] This four-page weekly periodical focused on 'current events,' leaving longer theoretical and educational articles to the monthly *Revista*.[25] Campaigns for prisoners formed a large part of the *Suplemento*. The paper administered funds, organised demonstrations and gave a voice to imprisoned workers, beginning in 1899 with the campaign for the reversal of the Montjuich trials (May 1899-May 1900), which was followed by campaigns for the prisoners of the Jerez uprising of 1892 and the 'Mano Negra' (January 1900-February 1901). As popular and industrial unrest spread across Spain in 1901, the paper became the focal point for campaigns against repression in Gijón (December 1900-March 1901), Lebrija and Sevilla (April-December 1901) and La Coruña (May-October 1901).[26] As well as these campaigns, the *Suplemento*'s 'Movimiento Social' section reported on growing anarchist activity across the whole of Spain, with news of propaganda groups, workers' societies, industrial action and educational centres, all of which saw a sharp increase from 1898 onwards. Both of these elements of the *Suplemento* gave the movement a sense of structure and purpose as it recovered from the disaster of the 1890s.[27]

Madrid is rarely cited as an anarchist stronghold, yet the presence of the Urales 'family' made the city the publishing centre of the movement in the early twentieth century. Urales saw the *Suplemento* as anarchism's 'central' periodical, while labelling all other papers 'local' publications.[28] Its writers were often self-congratulatory, informing readers of its expanding circulation and the influence it had on the movement.[29] At times this attitude did not sit comfortably with the wider movement. For example, in 1899, the Spanish anarchists were sent an open invitation to send delegates to the International Anti-Parliamentarian Congress, to be held in Paris alongside the Fifth Congress of the Second (Socialist) International the following September.[30] Lacking any formal means of electing a representative, the movement turned to its press.

Anarchist groups from around the country were invited to send in their nominations to Ernesto Álvarez's new publication, *La Protesta* (Valladolid). Problems arose when the *Suplemento* suggested three members of its own editorial group as delegates, which Álvarez rejected as being too costly.[31] In response, the *Suplemento* began its own, separate commission, which it funded with special double-price editions of the paper.[32] Neither commission raised enough money to send their own delegate, so eventually the two funds were combined and handed over to Ricardo Mella, who received the overwhelming majority of nominations received by Álvarez's commission.[33] In the event, the Congress was shut down by the Parisian police and the foreign delegates were forced to hold their meetings in secret, separate from their French counterparts. According to Emma Goldman, visiting Europe from the USA, the Congress was a disaster, as the intervention of the police had 'made constructive work impossible'.[34]

Despite occasional criticism, the *Suplemento* was generally respected and appreciated by the wider movement. It drew the largest and most geographically diverse readership of any anarchist periodical of the time, and was at the forefront of every major development within the movement. As such, the paper and its editors maintained an informal position of authority over their colleagues. At this point, the elite role of the Urales 'family' and their publications was appreciated by anarchists, who were buoyed by the return to legality and the subsequent expansion of the movement.

As the figurehead of the movement, the *Suplemento* felt obliged to educate its readers on the meaning of anarchism, including a commitment to the cultural, educational programme championed by its parent journal and publishing house, the 'Biblioteca de la Revista Blanca'. The Biblioteca produced a vast range of pamphlets and books, including original works from figures such as Mella and Lorenzo, and reissues of popular publications such as Kropotkin's *La Conquista del Pan*.[35] One of the main jobs of the *Suplemento* was to advertise new publications and maintain the distribution networks of the publishing house. A good example of the bottom-up nature of anarchist print culture came in October 1900, when the *Suplemento* called upon its readers for assistance. The Biblioteca wanted to reprint Errico Malatesta's *Entre campesinos*, but did not possess any of the previous editions of the pamphlet.[36] Within a fortnight a copy had been sent in and the new edition, translated by José Prat, went on sale through the paper's offices.[37] The *Suplemento*'s influence soon surpassed that of its parent publication. By 1901 it was distributing 10,000 copies across Spain and by 1902 its print run was almost double that of *La Revista Blanca*.[38] Shortly afterwards, the *Suplemento* changed its name to *Tierra y Libertad* in order to make it an 'independent platform' from the *Revista*. Nevertheless, the editorial board, contributors and content of *Tierra y Libertad* remained broadly the same as its predecessor.[39]

Numerous similar projects sprung up in the wake of the success of *La Revista Blanca* and its *Suplemento*. Outside Cataluña, few publications copied the long, journal-style of *La Revista Blanca*.[40] One exception was the short-lived *Libre Concurso* (Mahón, 1902, 3 issues), a monthly magazine of 'sociology, science and pedagogy' which published articles such as 'Glory to Science!', which claimed that it would soon be possible to feed the world's population with synthetic, test-tube cultivated food.[41] Although the business model of most anarchist papers was questionable, to say the least, this journal stands out as one of the most optimistic (or naïve) of the period. 20,000 copies of its first issue were printed and distributed for free, yet, unsurprisingly, this model proved to be unsustainable. Distribution dropped to 10,000 and 8,000 in the following two issues, after which the publication closed.

In the four-page periodical press, publishers made a noticeable effort to publish content which was in-line with the 'mission' of *La Revista Blanca* to educate the Spanish people. This cultural programme was evident in the titles and subtitles given to the anarchist papers launched at this time: 'fortnightly publication of sociology, science and the arts' (*El Obrero*, Badajoz, 1899–1902); 'literature, arts, science, sociology,' (*La Protesta*, Valladolid-Sabadell-La Línea, 1899–1902); 'in collaboration with the most renowned sociologists in the world,' (*La Justicia Obrera*, Haro, 1900); *La Razón Obrera* (*Workers' Reason*: Cádiz, 1901–1902); 'workers' sociological weekly: solidarity—science,' (*Adelante*, Santander, 1902–1903); 'sociological newspaper' (*El Corsario*, Valencia, 1902); *El Faro del Progreso*, (*The Beacon of Progress*: Mazarrón, 1904–1905). Through all of these papers, anarchism was defined as a movement which valued education as a key revolutionary strategy. The example of *La Revista Blanca* and its *Suplemento* was taken up in local contexts across the whole of Spain [see Map 3.1], as anarchists sought to engage in the new cultural drive of the movement by engaging in print culture. Publishing levels soared after 1900 [refer to Chart 0.2], as producing a periodical became seen as the best means to spread education and thus the height of revolutionary activity, as defined by *La Revista Blanca* in 1898.[42]

Relatives and Enemies

As well as defining what anarchism was, publications such as *La Revista Blanca* and the *Suplemento* outlined what anarchism was not. Above all, it was not 'political,' which was a dirty word within anarchist rhetoric, signifying corruption, authority and the pursuit of money.[43] By 'politics,' anarchists referred solely to politics of government, while their extra-parliamentary activity and concentration on social and cultural forms of authority were 'apolitical,' since they did not participate in the 'electoral farce' or advocate change through the mechanisms of the state. This was not only a critique of established Liberal and Conservative parties, but also all 'progressives' who sought to use 'politics' and the state in order to bring change.

The *Suplemento* was therefore hostile to the 'political' socialist movement and its paper *El Socialista*, edited by Pablo Iglesias, also the head of the PSOE and UGT.[44] Urales and Iglesias constantly bickered with one another through their papers. To *El Socialista*, the anarchists were naïve and lacked organisation, and their impetuous calls for revolution did nothing to help Spain's workers.[45] In turn, Urales kept up a constant stream of criticism towards the socialists, frequently dedicating a quarter of the *Suplemento* to refuting articles in *El Socialista*. At times the dispute extended beyond the pages of the press, as in 1901, when the *Suplemento* accused the president of the socialist Centro Obrero in Madrid of stealing 4,000 pesetas from workers' funds, and was taken to court for libel.[46] This did not deter Urales, who constantly mocked the PSOE's commitment to the 'electoral farce' and their 'false' interpretation of socialism (as opposed to the 'correct,' anarchist interpretation of the term), which led them to accept a hierarchical party structure and discipline.

Like the anarchist movement, the socialist PSOE and UGT were rapidly expanding over the turn of the century.[47] On the ground there was often little difference between these two movements. Their members came from similar working backgrounds, as shown by the distribution of trades in the UGT and the anarchist-orientated FSORE in 1900–1903 [see Table 3.1]. This spread of trades broadly corresponds to the thesis of van der Linden and Thorpe, which claims that early twentieth-century syndicalism was most noticeable in casual work and in trades going through a process of deskilling and labour intensification during the second industrial revolution.[48] However, the similarities between FSORE and UGT membership suggest that occupation did not determine whether a worker joined an anarchist or socialist organisation, at least in Spain. Rather than a fixed ideological position, it is likely that members of both movements often moved freely between the two identities of 'anarchist' and 'socialist'. The efforts of anarchist and socialist publications to maintain a distance between their affiliates also suggests that the two movements were close enough to cause alarm to their respective elites. *El Socialista* and the *Suplemento* stressed the rigid boundaries between anarchism and socialism, creating an image of a zero-sum game in the competition for membership. The most vitriolic attacks in the *Suplemento* against 'political socialists' often came from areas where the socialists had more support, such as Vizcaya, Oviedo and Madrid. In contrast, critiques against 'politicians' from anarchist strongholds in Andalucía and Cataluña were usually targeted against republicans.

The relationship between anarchism and republicanism in Spain was more complex than the fairly clear lines between the anarchist movement and the PSOE-UGT. In some respects, anarchists saw themselves as the inheritors of the original Spanish republican tradition, particularly

Table 3.1 Societies Adhered to FSORE and UGT Congresses, 1900–1903 by Trade

FSORE

Trade	No. Societies	%
Construction and Decoration	91	18.13
Workers' Centres, General Trades & Mixed	82	16.34
Woodwork and Furniture	61	12.15
Textiles	39	7.77
Tailoring	39	7.77
Agriculture	37	7.37
Metalwork, Mechanics and Engineering	35	6.97
Artisans	25	4.98
Cork and Paper Manufacturers	19	3.78
Masons and Quarrymen	11	2.19
Dockers, Longshoremen and Colliers	11	2.19
Miners	10	1.99
Food and Drink Production	10	1.99
Brick and Ceramic Works	9	1.79
Printing and Graphics	7	1.39
Hairdressers and Barbers	5	1.00
Transport	4	0.80
Sales and Shop Assistants	4	0.80
Cooks and Waiters	2	0.40
Women's Sections	1	0.20
Total	502	

UGT

Trade	No. Societies	%
Construction and Decoration	157	25.00
Tailoring and Clothing	88	14.01
Metalwork, Mechanics and Engineering	68	10.83
Woodwork and Furniture	55	8.76
Printing and Graphics	49	7.80
Textiles	33	5.25
Workers' Centres, General Trades & Mixed	32	5.10
Food and Drink Production	31	4.94
Transport	23	3.66
Agriculture	19	3.03
Masons and Quarrymen	16	2.55
Lighting and Heating	12	1.91
Miners	11	1.75
Sailors and Dock Workers	11	1.75
Brick and Ceramic Works	7	1.11
Plumbers, Tinsmiths and Glaziers	6	0.96
Hairdressers and Barbers	4	0.64
Ropemaking	3	0.48
Cleaners	2	0.32
Cooks and Waiters	1	0.16
Total	628	

Sources: FSORE: *Suplemento a La Revista Blanca* (Madrid): 20 October 1900, 2; 19 October 1900, 2; *Tierra y Libertad* (Madrid), 21 May 1903, 1.

UGT: Santiago Castillo, *Historia de la UGT*, Vol. I, *Un sindicalismo consciente, 1873–1914*, (Madrid, 2008), 160.

federalism, which had reached its peak under the brief presidency of Pi y Margall during the First Republic (1873–1874). The common history between federalism and anarchism was personified in figures such as Ricardo Mella, whose father had been a federalist and friend of Margall, and Fermín Salvochea, who had served as the federalist mayor of Cádiz during the First Republic.[49] Anarchists saw federalism as an early manifestation of their own ideas, particularly its critique of central state power; yet federalism had been too timid, calling for limits on this authority rather than its destruction. By the turn of the century anarchists felt they had left federalism in their wake.[50] When Margall died in 1901 the anarchist press was full of praise and respect for his ideas, which they claimed for their own movement rather than the fading Federalist Party.[51]

Despite the common ground between anarchism and republicanism, over the turn of the century these groups differed fundamentally on several issues, including their reaction to the loss of Empire.[52] Defeat in Cuba and the Philippines had provoked public unrest and calls for a 'regeneration' of Spain from political commentators, including most republicans.[53] Yet anarchists were not party to this 'regeneration' discourse. They had not needed the 'Disaster' of 1898 to see that Spain was a moribund state, and had called for many of the changes encapsulated in the 'regeneration' debate—an upheaval of the political system, the abolition of Church's role in society and an overhaul of education—for decades. This new, 'decadent,' call for republican 'regeneration' was no remedy, since it would leave the 'body' of Spain 'as gangrenous as it was before,' enthralled to 'the clergy, the barracks, the law, authority, capital, the bourgeoisie'.[54] Rather than a revitalised Spanish nation, anarchists wanted no nation at all, a 'world *patria*' without borders or war.[55] There was no need for the debates which were ongoing in Spain, no need for lengthy discussions about national character. The state did not require regeneration but 'elimination' through revolution, 'beneath the folds of the libertarian flag'.[56]

The close, yet distinct, perspectives of anarchists and republicans was also revealed in their educationalist rhetoric. The turn towards education brought with it a new vocabulary for anarchism in Spain. One of the most notable linguistic shifts in this period was the increasing use of the word 'germinal,' which was used as the title of three papers (Cádiz, 1903; La Coruña, 1904–1905; Tarrasa, 1905–1906) and numerous anarchist groups and institutions.[57] 'Germinal' was also a popular name for the children of anarchist parents, such as 'Libertario Germinal' and 'Acracio Germinal,' both of whom were registered in Algeciras (Cádiz) in 1900.[58] The uptake of this term within the anarchist movement was mirrored in Spanish republicanism, which, like anarchism, embraced the term 'germinal' as an evocation of nature and revolutionary cultural development.[59] Both republicans and anarchists also celebrated *Germinal*, by Emile Zola, as a literary masterpiece.[60]

'Germinal' was also the name of a nationwide network of republican centres, groups and newspapers and a large library-bookshop based in Madrid, led by the intellectual and journalist Ernesto Bark, an Estonian political refugee who had worked for Spanish republican papers since the 1880s.[61] Bark's aims for the 'Germinal Association' appeared similar to those of anarchist cultural educators: 'to develop the revolutionary consciousness of the people,' even 'to join with the radical forces of the libertarians'. However, Bark saw the revolution as the establishment of a Republic, modelled on the French experience in 1789, and did not share the anarchist ambition of a stateless future.[62] Nevertheless, Bark was respected by a number of anarchist commenters, including Soledad Gustavo, who was invited to give a lecture at the Madrid 'Germinal' association in 1899.[63] If the grassroots of Spanish anarchism had more in common with socialists, the elite of the movement clearly identified more with republicans such as Bark. In cities where republicanism had a strong presence, such as Gijón, anarchist and republican educational programmes were almost identical in their ambitions, terminology and practice.[64] Likewise, in the Islas Canarias, the anarchist periodical *Luz y Vida* (Santa Cruz de Tenerife) and the republican *Germinal* (Las Palmas) had a mutual respect and understanding, and saw it as their duty to help one another in their joint mission of bringing forth 'the empire of Reason [*sic*]'.[65]

'Politics' was another dividing line between republicans and anarchists. As detailed in Chapter 2, in 1898 many prominent figures within the anarchist movement joined a campaign against repression in Barcelona, led the republican journalist Alejandro Lerroux.[66] Many members of the *Revista Blanca* publishing group, including Urales, Gustavo and Anselmo Lorenzo, continued to have close contacts with Lerroux in the following years, and contributed regularly to his paper *Progreso*. Lerroux's professed antipathy to electoral politics and 'libertarian' stylings had much in common with anarchist rhetoric, and tapped into the widespread distrust in electoral politics in Spain.[67] Yet Lerroux was far from universally popular amongst anarchists. Many anarchist individuals, groups and publications—particularly those based outside Madrid—had little association with Lerroux and were wary of his proximity to their comrades.

The ambiguity towards Lerroux came to a head in May 1901 when he successfully stood for a seat in the Cortes for a constituency in Barcelona.[68] By violating the most obvious principles of anarchism, Lerroux tainted his associates with the stain of 'politics' and, more pointedly, was now offering an alternative to the anarchist movement in one of the few places it claimed mass support. A wave of indignation in the anarchist press followed, not least from Lerroux's erstwhile colleagues, including Ricardo Mella, who kindly reminded the new deputy that 'to say one is an anarchist and to mean it, one must clean oneself in the revolutionary Jordan [River] of all political filth'.[69] The *Suplemento* ran several bitter articles addressed to Lerroux in 1901, attacking the hypocrisy of his claim to be a 'libertarian' while standing for election, claiming that he had 'pretended to be an anarchist'.[70] The paper also celebrated anarchist groups which publicly rejected Lerroux, such as the Algeciras workers' centre, which refused to distribute *Progreso* because it was now affiliated to a politician. Its presence in the centre might cause 'discord,' unlike the 'apolitical' *Suplemento*.[71] Episodes such as this demonstrate how print was seen as a political marker in local contexts, where subscriptions to periodicals were seen as a means to identify with wider, national movements, and factions within them. Ideological differences and personal quarrels between publishers were thus played out at a grassroots level, where a choice of periodical signified allegiance to the individuals and values it represented.

Unlike many of the movement's elite, Ernesto Álvarez had never worked with Lerroux and distrusted his motivations in the late 1890s. Following Lerroux's election in 1901, Álvarez opened the pages of *La Protesta*, to 'public opinion' (i.e. anarchist opinion) on those anarchists who had worked with Lerroux. They were clearly inviting criticism of *La Revista Blanca*, prompting contributors such as Lorenzo to write to *La Protesta* to condemn Lerroux.[72] Underlying this debate was a feeling of apprehension and embarrassment following Lerroux's election, yet he continued to pass through the movement's orbit, particularly in Barcelona, and he maintained close personal relationships with anarchist figures such as Francisco Ferrer. He also continued to attract contempt, not least from his former colleagues in *La Revista Blanca*, who stopped publishing his works, since 'as anarchists' they could not 'defend the legal battle, nor the political battle, nor republican propaganda,' since 'he who does as much cannot be an anarchist'.[73]

These distinctions also played out in local arenas where anarchism and republicanism had previously been close. As both groups expanded in the early twentieth century, individuals and papers switched allegiances from anarchism to republicanism and vice versa. For example, in Mahón (Menorca), the periodical *El Porvenir del Obrero* began life as a part of the republican 'Germinal' association in 1899.[74] The paper was primarily concerned with attacking the Catholic Church in Menorca, which it accused of promoting ignorance on the island and for being 'guilty' of crimes 'against humanity'.[75] While it showed some signs of sympathy with anarchist ideas, the paper also published articles of a regenerationalist style, bemoaning the loss of the Cuba and the Philippines (sentiments which never appeared in the anarchist press), critiques of anarchist marriages, and praise of the 'Belgian model' of organising the working class, which was shared by Spanish socialists and derided by anarchists.[76] From October 1900 onwards these articles gradually disappeared, while anarchist ideas became more prominent. The paper dropped its 'Echo of the Germinal Association' subtitle and its editor, Juan Mir i Mir, began to correspond more regularly with other anarchist editors, and boasted of growth in the readership of anarchist papers in Mahón as evidence of a growing political awareness in the city.[77] The following year an article by Mir i Mir confirmed the paper's realignment, stating that 'as men of progress, [republicans] are our relatives; in regards to politics, they are our enemies'.[78]

El Porvenir del Obrero went on to be one of the longest-lasting anarchist papers of the period, publishing a total of 296 issues before it closed in 1907. As in its former, republican period, *El Porvenir del Obrero* strongly emphasised the revolutionary potential of education. The paper was vociferous in its criticism of religion (even by anarchist standards), it was an ardent supporter of secular schooling and 'integral' education, and it maintained a prominent campaign against social and cultural 'plagues' which inhibited the working class from self-emancipation.[79] These plagues included intoxicants, including tobacco—which caused 'apathy, indifference for important matters, cowardly fatalism . . . and laziness'—and alcohol, which was a waste of the worker's money and the cause of physical defects (trembling of the hands, loss of appetite, dementia), moral defects (diminishing of intellect, loss of memory, violence, moral degradation), addiction, misery, crime, premature ageing, epilepsy, madness and death.[80] Thus, in *El Porvenir del Obrero* sobriety was tied closely to a code of moral behaviour, justified with a (largely spurious) 'scientific' rationale.[81] Greater education, assisted by the anarchist press, in matters of 'hygiene' and health would enable the otherwise ignorant worker to resist these temptations.[82]

El Porvenir del Obrero had a clear position on the role of 'intellectuals' in the revolution. In 1901, Mir stated that although 'the emancipation of the working class must be conquered by the working class themselves,' they needed guidance towards the reason evident in anarchism. He proposed a new slogan for the movement which was more acceptable to his argument: '*the workers will SURELY emancipate themselves the day— BUT NOT BEFORE—that their emancipation can be their own work*'.[83] This attitude exemplifies the change in direction of the anarchist movement in this period. Education was no longer something to be achieved after the revolution, rather if the masses were denied access to modern ideas by the Church, if they were schooled badly, and if they were stifled by vice, then the revolution would not happen at all. Thinkers and propagandists needed to fight on behalf of the worker, bringing culture to the masses through the pages of the anarchist press.

Schooling, Literacy and Power

The 'culture' and 'education' sought by anarchists was valued according to its harmony with anarchist ideology. The content of the press, whether it was science or art, portrayed a social 'truth' which would lead its audience to see the world 'as it was' and inspire 'frank and bold ideas, of true liberty and justice, of noble feelings [of] fraternity, peace and love'.[84] Anarchist education was thus far from 'neutral' or 'objective'. Nevertheless, the anarchist cultural programme did provide the Spanish working class with access to contemporary scientific thought, which they could not receive from any other source.

This new commitment to education and science required a new pantheon of heroes. As the names of the martyrs of the 1890s gradually disappeared, as discussed in the previous chapter, they were replaced with those of scientists, explorers and intellectuals, particularly those regarded as in conflict with the Catholic Church. Galileo was frequently referenced as a figure who had assisted in the 'descent of religious arrogance,' as was Giodarno Bruno, Copernicus, Newton and Columbus.[85] These names were often intermingled with those of philosophers and sociologists, as in one article which suggested that Darwin, Schopenhauer, Marconi and Kropotkin belonged to a single cause of progress and revolution.[86] These new heroes and martyrs framed the anarchist movement as the inheritor of a scientific, educational lineage. Like their forebears in the natural sciences, anarchist theorists were the pioneers of a new, scientific understanding of society. Discoveries and events were celebrated as evidence of further advancements along the road of progress, for example, Camille Flammarion's investigations into solar eruptions and John Butler Burke's experiments with radium were reported with awe and respect for the 'distinguished men of science'.[87]

More broadly, advances in the fields of public health, oceanography, social geography and biology were all discussed in the anarchist periodical press, in articles brimming with enthusiasm for all things 'scientific'.[88] There was a genuine belief amongst anarchists that if people knew about science, sociology and art they would better themselves and the society around them. They believed that anarchism was a natural truth, provable by scientific methods, an 'on-going commitment to the appropriation of new knowledge and its use in working-class culture'.[89] This was an educational mission that was conceived of and created by those who considered themselves working-class; a bottom-up appreciation of culture and science which expanded the scope of what anarchism meant.

The press could not fulfil these educational ambitions alone. As well as the broad, general efforts to 'raise the consciousness' of the Spanish people with print, the movement developed a theory of schooling which would give the working class the skills they required to understand the anarchist message. The poor level of basic schooling in Spain was a particular concern to the movement. The country had one of the worst illiteracy rates in Europe: in 1887 over 70 per cent of the population could not read or write to a recognised standard of literacy, a figure which was even higher amongst women (81.2 per cent).[90] Although this had improved slightly by the turn of the century, illiteracy remained prevalent (1900:

63.8 per cent), particularly in rural areas and amongst the working class.[91] Despite the introduction of compulsory early-years schooling in 1857, schools were crippled by underfunding and remained inaccessible to many families.[92] Many children were sent to work instead of school as a means of supplementing meagre household incomes.[93] Anarchists thus saw the issue of child labour as the point where the immoral influence of capitalism reached into the cultural sphere, dragging children away from education so that their parents could eat.[94] Many papers pleaded with mothers to keep their children in education and praised those who taught their children to read on their own volition.[95] It was not parents but the government, in thrall to capital and religion, which was responsible for this situation. The only solution was a new society, based upon 'the natural, sole and true law' of anarchism.[96]

For anarchists, the solution to Spain's educational problems could not be found in official education programmes. Public, state-led schooling was 'a remedy worse than the disease,' making workers and their children 'less ignorant . . . but no less docile'.[97] When children were lucky enough to receive any form of education they were susceptible to the influence of the Catholic Church, which dominated the Spanish education system.[98] The Church's practice of dividing education by sex was regarded as the root cause of female oppression. Girls' schools taught gender-specific tasks such as needlework and housekeeping, and only gave rudimentary education in the sciences. Although boys had access to a wider range of education, their schooling remained unacceptable.[99] State education was not the modern, 'sociological' education anarchists advocated, but a means of reinforcing the hegemony of authority into boys of a young age.[100] While existing books on geography, grammar, arithmetic, and geometry were necessarily 'secular' because of their scientific basis, subjects such as history were simply vehicles for nationalistic and religious propaganda.[101] Anarchist educators thus called for new history books to be written, which would 'teach the life of the people rather than the lives of kings' and 'cleanse' the study of the past from the 'crimes which enclose it'.[102]

For anarchists, 'free,' 'integral,' 'modern' schooling was the only means by which the Spanish population could haul itself out of its miserable condition of ignorance.[103] These (largely interchangeable) terms implied an education which attuned to the individual wants and needs of every student.[104] Anarchist education would be experiential, non-religious, and gender-free; an education of both body and mind that broke down spurious, bourgeois boundaries between intellectual and physical work.[105] Many of these educationalist ideas overlapped with liberal and republican projects, such as the Institución Libre de Enseñanza (ILE), founded by Giner de los Ríos in 1876, which shared the ambition of anarchist educators to challenge the Church's monopoly on education.[106] Yet these middle-class efforts to alter public education did not go nearly far enough for the anarchist movement, and would only impoverish working-class families who would be better served by higher wages.[107] Instead, anarchists wanted advanced, radical education to be available to all of society, free from the influence of the state, capital and religion.[108] Their aim was not the creation of a privileged intellectual elite, who would steer society, but an enlightened working class who would lead the revolution for themselves, after which there would be 'fewer universities and more useful and profitable instruction'.[109]

Schooling was also needed for adults who had been failed by the education system. Unlike contemporary middle-class educators, anarchists did not see literacy and education as a means to pacify the Spanish working class, but to radicalise them. Literacy was thus seen as synonymous with a revolutionary mentality, an attitude laid out clearly in an article published in the *Suplemento* in 1899:

> How many [anarchists] do not know how to read? One in every hundred. On the other hand, for every hundred workers which form a part of the other parties, ninety do not know how to write their name. Where is the worker most educated? In the capitals. Which region is most educated? Cataluña. Where are the workers most advanced in ideas? In Cataluña. Practice demonstrates to us that ignorance is the element which nourishes reaction and sustains the privileged.[110]

Groups which were hostile to the movement also acknowledged the subversive power of education, including the reactionary Catholic newspaper *El Correo*, which declared that 'between a worker who does not know how to read, and one who reads . . . anarchist newspapers that attack . . . all the fundamental principles of the social order, we would always and in any case prefer the first'.[111]

Illiterate workers were cut off from the primary means by which anarchism was communicated. Although some of the problems posed by mass illiteracy were mitigated by oral reading culture, literacy continued to stratify the movement. Skills such as reading and writing were fundamental to the formation of the ideal, and untypical, *obrero ilustrado* ['educated worker'], an autodidact who required nothing other than his or her own reason to see the truth of anarchist ideas.[112] For printing groups, such educated individuals played a crucial role in distributing material, yet because they were so rare, they became local, informal elites, performing the roles of press correspondents, orators, union leaders and teachers in secular schools.[113] Disparities in reading ability thus created a hierarchy between educated militants, ordinary members of the movement, and the working class. This was not desired by anarchist publishers, but was recognised nonetheless.[114]

This connection between an 'advanced,' militant working class and their level of education was indicative of the general tone of the anarchist press over the turn of the century. Anarchist publishers saw it as their mission to spread culture and knowledge, raising the level of education across Spain, making every worker an *obrero ilustrado*. In the process, they reoriented the movement away from the controversial and damaging strategy of violence, replacing it with the broad, universally-accepted ambition to educate as a means of emancipation. In doing so publishers defined the movement's aims as synonymous with the spread of the anarchist press, and in the process made those involved in print culture the de facto elite of anarchism in Spain.

Education as Emancipation: The Growth of Anarchist-Feminism

The anarchist belief in the emancipatory value of education was exemplified in its attitude to women. The anarchist promise of liberation was intended for all: men and women of all social classes were to be freed from the interconnected forces of authority which enslaved them.[115] To anarchists, men felt the effects of oppression most tangibly in the workplace, where the authority of capital was absolute, while women were more likely to be affected by the cultural violence emanating from the Catholic Church.[116] Religion ensured that women remained in a state of ignorance: for them 'the doors to the university were closed as those of the convent were opened'.[117] Sections of the anarchist movement had recognised the need to organise women and combat sexism since the 1870s, yet little had been done to put these ideas into practice. Tentative efforts to work for gender equality began a decade later, through the activism of women workers such as Teresa Claramunt, who in 1884 formed a female textile workers' union affiliated to the FTRE.[118] Aside from these small developments, however, the movement's continuing focus on (overwhelming male) labour organisation meant that broader questions of female emancipation remained neglected. While there was no 'theoretical void' between anarchism and gender politics in the nineteenth century, there was a distinct lack of activity.[119]

As the movement turned towards education over the turn of the century, it made significant efforts to incorporate feminism into its ideology and practice.[120] This was not without problems: misogyny and deep-rooted gender stereotypes remained an element of anarchist discourse regarding women, while female emancipation remained largely secondary to the emancipation of the working class in general, despite the best intentions of many contributors to the anarchist press.[121] Nevertheless, anarchism provided a radical and subversive discussion of women's liberation, and established gender equality as a central component of the new society it advocated. This made anarchism unique amongst other progressive movements in Spain. Like most European socialist movements, the PSOE advocated equal rights for women in work, yet saw gender liberation as secondary to establishing working-class emancipation through parliamentary means. Women formed a very small part of both the UGT and the PSOE, and large sections of the socialist movement strongly objected to female suffrage, as it was claimed that women lacked a true sense of class consciousness and were predisposed to vote for reactionary or conservative (i.e. Catholic) candidates.[122] For the PSOE, women had to be educated to prepare them for the future, but until then socialism must remain 'anti-feminist in political questions'.[123]

Anarchist-feminism was also distinct from 'domesticated' middle-class feminism in Spain, which concentrated its demands on specific rights—predominantly the vote—while remaining largely unconcerned with the concerns or participation of working-class women.[124] Anarchist feminists were critical of this 'bourgeois' feminism for its neglect of the economic oppression of women, exemplified in articles such as 'Victim of Capital' by Claramunt, which derided liberals who praised the 'beautiful sex,' while allowing proletarian women to suffer and die at the hands of industrial production. She asked these 'infamous hypocrites' why they were so blind to the concerns of proletarian women: 'is it perhaps that the working woman does not belong to the same sex as the bourgeois woman?'[125] Anarchist feminists saw the right to vote as a pointless exercise that reinforced political authority, and instead sought to overturn the social constructs that oppressed women, rather than gain admittance to them.[126] To achieve this goal, women needed an 'education' which would free them from their social subjugation, which had to be both practical (i.e. better schooling) and a part of the broad cultural enlightenment that was needed across Spanish society.[127]

Gender equality and education were closely related concepts in the anarchist press. *La Revista Blanca* was an early and consistent supporter of gender liberation, and was one of the first anarchist publications to regularly use the term 'feminism'.[128] Other papers took up the subject enthusiastically. *Fraternidad* (Gijón) for example, maintained a regular column addressed to women, and many other papers, including *La Protesta, Adelante, Germinal* and *El Cosmopolita* discussed the role of women in the revolution far more frequently than their predecessors of the 1890s.[129] Through these papers, women's liberation and anarchism began to be seen as complementary and reinforcing. Neither could be realised without the other: anarchism without gender equality could not call itself truly emancipatory, while women could not be truly emancipated unless by anarchism.[130]

Anarchist papers were keen to stress that education, particularly in the sciences, would rid women of their 'fanaticism' and pave the way for a shared women's consciousness.[131] These views rested on the belief that women were more predisposed towards religious belief than men.[132] Many anarchist commentators believed that this issue could be resolved by repeatedly informing women of the truth of science and reason. One contributor to the Santander paper *Adelante*, for example, dedicated a discussion of astronomical processes explicitly 'to women', hoping that he could demonstrate 'as concretely as possible' that creation was a process of Nature [*sic*.] and not the work of God, who was merely 'the personi-fication . . . of ignorant fantasy'.[133] This patronising tone was common to many periodicals. In a four-part series named 'The Fanaticism of the Woman' published in *La Protesta*, women were portrayed as 'the weak-est part of society,' and in need of direction away from 'all worries and with knowledge of what was just and what was unjust'.[134] Women were at times depicted as 'weak,' 'beautiful,' 'strong' and 'slaves to maternal love'.[135] Gendered language was often negatively employed in anarchist discourse, as when *El Porvenir del Obrero* claimed that smoking tobacco weakened the worker as it caused 'effeminacy'.[136] Female anarchists were just as keen to employ gender stereotypes in their discussions of women. Claramunt in particular was fond of rounding on apathetic *compañeras*, who were concerned only with 'comfort, vanity and gossip'.[137]

Despite this problematic rhetoric, anarchist discussions of women did not claim that it was natural that women should be dominated by men. Ignorance was a product of society, not nature, and women possessed the same qualities of reason as men, as proven by science: 'the most exact anatomy has not been able to observe cerebral differences between man and woman'—wrote an anarchist group in Jerez—therefore women had to be 'prepared for science and art' as much as their male counterparts.[138] Women were thus 'victims of tradition,' enslaved by men from birth, domesticated and routinized, denied them access to education, and sub-ject to 'ridiculous and false' laws.[139] Just as it was unnatural for men to oppress men—for the bourgeoisie to oppress the working-class, and for the state to oppress its subjects—it was unnatural for men to oppress women. When a natural, anarchist, order was established, this oppres-sion would end; once 'ignorance' and 'false education' had been removed, so too would differences of sex.[140] The 'ignorance' of women, which maintained their subjugation, was thus seen a feature of society which anarchism wanted to change, rather than a justification for patriarchal dominance.

Although society had created these problems, it was the task of individual women to emancipate themselves.[141] Women were frequently addressed directly in a manner designed to cajole them into self-emancipation, as in one article by the anarchist educator Gabriela Alcalde: 'if we have wit-nessed an intellectual backwardness it is perpetuated by our ignorance; if we have seen reaction it nourished itself from our lack of the love of liberty . . . we will educate ourselves'.[142] Antonia Yzurieta, writing in 1899, stressed that women could not wait for liberation to come from men, since republicans, socialists, Catholics and 'why not say it? some so-called anarchists' were seeped in patriarchal tradition. Women 'must associate . . . study, convene at workers' meetings and conferences,' work-ing for their own emancipation as the first step towards the liberation of their sex.[143] Nature had given women all the tools they needed, all the 'distinctive signs of being rational', so they had to throw themselves into the 'social battles, in the turbulent life of the revolutionaries' with 'love, lots of love; liberty, lots of liberty; education, lots of education'.[144]

Sex, Love and the Family

Sex was not a common theme in the anarchist press at the turn of the century. When it was discussed, it was often medicalised, as in the movement's relationship with neo-Malthusian theories of population, sexual behaviour, and public health. These ideas were introduced into Spain in the early twentieth century through the national section of the League of Human Regeneration, led by the anarchist Luis Bulffi in Barcelona. This group saw access to contraception as a remedy for poverty, giving the working poor a choice which was otherwise denied to them by their ignorance and the religious qualms of the state. Although Bulffi's publication *Salud y Fuerza* (Barcelona, 1904–1914; 61 issues) claimed to have fostered numerous neo-Malthusian groups across Spain, the impact of such ideas is difficult to gauge. *Salud y Fuerza*'s audience was primarily in Cataluña and even there it was small: in 1914 the paper had fewer than 60 subscribers in Barcelona, and only 9 in Madrid.[145] More generally, neo-Malthusian ideas were almost entirely absent from the four-page periodical press outside Cataluña, and were opposed by prominent figures such as Urales and Leopoldo Bonafulla (pseud. Juan Bautista Esteve), a prolific pamphleteer and editor of *El Productor* (Barcelona).[146]

Sex was more commonly discussed in terms of the oppressive sexual practices of men, in which women were portrayed as passive victims. Prostitution and human trafficking were common themes in the La Coruña paper *Germinal*. In December 1904, the paper printed sordid details of a local bourgeois club named 'The Caliphate', which was accused of tricking working-class girls into joining a prostitution racket. The cause of this 'vice' was 'the injustice of the present society, which in its decrepitude wants to pervert and abuse the blossom of flowers barely in the spring of life'. *Germinal* claimed that 'the smallest influence of modern sociology' would rid society of such *higueras* (figs: a fruit linked with both female sexuality and homosexuality) who wanted to violate fourteen-year-old girls.[147] This critique had resonances with broader, mainstream feminist campaigns against prostitution, yet to anarchists the solution to this issue lay not in a 'desexualisation' of men and women—which is how anarchists perceived middle-class 'abolitionists' of 'white slavery'—since existing morality was as oppressive as prostitution. Instead, anarchists proposed to end prostitution through a broadening of cultural and sexual freedom.[148]

Marriage and the family are often identified as the key targets of the anarchist-feminist critique of society, viewed as a manifestation of property (since women became a man's chattel upon marriage) and authority (as the family structure necessarily involved hierarchies of power).[149] Occasionally such attacks drew on 'science' to prove the 'unhygienic nature' of conjugal life. For example, one article published in *Germinal* stated that although men and women should continue to have sex, they must learn to 'sleep alone' at night to ensure that both parties received sufficient rest.[150] Marriage was contrasted with the concept of 'free love', a scientific and socially acceptable alternative to matrimony, which allowed women and men to select their partners freely.[151] Free love was understood as a 'contractual act'—'an exchange of services agreed upon freely and voluntarily by two autonomous and equal beings in love'— and was not to be confused with either 'lust,' promiscuity, or polyamory, all of which remained disagreeable to most anarchist commentators.[152] Such moral positions on sexual conduct were often articulated through a scientific discourse, which depicted acceptable behaviour as 'healthy,' in contrast to 'deviant,' perverse practices, which only existed because 'hygienic' sexual behaviour was denied by Catholic tradition. For one contributor to *La Protesta*, for example, 'free love' would rid society of all sexual vice, allowing the free expression of 'physiological necessity' to do away with 'this onanistic and paedophilic, lesbian and sodomitic society'.[153] 'Free love' would thus reinforce most accepted sexual norms, with no suggestion that men and women would engage in anything other than heterosexual relationships.[154] Where 'free love' differed from traditional marital practice was in allowing for couples to separate and chose new partners, providing an ideological rationale for 'serial monogamy'.[155]

Anarchist attitudes to marriage exposed one of the many seeming contractions between theory and practice in the movement. In anarchist ideology, marriage was regarded as 'a contract of flesh legalised by the judge and sanctified by the priest,' yet over the turn of the century acts of civil marriages were widely celebrated in the anarchist press, and never criticised for conforming to a patriarchal legal culture that oppressed women.[156] Instead, they were presented in terms of a victory over religion and obstructionist local civic authorities.[157] Federico Urales was very proud of his civil marriage to Soledad Gustavo; indeed, he claims in his autobiography that they had met after Urales had actively searched for someone who would be prepared to marry him in a civil ceremony.[158] Urales was comfortable with the idea of marriage, and claimed that 'free love . . . can only implement itself in a society which, *beforehand*, guarantees the right of life, of liberty and of pleasure to all creatures'.[159] Like Gustavo, Teresa Claramunt did not refrain from marriage. In 1884 she and Antonio Gurri Vergés celebrated a civil marriage and went on to have children, including Proletaria Libre (who died shortly after birth) and Acracia. Although this marriage broke down in the following years, Claramunt is then reported to have married the anarchist José López Montenegro in 1901, or in other accounts, to have had a relationship with Leopoldo Bonafulla, her colleague in *El Productor*.[160] Rather than dissuade women from marriage, anarchist feminism sought to refigure it as an act conducted between two equal partners, stripping it of any religious or legal implications of oppression, without giving up on the practice altogether.[161] This was how anarchists 'loved freely' at the turn of the century: free from the Church, but not from marriage as a societal or legal practice. Radically different forms of behaviour, such as those posed by the concept of 'free love' (if not its practice) would have to wait until after revolution.

Marriage could also be used to empower women to act as part of the broader struggle against the state. In theory, 'free love' and independence from marriage were the only means by which women could gain economic emancipation, since women would no longer have 'to think who would work for her and provide for her table'.[162] Yet in the context of Restoration Spain, anarchists could not deny that marriage offered women protection and economic security. Few people lived alone in Spain, and single adult women were often exposed to exclusion, derision and poverty. Rather than advising women to risk these dangers, anarchist commentators suggested ways in which marriage practices and choices could benefit the wider movement. For example, after the violent suppression of a demonstration in La Línea in 1902, Constancio Romeo called for a campaign to dissuade working-class women from marrying members of the Civil Guard, emasculating these 'enemies of the people' through 'enforced celibacy'.[163]

As with marriage, the traditional family unit was celebrated in the anarchist press. One of the few photographs published in the *Suplemento* depicted Tarrida del Marmól with his child, accompanied by a piece which explained that although anarchist families were maintained 'without theological impositions,' this did not mean that anarchists were 'enemies of the family' nor was it true that they 'do not love their children,' as was claimed by critics of the movement.[164] As with civil marriages, the civil registration of children was framed as a victory over religion, often accompanied by sarcastic comments such as 'blessed are those that spurn baptism,' praising parents who had saved their children from the 'brutal soaking'.[165] Such registrations were often accompanied by a communal event, where revolutionary hymns were sung and anarchist readings were given, often by other children from the locality.[166] A similar, although more sombre, tone was used for anarchist funerals—many of which were also for children— held in local civil cemeteries, turning these often 'unkempt, undignified' spaces into sites of public manifestations against religion.[167] Cultural practices such as civil weddings and naming ceremonies helped to affirm what familial practice meant as an anarchist.[168] Anarchists were willing to marry and have children, as long as their ceremonies were free from any connection to the established Church. That they were similar to traditional, religious practices was not troubling to anarchist commentators, indeed, the *Suplemento* was fully aware of these similarities, and briefly published all reports of births, deaths and marriages in a column ironically titled 'Anarchic Jesuitism'.[169]

Parents demonstrated their commitment to the movement by giving their children appropriately revolutionary names. The bestowal of an anarchist name brought the child into the 'social world' of the movement, giving them an identity within a specific, alternative sub-culture.[170] Broad, conceptual names such as 'Germinal,' 'Aurora' or 'Acracia' were popular choices for the children of anarchists, as were the names of figures respected in the movement, such as 'Parsons Lingg y Spies,' (the surnames of three of the Chicago martyrs), 'Kropotkin,' 'Darwin' (particularly unfortunate choices in a language which does not use the letter 'K' or 'W'), 'Archimedes,' 'Galileo,' 'Spartacus' or in one case 'Proudhon y Washington'.[171] One particularly popular name for children was Palmiro/a, a reference to the ancient Middle-Eastern city Palmyra, known in classical history as a free city and the location of a prolonged rebellion against the Roman Empire, led (appropriately) by a female leader, Queen Zenobia.[172] The legend of Palmyra was the subject of one of the most popular history texts in the movement, Comte de Volney's *Las ruinas de Palmyra*, which Anselmo Lorenzo cited as one of the main causes of his 'conversion' to anarchism.[173] This upsurge of revolutionary naming practices was a generational development which took place over the turn of the century. The parents of the 'Germinals,' 'Acracio/as' and 'Palmiro/as' almost always had traditional Spanish names, as was the case with Vicente García (one of the most ubiquitous names in northern Spain), who named his daughter 'Fraternidad,' despite protests from a local civil registrar.[174] Such responses from officials to anarchist parents were common, and were seen as proof of the influence of religion into the lives of children and the functioning of the state.

The practice of raising children in a familial context was never questioned, nor was the assumption that the responsibility for this lay with women.[175] What mattered was that children were part of an anarchist family, which would ensure that they grew up as 'defender[s] of the redeeming ideas of anarchists,' maintaining anarchist ideas and culture through future generations.[176] Women were seen as particularly responsible for their children's education, and asked to intervene in the 'imagination' of young boys to lead them away from undesirable choices, such as joining the military.[177] One female correspondent to the *Suplemento* saw the 'production' and education of 'the free man of the future' as the most important 'mission' of revolutionary women, who should accept a gendered role as a means to demonstrate their value to the movement.[178]

Women in Print Culture

The upsurge of feminist ideas in the anarchist press was exemplified by the Valencian anarchist-feminist paper *La Humanidad Libre*. This paper was launched in 1902 with the explicit purpose of publishing a 'defence of the woman,' a term which resonated with the broader debates on the role of women in Spanish society.[179] Funds for the paper were raised through a raffle of books by (male) authors including Vicente Blasco Ibáñez, Emile Zola and Sebastián Faure.[180] When launched, the paper was adorned with an elaborate half-page frontispiece, depicting naked children skipping between flowers and leaves, books titled *Germinal*, *Work*, *Future Society*, *The Conquest of Bread*, *Justice* and *Resurrection*, with a sun blazing the word 'Truth' over the whole scene. To the left stands a well-dressed, heterosexual, nuclear family, composed of a tall, affectionate father, a dainty mother tilting to receive his kiss and a young, studious girl, foregrounded by an open book entitled 'Amor Libre [Free Love]'.[181] This image invoked many of themes within anarchist culture and education: nature, learning, youth and love, bound together by the ultimate goal of women's liberation, while remaining broadly in-line with conventional sexual, marital and familial practices.

La Humanidad Libre aimed to unify radical female writers from across Spain and abroad. Amongst the more prominent names involved in the paper were Teresa Claramunt and Soledad Gustavo, whose articles appeared alongside contributions from less well-known female anarchists, such as Luciana Rico, a correspondent from Badajoz who saw the paper as 'one of the means to recuperate the woman' and called for a 'new education . . . directed to the good of all'.[182] Foreign anarchist feminists such as Louise Michel and Emma Goldman were also cited as supporters of the paper, as was the Italian socialist campaigner Ana Mozzoni. None of these international *compañeras* made direct contributions to *La Humanidad Libre*, thus their 'support' for the paper may have been assumed, rather than explicitly given. By using these names the editors of *La Humandiad Libre* cast their paper as part of an international network of radical feminists, which did not subscribe to the aims or tactics of mainstream international feminist organisations.[183] In doing so they followed the example set by the Argentine anarchist-feminist periodical *La Voz de la Mujer* (1896–87), which was distributed across Spain and claimed a similar list of international *compañeras* who supported the paper, and almost certainly influenced the founders of *La Humanidad Libre*.[184] *La Voz de la Mujer* was, in turn, largely inspired by anarchist-feminists in Spain such as Gustavo, whose works appeared in the paper.[185] Though both papers were small, and short-lived, they demonstrate the reciprocal nature of transnational exchanges of ideas, practice and print that existed between anarchist movements across different countries and continents, which, in the case of anarchist-feminism, would continue into future decades with more established publications such as *Nuestra Tribuna* (Buenos Aires, 1922–1925), which was edited by the Spanish emigre Juana Rouco Buela, and the hugely influential *Mujeres Libres* (Barcelona, 1936–38).[186]

Despite clear enthusiasm from its readers—including the 'Humanidad Libre' women's youth group in Lebrija (Sevilla), which formed soon after the paper was launched and aimed to 'study the ideal' and 'spread propaganda'—*La Humanidad Libre* was 'paralysed' by financial problems and closed after just three issues.[187] Its editors returned to publishing three months later with *El Corsario* (Valencia, 1902, 27 issues), although after discussion with 'various friends' the publishing group had decided to tone down the feminism of their previous publication, resuming their defence of the 'trampled, exploited and ridiculed *without any distinction of sex*'.[188] Nevertheless, female emancipation remained one of the key elements of *El Corsario*, evident in articles such as 'Entidades' by María Losada, which called for an end to the social barriers which prevented women and men from uniting in common cause against the oppression of authority.[189]

More broadly, the inferior position of women in Spain had a direct impact on their role within anarchist publishing. Although the vast majority of editors and publishers within the movement were male, women did occasionally hold positions in editorial groups, such as those of *El Productor* (Claramunt) and *La Revista Blanca* (Gustavo). This could invite difficulties. In 1902, for example, Gustavo was named as the editor of the newly-launched *Tierra y Libertad*, but could not accept the role, since the Press Law required that an editor had to be 'in full possession of civil and political rights,' which, under the 1889 Civil Code, women were not.[190] Thus, while a woman could legally own a paper, the named editor had to be a man. In the case of *Tierra y Libertad*, this became Gustavo's husband Urales, who was also obliged to stand in for Gustavo when she was sued for libel as the court did not recognise a woman's capacity to defend herself in court, much to her indignation.[191]

Such problems were rare, or at least not particularly visible, simply because very few women within the movement were fully engaged in the workings of the press. Women generally appeared as contributors to anarchist papers, rather than as editors or owners. This reflected the broader disparity within the movement, where men held almost all prominent positions on both a local and national level. For example, Gustavo was considered an unsuitable delegate during nominations for the 1900 Paris Congress, discussed above. The commission stressed that this judgement was made not because she was a woman—stating that 'it would please us in the extreme [if] the feminine sex was to have representation'—but because she could not speak a foreign language. This lack of education would leave her in a passive, 'secondary' role, unlike her male counterparts Mella and Prat, who between them could speak English, French and Italian.[192] Lacking sufficient 'education' could thus be a barrier to advancement and equality within the anarchist movement, as in wider society.

Working for the Cause

Women were advised by anarchists to think beyond 'women's issues' and engage in the struggle against the oppression of capitalism and the state, which affected all of the working class.[193] While gendered language appeared throughout the anarchist press, it was in discussions of labour that it was articulated most clearly. Women were called on to associate and form a 'muscular power' they otherwise lacked, 'imitating' their husbands, 'the strong men who fight and fight' against their economic exploitation. When united, women would no longer be 'weak nor sterile' but a potent, collective and necessary addition to the anarchist cause.[194] Such statements were often made by women themselves, and reveal an underlying assumption that women could only participate in the struggle against capitalism if they took on male qualities and were prepared to engage in aggressive, masculine conflict.

Reports of women's meetings and societies appeared much less frequently in the press than those of men. When they did appear, they were celebrated as evidence of growing enthusiasm for anarchism amongst women, as in the reports of 'La Unión', a working-women's union of 416 members based in Elche (Alicante) which promoted activity that would liberate 'every human'.[195] Female support for anarchism was used as a symbol of the growing strength and health of the movement, and its ability to connect with the Spanish working class beyond its traditional base in male labour organisations.[196] At feminist meetings women took the floor, denouncing repression, calling for solidarity and declaring a 'war to the death' with capitalism. One such meeting was held in La Línea de la Concepción in July 1901, with several women speakers, including Ana Villalobo, the colleague and wife of José Sanchez Rosa (a prominent anarchist writer and boot-maker), both of whom worked at the Centre for Social Studies in Los Barrios, 20km from La Línea. Their twelve year-old daughter Francisca ('Paca'), also spoke at the meeting, reading 'a work eulogising the anarchist ideal' for which she would give 'her blood'.[197] In meetings such as these, women began to play an increased role in discussions of economic and labour matters. The publications of anarchist worker societies, such as the railworkers' publication *La Solidaridad Ferroviaria* (Madrid), called upon its affiliates to educate their wives and allow them to take part in union meetings, which would prepare them for the 'decisive battle'.[198] Working-women's societies began to proliferate, forming pacts of solidarity with their local male counterparts. One such group, 'La Igualdad' of Cádiz, held regular meetings in the premises of the local stokers' union, where they demanded association and education, uniting these two strands of anarchist action in the form of the emancipated woman as both worker and mother.[199] Tentative steps towards national recognition of female labour were also made at the III Congress of the FSORE in 1903, which saw its first female representative, Dolores Gómez, representing women workers in the Santander canning industry.[200]

Anarchist feminism thus did not rest on the assumed 'difference' of women, who should be kept far away from the world of labour.[201] Rather, women workers were invited to take part in the struggle with their male counterparts, so long as they accepted the masculine terrain on which it was fought. This would ensure that female labour was recognised as part of the collective struggle against capital. Together with men, they would form a united 'movement of progressive advance for the proletariat and femininity'.[202] Women's active participation in the class struggle was also evident outside organised labour. In Spain, as elsewhere, women took a particularly prominent role in strikes, protests and demonstrations.[203] The movement embraced this activity as revolutionary, anarchist action, relating it to previous examples of radical female agitation such as the mythical *pétroleuses* of the Paris Commune. *Compañeras* who followed this lineage were used as examples of female solidarity with the wider anarchist cause, including Elisa Aragón, who was imprisoned following a violent protest in 1902 'for the crime of being secretary of a feminist association'.[204]

Feminism was a key component of the anarchist ambition to emancipate the Spanish working class through education. The press played a particularly important role in the development of these ideas, both through dedicated publications such as *La Humanidad Libre*, and more broadly, in articles and reports of practices which appeared in almost every paper of the movement. Female writers and activists were important in this endeavour (in particular Gustavo and Claramunt) but so too were less prominent anarchists, both women and men, who shared their thoughts and accounts of their activities with comrades across Spain. The idea of women's equality increasingly shaped the meaning of anarchism, adding a new dimension to how life as an anarchist in Spain was understood. This understanding of the multifaceted ways in which women were oppressed in society, and the search for solutions beyond the right to vote, was rare and laudable, particularly in the context of early twentieth-century Europe.

Nevertheless, anarchist feminism had its limits. For all the theoretical arguments for gender equality within the anarchist press, anarchists could not fully shed the misogynistic culture in which they operated. Many of the discussions and practices associated with anarchist-feminism remained couched in traditional assumptions about the 'qualities' of women and their role in society. This underlying tension was never fully resolved. Twenty years later, female members of the movement still complained in the anarchist press that '*compañeros*, however radical they may be in cafés, unions and even affinity groups . . . seemed to drop their costumes as lovers of female liberation at the doors of their homes . . . they behave with their *compañeras* just like common "husbands"'.[205] The growth of anarchist-feminism in Spain can thus be seen as a development of a genu-inely emancipatory sentiment, but in practice it offered only 'a *relatively* less sexist milieu . . . than the framework provided by the political norms of the dominant political culture'.[206]

'Andando se prueba el movimiento': Education in Practice

In anarchist thought education was not a static concept, never simply a policy or the attainment of a specific set of skills, such as reading and writ-ing. Education was a process, through which emancipation from ignorance would emerge. To set this in motion, the working class needed guidance towards the reason inherent in anarchism, and contexts where such pro-cesses could flourish. Putting education into practice often began with a 'propaganda group', formed of individuals who came together to think, discuss and act towards their commonly-shared ideas. From 1899 onwards hundreds of these groups formed across Spain. One report produced for the Real Academia de Ciencias Morales y Políticas in Madrid counted over 120 anarchist groups in Spain in 1905.[207] By adding reports in the anar-chist press, I would suggest the figure was at least three times larger and evident in every region of the country over the period 1899–1906.

Propaganda groups were immersed in print culture. Some were cre-ated specifically to assist publishing groups, such as 'Vida del Periódico' in Aznalcóllar (Sevilla), which formed to distribute *Tierra y Libertad* (Madrid) across south-west Andalucía.[208] Such propaganda groups would receive papers and pamphlets, distribute them either physically or orally in public meetings, and send information back to publishers.[209] Propaganda groups formed the cultural 'vanguard' of the movement, hoping to spread anarchism within existing workers' groups and insti-gate cultural projects.[210] A frequent request of newly-formed groups was for 'one copy of all our newspapers and pamphlets' so that propaganda could be distributed freely in their local area.[211] These requests also came in from Spanish-speaking migrants based across Europe, the Americas, and North Africa, revealing a desire from emigrants to keep in contact with the movement; indeed in many cases these international groups were amongst the first to subscribe to new periodicals and make requests for new pamphlets, revealing a clear enthusiasm to establish and sustain links back to their comrades in Spain.[212]

Requests for periodicals were also sent by anarchist workers' societies and unions, many of which had roles for 'propaganda commissions' and 'librarians'. Anarchist labour activists saw themselves as educators, and regarded the anarchist press as an invaluable step in the cultural enlight-enment of their colleagues. For example, when a boot-makers' society in Granada formed in 1902, one of its first communiques advised its mem-bers to 'read valiant newspapers such as *Tierra y Libertad, El Corsario,*

Adelante and others'.[213] In promoting the anarchist press, these workers' groups fused the cultural struggle with the economic, aiming to inspire their members towards an all-encompassing revolutionary outlook. The press was also a means to achieve greater unity of action. Groups of all kinds used periodicals to publish notices 'to all the anarchist press,' which detailed their aims and addresses for correspondence, reflecting a desire to establish themselves within the movements' networks of communication and exchange.[214] Groups and newspapers were dependent on one another: just as groups needed newspapers to assist them in spreading ideas, newspapers needed willing individuals to receive, distribute, and pay for their materials, particularly in areas where anarchism had a limited presence.

It is often difficult to establish detailed information about these groups, beyond the fact that they existed. They were acutely ephemeral: groups continuously formed, dissolved or split and reformed under a new name. Their shared purpose—to educate and spread propaganda—did not require formalised processes or statutes which members had to follow. Propaganda groups generally only became a fixed presence in the press when they began taking the message of anarchism outside their locality, either in person or through print.

The New Geography of Spanish Anarchism

Anarchists could not rely on a party or national union to lead the way in expanding the movement into new areas. This task had to be undertaken by anarchists themselves. One way of expanding the reach of the movement was to take the message of anarchism to new localities in person, in the manner of a travelling missionary or proselytiser. By far the most famous example of this was Giuseppe Fanelli, who travelled from Italy to Barcelona and Madrid in 1868 in what is generally, and questionably, credited as the 'introduction' of anarchism into Spain.[215] Such proselytisers continued to play an important role in the expansion of anarchism through the late nineteenth century, when 'excursions' became more formalised with speakers banding together to give a travelling series of lectures throughout a region, known as a 'propaganda tour'.[216] One such tour was undertaken by the anarchist publishers Teresa Claramunt and Leopoldo Bonafulla through Andalucía in the late summer of 1902, financed by raffles managed by the *Suplemento* and later *Tierra y Libertad*.[217] Claramunt and Bonafulla passed through numerous towns in the provinces of Cádiz, Sevilla, Huelva, Málaga and Granada, joining local activists in meetings of thousands of people.[218] The speakers were stalked by the authorities wherever they went, meetings were broken up and cancelled, and Claramunt was arrested in Montejaque, Puerto Real and Sevilla.[219] Despite these difficulties the tour was seen as a great success by local anarchist press correspondents, some of whom were so inspired that they immediately began organising follow-up events and future tours.[220] A more extensive tour was organised by *Tierra y Libertad* in 1904, in which many of the most celebrated anarchists of the period visited every region of Spain.[221] Distributing print was one of the most important functions of travelling individuals and tours.[222] 'Able and enthusiastic propagandists' such as Claramunt and Bonafulla could 'plant the seed' of anarchism in 'fertile terrain,' but the longer process of 'germination' required cultural markers such as printed materials, which gave anarchist ideas a presence after a propaganda tour had passed on.[223] After the speeches were over and the rallies had dispersed, periodicals and pamphlets ensured that new adherents had a material reference to anarchist ideas and a means to communicate with the wider movement.[224]

An example of this process comes from the Asturian port city of Gijón, which became an area of significant anarchist support over the turn of the century.[225] The spread of anarchist ideas in the city has been attributed to the arrival of a Catalan metalworker, Ignacio Martín, in 1892. Martín is credited with single-handedly splitting the workers of Gijón into anarchist and socialist factions through his relentless proselytising in factories, taverns and workers' centres.[226] Yet this 'arrival' of anarchist ideology was not enough to establish a lasting anarchist presence in Gijón. Anarchist activity remained 'vague and sporadic,' repressed during the 1890s and challenged by the growing strength of the socialist movement.[227] This situation improved after 1898, when the city saw a remarkable growth in socialist, anarchist and unaligned workers' associations, which went hand-in-hand with renewed efforts to spread political literature.[228] Federico Urales, for example, visited the city in 1898 in order to encourage sales of his publications. Three years later the *Suplemento* boasted of its expanding readership in the city, and stated that more requests for anarchist pamphlets came from Asturias than any other province in Spain.[229]

Around the same time as Urales's visit, the first Asturian anarchist newspaper, *La Fraternidad*, was launched in Gijón, becoming the fortnightly *Fraternidad* in 1899.[230] This paper was one of the first to emerge in Spain following the repression of the mid-1890s. It soon gained prominence in the national movement, publishing contributions from both national figures (such as Lorenzo, Claramunt, Urales and Prat) and local anarchists, such as José Valdez, the president of the Gijón stone masons' guild, and the Rogelio 'The Boot-Maker' Fernández Fuey, who used his workshop in Gijón as an anarchist school.[231] A succession of anarchist papers followed: *La Defensa del Obrero* (1901), *La Organización* (1902), *El Perseguido* (c.1903) and *Tiempos Nuevos* (1905–1906). These initiatives cemented an anarchist presence in Gijón, from where it expanded into other areas in Asturias, such as the metallurgical centre of La Felguera.[232]

Similar processes were taking place across Spain over the turn of the century. Groups were formed, often launching new periodicals which marked their area out as new 'nodes' within the expanding geography of Spanish anarchism [see Map 3.1, compare with Map 0.1]. The upsurge in print was a key element of the movement's geographic expansion. Periodicals projected the local and regional concerns of anarchists into the national discourse of the movement. They also put new affiliates into contact with one another, creating a network in which groups and individuals shared experiences and joined in the collaborative construction of anarchist ideology and practice.[233] Yet one area initially remained absent from this publishing activity. Repression lingered in Cataluña until 1901, making it difficult for groups to join the upsurge in anarchist publishing evident in the rest of Spain. Aside from *La Protesta*'s brief stay in Sabadell (June-September 1900) and two workers' society papers, no anarchist newspaper appeared in Cataluña until *El Productor* was launched by Teresa Claramunt and Leopoldo Bonafulla in 1901.[234] After this point, however, Barcelona soon became the epicentre of anarchist publishing, and the movement in general.[235]

Centres for Social Studies

As well as taking the message of the movement into new areas, anarchist propaganda groups aimed to cement their presence in local contexts. Many hoped to secure premises, or 'locales of resistance,' in which they could conduct their activities, such as centres, libraries and meeting halls.[236] Various forms of associational bodies had developed in Spain

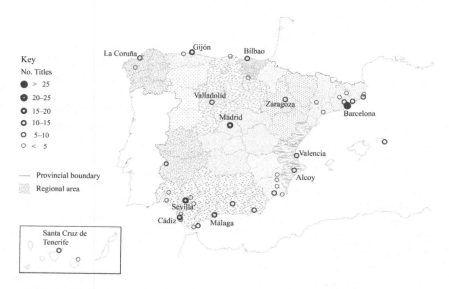

Map 3.1 Areas of Anarchist Publishing in Spain, 1899–1906.

Source: Map created by James G. Pearson.

through the nineteenth century: *casinos*, used predominantly for leisure; *ateneos*, institutions set up to provide popular education; *cooperativas*, for members of the co-operative movement; and *mutuas de socorros mutuos* (mutual assistance societies), which provided members with credit, basic medical care and assistance following industrial accidents.[237] More informal meeting places had been utilised by the anarchist movement since the 1870s, providing a bedrock for the movement during the early years of the Restoration.[238] In the 1880s the movement in Cataluña had established more formal spaces, yet these early initiatives ended in 1893 with the advent of anarchist terrorism and the repression which followed. The return and expansion of these efforts after 1899 formed a key component of the revitalisation of anarchism across the whole of Spain.

Outside Cataluña, anarchist spaces were often disputed, ephemeral and ramshackle affairs. They were often based within unused premises, such as a spare room in a tavern, or shared with rival political groups.[239] To anarchists, locales were a form of *ateneo*, providing leisure space, education, exchange, and economic assistance, all operating according to rational, communal principles. These locales were, however, different to conventional *ateneos*, which were adjudged to promote the 'bourgeoisification' of the working class.[240] This was evident in the anarchist critique of the literature offered by 'traditional' spaces of sociability, which were full of 'rank' popular fiction and the works of liberal theorists, rather than 'the recent works of French positivists or English sociologists, or the eternal scientific and philosophic reflections of Germans'.[241] Rather than *ateneos*, anarchists called their spaces 'Centres for Social Studies,' reflecting the movement's increased emphasis on education. This term also set them apart from the socialist 'centros obreros' and 'casas del pueblo', which were also proliferating at this time.[242]

Centres and locales formed the backbone of anarchist cultural infrastructure in a locality, providing 'platforms of reunion and meeting, exchanges of experiences, education and instruction'.[243] They were used for communal practices and celebrations, such as naming ceremonies, civil marriages, and wakes, as well as providing something of a refuge, where trusted comrades could form a parallel community in which anarchism could be practiced 'as if they actually lived in a world they would wish to live in'.[244] At times, locales were also places where illegal activity could be planned and carried out, as well as a place where an anarchist community could reconstitute itself following periods of repression.[245] Anarchist centres proliferated across Spain over the turn of the century, both in areas of traditional anarchist support, such as the provinces of Sevilla and Cádiz, and in areas where the movement had previously had little support, such as Córdoba, Santander, Baracaldo, Badajoz, Cartagena, Huelva, Tenerife, Elche, and Marbella. Together these locales formed the physical markers of the new geography of Spanish anarchism.[246] While the movement still drew the bulk of its support from Cataluña and south-west Andalucía, these scattered, often isolated, spaces became centres of gravity for anarchist practice in almost every province in Spain. Many maintained lasting pockets of anarchist support well into the twentieth century.[247]

Centres were not regarded as places that separated the movement from the outside world. Anarchism was intended to look outwards, creating an 'alternative geography' between and beyond their centres.[248] For example, the Manzanares (Ciudad Real) workers' centre—formed in October 1899 to provide 'education . . . without any form of political colour'—kept in constant contact with anarchist periodicals. Once established, this centre wanted to form lasting bonds with other centres in the province and help in the spread of anarchist locales.[249] Similar calls for nation-wide networks of locales were common in the anarchist press. Anarchist spaces were to be celebrated. Their openings were heralded as moments of great importance and were often accompanied by recitals of articles from the press, as at the opening of the new Bilbao Centre for Social Studies in 1904, where an article by Soledad Gustavo on the value of education published in *La Revista Blanca* was read aloud, alongside a collection of poems and a short play.[250] Once created, a locale formed a hub through which the anarchist press would be distributed. The 'Germinal' centre in La Coruña, for example, became a key supplier of pamphlets across Spain and to other countries such as Cuba.[251]

The presence of printed material inscribed spaces with an anarchist significance and meaning, transforming a mere 'room' into a 'library'.[252] Groups often sent in requests to newspapers for back issues, so that their library had a complete collection on offer to those visiting.[253] Special issues printed to mark certain dates were particularly valuable to such collections, a fact noticed in *La Protesta*, which in 1899 printed 300 extra copies of its commemorative 11 November edition 'on good quality paper'.[254] Libraries were not solely places to visit; they also acted as distribution centres, as in the 'Biblioteca de pedagogía' in Bilbao, which aimed to supply schools across Spain with anarchist 'sociological' literature.[255] Libraries identified centres as sites of learning, and were often the first step towards creating the most cherished anarchist space of all: the school.

Modern Schools

Prior to 1899, the 'integral' education and advanced pedagogy called for by anarchist educational theory was an ambitious and largely unachievable goal.[256] Educators wishing to implement such innovative methods usually found employment in secular or 'free-thinking' schools, often run by republicans, where they could 'combine the cause of popular education with their need to earn a living'.[257] These schools suffered during the 1890s. Although not 'anarchist' in name, many—including the school where Gustavo and Urales worked in Reus (Tarragona)—were seen as centres of sedition and forced to close.[258] After 1899, however, anarchist educators again started to put their ideas into practice and began founding their own schools. The term 'school' encompassed a wide range of establishments, from rooms within a centre (here named 'local schools'), which offered occasional, rudimentary classes in basic skills, to large, well-established institutions which aimed realise the ideas of integral education.

By far the most prestigious and celebrated school founded in this period was Francisco Ferrer's Escuela Moderna, which opened in Barcelona on 8 September 1901.[259] The Escuela was 'neither the first nor the most distinguished' of its kind in Spain, nor was Ferrer 'a theorist, [or] a conceiver of new ideas'.[260] Yet his school quickly became a symbol of the 'modern' schooling called for by anarchists across the country. By 1905, 126 students of both sexes were enrolled in the Escuela, receiving an education which imparted 'the positive value of education, progress and social equality, and the negative value of the government, property, religion, the army . . . and bull-fighting,' through a faculty comprised of freethinkers, masons, radical republicans and anarchists.[261]

For educators outside the movement, the Escuela was 'little more than a well-financed and organised version of the "nurseries of revolutionaries"' established by anarchists in the 1870s and 1880s. Ferrer's 'innovative' methods promoted a 'perversion' of rational education: 'maths problems, for example, illustrated principles of economic distribution . . . a field trip in 1904 to a chemical factory in Badalona was followed by a lecture on the evils of capitalism'.[262] Other progressive educators, such as those of the ILE, 'remained aloof' from the Escuela and shunned Ferrer, seeing him as 'an agitator who was exploiting the cause of education'.[263]

The school also drew criticism from within the movement, not least because it was clearly an elite institution. Despite Ferrer's desire for 'co-education of the social classes,' none of the school's intake were the children of the working class, who could not afford the monthly fees of 15 pesetas.[264] Some anarchist educators also critiqued its curriculum, which they saw as a 'betrayal' of free education and no better than the indoctrination which took place in religious schools. Advocates of free education, such as Ricardo Mella, saw Ferrer as an ideologue who had abandoned 'neutrality' in education in order to teach anarchist 'doctrine' and 'dogma'.[265] For Mella, children should not be forced to follow the principles of anarchism, but rather should be given a 'free, scientific education,' through which they would be given the power to reason for themselves, 'and if [they believe], as we believe, the fundamental truth of anarchism, they will become anarchists . . . through free choice, through their own conviction, not because we have moulded them'.[266] This dispute reveals, once again, the problematic question of leadership within the anarchist movement. While Ferrer undoubtedly used his school to spread anarchist ideas to his students, it is difficult to see how Mella expected 'neutral' education to avoid this issue, given that what he understood as 'free thinking' aligned closely to his conception of anarchism. As with the Jerez uprising in 1892 and the disputes which emerged in later years over organisation, putting education into practice raised concerns between the ideal of 'free' education and 'manipulative' indoctrination which were never fully resolved.

When the Barcelona Modern School opened in 1901 Ferrer was not well-known within the movement. *El Porvenir del Obrero* was one of the few papers to give the school significant attention, after its editor, Juan Mir i Mir, took a tour of the premises which left him feeling 'stronger, with a more optimistic concept of the future'.[267] In contrast, only two references to the Escuela were published in the *Suplemento* in 1901, and neither Ferrer nor his school were mentioned in most other anarchist titles in print.[268]

Nevertheless, the Escuela soon grew in prestige within the movement outside Catalonia, primarily because of its relationship to print culture. The second largest paper of the time, *La Protesta*, was particularly interested in the school's monthly journal *Boletín de la Escuela Moderna*.[269] *La Protesta* was keen to advertise the arrival of each new issue of the *Boletín*, each one 'better than the last, if that is possible' and highly recommended 'to all lovers of true education'.[270] *La Protesta* was also keen to stress the value of the textbooks and pamphlets produced by Ferrer's printing house, the 'forty . . . compact, red-covered volumes ranging from primers of arithmetic and grammar to popular introductions to the natural and social sciences and serious treatise on geography, sociology and anthropology'.[271] Most of these works were French translations, including the anti-war reading primer *Patriotism and Colonisation*, which contained hundreds of anti-militarist quotes from European thinkers such as Voltaire and prominent anarchist writers such as Elise Reclus.[272] The most well-known publication of the school was *The Adventures of Nono* by Jean Grave, in which a small child embarked upon a series of 'laboriously allegorical experiences' through the fantasy world of 'Autonomy'—where animals talk and the people are free, happy and good—and the miserable land of 'Agriocracy,' ruled over by a despotic King, capitalism, the military and the police.[273] When the book appeared in early 1902 it was well received by the anarchist press, including *Tierra y Libertad*, which declared it a 'beauty'.[274] *The Adventures of Nono* was also very popular in the Escuela itself, and went through at least six editions over the following ten years.[275] The Escuela maintained a presence in the movement through these publications, which carried Ferrer's ideas to areas outside Barcelona, where few had access to the type of advanced schooling he offered.[276] In subsequent years, many publishing groups followed the example of the Escuela and began to supply schools and centres with textbooks. The 'Archivo Social' in Tenerife, for example, offered a range of books at a discount price for anarchist centres, including the complete works of Victor Hugo, histories of France and ancient Greece, biology textbooks, and a biography of Garibaldi.[277]

The Escuela Moderna was a substantial achievement and stands as the high-point of the movement's educational programme. Ferrer's school was an inspiration for many within the movement, such as the 'Trabajo y Voluntad' educational group in Santa Cruz de Tenerife, which aimed to 'adopt the same [methods and procedures] as the Escuela Moderna of Barcelona'.[278] Numerous other modern schools opened in the wake of the Escuela, predominantly in Cataluña. By Pere Solà's data, 44 secular and rational schools opened in Spain in the following decade, 24 of which were in the province of Barcelona and a further six in the provinces of Tarragona and Gerona (both Cataluña), some of which were direct branches of the original Escuela.[279] The strength of the Modern School movement in Cataluña was demonstrated on Good Friday (April 12) 1906, when Ferrer led a procession of 1,700 children to the Tibiado Park on the outskirts of Barcelona, where they held a picnic and 'secular commemorative exercises'.[280] Ferrer's reputation as a pioneer of radical education was not, however, cemented only by the success of the Escuela, but also by its collapse, and his later martyrdom.[281] In 1906, Mateo Morral, an employee at the Escuela Moderna, attempted to assassinate King Alfonso XIII.[282] Ferrer was accused of conspiring with Morral and was arrested, and although he was eventually absolved, his school was permanently closed.[283] Three years later, Ferrer was executed after being found guilty of the (unconvincing) charge of having orchestrated the Barcelona Tragic Week. He was immediately made a martyr by freethinking circles across Europe and the Americas, which elevated his work in the previous decade to almost mythical status.[284] He has since been the main, and often the only, subject of study for historians of anarchist education in turn-of-the-century Spain.[285]

Outside Cataluña, followers of Ferrer began to open Modern Schools only after the original Barcelona Escuela was closed. In 1907 a new Escuela Moderna opened in Valencia, in a modest building (c.150m²), consisting of a single large classroom and a small adjacent library.[286] The school was run by Samuel Torner, an educator from Majorca who had previously worked with Ferrer in Barcelona.[287] Like the Barcelona Escuela, it offered co-education and rejected examinations. Although its curriculum had much in common with other schools, offering languages, mathematics, geography, history and the sciences, it also provided courses in manual work, agricultural labour and physical education, which were not common school subjects, even in other radical educational institutions.[288] Toner made efforts to make his school more inclusive than the Barcelona Escuela, and, like Ricardo Mella, he believed that the Ferrer had been overly dogmatic in his educational approach and sought a more 'neutral' method of schooling.[289] Although teaching was suspended on a number of occasions, the Valencia Escuela continued as the most tangible example of the programme advocated by Ferrer outside Cataluña, until its final closure in 1926.

A year after the Valencia Escuela opened, Torner's periodical *Humanidad Nueva* released a special issue dedicated to the Modern Schools, honouring the Barcelona Escuela and Ferrer for having 'inaugurated a new education, whose expansion could not be halted'.[290] This issue contained reports on over 20 'modern' and 'rational' schools which had been founded across Spain, including letters from school directors and photographs of students. Although the majority were based in Cataluña, above all in Barcelona, a handful of schools were founded in other areas, such as Zaragoza, Algeciras and Cullera (Valencia). Like Toner, many of those who ran these schools were self-declared anarchists, including Federico Forcada, who ran schools in Irún (Gipuzkoa) and Valladolid, and José Sánchez Rosa, who founded the 'Agrupación Escolar de Enseñanza Racionalista' in Aznalcollár (Sevilla) in 1905.[291] Many of these smaller 'Modern' schools were affected by legislation passed by the Ministry of Public Education in January 1907, which sought to regulate and inspect primary education.[292] Sánchez Rosa's school, for example, was deemed unfit for purpose and was closed, although he continued to provide lessons in the homes of local workers.[293] The movement also continued to produce educational literature in the style of Ferrer's publishing house. Inspired by the output of the Escuela Moderna, from 1909 onwards Sánchez Rosa began to produce his own educational pamphlets on subjects such as arithmetic and grammar, which became 'almost obligatory for any workers' centre of libertarian tendencies'.[294] Similarly, other educators began to produce educational periodicals in the manner of the *Boletín de la Escuela Moderna*, most notably Toner's *Humanidad Nueva* and *Esculea Moderna* (Valencia, 1910–1911, 71 issues), and Forcada's *La Enseñanza Moderna*, (Irún, 1908–1909, 9 issues), *La Enseñanza Moderna* (Valladolid, 1910, 3 issues) and *Esculea Libre*, (Valladolid, 1911, 3 issues).

Local Schools

The relative success of the Escuela Moderna of Barcelona was not typical. Many of the elements which made the Escuela possible—international links, available space, and assistance of experienced, radical educators— were not available to other educational centres. Outside Cataluña, most anarchist 'schools' were little more than rooms, with 'no equipment or trained personnel'.[295] These rooms were frequently used for other purposes. In Ronda (Málaga) the anarchist educational centre was shared with the local bakers and quarrymen, while in Cádiz a school for the children of local workers was based in the meeting room of the city's metalworkers' society.[296] Other anarchist 'schools' and 'centres' were spaces within larger educational establishments, such as the 'Centre for Social Studies' founded within the La Coruña secular school in 1901–1902, and the 'Mundo Libre' centre in Langreo (Asturias)—where 'all the children of the pueblo can learn what is good and what is sane'—which was based within the larger republican *ateneo*.[297]

The movement's periodicals were crucial in establishing support for new educational spaces. One project for a school in Cádiz attracted support from almost all the leading anarchists in Spain following a campaign published in the city's anarchist papers *El Proletario* and *Germinal*.[298] These papers also published messages of support from figures from across Europe, including former Communard Louise Michel (then in London), the sociologist Augustin Hamón (in Neuilly-Sur-Seine) and historian Dr Konrad Haebler (in Dresden).[299] Again, this emphasises the importance of print to the functioning of the movement. Without *El Proletario* and *Germinal*, the Cádiz school project would have been isolated from potential support in Spain and abroad. Yet the city's anarchist press ensured that the ambitions of local activists were plugged into a national and international network of like-minded individuals, who shared an appreciation of education as a revolutionary tactic and wanted to see it in action wherever possible.

Figures involved in publishing frequently helped to set up and run schools, employing their skills in written propaganda, good levels of literacy, and the ability to comprehend and communicate complex ideas to audiences with little or no formal education. Teachers and publishers were thus important figures in local contexts, where they performed multiple roles within anarchist communities. For example, the commission for the La Coruña educational centre was led by Enrique Taboada, who worked on the editorial of the city's 'Biblioteca El Sol' and was a co-founder of both the 'Biblioteca La Internacional' (1911–1914) and the 'Biblioteca Aurora', while also serving as the secretary of the local sailors' union.[300] Urales, a former teacher himself, left *Tierra y Libertad* in the hands of two secular teachers, Francisco Sola and Abelardo Saavedra in 1904.[301] The Basque correspondent Vicente García also ran a free school in Sestao (Vizcaya) in 1900, which was based in the local republican *ateneo* before moving to a more suitable and 'hygienic' building.[302] Despite having no background in education, García made do with his 'will to teach' and subscription to educational journals.[303] Formal training was thus unnecessary to educators like García, as the anarchist conception of education was much broader and less tangible than that of the official education system. The connection between publishers and teachers continued in the following years. For example, Eleuterio Quintanilla—a key figure in the Asturian CNT until the Civil War—taught languages and ran the library of the Gijón *ateneo* from 1904 onwards, before publishing a string of papers in the city, including *Tribuna Libre* (1909), *Acción Libertaria* (1910–1911; 1915–1916) and *El Libertario* (1912–1913).[304]

Reports of these schools in the press often contained only small snippets of information, making it difficult to reconstruct a thorough account of local anarchist schooling.[305] Notices in the press usually discussed one-off events at schools, as when 200 students in Algeciras were visited by the pardoned prisoners of the 1892 Jerez uprising. The students reportedly met these 'martyrs' with cries of '*¡viva la acracia!*', entertained their guests with speeches against religion, and were rewarded with sweets from their teachers for this demonstration of their 'good education'.[306] While such teaching methods were derided by critics of the movement, for local anarchist educators it was liberation, as it provided children with the foundations for a 'scientific,' critical mentality. Without more detailed sources it is hard to evaluate the quality of education provided in these local contexts. The blanket condemnation of anarchist schools as 'centres of sedition' by their critics overlooks the real benefits that this education could potentially have on the lives of working class children, particularly in areas where access to any form of schooling was limited.[307] On the other hand, reports in the anarchist press almost certainly exaggerated the impact of these schools on the 'moral' (education as a political strategy, designed to pass on anarchist ideology) and 'material' (education as the teaching of practical skills, such as literacy) development of their students, and the numbers they claimed to reach. It is likely that far fewer students attended these schools than was reported, and those that did attend received an education which was never as straightforward as either enlightenment or indoctrination.

One of the better-documented schools was based in the Centre for Social Studies in La Línea de la Concepción (Cádiz), a large town of around 40,000 on the Spanish border with Gibraltar.[308] At the turn of the century a series of initiatives in La Línea caught the attention of Ernesto Álvarez, the former editor of *La Anarquía* and *La Idea Libre*, who was at that time living in Valladolid. Álvarez was particularly interested in the local workers' centre, which had been dominated by anarchist workers' societies and 70 members of a local 'feminist section' since its foundation in 1898.[309] Álvarez's current publication, *La Protesta*, praised the work of the centre in improving the moral condition of the La Línea workers, particularly in reducing alcohol consumption and petty crime.[310] In 1901 the centre opened a school within its premises, which was inaugurated by poetry readings and the unveiling of portraits of Fermín Salvochea and Emile Zola, alongside a large banner bearing the frontispiece of the *Suplemento*. Lectures were given by local comrades on subjects such as God, State and Capital, and the history of the 'supposed' Mano Negra (which was greeted with cries of '*¡Viva la Anarquía!*'). Within hours it was impossible to enter the building, where a large crowd had gathered, including 'numerous representatives of the feminine sex'.[311]

In May 1901 Álvarez accepted a position as a teacher in the school, which provided his accommodation and paid him 25 pesetas a month from the membership fees of local societies.[312] He brought his periodical with him as he relocated 400 miles south, re-establishing *La Protesta* in the La Línea workers' centre. By the end of the year the school was holding classes in reading and writing for around 180 children—more than Ferrer's Escuela Moderna ever taught at one time—and was expanding into adult education in grammar, science and arithmetic. Álvarez also ran French night classes, in which the method of teaching and classroom rules were decided by the students. Another teacher, Gabriela Alcalde, ran night classes for women in embroidery and needlework.[313] Such classes were designed to provide skills which would give women economic independence, helping them to find work outside domestic service.[314] They also provided an alternative to similar projects run by the Church, ensuring that their students developed a 'sane and altruistic morality, full of love towards all of humanity,' in contrast to Catholic women's schools 'where they dull the senses and make the woman a slave and not the true comrade of the man'.[315] By 1902 the school was reportedly offering an education to 400 children and 22 adults from La Línea and the surrounding *campo*.[316]

Álvarez fell ill in the spring of 1902 and was forced to retire. His colleagues in *La Protesta* took over editorial responsibility and set up a collection to cover his medical expenses.[317] His absence came at a time of intense financial difficulty for the paper, which was forced to suspend publication in June that year.[318] Álvarez died on 5 October and was buried in La Línea in a 'modest pine coffin,' accompanied by a reported 5,000 people.[319] Reports of this event appeared in every anarchist paper in print, which praised Álvarez's humble nature and his commitment to spreading the anarchist message.[320]

The La Línea school closed only days after Álvarez's death. Over the summer of 1902 anarchists and workers' groups in Sevilla had agitated for city-wide general strikes across Andalucía, demanding that the provincial governor re-open centres which had been closed since 1901. A strike in Sevilla on 9 October was a failure, although workers in towns such as Algeciras took to the streets in solidarity.[321] The first mass public protest in the history of La Línea was also called, as workers' societies petitioned the local mayor for the right to demonstrate in solidarity with the Sevilla strike. This was denied, and the centre was closed on 8 October. The following day thousands of men, women and children assembled around Calle Pedreras to protest. As the local Civil Guard attempted to disperse the crowds they were met with a hail of stones and possibly some revolver shots. Their response was to fire on the crowd, which left five dead and the same number seriously injured. The protesters then split up and began attacking public buildings. In response, a state of war was declared in the town and the authorities began indiscriminately arresting workers.[322] The centre and the school remained closed, and a number of those arrested spent lengthy spells in prison.[323] Yet this did not stop the commitment to educational practice in La Línea. In 1903 a new centre was opened in the town, named 'El Porvenir', which began running twice-weekly conferences and lectures on subjects such as 'Democracy and Anarchism,' which were regarded as 'true acts of sociological propaganda'.[324]

The problems faced by the La Línea school were common to all anarchist educational projects. Many struggled to open at all, as they required legal approval which was often denied by local public officials, almost all of whom owed their position to patronage and clientelism.[325] These networks of local power—named *caciquismo* (from the word *cacique* meaning local political 'boss')—were characterised by opaque dealings and corruption. *Caciquismo* was loathed by all sections of progressive Spanish society, including the anarchists, who felt their legal rights of association were stifled by personal enmity towards the movement from local employers and the Church.[326] Conflicts with local authorities regarding locales and schools were publicised in the anarchist press to rouse indignation and spur further activity.[327] In 1901, for example, a group in the small pueblo of Jimena de la Frontera (Cádiz) attempted to found a centre to provide education to children of the surrounding *campo*. Their efforts were stifled through weeks of petty obstruction by the local mayor, who claimed to have lost the statues for the centre and could therefore not approve them.[328] The centre was eventually opened and named 'La Razón,' which contained a small school, yet was closed shortly afterwards by the mayor because the building was deemed to be 'unhygienic'—the most common reason given by local authorities for such decisions—and because the school's 'maestro,' Manuel Canas Guerrero, denied the existence of God in one of his lessons.[329] Once established, centres became a subject of enquiry and interference. In Morón de la Frontera (Sevilla), an anarchist agricultural workers' centre was closed after a strike in the town, as it was seen (probably with good reason) as a source of worker agitation.[330] In another incident, a centre based in Zaragoza was visited by a representative of the local governor and two 'secret policemen', who demanded access to the membership lists of the societies based there, including the anarchist workers' federation 'La Autonomía'. In accordance with their legal rights, the centre's administrative secretary refused, leading to a spat with the governor and the threat of closure.[331]

Centres and schools also faced internal problems, above all, a crippling lack of funds. According to one professor at the University of Barcelona, all one needed to open a school in Spain in the early twentieth century was '"money, money, money,"' which was the one thing anarchist schools lacked above all else.[332] Unlike the Escuela Moderna, most anarchist educational spaces did not have external funding. Their fees were also much smaller—for example, one school in Linares (Jaén) charged 5 céntimos a day—which was paid for either by parents, through subscriptions managed by local papers, or through membership fees of workers' associations.[333] They ran on a shoestring budget, and made frequent requests to the anarchist press for support.[334] Some centres, as in Manzanares, ran at a small profit and established a reserve fund for future expenses. Unfortunately, such funds were often stolen or quickly exhausted in the event of strikes or legal proceedings.[335] Many schools also lacked books to carry out lessons and sent requests through the anarchist press for spare materials.[336] Publishing groups linked donors to schools, maintaining a supply of unused textbooks, folders, picture cards, atlases, reading primers, pamphlets, periodicals, and journals, as well as clothes for students from poor families.[337] Periodicals also helped to match up teachers with schools, carrying adverts for vacancies and available staff, such as the qualified teacher who worked for *El Corsario* (Valencia), who had been forced to leave his job in mainstream education following an 'underhand war' waged against his 'free ideas' by 'filthy politicians'.[338]

Schools and centres also suffered from internal disputes. In Puerto Real, for example, the Society of Social Studies broke apart following an argument between 'libertarians' and a local 'charlatan'.[339] Arguments about the proper use of centres could also flare up between anarchists and rival groups who shared the premises, as in the early days of the Gijón workers' centre, which eventually led to the creation of separate socialist and anarchist locales.[340] Disputes over newspapers in mixed centres were common, as in Logroño, where the president of the supposed 'apolitical' workers' centre banned the reading of the anarchist *Tierra y Libertad* and *El Rebelde*, and suggested that members should read the socialist *El Obrero* and *La Lucha de Clases* instead.[341] As in the case of the workers' groups who ended their subscription with Lerroux's *Progreso* in 1901 discussed above, the conflict between ideologies within the Logroño centre was articulated in arguments over print, which was the prime means by which the groups defined themselves and their relationship with the wider socialist, anarchist and republican movements.

Problems could also develop between anarchist groups within centres and schools. Although education was presented as a unifying ambition within the anarchist movement, tensions over its proper application surfaced when groups attempted to put their ideas into practice. Like anarchism itself, education was a loose, multifaceted concept, without a set doctrine or strategy for implementation. Papers, groups and individuals all had their own ideas about how education should be valued and understood, and, without a universally-accepted figure or text to give direction on the matter, disagreements were rarely settled amicably. In Sevilla, for example, the Centro Instructivo Obrero Hispalense was the site of constant arguments between those who advocated educational methods and a group of anti-intellectual 'intransigents' who demanded immediate revolutionary action.[342]

Schools could also suffer from a lack of engagement with their local community. In Cádiz, for example, one sociology lecture was so badly attended that local militant Manuel de los Reyes used the local anarchist periodical *El Proletario* to publically denounce the 'cowards' and 'traitors' who had failed to show up. De los Reyes was incredulous, asking his apathetic colleagues 'why do you not frequent the society where they are able and want to educate you, and not the taverns that are nothing more than centres of corruption? . . . why do you not school yourselves?'[343] Similarly, the directors of a school based within the Aznalcóllar (Sevilla) workers' centre were incensed when no 'mothers' enrolled their children for lessons in early 1904. In an angry letter to *El Rebelde* (Madrid) the directors warned these 'ignorant' parents that they would be 'culpable' when their children 'become murderers of their comrades'.[344] Even in areas where the movement was strong, workers continued to enjoy the 'vices' attacked in the anarchist press, and remained largely indifferent to campaigns against alcohol, smoking, fiestas and bull-fighting.[345] This lack of commitment to the cause revealed the fragilities of a movement based on individual conviction. As support for anarchism ebbed and flowed, only the most dedicated, educated militants could be relied upon to maintain the message of the movement in local contexts.

Taken as a whole, efforts to realise educational ambitions increased significantly in the early years of the twentieth century. Yet this was not a linear story of success. Centres and schools opened, closed and reappeared with regularity.[346] Waves of repression forced the closure of many anarchist spaces, often on the basis that they were 'unhygienic,' or the more substantive charge that they were 'seditious' and 'blasphemous'. Many of the conditions which affected anarchist spaces were specific to local contexts, such as the activity of the local movement, the availability of funds and the attitude of local authorities. Educational practice therefore had multiple rhythms and trends, with no one clear chronology which encompassed the entire movement. Andalucía, in particular the Cádiz region, saw a dramatic spike in educational efforts from 1900 onwards. Writing in La Línea in 1901, Ernesto Álvarez saw this upsurge of educational practice as a source of optimism and pride, and upon hearing of the opening of a school in Puerto Real he declared 'andando se prueba el movimiento' ['actions speak louder than words'], seeing the newfound energy and activity in the field of education as emblematic of a 'resurrection' of anarchism in Spain.[347] Yet by 1903 most of these efforts had been curtailed, as anarchism in Andalucía once again attracted hostility from local and regional authorities.[348] In contrast, in La Coruña, the 'Germinal' centre was established somewhat later than those in Cádiz province, yet managed to maintain a more stable existence than locales in other areas, providing the anarchists of the city with a base of operations well into the twentieth century.

Both Modern Schools and smaller scale educational centres continued to emerge over the following years. These initiatives were later endorsed by the CNT at every national congress, affirming the movement's continuing commitment to the initiatives which took shape over the turn of the century. During the Second Republic, particularly in the early stages of the Civil War, schools continued to represent the pinnacle of anarchist education in practice.[349] These developments were built on the cultural infrastructure established over the turn of the century, both by the theorists and pedagogues of the Escuela Moderna and, more importantly in many areas, the local militants who wanted to teach their children and comrades how to read.[350]

Organisation and Collapse

Organisation and education were complementary strategies for the anarchist movement. In an anarchist understanding, the Spanish working class required education in order to recognise the malicious influence of capitalism. 'Ignorance' of these matters was regarded as the main reason for the passivity of the majority of the Spanish people. Workers could be deceived by their employers, or misguided by the incorrect analysis provided by rival progressive movements, especially the socialists of the PSOE and UGT.[351] What was required was a 'true,' 'reasoned' interpretation of labour organisation, which corresponded to the broader principles of anarchism. After 1899 workers' organisations expanded dramatically across Spain. Anarchists saw this as a source of immense potential, which could be directed towards mass revolutionary activity, prompting a return to the debates surrounding collective action which had largely been abandoned during the 1890s.[352] The number of articles concerning 'organisation' and 'association' exploded in the anarchist press after 1899, while anarchist unions formed in a number of areas, employing the discourse of the anarchist press to articulate labour struggles.[353] Yet workers' societies alone were not enough. A growing number of anarchist activists sought a national federation of workers' groups, which could articulate 'collective needs, collective ideas [and] collective ends'.[354]

Following two failed attempts to fashion a national federation in the winter of 1899–1900, a third project, entitled the Federación Regional de Sociedades de Resistencia de la Región España (FSORE) was inaugurated in Madrid in October 1900.[355] Like its predecessors the FRE and FTRE, the FSORE was a federal organisation, built up by local and regional 'societies of resistance to capital' (unions). Although it was initially a politically 'mixed' organisation, and contained many republican societies and figures—including Lerroux and the Badajoz 'Germinal' centre— the organisation was soon dominated by anarchist workers' groups.[356] Between 1900 and 1903 the FSORE briefly stood as a source of pride for the anarchist movement: a 70,000 strong federation of workers, which operated on anarchist organisational principles and was imbued with anarchist revolutionary rhetoric.[357] This was more than double the size of the UGT at this time (Sep. 1901: 31,558 affiliates), a fact not lost on anarchist commentators such as Sidón Sequano, who wrote to *La Protesta* to praise the FSORE and proclaim its growing strength as a 'symptom of death' for the 'political socialists'.[358]

Like its predecessors, much of the FSORE's membership was concentrated in Cataluña. Support from outside this region was far from 'meagre'—constituting around 60 per cent of federated societies—but it was more diffuse, based in provinces including Cádiz (9 per cent), Málaga (5.5 per cent), Valencia (5 per cent), Murcia (5 per cent), Asturias (4.5 per cent) and Madrid (3 per cent).[359] Yet despite the optimism generated by the creation of the FSORE, the organisation failed to inscribe itself in the daily life of its members and was unable to instigate, coordinate, or support actions such as strikes and protests. A failed general strike in Barcelona in early 1902 was particularly damaging to the organisation, as it resulted in the repression of organised labour across the whole of Spain.[360] Many of the FSORE's key activists were imprisoned and its newly-adopted tactic of the general strike had proved to be an utter failure.[361] Support for the FSORE soon drained from most anarchist periodicals, as groups and individuals who had previously called for a national organisation now began to assert that anarchism was incompatible with union structures.[362] The most significant blow came in 1903, when *Tierra y Libertad* dropped its support for the federation, stating that any attempt to unify the anarchists of Spain was hypocritical.[363] A year later support for the FSORE had waned dramatically and it was reduced to a shell of an organisation, whose formal dissolution in 1907 went largely unnoticed by the anarchist press.[364]

The Return of Violence

It was not only the FSORE which suffered during this period. In the summer of 1903 a wave of strikes broke out in the agricultural towns of Cádiz province, followed by the arrest of labour leaders and a media blackout. In response, a general strike was called in the town of Alcalá del Valle on 1 August, which led to violent confrontations with the Civil Guard. A 15-year-old boy was killed and several townspeople were wounded in these clashes, and the local archives were burned down. The response from the local authorities surpassed anything seen since the repression of the 1890s. Over 100 *alcalareños* were arrested and sent to prison in Ronda (Málaga), where many were tortured—including the infliction of genital mutilation, which was claimed to have caused the death of two prisoners—in an effort to discover who had planned the strike. Leaders of workers' societies across Andalucía were arrested, workers' centres and newspapers were closed, and anarchist figures fled the province. The movement in Cádiz was forced underground, and did not recover its strength for almost a decade.[365]

The repression in Alcalá brought the discourses of state violence and martyrdom back into a prominent position in the anarchist press.[366] The condemned were immediately embedded into a discourse of martyrs and inquisition almost identical to that of the 1890s.[367] Individual violence also returned at this time. The first act of anarchist 'propaganda by the deed' since 1897 took place in April 1904, when Prime Minister Antonio Maura was (non-fatally) stabbed by the 19-year-old Joaquín Miguel Artal during a royal visit to Barcelona. Like Pallás in 1893, Artal stayed at the scene and cried 'Viva la Anarquia!' as he was arrested, and remained unrepentant throughout his trial.[368] In a letter sent to the anarchist press, Artal explained that he had been motivated by the 'cries of pain from the tortured of Alcalá del Valle' that resonated in his ears.[369] Resentment of Maura ran deep throughout the movement. Like Cánovas in the 1890s, he was seen as directly responsible for repression and was cast as the personification of the inquisitorial nature of the Spanish state. In an open letter to the anarchist press, one group in La Línea stated that if Artal had succeeded, Maura's death would have represented 'a triumph towards human emancipation'.[370] Yet Artal was not martyred, nor did his act of violence leave a lasting mark upon the movement. Unlike the prisoners of Alcalá and former terrorists such as Pallás, Artal did not receive any special collections or particular attention in the anarchist press. No pamphlets were written in his name and no campaign was launched for his release. He remained in prison in Ceuta, where he died in 1909.[371]

Artal's attack came at a time when discourses of violence were returning to the anarchist press. As the failures of the FSORE revealed the weakness of anarchist efforts to organise the working class, there was a brief flourishing of individualist-anarchist papers, which sought to promote the writings of Friedrich Nietzsche within the movement.[372] Nietzsche had previously been treated with caution by anarchists. His philosophy was 'good at destruction' but lacked 'a sense of human solidarity,' and was fundamentally at odds with the anarchist conception of the future society.[373] For his own part, Nietzsche had claimed to loathe anarchism, which he saw as an extreme version of Judeo-Christian 'slave-mentality' and 'poisoned at the root by the pestiferous weed of *ressentiment* and the spiteful politics of the weak and pitiful'.[374]

Despite this mutual antagonism, a string of anarchist papers in Spain tried to rehabilitate Nietzsche's works from 1903 onwards. The first of these papers, *Juventud* (Valencia, 1903), regarded Nietzsche as 'the most brilliant thinker of the last quarter of a century'.[375] Despite his lack of understanding of 'Love' [sic], Nietzsche had recognised that the revolution was not 'solely a simple economic question,' but also one of individual perfection, which was incompatible with contemporary Christian society.[376] This led *Juventud* to valorise 'great art' and the appraisal of science as the first step towards a new society, framing education and self-enlightenment as a revolutionary act.[377] The caution of *Juventud* towards labour activism was shared by *Luz y Vida* (Santa Cruz de Tenerife, 1905–1907), which labelled all organisations which 'did not respond to the free and spontaneous will' as anti-anarchist.[378] This paper spoke highly of Nietzsche and published several extracts from his works.[379] Unlike *Juventud*, however, this paper saw education as a waste of time, stating that 'neither philosophy, nor art, nor science, are enough . . . to liberate ourselves from . . . the black physiological inheritance' of Christianity.[380] The paper called for revolutionary 'action,' 'energy' and 'will,' and was one of the very few papers of the period to explicitly valorise terrorism.[381] Likewise, the most ardently Nietzschean paper of the period, the short-lived *Anticristo* (La Línea de la Concepción, 1906), was critical of the movement's 'superficial and dogmatic' veneration of 'sociology,' and saw nothing of value in the 'idiotic class struggle'.[382] Instead, the paper saw Nietzsche's thought as a means of rejuvenating the 'old anarchism,' which had become as 'mystified' as Christianity, enthralled to passive subjection, exemplified by its obsession with education.[383] *Anticristo* was one of the most tonally distinct anarchist periodicals published over the turn of the century, with its bombastic, misogynistic language and aggressive grandstanding that was entirely at odds with the majority of the movement's press. The sense of superiority emanating from the paper was, however, slightly undercut by a letter written by its editors to *El Productor*, which apologised for the large number spelling mistakes in its first issue.[384] These papers represented only a small minority of the anarchist movement. Nevertheless, their appearance from 1903 onwards was indicative of a growing discomfort with the perceived 'orthodox' anarchist position of the early twentieth century, leading to a growing prominence of dissenting voices which called for a return to immediate revolutionary action.

Division and Fragility

Over the turn of the century the anarchist movement in Spain relied upon the loose, decentred system sustained by print culture, rather than the formal structures of a labour organisation. As has been shown, print was essential in binding the movement together around the strategy of education during the movement's recovery and expansion. This had created elites, whose position in the movement was based upon their standing in print culture, both in local contexts, in the form of correspondents to the press and the educated *obreros conscientes*, and on a national level, where the leading figures of the movement coalesced around important publications. One of these national figures was Antonio Apolo, a typographer working at the Imprenta de Antonio Marzo, which published both *La Revista Blanca* and its *Suplemento*. Apolo also wrote for *El Progreso*, until he fell out spectacularly with its editor Lerroux. Apolo subsequently published a pamphlet which portrayed his former employer as an ostentatious liar and a drunk, who had used the campaign for the release of the Montjuich prisoners simply to advance his own position and make money.[385]

Apolo remained with the editorial of the *Suplemento* as it was transformed into *Tierra y Libertad* in 1902, where he was joined by Julio Camba, who had recently returned to Spain after being expelled from Argentina.[386] Like the *Suplemento*, *Tierra y Libertad* acted as the unofficial 'central' publication of the movement. It instigated the major campaigns of the time and managed the huge subscription funds which had been on-going since 1899. Confident that it had enough support from the movement for expansion, *Tierra y Libertad* was transformed into a daily in August 1903.[387] This move brought with it an unsustainable strain on the paper's finances. After just four months the paper returned to a weekly publication, and disappeared altogether the following August.[388] The failure to sustain a daily *Tierra y Libertad* provoked bitter recriminations within the paper's former publishing group, and in December 1903 Apolo and Camba left the paper and launched their own publication, *El Rebelde*. In response, Urales used *Tierra y Libertad* to publically attack *El Rebelde* and its editors, who he blamed for the failure of his project. He claimed that Apolo and Camba had turned up to work late, smoked all day, did as little work as possible and spent their evenings 'having coffee with the *intellectuals*'.[389] He later labelled Apolo a 'cancer within Spanish anarchism'.[390] As these arguments intensified, an increasing portion of the movement turned against the Urales group and attacked them through periodicals and pamphlets, such as the scathing *Por la muerte de los ídolos*.[391] Urales and Gustavo soon stepped back from anarchist print culture. *La Revista Blanca* folded in 1905, while *Tierra y Libertad* was re-launched under a new editorial group, the '4th May,' which included the educators Francisco González Sola and Albelardo Saavedra del Toro, but neither Urales nor Gustavo.[392] A year and half later, this new editorial was arrested as part of a wave of repression against anarchist publishers, which had intensified after Morall's attack on Alfonso XIII. As anarchist publishing in the capital became increasingly unsustainable, González Sola and Saavedra left Spain for Cuba, where they were influential in the development of anarchist education and wrote for the Havana periodical *¡Tierra!*, before being deported back to Spain in 1911 and 1912 respectively.[393] *Tierra y Libertad* relocated to Barcelona, where it became one of the most successful and prominent publications in the history of the movement.[394]

Apolo and Camba asked former contributors and correspondents of *Tierra y Libertad* to align themselves to their new publication, with the hope of becoming the 'platform of all anarchists'.[395] Like *Tierra y Libertad*, *El Rebelde* positioned itself as a campaigning publication, filling every issue with reports of arrests, trials, protests against repression and letters from imprisoned comrades. The paper reflected the state of the movement in 1904, which had been battered by repeated waves of arrests, failed strikes and the closure of centres.[396] *El Rebelde* also voiced a growing dissent against the hegemonic status of 'education' within Spanish anarchism. Contributors, including Apolo and Camba wrote scathing articles against the 'platonic passivity' which had developed within the movement, which had led to endless theorising about how to '*intellectualise ourselves*' at the expense of the 'principal object' of revolution.[397] In the words of a later observer of this period, the movement had done little more than foster a 'cult of reason,' which was useless in the face of repression and left it exposed as 'decadent' and toothless while 'the prisons continually devour comrades'.[398] In February 1904 Camba declared that 'we have had too much culture, too much education . . . while our brain evolved in an ascendant sense our muscles were losing their all-powerful strength'.[399]

El Rebelde was constantly denounced, and its editors spent stretches in prison following the publication of inflammatory articles.[400] Its editors were bullish in their response to their constant harassment by the police, wearing their denunciations—35 of which were made against in paper its first 50 issues—and prison sentences as a badge of honour.[401] Despite these severe pressures, the paper survived much longer than most of its contemporaries, and managed to establish a solid print-run of around 8,000 copies by mid-1904.[402] Yet six months later *El Rebelde* folded, following financial problems caused by non-paying correspondents. Apolo, who had once believed himself and his paper to be 'all powerful,' now saw himself as a failure: a 'César, who crossed the Rubicon . . . brought to a standstill before a dungheap'.[403] Apolo had little further input into anarchist print culture, or the movement in general.[404] This collapse, followed by the departure of *Tierra y Libertad* marked the end of Madrid's brief status as the centre of anarchist publishing in Spain.

When divisions were accommodated, as in 1899–1903, an informal system of publishers and local correspondents helped the movement to expand in size and scope. Yet when the elites of this system fell out, the movement had no means to mediate or resolve issues and the fragility of its structure was left exposed. Publishers turned on one another, publically undermining their erstwhile comrades and provoking rifts between rival groups of readers. The last time that these issues had emerged was during the late 1880s and early 1890s, when anarcho-collectivists and communists used their papers to attack one another, contributing to the collapse of the FTRE and the fragmentation of the movement into rival camps. The divisions of 1903 onwards had a similar result. The movement fragmented, and many supporters were left exasperated by internal bickering. Looking back on this period, a former correspondent to *El Rebelde* based in Cartagena labelled these disputes as evidence of the

'ruin' of Spanish anarchism, which sparked an exodus from the anarchist movement towards the socialists and republicans in the movement's
strongholds of Sevilla, Cádiz, Gijón and Barcelona.[405]

After the dramatic recovery of anarchism over the turn of the century,
the movement started to overreach itself, inviting external repression and
internal disputes. By 1903 these pressures had eroded many of the movement's foundations. Education had been a unifying strategy, but there
was still a long way to go before it could be seen as a success. A sense of
stagnation hung over the movement. Correspondents wrote of the 'apathy' of local workers, who were little more than 'animated corpses,' while
their centres had been left as 'necropolises'.[406] The decline of the movement was accompanied by a contraction in anarchist publishing. After
years of relative tolerance, the press was targeted for repression and editors imprisoned for breaches of the law of publications.[407] This added to
a reversal of the dramatic growth of anarchist publishing seen in previous years, so much so that by 1907 the number of anarchist periodicals
in Spain was around half that of 1905 [refer to Chart 0.2]. It appeared
that only the dedicated remained in the movement, as the surge in anarchist support after 1899 drained away, replaced by indifference from the
Spanish working class. One letter sent to *El Rebelde* in 1904 summed up
the problems with the movement at this time, claiming that the movement had failed because the Spanish working class remained 'politically
castrated' and unable to understand the ideas of anarchism. Despite all
the advances of the previous years, the workers still required 'free Education [sic.] . . . to assure the liberty of the man of tomorrow and of today;
permanent propaganda action and action in all of the populaces of Spain
by the meeting, the newspaper, the pamphlet, the book [and] the conference'. Only then could the 'weak cries and partial protests' of anarchism
transform into a revolutionary force.[408]

Despite the despondent tone of this letter, anarchism in Spain had come
a long way since the late 1890s. Its educational practices had proliferated
across Spain, increasing the scope of the movement beyond any previous
point in its history. While the FSORE was a failure, the cultural framework which underpinned the expansion of the movement from 1899–
1906 was a lasting and important success. The ideas of anarchism had
developed and spread into new areas, largely as a result of the efforts of
figures connected to the print culture. Centres and schools had formed,
grounding anarchist practice in hundreds of localities across the country.
Many of these practices faltered in the face of repression, but the movement was never in danger of complete collapse as it had been a decade earlier. This was because anarchists resumed activity in 1907, drawing upon
their experiences over the turn of the century, re-founding centres and
schools, and forming new publishing groups and periodicals. All of this
activity drew upon the networks and ideas that had been established from
1899 onwards. If we want to understand how anarchism became a mass

movement in Spain in the twentieth century we must look to these years, in which the movement looked to 'educate', expand and develop. Print culture was at the heart of this process, carrying the ideas and providing a structure for anarchism in Spain. In future years the CNT would come to absorb and formalise many of the roles performed by the anarchist press at this time. This task was far from easy; many anarchist individuals and groups were unwilling to leave behind the plural, dispersed, and grassroots structure of the press which had shaped the movement during its recovery. It took years of conflict, compromise and negotiation, mediated through the anarchist press, for the movement to accept this change.

Notes

1. See comments on the relaxation of the law in *Suplemento a la Revista Blanca* (Madrid), 8 September, 1900, 4; 8 December, 1900, 4; 19 January, 1900, 4. See also Gonzalo Rojas Sánchez, 'Legislación sobre asociaciones anarquistas en España: 1890–1910,' *Revista Chilena de Derecho* 8 (1981): 79.
2. *Suplemento a la Revista Blanca* (Madrid), 5 August, 1899, 2.
3. Francisco Madrid Santos, 'La prensa anarquista y anarcosindicalista en España desde la I Internacional hasta el fin de la Guerra Civil,' (PhD thesis, Barcelona: Universidad Central de Barcelona, 1988–89), 145.
4. Key studies which exclude this period include George Esenwein, *Anarchist Ideology and the Working-Class Movement in Spain, 1868–1898* (Berkeley: University of California Press, 1989), while others which cover the period as part of a broader, pre-CNT timeframe, for example José Álvarez Junco, *La ideología política del anarquismo español (1868–1910)* (Madrid: Siglo XXI, 1991) and Lily Litvak, *Musa libertaria: Arte, literatura y vida cultural del anarquismo español (1890–1913)* (Madrid: Fundación de Estudios Libertarios Anselmo Lorenzo, 2001).
5. For example see Antonio Bar, *La CNT en los años rojos: Del sindicalismo revolucionario al anarcosindicalismo (1910–1926)* (Madrid: Akal, 1981).
6. *Suplemento a la Revista Blanca* (Madrid), 24 June, 1899, 2.
7. *Suplemento a la Revista Blanca* (Madrid), 20 January, 1900, 1; *Fraternidad* (Gijón, II), 3 November, 1900, 2.
8. *Juventud* (Valencia), 18 January, 1903, 3. Second quote from Owen Chadwick, *The Secularisation of the European Mind in the 19th Century* (Cambridge: Cambridge University Press, 1975), 15.
9. Clara Lida, 'Educación anarquista del ochocientos,' *Revista de Occidente* 97 (1971): 33–47.
10. See Álvarez Junco, *La ideología política*, 63–114; Richard Cleminson, *Anarchism, Science and Sex: Eugenics in Eastern Spain, 1900–1937* (Oxford: Peter Lang, 2000), 117–118.
11. Marie-Madeleine Compère, cited in D.J. O'Connor, *Crime at El Escorial: The 1892 Child Murder, the Press and the Jury* (San Francisco: International Scholars Publications, 1995), 45.
12. Francisco Javier Navarro Navarro, *El paraíso de la razón: La revista Estudios (1928–1937) y el mundo cultural anarquista* (Valencia: Ediciones Alfons de Magnánim, 1997), 18. My thanks to Dr Robyn Orfitelli [unborn] for her thoughts on this subject (personal communication, 13 March, 2018).
13. Several elements of the anarchist view of the emancipatory quality of education, the role of print and the benefits for correspondents engaging in the

press can be compared with early NEP Soviet Russia (1921–1925), see Matthew Lenoe, *Closer to the Masses: Stalinist Culture, Social Revolution, and Soviet Newspapers* (Cambridge: Harvard University Press, 2004), 31–32.

14. Carolyn P. Boyd, 'The Anarchists and Education in Spain, 1868–1909,' *The Journal of Modern History* 48, 4 (1976): 131–132.
15. Carlos Serrano Lacarra, '*Acracia*, los anarquistas y la cultura,' in *El anarquismo español y sus tradiciones culturales*, ed. Bert Hofmann, Pere Joan i Tous and Manfred Tietze (Frankfurt/Madrid: Vervuert/Iberoamericana, 1995), 347.
16. Esenwein, *Anarchist Ideology*, 126.
17. *Vía Libre* (Zaragoza), 16 December, 1906, 3–4.
18. On anarchist culture in this period see Manuel Morales Muñoz, *Cultura e ideología en el anarquismo Español (1870–1910)* (Málaga: Centro de Ediciones de la Diputación de Málaga, 2002). See also comments in Chapter 1 on the role of *certámenes* within the movement.
19. Esenwein, *Anarchist Ideology*, 203–204.
20. Susanna Tavera i García, 'La premsa anarco-sindicalista, (1868–1931),' *Recerques* 8 (1978): 88.
21. *La Revista Blanca* (Madrid), 1 July, 1898, 1–2.
22. *La Revista Blanca* (Madrid), 1 July, 1898, 1. See also David Ortiz, Jr., 'Redefining Public Education: Contestation, the Press and Education in Regency Spain, 1885–1902,' *Journal of Social History* 35, 1 (2001): 82.
23. *La Revista Blanca* (Madrid), 15 July, 1898, 58.
24. The *Suplemento* was launched with the support of 10,000 pesetas received from Francisco Ferrer (5,000) and Juan Greaghe (an Argentinian doctor; 5,000), see Federico Urales, *Mi vida*, Vol. 2 (Barcelona: La Revista Blanca, 1930), 153 and Francisco Madrid Santos, *Solidaridad Obrera y el periodismo de raíz ácrata* (Badalona: Ediciones Solidaridad Obrera, 2007), 74, n.149.
25. *Suplemento a la Revista Blanca* (Madrid), 23 March, 1901, 4.
26. On the Gijón general strike see Pamela Beth Radcliff, *From Mobilization to Civil War: The Politics of Polarization in the Spanish City of Gijón, 1900–1937* (Cambridge: Cambridge University Press, 1996), 253–254 and Ángeles Barrio Alonso, 'Cultura del trabajo y organización obrera en Gijón en el cambio de siglo,' *Historia Contemporánea* 5 (1991): 40–46. On the strikes in Sevilla see Custodio Velasco Mesa, 'Revolutionary Rhetoric and Labour Unrest: Liège in 1886 and Sevilla in 1901,' *International Review of Social History* 56, 2 (2011): 237–238. On the protest, strike and repression in Coruña in 1901, and the support of the *Suplemento*, see Antón Capelán, *Da violencia que non condenan: O centenario da folgo xeral de maio na Coruña* (La Coruña: Ateneo Libertario Ricardo Mella, 2003), 14–31.
27. Madrid Santos, 'La prensa anarquista,' 147–148.
28. *Suplemento a la Revista Blanca* (Madrid), 10 August, 1901, 4.
29. *Suplemento a la Revista Blanca* (Madrid), 16 June, 1900, 2–3.
30. *La Protesta* (Valladolid), 3 November, 1899, 2; *Fraternidad* (Gijón, II), 25 November, 1899, 3.
31. *La Protesta* (Valladolid), 1 December, 1899, 2; 15 December, 1899, 2; *Suplemento a la Revista Blanca* (Madrid), 30 December, 1899, 2.
32. *Suplemento a la Revista Blanca* (Madrid), 6 January, 1900, 3–4 and *La Protesta* (Valladolid), 12 January, 1900, 2–3.
33. The total amount raised by the separate funds was published in *Suplemento a la Revista Blanca* (Madrid), 22 December, 1900, 4, showing that the commission based in the *Suplemento*' raised 148.50 pesetas while *La Protesta* s fund raised 107.70. See reports from Raul [R. Mella] in *Suplemento a la Revista Blanca* (Madrid), 29 September, 1900, 2; 13 October, 1900, 2;

27 October, 1900, 1; 3 November, 1900, 1; and in *La Protesta* (Sabadell), 29 September, 1900, 1; 5 October, 1900, 4.

34. Quote from Emma Goldman, *Living My Life*, Vol. 1 (New York: Dover Publications, 1970), 401. See also Constance Bantman, 'Internationalism without an International? Cross-Channel Anarchist Networks, 1890–1914,' *Revue belge de philology et d'histoire* 84, 4 (2006): 967 and Teresa Abelló Güell, *Les relacions internacionals de l'anarquisme català (1881–1914)* (Barcelona: Edicions 62, 1987), 115–120.

35. For example, see *Suplemento a la Revista Blanca* (Madrid), 8 September, 1900, 4 and 3 November, 1900, 4.

36. *Suplemento a la Revista Blanca* (Madrid), 13 October, 1900, 4.

37. *Suplemento a la Revista Blanca* (Madrid), 27 October, 1900, 1.

38. *Suplemento a la Revista Blanca* (Madrid), 3 August, 1901, 4. See also Tavera, 'La premsa anarco-sindicalista,' 88.

39. See *Suplemento a la Revista Blanca* (Madrid), 11 November, 1899, 4 and 4 January, 1902, 1. See also Madrid Santos, *Solidaridad Obrera*, 74.

40. In contrast, a number of Barcelona papers did follow this style, including *Natura* (Barcelona) and *Buena Semilla* (Barcelona).

41. *Libre Concurso* (Mahón), July 1902, 2.

42. Madrid Santos, 'La prensa anarquista,' 24–25.

43. See for example *El Corsario* (Valencia), 8 June, 1902, 4.

44. See Santiago Castillo, 'La labor editorial del PSOE en el siglo XIX,' *Estudios de Historia Social* 8–9 (1979): 188–195.

45. For example, see comments on 1901 repression in *El Socialista* (Madrid), 7 February, 1902, 2–3.

46. *Suplemento a la Revista Blanca* (Madrid), 6 July, 1901, 4; 27 July, 1901, 2; 3 August, 1901, 2; 10 August, 1901, 2.

47. Santiago Castillo, *Historia de la UGT: Un sindicalismo consciente, 1873–1914* (Madrid: Siglo XXI, 2008), 157–158.

48. Marcel van der Linden and Wayne Thorpe, 'The Rise and Fall of Revolutionary Syndicalism,' in *Revolutionary Syndicalism: An International Perspective*, ed. Marcel van der Linden and Wayne Thorpe (Aldershot: Scolar Press, 1990), 7–11.

49. See Antón Fernández Álvarez, *Ricardo Mella o el anarquismo humanista* (Barcelona: Anthropos, 1990), 65–71 and Mella's defence of Margall in *Suplemento a la Revista Blanca* (Madrid), 12 August, 1899, 2–3. See also Jean-Louis Guereña, 'Fermín Salvochea: Del federalismo al anarquismo,' in *Fermín Salvochea: Un anarquista entre la leyenda y la historia*, ed. Jacques Maurice (Cádiz: Quorum, 2009), 73–74.

50. *Juventud* (Valencia), 25 January, 1903, 3.

51. *Suplemento a la Revista Blanca* (Madrid), 7 December, 1901, 1; *El Porvenir del Obrero* (Mahón), 7 December, 1901, 4; *Juventud* (Valencia), 1 March, 1903, 3.

52. *El Rebelde* (Madrid), 14 April, 1904, 1 and 21 April, 1904, 1. José Álvarez Junco, *El emperador del Paralelo: Lerroux y la demagogia populista* (Madrid: Alianza Editorial, 1990), 98–100.

53. Sebastian Balfour, 'The Impact of the War within Spain: Continuity or Crisis?,' in *The Crisis of 1898: Colonial Redistribution and Nationalist Mobilization*, ed. Angel Smith and Emma Dávila-Coz (Basingstoke: Macmillan, 1999), 180–194. See also Pol Dalmau, *Press, Politics and National Identities in Catalonia: The Transformation of La Vanguardia, 1881–1931* (Brighton: Sussex Academic Press, 2017), 93–115.

54. *Suplemento a la Revista Blanca* (Madrid), 2 December, 1899, 2–3.

55. *Suplemento a la Revista Blanca* (Madrid), 20 May, 1899, 1.

56. *La Idea Libre* (Madrid), 29 October, 1898, 1; *Suplemento a la Revista Blanca* (Madrid), 30 December, 1899, 3.

57. For example, the 'Germinal' centre in La Coruña, and 'Germinal' groups in La Línea, Palafrugell, Palma del Río, Gijón, Jerez de la Frontera, Barcelona and Sallent. See *Suplemento a la Revista Blanca* (Madrid), 16 September, 1899, 4; *El Obrero del Río-Tinto* (Río-Tinto), 30 June, 1900, 2–3; *La Protesta* (La Línea de la Concepción), 5 November, 1901, 4; *El Corsario* (Valencia), 12 December, 1902, 4; and Gustavo La Iglesia y García, *Caracteres del anarquismo en la actualidad* (Barcelona: Gustavo Gil, 1907), 293–294, n.1.

58. *La Protesta* (La Línea de la Concepción), 1 August, 1901, 4 and 29 August, 1901, 4.

59. Álvarez Junco, *La ideología política*, 43–62 and Litvak, *Musa libertaria*, 43–67.

60. See *La Revista Blanca* (Madrid), 15 October, 1902, 226–228 and Litvak, *Musa libertaria*, 154, 283–286.

61. Dolores Thion Soriano-Mollá, *Ernesto Bark: Un propagandista de la modernidad, 1858–1924* (Alicante: Instituto de Cultura Juan Gil-Albert, 1998), 48–50; Encarnación Medina Arjona, 'El Grupo Germinal de 1901 y Zola: El carácter programático de una carta inédita,' *Ull Crític* 7 (2002): 169–181. See also Madrid Santos, 'La prensa anarquista,' 154, n.806.

62. *El Porvenir del Obrero* (Mahón), 1 February, 1900, 2. See also Soriano-Mollá, *Ernesto Bark*, 91–194.

63. *Suplemento a la Revista Blanca* (Madrid), 24 June, 1899, 4.

64. Radcliff, *From Mobilization to Civil War*, 35–43.

65. *Luz y Vida* (Santa Cruz de Tenerife), 30 December, 1905, 3.

66. Álvarez Junco, *El emperador*, 165–166.

67. In 1900 Gustavo and Lerroux campaigned together in Andalucía, calling for the release of the prisoners of the Jerez uprising in 1892, see *Suplemento a la Revista Blanca* (Madrid), 1 September, 1900, 1 and 8 September, 1900, 1. See also Álvarez Junco, *El emperador*, 162.

68. *La Protesta* (La Línea de la Concepción), 31 May, 1901, 2. See Álvarez Junco, *El emperador*, 225–228 and Dalmau, *Press, Politics and National Identities*, 125–130.

69. *Suplemento a la Revista Blanca* (Madrid), 6 July, 1901, 2.

70. *Suplemento a la Revista Blanca* (Madrid), 27 April, 1901, 2; 4 May, 1901, 2; 9 November, 1901, 2; 7 December, 1901, 2.

71. *Suplemento a la Revista Blanca* (Madrid), 30 March, 1901, 3.

72. *La Protesta* (La Línea de la Concepción), 31 May, 1901, 4; 22 June, 1901, 2–3; 11 July, 1901, 3–4.

73. *Tierra y Libertad* (Madrid), 28 May, 1903, 1. See also *El Rebelde* (Madrid), 28 April, 1904, 2.

74. Adverts for Bark's 'Biblioteca Germinal,' in *El Porvenir del Obrero* (Mahón), 11 January, 1900, 4 and 17 May, 1900, 2.

75. *El Porvenir del Obrero* (Mahón), 18 January, 1900, 1–2.

76. *El Porvenir del Obrero* (Mahón), 5 April, 1900, 3–4 and 25 October, 1900, 1–2; 10 May, 1900, 3; 3 May, 1900, 1. Jean-Louis Guereña, 'European Influences in Spanish Popular Education: The Case of the Socialist *Casa Del Pueblo* of Madrid and the Belgian Model (1897–1929),' *History of Education* 35, 1 (2006): 27–45.

77. *El Porvenir del Obrero* (Mahón), 4 October, 1900, 1 and 7 November, 1900, 3–4.

78. *El Porvenir del Obrero* (Mahón), 21 December, 1901, 1–2.

79. For example, *El Porvenir del Obrero* (Mahón), 24 January, 1901, 3–4; 14 March, 1901, 3; 20 April, 1901, 3–4; 4 May, 1901, 3; 1 August, 1901, 1; 24 August, 1901, 1 and 2; 21 September, 1901, 2; 28 September, 1901, 3.

80. *El Porvenir del Obrero* (Mahón), 21 September, 1901, 3–4; 17 June, 1904, 3–4. See also Ángel Herrerín López, 'Anarchist Sociability in Spain: In Times of Violence and Clandestinity,' *Bulletin for Spanish and Portuguese Historical Studies* 38, 1 (2013): 169–170. Critiques of alcohol featured as one of the main talking points of the International Congress of Anarchists held in Amsterdam in 1907, see Joan Zambrana, 'El anarquismo organizado en los orígenes de la CNT: *Tierra y Libertad*, 1910–1919,' (2009), 1067. Published online, accessed 21 January, 2013, http://cedall.org/Documentacio/IHL/Tierra%20y%20Libertad%201910-1919.pdf.

81. See *Vía Libre* (Zaragoza), 16 December, 1906, 1–2.

82. Álvaro Girón Sierra, 'Metáforas finiseculares del declive biológico: Degeneración y revolución en el anarquismo español (1872–1914),' *Asclepio* 51, 1 (1999): 247–273.

83. *El Porvenir del Obrero* (Mahón), 14 December, 1901, 1. Emphasis in original.

84. Felip Cortiella, cited in Litvak, *Musa Libertaria*, 274.

85. *Luz y Vida* (Santa Cruz de Tenerife), 17 February, 1906, 1–2.

86. *El Rebelde* (Madrid), 26 December, 1903, 2–3.

87. *La Protesta* (Valladolid), 1 June, 1900, 4; *Germinal* (La Coruña), 8 July, 1905, 1.

88. Public health and disease in *La Protesta* (Valladolid), 19 August, 1899, 3–9 September, 1899, 3; 24 September, 1899, 2–12 October, 1899, 4; 29 December, 1899, 2; 2 February, 1900, 2; 11 May, 1900, 1–2; 7 December, 1900, 1–2; 31 January, 1901, 4; 1 March, 1901, 1–2; 8 March, 1901, 2; *La Protesta* (La Línea de la Concepción), 8 August, 1901, 4; 5 December, 1901, 1–2; 8 March, 1902, 3. See also *Germinal* (La Coruña), 12 November, 1904, 2. Economics: *La Protesta* (La Línea de la Concepción), 23 January, 1902, 1. Oceanography: *La Protesta* (La Línea de la Concepción), 7 June, 1902, 4. Evolution: *El Cosmopolita* (Valladolid), 17 August, 1901, 1; *Germinal* (La Coruña), 10 December, 1904, 4. Geography: *Germinal* (La Coruña), 18 March, 1905, 2 and 15 April, 1905, 2.

89. Cleminson, *Anarchism, Sex and Science*, 119.

90. O'Connor, *Crime at El Escorial*, 27; Ortiz, Jr., 'Redefining Public Education,' 76.

91. Mercedes Vilanova Ribas and Xavier Moreno Juliá, *Atlas de la evolución del analfabetismo en España de 1887–1981* (Madrid: Ministerio de Educación y Ciencia, 1992), 68 and 189–190. See also Alejandro Tiana Ferrer, 'The Workers' Movement and Popular Education in Contemporary Spain (1868–1939),' *Paedagogica Historica* 32, 3 (1996): 651–652.

92. Boyd, 'The Anarchists and Education,' 135–136.

93. Tiana Ferrer, 'The Workers' Movement,' 652–653. See also Pilar Muñoz López, *Sangre, amor e interés: La familia en la España de la Restauración* (Madrid: Marcial Pons Historia, 2001), 342–351.

94. *El Proletario* (Cádiz), 1 April, 1902, 3 and 5.

95. *La Protesta* (La Línea de la Concepción), 15 February, 1902, 4; *Germinal* (La Coruña), 26 November, 1904, 2 and 4 March, 1905, 2.

96. *Adelante* (Santander), 10 August, 1902, 3.

97. Boyd, 'The Anarchists and Education,' 127.

98. *Fraternidad* (Gijón, II), 1 December, 1900, 2–3. Much of the language and metaphors used in the anarchist press suggest that many members of the movement had at least some religious education. For example see *Suplemento a la Revista Blanca* (Madrid), 2 September, 1899, 2 and 1 September, 1900, 2; *Juventud* (Valencia), 15 February, 1903, 1. See Joël Delhom, 'Esbozo de una tipología temática y funcional de los usos de la biblia en el anarquismo hispánico,' in *Cuando los anarquistas citaban la biblia: Entre mesianismo y propaganda*, ed. Joël Delhom and Daniel Attala (Madrid: Catarata, 2014), 233–274.

99. *El Proletario* (Cádiz), 15 April, 1902, 2.
100. Till Kössler, 'Human Sciences and Child Reform in Spain, 1890–1936,' in *Engineering Society: The Role of the Human and Social Sciences in Modern Societies, 1880–1980*, ed. Kerstin Brückweh, Dirk Schumann, Richard F. Wetzell and Benjamin Ziemann (Basingstoke: Palgrave Macmillan, 2012), 180.
101. *Suplemento a la Revista Blanca* (Madrid), 1 December, 1900, 4.
102. *Tiempos Nuevos* (Gijón), 1 December, 1905, 3. See also *La Protesta* (Valladolid), 22 March, 1901, 1; *La Acción* (La Coruña), 30 November, 1908, 1–2.
103. *La Revista Blanca* (Madrid), 15 December, 1901, 353–357.
104. Francisco José Cuevas Noa, *Anarquismo y educación: La propuesta sociopolítica de la pedagogía libertaria* (Madrid: Fundación de Estudios Libertarios Anselmo Lorenzo, 2003), 83.
105. *Luz y Vida* (Santa Cruz de Tenerife), 10 February, 1906, 3. See also Paul Avrich, *The Modern School Movement: Anarchism and Education in the United States* (Princeton: Princeton University Press, 1980), 3–19.
106. One example of this overlap can be found in *La Solidaridad Ferroviaria* (Madrid), 15 December, 1901, 2–6. On the ILE see Antonio Jiménez-Landi, *La Institución Libre de Enseñanza y su ambiente: Los orígenes de la Institución* (Madrid: Editorial Computense, 1996).
107. *Suplemento a la Revista Blanca* (Madrid), 3 November, 1899, 2.
108. *Luz y Vida* (Santa Cruz de Tenerife), 30 December, 1905, 2.
109. *La Solidaridad* (Madrid), 15 October, 1870, 3, cited in Boyd, 'The Anarchists and Education,' 129.
110. *Suplemento a la Revista Blanca* (Madrid), 25 October, 1899, 2. See also *Juventud* (Valencia), 11 January, 1903, 1.
111. Cited in Joan Connelly Ullman, *The Tragic Week: A Study of Anticlericalism in Spain* (Cambridge: Harvard University Press, 1968), 320.
112. Javier Navarro Navarro, 'Los educadores del pueblo y la "Revolución Interior": La cultura anarquista en España,' in *Tierra y Libertad: Cien años de anarquismo en España*, ed. Julián Casanova (Barcelona: Crítica, 2010), 203.
113. An example of the role of educated workers in a local context in Jerome R. Mintz, *The Anarchists of Casas Viejas* (Chicago: University of Chicago Press, 1982), 28. Concept of 'informal elites' from Andy Cumbers, Paul Routledge and Corinne Nativel, 'The Entangled Geographies of Global Justice Networks,' *Progress in Human Geography* 32, 2 (2008): 188–189 and 196.
114. *El Cosmopolita* (Valladolid), 21 September, 1901, 1. See also Navarro Navarro, 'Los educadores del pueblo,' 194.
115. *Fraternidad* (Gijón, II), 23 December, 1899, 3.
116. Martha A. Ackelsberg, 'It Takes More Than a Village!: Transnational Travels of Spanish Anarchism in Argentina and Cuba,' *International Journal of Iberian Studies* 29, 3 (2016): 214.
117. *Suplemento a la Revista Blanca* (Madrid), 12 October, 1901, 1. See also *El Proletario* (Cádiz), 1 June, 1902, 2–3.
118. Geraldine M. Scanlon, *La polémica feminista en la España contemporánea (1868–1974)* (Madrid: Siglo XXI, 1976), 102–103; Temma Kaplan, *Anarchists of Andalusia, 1868–1903* (Princeton: Princeton University Press, 1977), 158–162; Antonio Prado, *Escritoras anarco-feministas en La Revista Blanca (1898–1936): Matrimonio, familia y estado* (Madrid: Fundación de Estudios Libertarios Anselmo Lorenzo, 2011), 41–45.
119. John Hutton, 'Camille Pissarro's *Turpitudes Sociales* and Late Nineteenth Century French Anti-Feminism,' *History Workshop* 24, 1 (1987): 41.
120. Sharif Gemie, 'Anarchism and Feminism: A Historical Survey,' *Women's History Review* 5, 3 (1996): 433–434. See also Prado, *Escritoras anarchofeministas*, 38–41.

121. Sharif Gemie, 'Counter-Community: An Aspect of Anarchist Political Culture,' *Journal of Contemporary History* 29, 2 (1994): 363–364; Martha A. Ackelsberg, *Free Women of Spain: Anarchism and the Struggle for the Emancipation of Women* (Edinburgh: AK Press, 2005), 38.
122. On similar trends in nineteenth-century Britain, see Denise Riley, *Am I That Name?: Feminism and the Category of Women in History* (Basingstoke: Macmillan, 1988), 87–93.
123. Scanlon, *La polémica feminista*, 151–152; Mary Nash, '"Ideals of Redemption": Socialism and Women on the Left in Spain,' in *Women and Socialism / Socialism and Women: Europe between the Two World Wars*, ed. Helmut Gruber and Pamela Graves (Oxford: Berghahn, 1998), 348–352.
124. Mary Nash, 'Experiencia y aprendizaje: La formación histórica de los feminismos en España,' *Historia Social* 20 (1994): 158–160.
125. *La Humanidad Libre* (Valencia), 1 February, 1902, 3. See also Marilyn J. Boxer, 'Rethinking the Socialist Construction and International Career of the Concept of "Bourgeois Feminism",' *The American Historical Review* 112, 1 (2007): 131–158. A comparison may be drawn with the critique of enslaved women in nineteenth-century USA, see Avtar Brah and Ann Phoenix, '"Ain't I a Woman?": Revisiting Intersectionality,' *Journal of International Women's Studies* 5, 3 (2004): 76–78.
126. *Suplemento a la Revista Blanca* (Madrid), 24 November, 1900, 2–3.
127. *La Protesta* (Valladolid), 16 September, 1899, 2; *El Cosmopolita* (Valladolid), 29 September, 1901, 1–2; *Adelante* (Santander), 11 January, 1903, 2.
128. *La Revista Blanca* (Madrid), 1 July, 1898, 23–24; 15 July, 1898, 37–38; 30 July, 1898, 88. See also Prado, *Escritoras anarcho-feministas*, 47–106 and Gloria Espigado Tocino, 'Las mujeres en el anarquismo español (1869–1939),' *Ayer* 45, 1 (2002): 66.
129. María Ángeles García Maroto, *La mujer en la prensa anarquista: España, 1900–1936* (Madrid: Fundación de Estudios Libertarios Anselmo Lorenzo, 1996), 233–239.
130. *La Protesta* (La Línea de la Concepción), 31 July, 1901, 1.
131. Compare with attitudes discussed in Riley, *Am I That Name?*, 10.
132. See also this attitude in the Cuban anarchist movement, in Kirwin R. Shaffer, *Anarchism and Countercultural Politics in Early Twentieth-Century Cuba* (Gainesville: University Press of Florida, 2005), 215.
133. *Adelante* (Santander), 11 May, 1902, 1.
134. *La Protesta* (Valladolid), 24 September, 1899, 3–4; 29 September, 1899, 2; 12 October, 1899, 1–2.
135. For example see *Suplemento a la Revista Blanca* (Madrid), 6 April, 1901, 4.
136. *El Porvenir del Obrero* (Mahón), 17 June, 1904, 3–4.
137. *La Humanidad Libre* (Valencia), 8 March, 1902, 2–3.
138. *Juventud* (Valencia), 8 February, 1903, 3.
139. *Luz y Vida* (Santa Cruz de Tenerife), 8 December, 1906, 4; *La Humanidad Libre* (Valencia), 8 March, 1902, 2–3.
140. *El Cosmopolita* (Valladolid), 28 September, 1901, 1.
141. A decade later the CNT agreed that more had to be done to organise women, but that this task should be left to women themselves, see *Solidaridad Obrera* (Barcelona, II), 15 September, 1911, 2.
142. *La Protesta* (La Línea de la Concepción), 28 November, 1901, 1.
143. *Fraternidad* (Gijón, II), 11 November, 1899, 2–3.
144. *La Protesta* (La Línea de la Concepción), 28 November, 1901, 1.
145. See Cleminson, *Anarchism, Science and Sex*, 133–134.
146. Leopoldo Bonafulla, *Generación libre: Los errores del neo-maltusianismo* (Barcelona: El Productor, 1905); *Juventud* (Valencia), 1 March, 1903, 4.

See also Cleminson, *Anarchism, Science and Sex*, 137–139. One example of support for Malthusian ideas in non-Catlalan press: *Luz y Vida* (Santa Cruz de Tenerife), 22 January, 1907, 2. The debate over the validity of Neo-Malthusianism continued over the following decade, see for example: *El Porvenir del Obrero* (Mahón, II), 6 June, 1912, 3; *El Látigo* (Baracaldo), 1 February, 1913, 1–2; *Acción Libertaria* (Madrid), 13 June, 1913, 2 and 18 June, 1913, 2.

147. *Germinal* (La Coruña), 10 December, 1904, 1 and 24 December, 1904, 1–2. See Richard Cleminson, '"Science and Sympathy" or "Sexual Subversion on a Human Basis"? Anarchists in Spain and the World League for Sexual Reform,' *History of Sexuality* 12, 1 (2003): 117–118 for later anarchist perspectives on prostitution.

148. *El Porvenir del Obrero* (Mahón), 21 September, 1901, 3. See also Jean-Louis Guereña, *La prostitución en la España contemporánea* (Madrid: Marcial Pons, 2003), 339–397 and Anne Summers, 'Liberty, Equality, Morality: The Attempt to Sustain an International Campaign against the Double Sexual Standard,' in *Globalizing Feminisms: 1789–1945*, ed. Karen Offen (London: Routledge, 2010), 26–35.

149. *Adelante* (Santander), 1 June, 1902, 2; *El Corsario* (Valencia), 8 June, 1902, 3. See also Scanlon, *La polémica feminista*, 126–137 and Álvarez Junco, *La ideología política*, 289–290 and Muñoz López, *Sangre, amor e interés*, 208–214.

150. See *Germinal* (La Coruña), 10 June, 1905, 1, which uses both of these attacks.

151. *Fraternidad* (Gijón, II), 3 February, 1900 3 and 1 December, 1900, 2; *Suplemento a la Revista Blanca* (Madrid), 12 May, 1900, 1–2; *Luz y Vida* (Santa Cruz de Tenerife), 24 December, 1906, 3. See also the collection of writings on free love by anarchist thinkers: Osvaldo Baigorria, ed., *El amor libre: Eros y anarquía* (Buenos Aires: Libros de Anarres, 2006).

152. *El Proletario* (Cádiz), 1 July, 1902, 2–3. See also Álvarez Junco, *La ideología política*, 297.

153. *La Protesta* (Valladolid), 2 March, 1900, 1–2. On anarchist discussions of masturbation see Richard Cleminson, *Anarquismo y sexualidad en España, 1900–1939* (Cádiz: Universidad de Cádiz, 2008), 129–150.

154. Gemie, 'Anarchism and Feminism,' 431–432. On later discussions of homosexuality within the movement see Acklesburg, *Free Women of Spain*, 49–50. On the broader discussions of male homosexuality in Spain see Richard Cleminson and Francisco Vásquez García, *"Los Invisibles": A History of Male Homosexuality in Spain, 1850–1939* (Cardiff: University of Wales Press, 2007), 265–276.

155. Ackelsberg, 'Transatlantic Travels,' 215–216.

156. See *Solidaridad Obrera* (Gijón), 23 June, 1910, 4.

157. For example see *La Protesta* (La Línea de la Concepción), 29 August, 1901, 4; *Germinal* (La Coruña), 4 February, 1905, 4.

158. Urales, *Mi vida*, Vol. 1, 54–58.

159. *Tierra y Libertad* (Madrid, II), 2 September, 1904, 2. Emphasis added.

160. María Amalia Pradas Baena, *Teresa Claramunt: La virgen roja barcelonesa: Biografía y escritos* (Barcelona: Virus, 2006), 32–33.

161. *La Protesta* (La Línea de la Concepción), 12 December, 1901, 1–2. See also Herrerín López, 'Anarchist Sociability,' 172.

162. *Tierra y Libertad* (Madrid, II), 2 September, 1904, 2.

163. *El Corsario* (Valencia), 7 November, 1902, 2; *El 4º de Febrero* (Huelva), 15 November, 1902, 2–3. See also agreement in III FSORE Congress to 'boycott' the children and wives of Civil Guardsmen, in *Tierra y Libertad* (Madrid), 21 May, 1903, 1.

164. Published in *Suplemento a la Revista Blanca* (Madrid), 8 June, 1901, 3.
165. *Germinal* (La Coruña), 12 November, 1904, 4; 26 November, 1904, 4; 21 January, 1905, 4; 26 August, 1905, 4.
166. *Suplemento a la Revista Blanca* (Madrid), 18 August, 1900, 3 and 2 November, 1901, 3.
167. For example *Fraternidad* (Gijón, II), 23 December, 1899, 4; *La Protesta* (La Línea de la Concepción), 29 August, 1901, 4 and 1 February, 1902, 4; *El Rebelde* (Madrid), 6 February, 1904, 4. Quote from Matthew Kerry, 'The Bones of Contention: The Secularisation of Cemeteries and Funerals in the Spanish Second Republic,' *European History Quarterly* 49, 1 (2019): 76. See also Muñoz López, *Sangre, amor e interés*, 266–269.
168. See *El Rebelde* (Madrid), 18 March, 1904, 4.
169. *Suplemento a la Revista Blanca* (Madrid), 22 June, 1901, 2.
170. Richard D. Alford, *Naming and Identity: A Cross-Cultural Study of Personal Naming Practices* (New Haven: HRAF Press, 1988), 30–34 and Stanley Lieberson, *A Matter of Taste: How Names, Fashion and Culture Change* (New Haven: Yale University Press, 2000), 138–141.
171. Parsons Lingg y Spies named in Barcelona: *La Protesta* (Valladolid), 10 November, 1900, 4 and 17 November, 1900, 4. Kropotkin named in Sevilla: *Suplemento a la Revista Blanca* (Madrid), 25 May, 1900, 3. Attempt to call child Darwin by Enrique Taboada denied by registrar and 'Archimedes,' named in Madrid, both *El Rebelde* (Madrid), 5 May, 1904, 4. Galileo in Valladolid: *La Protesta* (La Línea de la Concepción), 9 June, 1901, 4. Spartacus was the name of Ernesto Álvarez's child, see *La Protesta* (Madrid), 11 August, 1901, 1. Proudhon, Lingg y Washington,' in *Suplemento a la Revista Blanca* (Madrid), 5 May, 1900, 3.
172. A small selection of 'Palmiro/as' in *Suplemento a la Revista Blanca* (Madrid), 31 March, 1900, 3; 25 May, 1900, 3; 21 July, 1900, 2; 27 April, 1901, 4.
173. Luis Monguió, 'Una biblioteca obrera madrileña en 1912–1913,' *Bulletin Hispanique* 77, 1–2 (1975): 161–162; Litvak, *Musa libertaria*, 282. Díaz del Moral cites Volney's book as one of the most popular in the movement, see *Historia de las agitaciones campesinas andaluzas-Córdoba: Antecedentes para una reforma agraria* (Madrid: Alianza, 1967), 191. The book was also published as a cut-out pamphlet in *La Organización* (Gijón), see Ignacio Soriano and Francisco Madrid Santos, 'Antología documental del anarquismo español VI.I: Bibliografía del anarquismo en España, 1868–1939, Enriquecida con notas y comentarios,' (5th edition, 2012), 366–367. Published online, accessed 12 December, 2012. http://cedall.org/Documentacio/Castella/cedall203410103.htm.
174. *Suplemento a la Revista Blanca* (Madrid), 16 February, 1901, 4 and 30 March, 1901, 3. See also James Michael Yeoman, '*Salud y anarquía desde Dowlais*: The Translocal Experience of Spanish Anarchists in South Wales, 1900–1915,' *International Journal of Iberian Studies* 29, 3 (2016): 281–282.
175. Ackelsberg, 'Transatlantic Travels,' 216.
176. *Adelante* (Santander), 1 June, 1902, 4.
177. *Suplemento a la Revista Blanca* (Madrid), 19 May, 1900, 4.
178. *Suplemento a la Revista Blanca* (Madrid), 16 June, 1900, 4.
179. *Suplemento a la Revista Blanca* (Madrid), 16 November, 1901, 3 and 28 December, 1901, 2. See also Theresa Ann Smith, *The Emerging Female Citizen: Gender and Enlightenment in Spain* (Berkeley: University of California Press, 2006), 17–39.
180. *La Humanidad Libre* (Valencia), 1 February, 1902, 3.
181. Appears in Álvarez Junco, *La ideología política*, 611, and can also be viewed at '1 febrero,' Efemerides Anarquistas, accessed 17 August, 2018, https://

alacantobrer.files.wordpress.com/2012/03/016_cab_humanidadlibre-valencia-01-02-1902.jpg.

182. *La Humanidad Libre* (Valencia), 1 February, 1902, 4.
183. See Karen Offen, *European Feminisms, 1700–1950: A Political History* (Standford: University of Stanford Press, 2000), 150–160, 213–214 and Sandra Stanley Holton, 'To Educate Women into Rebellion: Elizabeth Cady Stanton and the Creation of a Transatlantic Network of Radical Suffragists,' in Offen, *Globalizing Feminisms*, 36–50.
184. *La Voz de la Mujer* (Buenos Aires), 15 May, 1896, 14 and 1 January, 1897, 15.
185. *La Voz de la Mujer* (Buenos Aires), 27 March, 1896, 6–7. Ackelsberg, 'Transatlantic Travels,' 215–216.
186. Ackelsberg, 'Transatlantic Travels,' 216–220.
187. *La Humanidad Libre* (Valencia), 8 March, 1902, 4.
188. *El Corsario* (Valencia), 8 June, 1902, 1. Emphasis added.
189. *El Corsario* (Valencia), 8 June, 1902, 2.
190. Carlos Soria, 'La ley española de policía de imprenta de 1883,' *Documentación de las Ciencias de la Información* 6 (1982): 25.
191. *Suplemento a la Revista Blanca* (Madrid), 27 July, 1901, 2 and 3 August, 1901, 2. See also Urales, *Mi vida*, Vol. 2, 152–153.
192. *La Protesta* (Valladolid), 12 January, 1900, 2–3.
193. *La Humanidad Libre* (Valencia), 1 February, 1902, 1 and 1–2.
194. *Germinal* (La Coruña), 10 June, 1905, 2; *La Defensa del Obrero* (Gijón), 20 November, 1901, 1.
195. *Suplemento a la Revista Blanca* (Madrid), 21 September, 1901, 3. See also announcement of feminist society in Cieza (Murcia), which claimed 230 affiliates, *Germinal* (La Coruña), 15 April, 1905, 4.
196. *Suplemento a la Revista Blanca* (Madrid), 12 October, 1901, 1.
197. *La Protesta* (La Línea de la Concepción), 31 July, 1901, 2 and 8 August, 1901, 1–2. See also José Luis Gutiérrez Molina, *La tiza, la tinta y la palabra: José Sánchez Rosa: Maestro y anarquista andaluz (1864–1936)* (Ubrique: Tréveris, 2005), 336–337.
198. *La Solidaridad Ferroviaria* (Madrid), 15 November, 1901, 7.
199. *La Razón Obrera* (Cádiz), 7 December, 1902, 2–3 and 11 January, 1902, 2; 8 February, 1902, 3.
200. *Tierra y Libertad* (Madrid), 21 May, 1903, 1; *El Productor* (Barcelona, III), 23 May, 1903, 2.
201. Contrast with misogynistic attitudes discussed in Gemie, 'Anarchism and Feminism,' 427–428.
202. *El Rebelde* (Madrid), 2 January, 1904, 3; *Luz y Vida* (Santa Cruz de Tenerife), 9 December, 1905, 1.
203. See account of protest of 300 women against high bread prices, *El Rebelde* (Madrid), 11 March, 1904, 3. See also Temma Kaplan, 'Female Consciousness and Collective Action: The Case of Barcelona, 1910–1918,' *Signs* 7, 3 (1982): 545–566 and 'Redressing the Balance: Gendered Acts of Justice around the Mining Community of Río Tinto in 1913,' in *Constructing Spanish Womanhood: Female Identity in Modern Spain*, ed. Victoria Lorée Enders and Pamela Beth Radcliff (Albany: State University of New York Press, 1999), 283–299; Pamela Beth Radcliff, 'Elite Women Workers and Collective Action: The Cigarette Makers of Gijon, 1890–1930,' *Journal of Social History* 27, 1 (1993): 85–108 and 'Women's Politics: Consumer Riots in Twentieth-Century Spain,' in Enders and Radcliff, *Constructing Spanish Womanhood*, 301–323; Carlos Gil Andrés, 'Mujeres en la calle: Trabajo, condición social y protesta de la mujer: La Rioja, 1885–1910,' in *El trabajo*

a través de la historia, ed. Santiago Castillo (Madrid: Asociación de Historia Social, 1996), 373–382.

204. *El Corsario* (Valencia), 7 November, 1902, 1.
205. Ackelsburg, *Free Women of Spain*, 115–120, at 115.
206. Gemie, 'Anarchism and Feminism,' 433–434. Emphasis added.
207. La Iglesia y García, *Caracteres del anarquismo*, 293–294, n.1. The same list appears in part in Litvak, *Musa libertaria*, 173.
208. Ángeles González Fernández, *Utopía y realidad: Anarquismo, anarcosindicalismo y organizaciones obreras: Sevilla, 1900–1936* (Sevilla: Diputación Provincial de Sevilla, 1996); 87, n.237. See also *El Rebelde* (Madrid), 2 June, 1904, 3.
209. For example see *Suplemento a la Revista Blanca* (Madrid), September 2, 1899, 4 and *La Razón Obrera* (Cádiz), 19 October, 1901, 4.
210. González Fernández, *Utopía y realidad*, 66–67, 85–87.
211. For example see *La Protesta* (La Línea de la Concepción), 5 December, 1901, 4; *El Rebelde* (Madrid), 13 January, 1904, 3.
212. Examples of North African propaganda groups can be found in *Suplemento a la Revista Blanca* (Madrid), 8 December, 1900, 3 and 2 March, 1901, 3. See also Yeoman, '*Salud y anarquía*,' 279–280.
213. *Adelante* (Santander), 10 August, 1902, 2–3. See also *La Protesta* (La Línea de la Concepción), 1 March, 1902, 4.
214. For example see the statement of the La Línea group 'Retoño Anarquista,' in *El Rebelde* (Madrid), 5 March, 1904, 3.
215. See introduction, note 51.
216. See Díaz del Moral, *Historia de las agitaciones*, 187–188.
217. *Suplemento a la Revista Blanca* (Madrid), 23 March, 1901, 1; 30 March, 1901, 4; 6 April, 1901, 2; 20 June, 1901, 4; 27 July, 1901, 3. See also Gutiérrez Molina, *José Sánchez Rosa*, 62, 341–341, n.199.
218. See *Tierra y Libertad* (Madrid), 6 September, 1902, 3 for the original plans for the tour. An extensive account of the tour's meeting in Cádiz is given in *El Proletario: Suplemento al número 14* (Cádiz), 19 October, 1901, 2–3.
219. *El Proletario* (Cádiz), 1 October, 1902, 7 and 8; 15 October, 1902, 8. See also González Fernández, *Utopía y realidad*, 88–93.
220. José Luis Gutiérrez Molina, *El anarquismo en Chiclana: Diego Rodríguez Barbosa: Obrera y escritor (1885–1936)* (Chiclana de la Frontera: Ayuntamiento de Chiclana, 2001), 24–26.
221. *Tierra y Libertad* (Madrid), 14 April, 1904, 1; *El Rebelde* (Madrid), 14 April, 1904, 1–2. See reports from the tour in both papers through the following months.
222. *Luz y Vida* (Santa Cruz de Tenerife), 19 May, 1906, 2.
223. *El 4º de Febrero* (Huelva), 15 November, 1902, 4. See also Gabriel Santullano, 'Algunas notas sobre la prensa obrera en Asturias en el siglo XIX (1868–1899),' *Boletín del Instituto de Estudios Asturianos*, 88–89 (1976): 527.
224. Herrerín López, 'Anarchist Sociability,' 168.
225. Another example of the spread of anarchism to new areas, in this case Casa Viejas (Cádiz) is given in Mintz, *The Anarchists*, 14–31. Anarchist papers were being sent to this area since at least 1904, see *El Rebelde* (Madrid), 13 February, 1904, 4.
226. Santullano, 'Prensa obrera,' 528.
227. Ángeles Barrio Alonso, *Anarquismo y anarcosindicalismo en Asturias, 1890–1936* (Madrid: Siglo XXI, 1988), 14 and 20–22. See also *Fraternidad* (Gijón, II), 11 November, 1899, 1.

180   *The Cult of Reason*

228. Jean-Louis Guereña, *Sociabilidad, cultura y educación en Asturias bajo la Restauración (1875–1900)* (Oviedo: Real Instituto de Estudios Asturianos, 2005), 77–113.
229. *Suplemento a la Revista Blanca* (Madrid), 23 March, 1901, 2. Barrio Alonso, *Anarquismo en Asturias*, 22–23.
230. Madrid Santos, 'La prensa anarquista,' 424 and 435.
231. Litvak, *Musa libertaria*, 214.
232. *Fraternidad* (Gijón, II), 1 December, 1900, 4.
233. Ackelsberg, *Free Women of Spain*, 85–86.
234. *Suplemento a la Revista Blanca* (Madrid), 29 June, 1901, 3.
235. Other notable papers from Cataluña in this period include *Salud y Fuerza*, (1904–1914, 61 issues) edited by Luis Bulffi, see Cleminson, *Anarchism, Science and Sex*, 109–158; *La Huelga General* (1901–1903, 21 issues), founded by Francisco Ferrer; *Natura* (1903–1905, 48 issues), edited by Anselmo Lorenzo and José Prat.
236. For example in Sevilla, see González Fernández, *Utopía y realidad*, 41. Comapre with observations in Tom Goyens, 'Social Space and the Practice of Anarchist History,' *Rethinking History* 13, 4 (2009): 439 and Bruce Christopher Nelson, *Beyond the Martyrs: A Social History of Chicago's Anarchists, 1870–1900* (New Brunswick: Rutgers University Press, 1988), 240–241.
237. Michel Ralle, 'La sociabilidad obrera en la sociedad de la Restauración (1875–1910),' *Estudios de Historia Social* 3, 50–51 (1989): 166–167; Pere Gabriel, 'Sociabilidad obrera y popular y vida política en Cataluña, 1868–1923,' *Bulletin d'Histoire Contemporaine de l'Espagne* 17–18 (1993): 147–148. See also Xavier Motilla Salas, 'Bases bibliográficas para una historia de la sociabilidad, el asociacionismo y la educación en la España contemporánea,' *Historia de la educación: Revista interuniversitaria* 31 (2012): 339–358.
238. Herrerín López, 'Anarchist Sociability,' 168–170.
239. *Suplemento a la Revista Blanca* (Madrid), 17 June, 1899, 3; *Fraternidad* (Gijón, II), 20 January, 1900, 3 and 21 April, 1900, 3–4. See also Guereña, 'European influences,' 29 and Herrerín López, 'Anarchist Sociability,' 170.
240. *Suplemento a la Revista Blanca* (Madrid), 10 June, 1899, 2 and 8 December, 1900, 2.
241. *Juventud* (Valencia), 15 February, 1903, 4. On popular libraries see Antonio Viñao Frago, 'A la cultura por la lectura: Las bibliotecas populares (1869–1885),' in *Clases populares, cultura, educación: Siglos XIX y XX*, ed. Jean-Louis Guereña and Alejandro Tiana Ferrer (Madrid: UNED, 1989), 301–335.
242. Jean-Louis Guereña, 'Las casas del pueblo y la educación obrera a principios del siglo XX,' *Hispania: Revista Española de Historia* 51, 2 (1991): 655–657.
243. Francisco Javier Navarro Navarro, *Ateneos y grupos ácratas: Vida y actividad cultural de las asociaciones anarquistas valencianas durante la Segunda República y la Guerra Civil* (Valencia: Biblioteca Valenciana, 2002), 13.
244. *Suplemento a la Revista Blanca* (Madrid), 2 November, 1901, 3 and 14 December, 1901, 2; *La Razón Obrera* (Cádiz), 30 November, 1901, 2. See also Goyens, 'Social Space,' 451.
245. For example, see role of 'Germinal' centre in La Coruña in *La Humanidad Libre* (Valencia), 1 February, 1902, 4. See also Capelán, *Da violencia*, 36–37, 115–118 and 121–122.
246. In Sevilla, 10 centres were formed between 1903 and 1905, see González Fernández, *Utopía y realidad*, 88. On the spread of anarchism in Tenerife see *Luz y Vida* (Santa Cruz de Tenerife), 17 February, 1906, 4.

247. For example, anarchist centres in Huelva, Algeciras and Córdoba confirmed their continuing adhesion to the movement and sent representatives to the early CNT congresses, see *Solidaridad Obrera* (Barcelona, II), 4 November, 1910, 1; 8 September, 1911, 1; 15 September, 1911, 1.

248. Goyens, 'Social Space,' 448.

249. *Suplemento a la Revista Blanca* (Madrid), 7 October, 1899, 4; 23 December, 1899, 4; 30 December, 1899, 4; 21 April, 1900, 4; 12 May, 1900, 3; 7 June, 1900, 3; 10 November, 1900, 2; 17 November, 1900, 3; 22 June, 1901, 3.

250. *El Rebelde* (Madrid), 24 March, 1904, 4. Article published in *La Revista Blanca* (Madrid), 15 February, 1904, 481–485.

251. See for example *Germinal* (La Coruña), 21 January, 1905, 4 and 4 February, 1905, 4.

252. Goyens, 'Social Space,' 451–452; Herrerín López, 'Anarchist Sociability,' 164. For a comparison with socialist efforts at this time see Monguió, 'Una biblioteca obrera,' 154–173.

253. *Suplemento a la Revista Blanca* (Madrid), 17 November, 1900, 4; *La Protesta* (Valladolid), 12 April, 1901, 4; *La Protesta* (Madrid), 11 August, 1901, 3.

254. *La Protesta* (Valladolid), 24 November, 1899, 3–4.

255. *Suplemento a la Revista Blanca* (Madrid), 16 June, 1900, 3; 21 June, 1900, 3; 22 December, 1900, 2.

256. Alejandro Tiana Ferrer, 'La idea enseñanza integral en el movimiento obrero internacionalista español, 1868–1881,' *Historia de la Educación* 2 (1983): 113–121; Herrerín López, 'Anarchist Sociability,' 164.

257. Boyd, 'The Anarchists and Education,' 138–141.

258. Urales, *Mi vida*, Vol. 1, 54–56, 104.

259. Juan Avilés Farré, *Francisco Ferrer y Guardia: Pedagogo, anarquista y mártir* (Madrid: Marcial Pons, 2006), 17–99. For Ferrer's account of the school's inauguration see Francisco Ferrer, *The Origins and Ideas of the Modern School*, trans. Joseph McCabe (New York: G.P. Putnam's Sons, 1913), 25–32.

260. Avrich, *The Modern School Movement*, 19; Lida, 'Educación anarquista,' 41. There are many notices of similar schools opening in Spain in the anarchist press prior to 1901, for example, *Suplemento a la Revista Blanca* (Madrid), 12 May, 1900, 4.

261. Boyd, 'The Anarchists and Education,' 149.

262. Boyd, 'The Anarchists and Education,' 150–151.

263. Ullman, *The Tragic Week*, 100.

264. Ferrer, *Origins and Ideas*, 44–46; Ullman, *The Tragic Week*, 97.

265. Mella's views were expressed years later in *Acción Libertaria* (Gijón), for example see 16 December, 1910, 1. See also Tiana Ferrer, 'The Workers' Movement,' 682.

266. *Acción Libertaria* (Gijón), 27 January, 1911, 1.

267. *El Porvenir del Obrero* (Mahón), 6 September, 1901, 1.

268. *Suplemento a la Revista Blanca* (Madrid), 24 August, 1901 and 7 December, 1901, 3.

269. On the *Boletín* see Madrid Santos, 'La prensa anarquista,' 163–164.

270. *La Protesta* (La Línea de la Concepción), 21 November, 1901, 4 and 26 December, 1901, 4. On the publications of the Escuela see Avrich, *The Modern School Movement*, 22–23; Madrid Santos, 'La prensa anarquista,' 162–164; Soriano and Madrid Santos, 'Antología documental,' 12–13; Litvak, *Musa libertaria*, 278–279; Avilés Farré, *Francisco Ferrer*, 114–116.

271. *La Protesta* (La Línea de la Concepción), 24 October, 1901, 1–2. Quote from William Archer, *The Life, Trial and Death of Francisco Ferrer* (London: Chapman and Hall, 1911), 39.

272. *Patriotismo y colonización: Cual es la patria del pobre?: Tercer libro de lectura*, preface by E. Reclus (Barcelona: Escuela Moderna, 1904).
273. A summary of the story is given in Archer, *Francisco Ferrer*, 39–49. On Grave, see Constance Bantman, 'Jean Grave and French Anarchism: A Relational Approach,' *International Review of Social History* 62, 3 (2017): 451–477.
274. *Tierra y Libertad* (Madrid), 25 January, 1902, 3.
275. Francsico Ferrer, preface to Jean Grave, *Las aventuras de Nono: Segundo libro de lectura*, tran. Anselmo Lorenzo (Barcelona: La Escuela Moderna, 1908), 2; Soriano and Madrid Santos, 'Antología documental,' 192.
276. *Luz y Vida* (Santa Cruz de Tenerife), 27 January, 1906, 3; 19 May, 1906, 4; 23 June, 1906, 3. See also *El Rebelde* (Madrid), 30 June, 1904, 4.
277. *Luz y Vida* (Santa Cruz de Tenerife), 17 March, 1906, 4 and 23 June, 1906, 4. See also *La Protesta* (La Línea de la Concepción), 29 August, 1901, 4.
278. *Luz y Vida* (Santa Cruz de Tenerife), 27 January, 1906, 3.
279. Pere Solà i Gussinyer, *Las escuelas racionalistas en Cataluña, 1909–1939* (Barcelona: Tusquets, 1976), 203–204 and 208–209.
280. Boyd, 'The Anarchists and Education,' 155.
281. See Chapter 4.
282. Enrique A. Sanabria, *Republicanism and Anticlerical Nationalism in Spain* (Basingstoke: Palgrave Macmillan, 2009), 102–106; Eduard Masjuan, *Un héroe trágico del anarquismo español: Mateo Morral: 1879–1906* (Barcelona: Icaria, 2009), 177–234.
283. *Luz y Vida* (Santa Cruz de Tenerife), 24 December, 1906, 4. Avilés, *Francsico Ferrer*, 167–193.
284. Pere Solà i Gussinyer, 'Los grupos del magisterio racionalista en Argentina y Uruguay hacia 1910 y sus actitudes ante la enseñanza laica oficial,' *Historia de la Educación* 1 (1982): 234–237; Kirwin R. Shaffer, 'Freedom Teaching: Anarchism and Education in Early Republican Cuba, 1898–1925,' *The Americas* 60, 2 (2003): 161–165; Matthew Thomas, '"No-One Telling Us What to Do": Anarchist Schools in Britain, 1890–1916,' *Historical Research* 77, 197 (2004): 417–419.
285. Lida, 'Educación anarquista,' 41–42.
286. Luis Miguel Lázaro Lorente, *La Escuela Moderna de Valencia* (Valencia: Generalitat Valenciana, 1989), 106–113, see 100 for a plan of the school.
287. Tiana Ferrer, 'The Workers' Movement,' 681; Lázaro Lorente, *Escuela Moderna de Valencia*, 123–137 and 313–314.
288. Lázaro Lorente, *Escuela Moderna de Valencia*, 197–208.
289. Tiana Ferrer, 'The Workers' Movement,' 681–682.
290. *Humanidad Nueva: Extraordinario de Humanidad Nueva* (Valencia), 12 June, 1907, 2 and 5.
291. Aitor Hernández Franco, 'Federico Forcada y la escuela moderna: educación, política y laicismo en el Irún de principios de siglo XX,' *Boletín de estudios del Bidasoa* 25 (2007): 9–70; Gutiérrez Molina, *José Sánchez Rosa*, 64.
292. Antonio Viñao Frago, *Escuela para todos: Educación y modernidad en la España del siglo XX* (Madrid: Marcial Pons, 2004), 23–24.
293. Gutiérrez Molina, *José Sánchez Rosa*, 63–64.
294. Gutiérrez Molina, *José Sánchez Rosa*, 63. See also *Humanidad Nueva: Extraordinario de Humanidad Nueva* (Valencia), 12 June, 1907, 6.
295. Ullman, *The Tragic Week*, 98; Boyd, 'The Anarchists and Education,' 154.
296. *El Proletario* (Cádiz), 15 June, 1902, 8; 15 September, 1902, 8; 15 April, 1902, 7–8. See also Gutiérrez Molina, *José Sánchez Rosa*, 52.
297. *La Razón Obrera* (Cádiz), 14 December, 1901, 1–2; *Tiempos Nuevos* (Gijón), 8 December, 1905, 4.

298. *El Proletario* (Cádiz), 16 January, 1903, 8; *Germinal* (Cádiz), 24 March, 1903, 7–8.

299. On this period of Michel's life, see Constance Bantman, 'Louise Michel's London Years: A Political Reassessment,' *Women's History Review* 26, 6 (2017): 994–1012.

300. *Suplemento a la Revista Blanca* (Madrid), 30 November, 1901, 3; *El Rebelde* (Madrid), 9 January, 1904, 3. Taboada was arrested in 1905 because of his anarchist activities in the city and was assaulted in prison, see *Tierra y Libertad* (Madrid, III), 13 January, 1905, 4. Soriano and Madrid Santos, 'Antología documental,' 29, 33 n.42, 348 and 389.

301. José Luis Guzmán García, *Perfiles en el olvido del anarquismo en Canarias: Francisco González Sola (1870–1934)* (Madrid/Tenerife: La Malatesta/Tierra de Fuego, 2009), 21–24.

302. *Suplemento a la Revista Blanca* (Madrid), 12 May, 1900, 4 and 25 August, 1900, 3. See also Jxto Estebaranz, *Breve historia del anarquismo vasco: Desde sus orígenes al siglo XXI* (San Sebastián: Txertoa, 2011), 37.

303. *El Porvenir del Obrero* (Mahón), 26 October, 1912, 2. In this respect García was closer to earlier anarchist educators than those of the 'Modern Schools,' see Lida, 'Eduación anarquista,' 41.

304. Ramón Álvarez, *Eleuterio Quintanilla: (Vida y obra del maestro): Contribución a la historia del sindicalismo revolucionario en Asturias* (México, DF: Editores Mexicanos Unidos, 1973), 19–21.

305. For example *Suplemento a la Revista Blanca* (Madrid), 29 December, 1900, 2 and 19 January, 1901, 3.

306. *Suplemento a la Revista Blanca* (Madrid), 9 March, 1901, 2; *Fraternidad* (Gijón, II), 23 December, 1899, 4.

307. Ackelsberg, *Free Women of Spain*, 83–84.

308. David Muñoz Martínez and Ángel J. Sáez Rodríguez, 'Apuntes para un estudio socio-económico de La Línea de la Concepción a comienzos del siglo XX,' *Almoraima* 13 (1995): 409.

309. *La Protesta* (Valladolid), 19 January, 1901, 4 and 9 February, 1901, 4. See also *El País* (Madrid), 21 October, 1902, 3 for a brief history of the centre. Anarchist affiliates in the workers' centre: 347 carpenters, 450 construction workers, 200 painters, 210 iron and metal workers, 80 quarrymen and stonemasons, 80 cork-makers, 120 boot-makers, 120 tobacco-workers and 423 from 'varied industries' (usually casual and farm labourers), see *La Protesta* (La Línea de la Concepción), 17 May, 1901, 2. Various reports put the total figure workers' affiliated to the centre between 4,000 and 8,000 in 1902, see *El Imparcial* (Madrid), 9 October, 1902, 3 (>8,000); *El Heraldo de Madrid* (Madrid), 10 October, 1902, 2 (4,000). See also Chris Grocott, Gareth Stockey and Jo Grady, 'Anarchism in the UK('s Most Famous Fortress): Comradeship and Cupidity in Gibraltar and Neighbouring Spain, 1890–1902,' *Labour History* 56, 4 (2015): 392–393.

310. *La Protesta* (La Línea de la Concepción), 2 January, 1902, 2–3.

311. *La Protesta* (Valladolid), 1 March, 1901, 2; 22 March, 1901, 4; 29 March, 1901, 2. See also Gutiérrez Molina, *José Sánchez Rosa*, 59.

312. *La Protesta* (La Línea de la Concepción), 31 July, 1901, 4. See also criticism of this decision by a local socialist in *El Socialista* (Madrid), 19 July, 1901, 3–4.

313. *La Protesta* (La Línea de la Concepción), 28 November, 1901, 1 and 4.

314. See Isidro Dubert, 'Modernity without Modernisation: The Evolution of Domestic Service in North-West Spain, 1752–1900,' *Gender & History* 18, 2 (2006): 200.

315. *Suplemento a la Revista Blanca* (Madrid), 2 November, 1901, 4. See also Federico Gómez R. de Castro, 'Las escuelas católicas privadas y la educación

popular,' in Guereña and Tiana Ferrer, *Clases populares, cultura, educación*, 233–239.
316. *La Época* (Madrid), 15 October, 1902; *El País* (Madrid), 21 October, 1902, 3.
317. *La Protesta* (La Línea de la Concepción), 29 March, 1902, 1 and 12 April, 1902, 4.
318. *La Protesta* (La Línea de la Concepción), 7 June, 1902, 3.
319. Report comes from Álvarez's former employers, the liberal daily *El Globo* (Madrid), 7 October, 1902, 3.
320. See *El Corsario* (Valencia), 11 October, 1902, 1; *El Proletario* (Cádiz), 15 October, 1902, 7 and *El Porvenir del Obrero* (Mahón), 25 October, 1902, 4. The longest and most informed eulogy for Álvarez came from his old colleague Anselmo Lorenzo in *Tierra y Libertad* (Madrid), 18 October, 1902, 2.
321. González Fernández, *Utopía y realidad*, 91–92.
322. See Chris Grocott, Gareth Stockey and Jo Grady, 'Anarchy in the UK,' 401 and 'Reformers and Revolutionaries: The Battle for the Working Classes in Gibraltar and Its Hinterland, 1902–1921,' *Labor History* 59, 6 (2018): 692–694; and Enrique Sánchez Cabeza-Earle, *La Línea de mis recuerdos* (La Línea de la Concepción, no publisher, 1975), 131–134. Published online, accessed 26 October, 2013, https://lalineaenblancoynegro.blogspot.com/2018/09/la-linea-de-mis-recuerdos-de-enrique.html.
   See also Luis Javier Traverso Vásquez, 'El suceso de las Pedreras a través de la prensa,' (2012). Published online, accessed 26 October, 2013, http://lalineaenblancoynegro.blogspot.co.uk/2012/08/el-suceso-de-las-pedreras-traves-de-la.html.
323. *El Rebelde* (Madrid), 23 January, 1904, 2; 6 February, 1904, 2; 20 February, 1904, 2.
324. *El Rebelde* (Madrid), 20 February, 1904, 3; 27 February, 1904, 4; 18 March, 1904, 3; 14 April, 1904, 4; 23 June, 1904, 4.
325. See González Fernández, *Utopía y realidad*, 90–91.
326. Examples of anarchist critique of *caciquismo*: *El Rebelde* (Madrid), 31 March, 1905, 3; 7 April, 1904, 4; 7 July, 1904, 3. On *caciquismo* see José Valera Ortega, *Los amigos políticos: Partidos, elecciones y caciquismo en la Restauración (1875–1900)* (Madrid: Alianza, 1977) and Javier Moreno Luzón, 'Political Clientelism, Elites and Caciquismo in Restoration Spain,' *European History Quarterly* 37, 3 (2007): 417–441.
327. *El Proletario* (Cádiz), 15 April, 1902, 5–6 and 15 May, 1902, 4–5.
328. *La Protesta* (La Línea de la Concepción), 31 October, 1901, 4 and 19 December, 1901, 4.
329. *El Rebelde* (Madrid), 16 January, 1904, 4. See also Gutiérrez Molina, *José Sánchez Rosa*, 52. See similar incident in Villafranca (Córdoba), reported in *El Rebelde* (Madrid), 30 June, 1904, 4.
330. *La Protesta* (La Línea de la Concepción), 21 May, 1902, 4 and 7 June, 1902, 4.
331. *La Protesta* (La Línea de la Concepción), 22 February, 1902, 2. See similar event discussed in *El Obrero del Río-Tinto* (Río-Tinto), 9 June, 1900, 3 and 28 July, 1900, 3.
332. Cited in Ullman, *The Tragic Week*, 97.
333. *El Obrero* (Badajoz), 27 January, 1902, 4; *El Rebelde* (Madrid), 16 January, 1904, 4 and 5 March, 1904, 4.
334. See *El Rebelde* (Madrid), 30 June, 1904, 4.
335. *Suplemento a la Revista Blanca* (Madrid), 21 September, 1901, 3.
336. *Suplemento a la Revista Blanca* (Madrid), 2 November, 1901, 4; *La Protesta* (La Línea de la Concepción), 1 February, 1902, 4.
337. *La Protesta* (La Línea de la Concepción), 28 November, 1901, 4.
338. *El Corsario* (Valencia), 5 December, 1902, 3.

339. *La Razón Obrera* (Cádiz), 7 December, 1901, 4 and 14 December, 1901, 4.
340. *Suplemento a la Revista Blanca* (Madrid), 17 June, 1899, 3; 7 April, 1900, 3. See also *Luz y Vida* (Santa Cruz de Tenerife), 19 May, 1906, 1.
341. *El Rebelde* (Madrid), 13 February, 1904, 4. See also 11 March, 1904, 4.
342. González Fernández, *Utopía y realidad*, 94–100.
343. *El Proletario* (Cádiz), 16 December, 1902, 7–8. See also *Suplemento a la Revista Blanca* (Madrid), 7 December, 1901, 3–4.
344. *El Rebelde* (Madrid), 27 February, 1904, 4. See also poor attendance at lectura in La Coruña centre: *El Rebelde* (Madrid), 11 March, 1904, 2.
345. Ralle, 'La sociabilidad obrera,' 161.
346. See *El Rebelde* (Madrid), 2 January, 1904, 2.
347. *La Protesta* (La Línea de la Concepción), 31 October, 1901, 4.
348. See *El Rebelde* (Madrid), 30 June, 1904, 3. The 'La lucha obrera,' section of this paper was full of reports of closures across Spain through 1904.
349. Tiana Ferrer, 'The Workers' Movement,' 674–675.
350. Navarro Navarro, *Ateneos y grupos*, 12–13.
351. *Suplemento a la Revista Blanca* (Madrid), 14 September, 1901, 1.
352. Ángel Durante, 'Entre el mito y realidad: Barcelona, 1902,' *Ayer* 4 (1991): 151–153.
353. For example, see *El Obrero del Río Tinto* (Río Tinto), 26 May, 1900–18 August, 1900. One exception to this trend can be found in an editorial of *Suplemento a la Revista Blanca* (Madrid), 30 September, 1899, 4, which declared that anarchists were 'enemies of all organisation,' provoking strong criticism in *La Protesta* (Valladolid), 6 October, 1899, 2 and 19 October, 1899, 2; *Fraternidad* (Gijón, II), 1 July, 1900, 1.
354. *Fraternidad* (Gijón, II), 14 July, 1900, 1.
355. On the failed 'International Workers' Alliance,' under the direction of Vicente García see *Suplemento a la Revista Blanca* (Madrid), 30 December, 1899, 3–4; 10 February, 1900, 3. Plans for a workers' congress in Manlleu (Barcelona) in *Suplemento a la Revista Blanca* (Madrid), 10 February, 1900, 4 and *El Obrero del Río-Tinto* (Río-Tinto), 14 July, 1900, 2–3. See also Xavier Cuadrat, *Socialismo y anarquismo en Cataluña (1899–1911): Los orígenes de la CNT* (Madrid: Ediciones de la Revista de Trabajo, 1976), 57. The FSORE is known by a number of other names and acronyms, including the simply the 'Federation Regional,' for example, *Suplemento a la Revista Blanca* (Madrid), 26 October, 1901, 2 and the FRSRRE in Castillo, *Historia de la UGT*, 322–324.
356. Antonio López Estudillo, 'El anarquismo español decimonónico,' *Ayer* 45, 1 (2002): 95, n.32.
357. The exact size of the Federation at its peak in late 1901 is contested. The figure most frequently used is 73,000, which can be found in Urales in *Mi vida*, II, 72. Ramiro de Maetzu claimed it was 75,000 in *El Imparcial* (Madrid), 6 December, 1901, 3, which is also cited by Cuadrat, *Socialismo y anarquismo*, 64.
358. *La Protesta* (La Línea de la Concepción), 26 December, 1901, 2.
359. Counter to claim made in Jason Garner, *Goals and Means: Anarchism, Syndicalism, and Internationalism in the Origins of the Federación Anarquista Ibérica* (Edinburgh: AK Press, 2016), 60. Information on FSORE membership: I Congress: *Suplemento a La Revista Blanca* (Madrid), 20 October, 1900, 2; II Congress: *Suplemento a La Revista Blanca* (Madrid), 19 October, 1901, 3 and *La Federación Regional Española: Manifestó, estatutos, delegaciones, adhesiones y acuerdos: Segundo Congreso* (Madrid: Antonio Marzo, 1901), 21–34; III Congress: *Tierra y Libertad* (Madrid), 21 May, 1903, 1.

360. Durante, 'Barcelona 1902,' 161–168; Angel Smith, 'Anarchism, the General Strike and the Barcelona Labour Movement, 1899–1914,' *European History Quarterly* 27, 1 (1997): 5–40.
361. Madrid, 'La prensa anarquista,' 169.
362. Earlier reservations include *El Cosmopolita* (Valladolid), 28 September, 1901, 3. See also González Fernández, *Utopía y realidad*, 70–71.
363. *Tierra y Libertad* (Madrid), 12 March, 1903, 2.
364. Cuadrat, *Socialismo y anarquismo*, 127–128.
365. Kaplan, *Anarchists of Andalusia*, 202–203; Gutiérrez Molina, *José Sánchez Rosa*, 60; Ángel Herrerín López, *Anarquía, dinamita y revolución social: Violencia y represión en la España entre siglos (1868–1909)* (Madrid: Catarata, 2011), 209.
366. See *Tierra y Libertad* (Madrid), 12 October, 1903, 2 and 4 February, 1904, 2; *El Rebelde* (Madrid), 18 August, 1904, 1–2. See also Avilés Farré, *Francisco Ferrer*, 140–141.
367. See *Tierra y Libertad* (Madrid) and *El Rebelde* (Madrid), from October 1903 onwards, both of which discussed the Alcalá prisoners in almost every issue.
368. See Herrerín López, *Anarquía, dinamita*, 215.
369. *El Rebelde* (Madrid), 28 July, 1904, 1.
370. *El Rebelde* (Madrid), 5 May, 1904, 4. The publication of this letter led to a the brief imprisonment of the paper's editor Antonio Apolo, see *El Rebelde* (Madrid), 23 June, 1904, 1 and 21 April, 1904, 2.
371. *Al Paso* (Sevilla, II), 16 December, 1909, 2; *El Libertario* (Madrid), 12 December, 1909, 2.
372. Madrid Santos, 'La prensa anarquista,' 161–162.
373. *Suplemento a la Revista Blanca* (Madrid), 1 September, 1900, 1.
374. Saul Newman, 'Anarchism and the Politics of Ressentiment,' in *I Am Not a Man: I Am Dynamite!: Friedrich Nietzsche and the Anarchist Tradition*, ed. John Moore and Spencer Sunshine (New York: Autonomedia, 2004), 107.
375. *Juventud* (Valencia), 5 June, 1903, 3.
376. *Juventud* (Valencia), 4 January, 1903, 1 and 5 June, 1903, 2–3.
377. *Juventud* (Valencia), 4 January, 1903, 1.
378. *Luz y Vida* (Santa Cruz de Tenerife), 17 February, 1906, 4.
379. *Luz y Vida* (Santa Cruz de Tenerife), 8 December, 1906, 3 and 22 January, 1907, 3. The paper's constant attacks on the local Church led to its excommunication by the Archbishop of Tenerife, see *Luz y Vida* (Santa Cruz de Tenerife), 17 February, 1906, 1–2.
380. *Luz y Vida* (Santa Cruz de Tenerife), 22 January, 1907, 1. See also 30 December, 1905, 1.
381. *Luz y Vida* (Santa Cruz de Tenerife), 22 January, 1907, 4.
382. *Anticristo* (La Línea de la Concepción), 31 March, 1906, 3–4.
383. *Anticristo* (La Línea de la Concepción), 19 May, 1906, 1. See also Francisco José Fernández Andújar, 'Anarquismo nietzcheano y el periódico *Anticristo*,' *International Journal of Iberian Studies* 29, 3 (2016): 257–272.
384. *El Productor* (Barcelona, IV), 19 April, 1906, 4.
385. Antonio Apolo, *La explotación de Montjuich: Farsantes sin careta: Apuntes biográficos para conocer a Lerroux* (Madrid: Antonio Marzo, 1901). See also Álvarez Junco, *El emperador*, 213, n.121.
386. *Suplemento a la Revista Blanca* (Madrid), 4 January, 1902, 1. See also James A. Baer, *Anarchist Immigrants in Spain and Argentina* (Chicago: University of Illinois Press, 2015), 52–54.
387. *Tierra y Libertad* (Madrid), 16 June, 1903, 1.

388. The paper briefly returned as *Suplemento Semanal a la Revista Blanca*, which published only seven issues. Madrid Santos, 'La prensa anarquista,' 146–147.
389. Urales, *Mi vida*, Vol. 2, 238–239. Emphasis in original.
390. *Suplemento Semanal de la Revista Blanca* (Madrid), 13 October, 1904, 1–3.
391. No copy of the pamphlet has survived, see Soriano and Madrid Santos, 'Antología documental,' 293. One of the signatories of the pamphlet had their subscription to *La Revista Blanca* publically cancelled by Urales, see *Suplemento Semanal a La Revista Blanca* (Madrid), 6 October, 1904, 16.
392. Madrid Santos, 'La prensa anarquista,' 146–149. The group's name was a reference to the Haymarket Riot which occurred on May 4, 1886.
393. Guzman Garcia, *Francisco González Sola*, 24–32 and Amparo Sánchez Cobos, 'La reorganización del trabajo libre: Los anarquistas españoles y la difusión del ideal libertario en Cuba,' *Millars* 33 (2010): 247–257. Saavedra returned to Cuba in 1913, before a further deportation to Spain in 1915.
394. Madrid Santos, *Solidaridad Obrera*, 76–84.
395. *El Rebelde* (Madrid), 26 December, 1903, 1 and 4.
396. See prisoner lists in *El Rebelde* (Madrid), 23 January 23, 1904–8; December 8, 1904.
397. *El Rebelde* (Madrid), 27 February, 1904, 2. Emphasis in original. See also 11 March, 1904, 2.
398. *Al Paso* (Sevilla, II), 31 December, 1909; *El Rebelde* (Madrid), 28 April, 1904, 3 and 14 July, 1904, 1.
399. *El Rebelde* (Madrid), 5 March, 1904, 1. Critical response to this article in *El Rebelde* (Madrid), 21 March, 1904, 2–3.
400. For example, see *El Rebelde* (Madrid), 12 May, 1904, 2; 2 June, 1904, 1; 10 June, 1904, 2; 23 June, 1904, 1.
401. *El Rebelde* (Madrid), 1 December, 1904, 3.
402. *El Rebelde* (Madrid), 30 June, 1904, 1.
403. *El Rebelde* (Madrid), 12 January, 1905, 1.
404. Miguel Íñiguez, *Esbozo de una enciclopedia histórica del anarquismo español* (Madrid: Fundación de Estudios Libertarios Anselmo Lorenzo, 2001), 46–47.
405. *Al Paso* (Sevilla, II), 7 January, 1910, 1. See also Kaplan, *Anarchists of Andalusia*, 203; Barrio Alonso, *Anarquismo en Asturias*, 57–60; González Fernández, *Utopía y realidad*, 108–116; Smith, 'Anarchism,' 13 and 24.
406. *El Rebelde* (Madrid), 14 July, 1904, 2–3.
407. List of editors arrested in *La Huelga General* (Madrid), 9 March, 1906, 1.
408. *El Rebelde* (Madrid), 24 July, 1904, 2–3 and 4 August, 1904, 3.

Bibliography

Archives

AFPI: Archivo Fundación Pablo Iglesias. Online.
BL: British Library.
BNE: Biblioteca Nacional de España. Madrid.
BVA: Biblioteca Virtual de Andalucía. Online.
CED: cedall.org. Online.
HMM: Hemeroteca Municipal de Madrid. Madrid.
IA: The Internet Archive. Online.

IISG: Internationaal Instituut voor Sociale Geschiedenis. Amsterdam.
UNSM: Universidad Nacional de San Martín: AméricaLee Digital Collection. Online.
US: University of Sheffield Library. Sheffield.

Primary Sources

Anarchist Press

Acción Libertaria. Gijón/Vigo, 1910–1911. HMM and IISG.
Acción Libertaria. Madrid, 1913. IISG.
Adelante. Santander, 1902–1903. IISG.
Al Paso. Sevilla, II, Epoch, 1909–1910. IISG.
Anticristo. La Línea de la Concepción, 1906. IISG.
Buena Semilla. Barcelona, 1905–1906. IISG.
El 4º de Febrero. Huelva, 1902. HMM.
El Corsario. La Coruña, 1890–1896. IISG.
El Corsario. Valencia, 1902. IISG.
El Cosmopolita. Valladolid, 1900–1901. IISG.
El Látigo. Baracaldo, 1912–1914. IISG.
El Libertario. Madrid, 1909–1910. IISG.
El Obrero. Badajoz, 1899–1902. IISG.
El Obrero del Río-Tinto. Río-Tinto, 1900. IISG.
El Porvenir del Obrero. Mahón, 1898–1907. BNE, HMM and IISG.
El Porvenir del Obrero. Mahón, II Epoch, 1912–1915. BNE, HMM and IISG.
El Productor. Barcelona, III Epoch, 1902–1904. IISG.
El Productor. Barcelona, IV Epoch, 1905–1906. IISG.
El Proletario. Cádiz, 1902–1903. IISG.
El Rebelde. Madrid, 1903–1905. HMM and IISG.
El Trabajo. Cádiz, 1899–1900. HMM.
Escuela Libre. Valladolid, 1911. IISG.
Fraternidad. Gijón, II Epoch, 1899–1900. IISG.
Germinal. La Coruña, 1904–1905. IISG.
Juventud. Valencia, 1903. IISG.
La Acción. La Coruña, 1908. IISG.
La Defensa del Obrero. Gijón, 1901. IISG.
La Huelga General. Madrid, 1906. IISG.
La Humanidad Libre. Valencia, 1902. IISG.
La Idea Libre. Madrid, 1894–1899. HMM and IISG.
La Protesta. Valladolid/Sabadell/La Línea de la Concepción, 1899–1902. BVA and IISG.
La Razón Obrera. Cádiz, 1901–1902. HMM.
La Revista Blanca. Madrid, 1898–1905. II, BNE, HMM and IISG.
La Solidaridad Ferroviaria. Madrid, 1901–1904. IISG.
La Voz de la Mujer. Buenos Aires, 1896–1897. UNSM.
Libre Concurso. Mahón, 1902. HMM.
Luz y Vida. Santa Cruz de Tenerife, 1905–1907. IISG.
Natura. Barcelona, 1903–1905. HMM.

Solidaridad Obrera. Gijón, 1909–1910. IISG.
Solidaridad Obrera. Barcelona, II Epoch, 1910–1911. CED and IISG.
Suplemento a la Revista Blanca. Madrid, 1899–1902. HMM and IISG.
Suplemento Semanal de la Revista Blanca. Madrid, 1904. IISG.
Tiempos Nuevos. Gijón, 1905. IISG.
Tierra y Libertad. Madrid, 1902–1904. IISG.
Tierra y Libertad. Madrid, II Epoch, 1904. IISG.
Tierra y Libertad. Madrid, III Epoch, 1905. IISG.
Vía Libre. Zaragoza, 1906. IISG.

Supplements and Almanacs to Periodicals

El Proletario: Suplemento al número 14. Cádiz, 19 October, 1901. IISG.
Humanidad Nueva: Extraordinario de Humanidad Nueva. Valencia, 12 June, 1907. IISG.

Other Press

El Globo. Madrid, 1875–1932. BNE.
El Heraldo de Madrid. Madrid, 1890–1939. BNE.
El Imparcial. Madrid, 1867–1933. BNE.
El Liberal. Madrid, 1879–1936. BNE.
El País. Madrid, 1887–1921. BNE.
El Socialista. Madrid, 1886–1939. AFPI.
La Época. Madrid, 1849–1936. BNE.

Memoirs, Books and Pamphlets by Contemporary Authors

Apolo, Antonio. *La explotación de Montjuich: Farsantes sin careta: Apuntes biográficos para conocer a Lerroux.* Madrid: Antonio Marzo, 1901. BNE.
Archer, William. *The Life, Trial and Death of Francisco Ferrer.* London: Chapman and Hall, 1911. US.
Bonafulla, Leopoldo. *Generación libre: Los errores del neo-maltusianismo.* Barcelona: El Productor, 1905. IISG.
Ferrer, Francisco. *The Origins and Ideas of the Modern School,* translated by Joseph McCabe. New York: G.P. Putnam's Sons, 1913. IA.
Goldman, Emma. *Living My Life,* 2 Volumes. New York: Dover Publications, 1970.
Grave, Jean. *Las aventuras de Nono: Segundo libro de lectura,* translated by Anselmo Lorenzo, preface by Francisco Ferrer. Barcelona: La Escuela Moderna, 1908. IISG.
La Federación Regional Española: Manifestó, estatutos, delegaciones, adhesiones y acuerdos: Segundo Congreso. Madrid, Antonio Marzo, 1901. Serialised in *Suplemento a la Revista Blanca* (Madrid): 26 October, 1901–4 January, 1902.
La Iglesia y García, Gustavo. *Caracteres del anarquismo en la actualidad.* Barcelona: Gustavo Gil, 1907. BL.
Patriotismo y colonización: Cual es la patria del pobre?: Tercer libro de lectura, preface by Eliseo Reclus. Barcelona: Escuela Moderna, 1904. IISG.
Urales, Federico. *Mi vida,* 3 Volumes. Barcelona: La Revista Blanca, 1930. IISG.

Secondary Sources

Abelló Güell, Teresa. *Les relacions internacionals de l'anarquisme català (1881–1914)*. Barcelona: Edicions 62, 1987.

Ackelsberg, Martha A. *Free Women of Spain: Anarchism and the Struggle for the Emancipation of Women*. Edinburgh: AK Press, 2005.

Ackelsberg, Martha A. 'It Takes More Than a Village!: Transnational Travels of Spanish Anarchism in Argentina and Cuba.' *International Journal of Iberian Studies* 29, 3 (2016): 205–223.

Alford, Richard D. *Naming and Identity: A Cross-Cultural Study of Personal Naming Practices*. New Haven: HRAF Press, 1988.

Álvarez, Ramón. *Eleuterio Quintanilla: (Vida y obra del maestro): Contribución a la historia del sindicalismo revolucionario en Asturias*. México DF: Editores Mexicanos Unidos, 1973.

Álvarez Junco, José. *El emperador del Paralelo: Lerroux y la demagogia populista*. Madrid: Alianza Editorial, 1990.

Álvarez Junco, José. *La ideología política del anarquismo español (1868–1910)*. Madrid: Siglo XXI, 1991.

Avilés Farré, Juan. *Francisco Ferrer y Guardia: Pedagogo, anarquista y mártir*. Madrid: Marcial Pons, 2006.

Avrich, Paul. *The Modern School Movement: Anarchism and Education in the United States*. Princeton: Princeton University Press, 1980.

Baer, James A. *Anarchist Immigrants in Spain and Argentina*. Chicago: University of Illinois Press, 2015.

Baigorria, Osvaldo, ed. *El amor libre: Eros y anarquía*. Buenos Aires: Libros de Anarres, 2006.

Balfour, Sebastian. 'The Impact of the War Within Spain: Continuity or Crisis?.' In *The Crisis of 1898: Colonial Redistribution and Nationalist Mobilization*, edited by Angel Smith and Emma Dávila-Coz, 180–194. Basingstoke: Macmillan, 1999.

Bantman, Constance, 'Internationalism without an International? Cross-Channel Anarchist Networks, 1890–1914.' *Revue belge de philology et d'histoire* 84, 4 (2006): 961–981.

Bantman, Constance. 'Jean Grave and French Anarchism: A Relational Approach.' *International Review of Social History* 62, 3 (2017): 451–477.

Bantman, Constance. 'Louise Michel's London Years: A Political Reassessment.' *Women's History Review* 26, 6 (2017): 994–1012.

Bar, Antonio. *La CNT en los años rojos: Del sindicalismo revolucionario al anarcosindicalismo (1910–1926)*. Madrid: Akal, 1981.

Barrio Alonso, Ángeles. *Anarquismo y anarcosindicalismo en Asturias, 1890–1936*. Madrid: Siglo XXI, 1988.

Barrio Alonso, Ángeles. 'Cultura del trabajo y organización obrera en Gijón en el cambio de siglo.' *Historia Contemporánea* 5 (1991): 27–51.

Boxer, Marilyn J. 'Rethinking the Socialist Construction and International Career of the Concept of "Bourgeois Feminism".' *The American Historical Review* 112, 1 (2007): 131–158.

Boyd, Carolyn P. 'The Anarchists and Education in Spain, 1868–1909.' *The Journal of Modern History* 48, 4 (1976): 125–170.

Brah, Avtar, and Ann Phoenix. '"Ain't I a Woman?": Revisiting Intersectionality.' *Journal of International Women's Studies* 5, 3 (2004): 75–86.

Cabeza-Earle, Enrique Sánchez. *La Línea de mis recuerdos*. La Línea de la Concepción, no publisher, 1975. Published online, accessed 26 October, 2013. https://lalineaenblancoynegro.blogspot.com/2018/09/la-linea-de-mis-recuerdos-de-enrique.html.

Capelán, Antón. *Da violencia que non condenan: O centenario da folgo xeral de maio na Coruña*. La Coruña: Ateneo Libertario Ricardo Mella. 2003.

Castillo, Santiago. 'La labor editorial del PSOE en el siglo XIX.' *Estudios de Historia Social* 8–9 (1979): 181–195.

Castillo, Santiago. *Historia de la UGT: Un sindicalismo consciente, 1873–1914*. Madrid: Siglo XXI, 2008.

Castro, Federico Gómez R. de. 'Las escuelas católicas privadas y la educación popular.' In Guereña and Tiana Ferrer, *Clases populares, cultura, educación*, 233–239.

Chadwick, Owen. *The Secularisation of the European Mind in the 19th Century*. Cambridge: Cambridge University Press, 1975.

Cleminson, Richard. *Anarchism, Science and Sex: Eugenics in Eastern Spain, 1900–1937*. Oxford: Peter Lang, 2000.

Cleminson, Richard. '"Science and Sympathy" or "Sexual Subversion on a Human Basis"? Anarchists in Spain and the World League for Sexual Reform.' *History of Sexuality* 12, 1 (2003): 110–121.

Cleminson, Richard. *Anarquismo y sexualidad en España, 1900–1939*. Cádiz, Universidad de Cádiz, 2008.

Cleminson, Richard, and Francisco Vásquez García. *'Los Invisibles': A History of Male Homosexuality in Spain, 1850–1939*. Cardiff: University of Wales Press, 2007.

Cuadrat, Xavier. *Socialismo y anarquismo en Cataluña (1899–1911): Los orígenes de la CNT*. Madrid: Ediciones de la Revista de Trabajo, 1976.

Cuevas Noa, Francisco José. *Anarquismo y educación: La propuesta sociopolítica de la pedagogía libertaria*. Madrid: Fundación de Estudios Libertarios Anselmo Lorenzo, 2003.

Cumbers, Andy, Paul Routledge, and Corinne Nativel. 'The Entangled Geographies of Global Justice Networks.' *Progress in Human Geography* 32, 2 (2008): 183–201.

Dalmau, Pol. *Press, Politics and National Identities in Catalonia: The Transformation of La Vanguardia, 1881–1931*. Brighton: Sussex Academic Press, 2017.

Delhom, Joël. 'Esbozo de una tipología temática y funcional de los usos de la biblia en el anarquismo hispánico.' In *Cuando los anarquistas citaban la biblia: Entre mesianismo y propaganda*, edited by Joël Delhom and Daniel Attala, 233–274. Madrid: Catarata, 2014.

Díaz del Moral, Juan. *Historia de las agitaciones campesinas andaluzas-Córdoba: Antecedentes para una reforma agraria*. Madrid: Alianza, 1967.

Dubert, Isidro. 'Modernity without Modernisation: The Evolution of Domestic Service in North-West Spain, 1752–1900.' *Gender & History* 18, 2 (2006): 199–210.

Durante, Ángel. 'Entre el mito y realidad: Barcelona, 1902.' *Ayer* 4 (1991): 147–168.

Enders, Victoria Lorée, and Pamela Beth Radcliff, eds. *Constructing Spanish Womanhood: Female Identity in Modern Spain*. Albany: State University of New York Press, 1999.

Esenwein, George. *Anarchist Ideology and the Working-Class Movement in Spain, 1868–1898.* Berkeley, CA: University of California Press, 1989.

Espigado Tocino, Gloria. 'Las mujeres en el anarquismo español (1869–1939).' *Ayer* 45, 1 (2002): 39–72.

Estebaranz, Jxto. *Breve historia del anarquismo vasco: Desde sus orígenes al siglo XXI.* San Sebastián: Txertoa, 2011.

Fernández Álvarez, Antón. *Ricardo Mella o el anarquismo humanista.* Barcelona: Anthropos, 1990.

Fernández Andújar, Francisco José. 'Anarquismo nietzcheano y el periódico *Anticristo.*' *International Journal of Iberian Studies* 29, 3 (2016): 257–272.

Gabriel, Pere. 'Sociabilidad obrera y popular y vida política en Cataluña, 1868–1923.' *Bulletin d'Histoire Contemporaine de l'Espagne* 17–18 (1993): 145–156.

García Maroto, María Ángeles. *La mujer en la prensa anarquista: España, 1900–1936.* Madrid: Fundación de Estudios Libertarios Anselmo Lorenzo, 1996.

Garner, Jason. *Goals and Means: Anarchism, Syndicalism, and Internationalism in the Origins of the Federación Anarquista Ibérica.* Edinburgh: AK Press, 2016.

Gemie, Sharif. 'Counter-Community: An Aspect of Anarchist Political Culture.' *Journal of Contemporary History* 29, 2 (1994): 349–367.

Gemie, Sharif. 'Anarchism and Feminism: A Historical Survey.' *Women's History Review* 5, 3 (1996): 417–444.

Gil Andrés, Carlos. 'Mujeres en la calle: Trabajo, condición social y protesta de la mujer: La Rioja, 1885–1910.' In *El trabajo a través de la historia,* edited by Santiago Castillo, 373–382. Madrid: Asociación de Historia Social, 1996.

Girón Sierra, Álvaro. 'Metáforas finiseculares del declive biológico: Degeneración y revolución en el anarquismo español (1872–1914).' *Asclepio* 51, 1 (1999): 247–273.

González Fernández, Ángeles. *Utopía y realidad: Anarquismo, anarcosindicalismo y organizaciones obreras: Sevilla, 1900–1936.* Sevilla: Diputación Provincial de Sevilla, 1996.

Goyens, Tom. 'Social Space and the Practice of Anarchist History.' *Rethinking History* 13, 4 (2009): 439–457.

Grocott, Chris, Gareth Stockey, and Jo Grady. 'Anarchism in the UK('s Most Famous Fortress): Comradeship and Cupidity in Gibraltar and Neighbouring Spain, 1890–1902.' *Labour History* 56, 4 (2015): 385–406.

Grocott, Chris, Gareth Stockey, and Jo Grady. 'Reformers and Revolutionaries: The Battle for the Working Classes in Gibraltar and its Hinterland, 1902–1921.' *Labor History* 59, 6 (2018): 692–719.

Guereña, Jean-Louis. 'Las casas del pueblo y la educación obrera a principios del siglo XX.' *Hispania: Revista Española de Historia* 51, 2 (1991): 645–692.

Guereña, Jean-Louis. *La prostitución en la España contemporánea.* Madrid: Marcial Pons, 2003.

Guereña, Jean-Louis. *Sociabilidad, cultura y educación en Asturias bajo la Restauración (1875–1900).* Oviedo: Real Instituto de Estudios Asturianos, 2005.

Guereña, Jean-Louis. 'European Influences in Spanish Popular Education: The Case of the Socialist *Casa Del Pueblo* of Madrid and the Belgian Model (1897–1929).' *History of Education* 35, 1 (2006): 27–45.

Guereña, Jean-Louis. 'Fermín Salvochea: Del federalismo al anarquismo.' In *Fermín Salvochea: Un anarquista entre la leyenda y la historia,* edited by Jacques Maurice, 73–117. Cádiz: Quorum, 2009.

Guereña, Jean-Louis, and Alejandro Tiana Ferrer, eds. *Clases populares, cultura, educación: Siglos XIX y XX.* Madrid: UNED, 1989.

Gutiérrez Molina, José Luis. *El anarquismo en Chiclana: Diego Rodríguez Barbosa: Obrera y escritor (1885–1936).* Chiclana de la Frontera: Ayuntamiento de Chiclana, 2001.

Gutiérrez Molina, José Luis. *La tiza, la tinta y la palabra: José Sánchez Rosa: Maestro y anarquista andaluz (1864–1936).* Ubrique: Tréveris, 2005.

Guzmán García, José Luis. *Perfiles en el olvido del anarquismo en Canarias: Francisco González Sola (1870–1934).* Madrid and Tenerife: La Malatesta and Tierra de Fuego, 2009.

Hernández Franco, Aitor. 'Federico Forcada y la escuela moderna: educación, política y laicismo en el Irún de principios de siglo XX.' *Boletín de estudios del Bidasoa* 25 (2007): 9–70.

Herrerín López, Ángel. *Anarquía, dinamita y revolución social: Violencia y represión en la España entre siglos (1868–1909).* Madrid: Catarata, 2011.

Herrerín López, Ángel. 'Anarchist Sociability in Spain: In Times of Violence and Clandestinity.' *Bulletin for Spanish and Portuguese Historical Studies* 38, 1 (2013): 155–174.

Hofmann, Bert, Pere Joan i Tous, and Manfred Tietze, eds. *El anarquismo español y sus tradiciones culturales.* Frankfurt and Madrid: Vervuert and Iberoamericana, 1995.

Holton, Sandra Stanley. 'To Educate Women Into Rebellion: Elizabeth Cady Stanton and the Creation of a Transatlantic Network of Radical Suffragists.' In Offen, *Globalizing Feminisms*, 36–50.

Hutton, John. 'Camille Pissarro's *Turpitudes Sociales* and Late Nineteenth Century French Anti-feminism.' *History Workshop* 24, 1 (1987): 32–61.

Íñiguez, Miguel. *Esbozo de una enciclopedia histórica del anarquismo español.* Madrid: Fundación de Estudios Libertarios Anselmo Lorenzo, 2001.

Jiménez-Landi, Antonio. *La Institución Libre de Enseñanza y su ambiente: Los orígenes de la Institución.* Madrid: Editorial Computense, 1996.

Kaplan, Temma. *Anarchists of Andalusia, 1868–1903.* Princeton: Princeton University Press, 1977.

Kaplan, Temma. 'Female Consciousness and Collective Action: The Case of Barcelona, 1910–1918.' *Signs* 7, 3 (1982): 545–566.

Kaplan, Temma. 'Redressing the Balance: Gendered Acts of Justice Around the Mining Community of Río Tinto in 1913.' In Enders and Radcliff, *Constructing Spanish Womanhood*, 545–566.

Kerry, Matthew. 'The Bones of Contention: The Secularisation of Cemeteries and Funerals in the Spanish Second Republic.' *European History Quarterly* 49, 1 (2019): 73–95.

Kössler, Till. 'Human Sciences and Child Reform in Spain, 1890–1936.' In *Engineering Society: The Role of the Human and Social Sciences in Modern Societies, 1880–1980,* edited by Kerstin Brückweh, Dirk Schumann, Richard F. Wetzell and Benjamin Ziemann, 179–197. Basingstoke: Palgrave Macmillan, 2012.

Lázaro Lorente, Luis Miguel. *La Escuela Moderna de Valencia.* Valencia: Generalitat Valenciana, 1989.

Lenoe, Matthew. *Closer to the Masses: Stalinist Culture, Social Revolution, and Soviet Newspapers.* Cambridge: Harvard University Press, 2004.

Lida, Clara. 'Educación anarquista del ochocientos.' *Revista de Occidente* 97 (1971): 33–47.

194   *The Cult of Reason*

Lieberson, Stanley. *A Matter of Taste: How Names, Fashion and Culture Change.* New Haven: Yale University Press, 2000.

Linden, Marcel van der, and Wayne Thorpe. 'The Rise and Fall of Revolutionary Syndicalism.' In *Revolutionary Syndicalism: An International Perspective,* edited by Marcel van der Linden and Wayne Thorpe, 1–24. Aldershot: Scolar Press, 1990.

Litvak, Lily. *Musa libertaria: Arte, literatura y vida cultural del anarquismo español (1890–1913).* Madrid: Fundación de Estudios Libertarios Anselmo Lorenzo, 2001.

López Estudillo, Antonio. 'El anarquismo español decimonónico.' *Ayer* 45, 1 (2002): 73–104.

Madrid Santos, Francisco. 'La prensa anarquista y anarcosindicalista en España desde la I Internacional hasta el fin de la Guerra Civil.' PhD thesis, Barcelona: Universidad Central de Barcelona, 1988–1989. Published online, accessed 12 May, 2012. http://cedall.org/Documentacio/Castella/cedall203410101.htm.

Madrid Santos, Francisco. *Solidaridad Obrera y el periodismo de raíz ácrata.* Badalona: Ediciones Solidaridad Obrera, 2007.

Masjuan, Eduard. *Un héroe trágico del anarquismo español: Mateo Morral: 1879–1906.* Barcelona: Icaria, 2009.

Medina Arjona, Encarnación. 'El Grupo Germinal de 1901 y Zola: El carácter programático de una carta inédita.' *Ull Crític* 7 (2002): 169–181.

Mintz, Jerome R. *The Anarchists of Casas Viejas.* Chicago: University of Chicago Press, 1982.

Monguió, Luis. 'Una biblioteca obrera madrileña en 1912–1913.' *Bulletin Hispanique* 77, 1–2, (1975): 154–173.

Morales Muñoz, Manuel. *Cultura e ideología en el anarquismo Español (1870–1910).* Málaga: Centro de Ediciones de la Diputación de Málaga, 2002.

Moreno Luzón, Javier. 'Political Clientelism, Elites and Caciquismo in Restoration Spain.' *European History Quarterly* 37, 3 (2007): 417–441.

Motilla Salas, Xavier. 'Bases bibliográficas para una historia de la sociabilidad, el asociacionismo y la educación en la España contemporánea.' *Historia de la educación: Revista interuniversitaria* 31 (2012): 339–358.

Muñoz López, Pilar. *Sangre, amor e interés: La familia en la España de la Restauración.* Madrid: Marcial Pons Historia, 2001.

Muñoz Martínez, David, and Ángel J. Sáez Rodríguez. 'Apuntes para un estudio socio-económico de La Línea de la Concepción a comienzos del siglo XX.' *Almoraima* 13 (1995): 409–424.

Nash, Mary. 'Experiencia y aprendizaje: La formación histórica de los feminismos en España.' *Historia Social* 20 (1994): 151–172.

Nash, Mary. '"Ideals of Redemption": Socialism and Women on the Left in Spain.' In *Women and Socialism/Socialism and Women: Europe between the Two World Wars,* edited by Helmut Gruber and Pamela Graves, 348–380. Oxford: Berghahn, 1998.

Navarro Navarro, Francisco Javier. *'El paraíso de la razón': La revista Estudios (1928–1937) y el mundo cultural anarquista.* Valencia: Ediciones Alfons de Magnánim, 1997.

Navarro Navarro, Francisco Javier. *Ateneos y grupos ácratas: Vida y actividad cultural de las asociaciones anarquistas valencianas durante la Segunda República y la Guerra Civil.* Valencia: Biblioteca Valenciana, 2002.

Navarro Navarro, Francisco Javier. 'Los educadores del pueblo y la "Revolución Interior": La cultura anarquista en España.' In *Tierra y Libertad: Cien años de anarquismo en España*, edited by Juliaán Casanova. Barcelona: Crítica, 2010.

Nelson, Bruce Christopher. *Beyond the Martyrs: A Social History of Chicago's Anarchists, 1870–1900*. New Brunswick: Rutgers University Press, 1988.

Newman, Saul. 'Anarchism and the Politics of Ressentiment.' In *I am Not a Man: I am Dynamite!: Friedrich Nietzsche and the Anarchist Tradition*, edited by John Moore and Spencer Sunshine, 107–126. New York: Autonomedia, 2004.

O'Connor, D.J. *Crime at El Escorial: The 1892 Child Murder, the Press and the Jury*. San Francisco: International Scholars Publications, 1995.

Offen, Karen. *European Feminisms, 1700–1950: A Political History*. Standford: University of Stanford Press, 2000.

Offen, Karen, ed. *Globalizing Feminisms: 1789–1945*. London: Routledge, 2010.

Ortiz, David, Jr. 'Redefining Public Education: Contestation, the Press and Education in Regency Spain, 1885–1902.' *Journal of Social History* 35, 1 (2001): 73–94.

Pradas Baena, María Amalia. *Teresa Claramunt: La virgen roja barcelonesa: Biografía y escritos*. Barcelona: Virus, 2006.

Prado, Antonio. *Escritoras anarco-feministas en La Revista Blanca (1898–1936): Matrimonio, familia y estado*. Madrid: Fundación de Estudios Libertarios Anselmo Lorenzo, 2011.

Radcliff, Pamela Beth. 'Elite Women Workers and Collective Action: The Cigarette Makers of Gijon, 1890–1930.' *Journal of Social History* 27, 1 (1993): 85–108.

Radcliff, Pamela Beth. *From Mobilization to Civil War: The Politics of Polarization in the Spanish City of Gijón, 1900–1937*. Cambridge: Cambridge University Press, 1996.

Radcliff, Pamela Beth. 'Women's Politics: Consumer Riots in Twentieth-Century Spain.' In Enders and Radcliff, *Constructing Spanish Womanhood*, 301–323.

Ralle, Michel. 'La sociabilidad obrera en la sociedad de la Restauración (1875–1910).' *Estudios de Historia Social* 3, 50–51 (1989): 161–199.

Riley, Denise. *Am I That Name?: Feminism and the Category of Women in History*. Basingstoke: Macmillan, 1988.

Rojas Sánchez, Gonzalo. 'Legislación sobre asociaciones anarquistas en España: 1890–1910.' *Revista Chilena de Derecho* 8 (1981): 71–86.

Romero Maura, Joaquín. *La rosa de fuego: Republicanos y anarquistas: La política de los obreros barceloneses entre el desastre colonial y la Semana Trágica*. Barcelona: Ediciones Grijalbo, 1975.

Sanabria, Enrique A. *Republicanism and Anticlerical Nationalism in Spain*. Basingstoke: Palgrave Macmillan, 2009.

Sánchez Cobos, Amparo. 'La reorganización del trabajo libre: Los anarquistas españoles y la difusión del ideal libertario en Cuba.' *Millars* 33 (2010): 243–260.

Santullano, Gabriel. 'Algunas notas sobre la prensa obrera en Asturias en el siglo XIX (1868–1899).' *Boletín del Instituto de Estudios Asturianos* 88–89 (1976): 509–534.

Scanlon, Geraldine M. *La polémica feminista en la España contemporánea (1868–1974)*. Madrid: Siglo XXI, 1976.

Serrano Lacarra, Carlos. '*Acracia*, los anarquistas y la cultura.' In Hofmann, Tous and Tietze, *El anarquismo español*, 347–360.

Shaffer, Kirwin R. 'Freedom Teaching: Anarchism and Education in Early Republican Cuba, 1898–1925.' *The Americas* 60, 2 (2003): 151–183.

Shaffer, Kirwin R. *Anarchism and Countercultural Politics in Early Twentieth-Century Cuba*. Gainesville: University Press of Florida, 2005.

Smith, Angel. 'Anarchism, the General Strike and the Barcelona Labour Movement, 1899–1914.' *European History Quarterly* 27, 1 (1997): 5–40.

Smith, Theresa Ann. *The Emerging Female Citizen: Gender and Enlightenment in Spain*. Berkeley: University of California Press, 2006.

Solà i Gussinyer, Pere. *Las escuelas racionalistas en Cataluña, 1909–1939*. Barcelona: Tusquets, 1976.

Solà i Gussinyer, Pere. 'Los grupos del magisterio racionalista en Argentina y Uruguay hacia 1910 y sus actitudes ante la enseñanza laica oficial.' *Historia de la Educación* 1 (1982): 229–246.

Soria, Carlos. 'La ley española de policía de imprenta de 1883.' *Documentación de las Ciencias de la Información* 6 (1982): 11–40.

Soriano, Ignacio, and Francisco Madrid Santos. 'Antología documental del anarquismo español VI.I: Bibliografía del anarquismo en España, 1868–1939, Enriquecida con notas y comentarios.' 5th edition, 2012. Published online, accessed 12 December, 2012. http://cedall.org/Documentacio/Castella/cedall203410103.htm.

Soriano-Mollá, Dolores Thion. *Ernesto Bark: Un propagandista de la modernidad, 1858–1924*. Alicante: Instituto de Cultura Juan Gil-Albert, 1998.

Summers, Anne. 'Liberty, Equality, Morality: The Attempt to Sustain an International Campaign Against the Double Sexual Standard.' In Offen, *Globalizing Feminisms*, 26–35.

Tavera i García, Susanna. 'La premsa anarco-sindicalista, (1868–1931).' *Recerques* 8 (1978): 85–102.

Thomas, Matthew. '"No-One Telling Us What to Do": Anarchist Schools in Britain, 1890–1916.' *Historical Research* 77, 197 (2004): 405–436.

Tiana Ferrer, Alejandro. 'La idea enseñanza integral en el movimiento obrero internacionalista español, 1868–1881.' *Historia de la Educación* 2 (1983): 113–121.

Tiana Ferrer, Alejandro. 'The Workers' Movement and Popular Education in Contemporary Spain (1868–1939).' *Paedagogica Historica* 32, 3 (1996): 647–684.

Ullman, Joan Connelly. *The Tragic Week: A Study of Anticlericalism in Spain*. Cambridge: Harvard University Press, 1968.

Valera Ortega, José. *Los amigos políticos: Partidos, elecciones y caciquismo en la Restauración (1875–1900)*. Madrid: Alianza, 1977.

Velasco Mesa, Custodio. 'Revolutionary Rhetoric and Labour Unrest: Liège in 1886 and Sevilla in 1901.' *International Review of Social History* 56, 2 (2011): 235–266.

Vilanova Ribas, Mercedes, and Xavier Moreno Juliá. *Atlas de la evolución del analfabetismo en España de 1887–1981*. Madrid: Ministerio de Educación y Ciencia, 1992.

Viñao Frago, Antonio. 'A la cultura por la lectura: Las bibliotecas populares (1869–1885).' In Guereña and Tiana Ferrer, *Clases populares, cultura, educación*, 301–335.

Viñao Frago, Antonio. *Escuela para todos: Educación y modernidad en la España del siglo XX*. Madrid: Marcial Pons, 2004.

Yeoman, James Michael. '*Salud y anarquía desde Dowlais*: The Translocal Experience of Spanish Anarchists in South Wales, 1900–1915.' *International Journal of Iberian Studies* 29, 3 (2016): 273–289.

Zambrana, Joan. 'El anarquismo organizado en los orígenes de la CNT: *Tierra y Libertad*, 1910–1919.' 2009. Published online, accessed 21 January, 2013. http://cedall.org/Documentacio/IHL/Tierra%20y%20Libertad%201910-1919.pdf.

Website Content

Efemerides Anarquistas. '1 febrero.' Accessed 17 August, 2018. https://alacantobrer.files.wordpress.com/2012/03/016_cab_humanidadlibre-valencia-01-02-1902.jpg.

Traverso Vásquez, Luis Javier. 'El suceso de las Pedreras a través de la prensa.' 2012. Published online, accessed 26 October, 2013. http://lalineaenblancoynegro.blogspot.co.uk/2012/08/el-suceso-de-las-pedreras-traves-de-la.html.

4 Our Love of Organisation
Anarchism and Syndicalism, 1907–1915

The period 1899–1906 revealed both the value and limitations of 'decen-tred propaganda and agitation' to anarchists in Spain.[1] While print culture and the networks which supported it had been central to the recovery of the movement, the subsequent unravelling of gains led an increasing number of anarchists in Spain to call for a more stable organ-isational structure, based around unions and mass working class support, like those which had formed in 1870 (FRE), 1881 (FTRE) and, to a lesser extent, 1900 (FSORE). Yet these earlier anarchist organisations had been unsuccessful and short-lived, not least because national bodies of this kind invited repression, due to their high profile and aggressive attitudes to labour struggles. Organisation also always involved compromises, which were unacceptable to some sections of the movement.[2] Together these factors had caused the disintegration of the FRE, the FTRE and the FSORE, all of which had followed a familiar cycle of enthusiasm to paralysis to collapse.[3] This chapter discusses the efforts of anarchists in Spain to break free from this cycle, through the implementation of syndicalism as a new form of organisational strategy, symbolised by the creation of the anarcho-syndicalist Confederación Nacional del Trabajo (CNT) in 1910, and its consolidation in 1915.

Print culture, which had been central to the movement since 1890, continued to serve as the movement's primary means of communication in this period. Yet by helping to create and sustain an alternative, more formal, structure within the movement, the anarchist press prompted a decline in its own heterogeneity and significance. As the CNT and its organ, *Solidaridad Obrera*, became the central institutions of the move-ment, they supplanted the heterodox system maintained by the anarchist press in earlier periods, promoting different identities and different forms of engagement. Individuals and papers which had been pre-eminent in anarchist print culture for decades were side-lined by a new generation of activists and writers, who employed alternative discourses and promoted new structures in which to operate.

In order to create a national organisation, anarchists had to confront a paradox at the heart of their ideology. On the one hand, anarchism aspired to an individualist future, free from organisational structures and hierarchies; on the other, it required supporters to act in a collective manner, most commonly through trade unions. Managing these two positions meant striking a balance between individual autonomy and collective action. Although at times the movement was capable of accommodating this 'cognitive dissonance,' perennial questions remained unresolved.[4] In the words of Constance Bantman:

> The problem of organisation lay at the core of anarchist ideology itself: how libertarian should one be with respect to political organisation? The rejection of traditional political hierarchies and the tyranny of party discipline was one of the basic tenants of anarchism—but clearly it left a broad margin for interpretation.[5]

For some sections of anarchist thought, any form of organisation was illegitimate. This individualist form of anarchism was rare in Spain, although it was discussed in the intellectual journals of the movement such as *La Revista Blanca* and *Natura* and found support in more ephemeral periodicals such as *Juventud* and *Anticristo*.[6] A more common position was that of anarcho-communism, which encouraged the organisation of small groups of dedicated militants, but regarded all formal organisations, including trade unions, as reformist and anti-revolutionary.[7] In contrast, anarcho-collectivism regarded worker associations as the building blocks of a mass revolutionary movement. For this faction, which had dominated the movement in the nineteenth century, national organisations were legitimate as long as they were made up from autonomous local and regional federations which could go against the wishes of a national central committee.[8] An anarchist organisation would also have to be revolutionary: it must be aggressive towards employers and the state, free from religious involvement, and independent from party politics. Collectivist ideas had dominated the FRE and FTRE. The FSORE, formed in 1900, had seen itself as an inheritor of these organisations, yet this project had been largely symbolic and had been unable to instigate, coordinate or support the actions of its members. In 1907 the FSORE was disbanded, representing an end to the tradition of collectivism within Spanish anarchism.[9]

At the same time, a new theory of organisation took hold within the movement. French theories of syndicalism gradually filtered into the anarchist movement in the first decade of the twentieth century, first in Cataluña, and then through the rest of Spain. This development culminated in the creation of the CNT, which eventually became the largest and most long-lasting articulation of anarchist ideology in world history. The CNT had a more 'realistic' approach to organisation, and benefitted from the ideological coherence of 'modern' syndicalism, compared to collectivism's antiquated tactics of *societarismo* [fraternalism].[10] Yet between 1907 and 1915 the CNT was elusive and illusory, often more of an idea than a stable, functioning organisation. Likewise, the adoption of syndicalism within the movement was far from straightforward. Many anarchists saw no difference between this form of organisation and collectivism, while others were hostile to any attempts to codify and centralise anarchist practice. The creation of the CNT was thus less a story of linear ideological development—from anarchism and revolutionary syndicalism, to anarcho-syndicalism, as claimed by many scholars of this period—than one of a waxing and waning of support for syndicalism, external pressures and internal conflict.[11] What made the CNT different from its predecessors was less its theoretical grounding, and more its ability to withstand these pressures during its early years, putting it in a position that enabled it to expand massively during the exceptional circumstances of the First World War.

Syndicalism, Solidaridad Obrera, and La Semana Trágica: 1907–1909

Anarchism and syndicalism were distinct, but potentially complementary theories. Syndicalism signified revolutionary trade unionism, combined with a commitment to collective, direct action that made workers the instrument of change.[12] Like nineteenth-century anarcho-collectivists, syndicalists regarded trade unions as the 'crucial vehicle of struggle' and 'the only means to achieve short-term gains within the current system and their long-term objective of the overthrow of capitalism'.[13] To some of its early supporters, syndicalist theory was a 'synthesis of Bakunin and Marx,' which was neither compromised by political participation—like parliamentary socialism—nor overly idealistic, like anarchism.[14] The development of syndicalism owed a great deal to ideas and practices from countries such as Britain, Ireland, the USA, Australia, Argentina, Brazil and South Africa, yet it was in France that it found its most prominent supporters and thinkers.[15] Sections of the international anarchist movement were inspired by the growing success of the French Confédération Générale du Travail (CGT), which adopted revolutionary syndicalism at its IX Congress in 1906.[16] One year later, the International Anarchist Congress in Amsterdam was dominated by questions about the relationship between anarchism and syndicalism, articulated in a dispute between Errico Malatesta, who warned of the dangers of uniting with 'reformist' trade unions, and supporters of syndicalism, such as Amédée Dunois and Pierre Monatte, who championed syndicalism as a 'new world' of opportunity.[17] The Congress eventually adopted a motion supporting anarchist activity within syndicates as a means to develop the 'revolutionary spirit' of the working class, although it stressed that syndicalist activity alone was not a 'substitute for revolution'.[18] Although the Spanish movement did not participate in this Congress, similar debates would be articulated within Spanish anarchism over the coming years.

Syndicalist ideas had been gradually filtering into Spain from France since the turn of the century. Early support for syndicalism came primarily from Cataluña, where advocates of syndicalism had translated a string of pamphlets by French syndicalists such as Emile Pouget from 1904 onwards.[19] At the same time they began to use the word *sindicato*—imported from the French *syndicat*—for their unions, replacing the nineteenth-century Spanish term *sociedad de resistencia*.[20] In 1907, 57 workers' societies in Barcelona came together to constitute the Federación Local Solidaridad Obrera de Barcelona (known as Solidaridad Obrera, hereafter SO), which sought to coordinate socialist, radical republican and anarchist groups in the city, providing a united organisation that represented the entire workers' movement.[21] SO portrayed itself as independent of all political positions—including anarchism—defining itself as a purely 'syndical' organisation which would fight solely for the economic interests of its affiliates.[22] In 1908 SO expanded into a regional federation, encompassing all of Cataluña and claiming the support of 20–25,000 workers. This expansion was aided by its organ, *Solidaridad Obrera*, launched in October 1907. In its early years this paper sustained a print run of approximately 3,000 issues and was run almost entirely by anarchists.[23]

SO's commitment to non-partisan syndicalism was challenged from the outset. Both socialists and radical republicans in Barcelona tried to use SO to forward their own electoral objectives and opposed the organisation when they failed to control it. In contrast, the anarchist majority in SO wanted to ensure that the organisation fulfilled its stated revolutionary goals, steering it away from parliamentary politics and towards confrontational industrial action.[24] They portrayed SO as both the inheritor of the anarchist tradition and a 'modern' organisation, suitable for the realities of the twentieth century.

Outside Cataluña, the collapse of the FSORE had left the movement fragmented over questions of strategy. Syndicalist theory remained marginal to discussions in the anarchist press, and few groups acknowledged the existence of SO or its periodical.[25] In 1907–08, papers such as *Humanidad Libre* (Jumilla) and *Humanidad* (Toledo) were largely concerned with attacking the Church and praising the emancipatory power of education, in a manner similar to the anarchist press of 1899–1906.[26] When these papers did discuss organisation, they simply lamented its absence.[27] In contrast, *La Voz del Obrero del Mar* (Cádiz) was explicitly directed towards worker organisation. This paper was launched to support the reformation of the Cádiz union of stokers, sailors and port workers, which had disbanded in 1906. It aimed to keep anarchist unionism alive in the city, reminding local workers of the dangers of socialist organisations—particularly the UGT-affiliated 'Comité de los Obreros del Mar de España'—and attacking the members of the local company union.[28] The latter, known as *amarillos* ['yellows'] were seen as class traitors, who had renounced 'their rights of liberty and social emancipation' by siding with their employers in order to line their own pockets, and were commonly identified as *esquiroles* (strike-breakers) and scapegoated when strikes and organisational initiatives failed to ignite revolutionary action.[29] The paper's sole concern was with the workers in the Cádiz area, and it made no reference to SO, *Solidaridad Obrera*, or syndicalism. *La Voz del Obrero del Mar* closed in 1908, marking the end of anarchist publishing in Cádiz—formerly one of the centres of the anarchist print network—for twelve years.[30]

Early Syndicalist Support

The scattered, diverse papers of 1907–1908 give little impression of a growing move towards syndicalism outside Cataluña.[31] A shift began towards the end of 1908, most notably in the north-west of the country. The first issue of *La Acción* (La Coruña, 1908, 3 issues) advocated organisation within the movement, stating that although most anarchists could 'never accept the impositions of a centralising power such as the socialists accept' they could agree 'to sustain . . . collective tension and supportive links' as long as they were 'sufficiently autonomous'.[32] Correspondents to the paper claimed that 'true' anarchists had maintained a tradition of organisation that stretched back to the First International.[33] Although this publication was small and short lived—1,000–1,500 copies of each issue were printed, yet very few were sold—*La Acción* represented a renewed sense of optimism in the idea of a national anarchist workers' organisation.[34] It was also one of the first papers outside Cataluña to be in contact with *Solidaridad Obrera*.[35]

Another paper to forge bonds with *Solidaridad Obrera* was *Tribuna Libre*, launched in Gijón in early 1909. The arrival of this publication went hand-in-hand with the reorganisation of the Gijón's workforce. Groups such as the city's *ebanistas* (cabinetmakers) had already made contact with *Solidaridad Obrera* in 1908, in a letter which affirmed their belief in syndicalism as the basis of an organised, revolutionary force.[36] A new generation of anarchist thinkers and activists in Gijón saw great potential in these developments, in particular Eleuterio Quintanilla and Pedro Sierra Álvarez, both of whom were heavily influenced by Ricardo Mella, who lived in Asturias from 1901 to 1909.[37] Quintanilla and Sierra Álvarez were the driving force behind *Tribuna Libre*, writing much of its content and supporting it financially.[38] They aimed to promote syndicalism within the anarchist movement, declaring that it was no longer good enough for anarchists to retreat into intellectualism, rather, what was needed was a new tactic aligned to workers' needs and addressed their struggle for 'bread'.[39] The paper was optimistic about the situation in Gijón, where anarchist societies of carpenters, masons, bakers, boilermakers, painters, iron workers and locksmiths had united into a Local Federation, named—in reference to their inspiration—Solidaridad

Obrera.[40] The paper also saw encouraging signs in Vigo, where several workers' societies had established an 'apolitical' alternative to the local UGT-affiliated Federation.[41]

Syndicalism was portrayed in *Tribuna Libre* as the most 'modern' anarchist organisational theory, epitomised by its innovative tactics of boycott and sabotage.[42] Both tactics were depicted as youthful, in contrast to 'old' and 'antiquated' agitation such as partial strikes. This attitude was demonstrated in the dialogue 'Opiniones acerca del sabotaje,' in which a youth and an old worker debated the validity of sabotage (to the old worker 'the weapon of cowards') and the strike (to the youth 'the struggle of empty stomachs').[43] Yet despite its enthusiasm for syndicalism, *Tribuna Libre* did not see organisation as an end in itself. Anarchism remained the ultimate goal, towards which worker organisation could help, but could not accomplish single-handed.[44] Nor did *Tribuna Libre* discuss syndicalist theory at length, and instead dedicated most of its content to critiquing the poor state of workers' education, attacking socialist organisational methods and praising the unifying quality of strike action.[45] The activity the paper called for was greater unionisation, the 'education' of union members about the value of direct action, and building greater cohesion between unions; in other words, largely the same activity that had been advocated by anarchist organisers since 1870.[46]

Elsewhere, the rhetoric of syndicalism was making inroads into anarchist publications, such as the one-off *¡Despertad!* (Madrid, 1909, 1 issue), which regarded syndicalism as an excellent method for bringing about 'the pure ideal of anarchy'.[47] In Málaga, the local workers' paper *Nueva Aurora* (1909, 2 issues) declared itself as a platform for 'syndicalist ideas'. In all of these papers, 'syndicalism' signified little more than 'newness', used to indicate support for worker organisation and 'modern' revolutionary activity, without engaging with the details of syndicalist theory. A comparable process had occurred a decade earlier, when the phrase 'general strike' had entered the vocabulary of the anarchist press, with little reflection on what a general strike was. For example, in 1901 the editorial of *La Protesta* reported on a 'general strike' of the locksmiths in a single, small provincial town.[48] In a similar manner, the early advocates of syndicalism often simply inserted the term into articles where formerly word 'anarchism' would have been used.[49] Thus while the term syndicalism appeared more frequently in the movement's press prior to 1910, it was not used in a manner which advocated substantially different aims or practices than had gone before.[50]

As in 1870, 1881, and 1900, enthusiasm for organisation within the movement led to plans for a national federation of anarchist unions. By 1909, the Catalan SO was receiving requests to enter the Federation from societies all over Spain, including the metal workers of La Felguera (Asturias) and newly founded workers' federations in La Coruña, Zaragoza and Granada.[51] At its 1909 Congress SO voted in favour of national expansion by twenty-six votes to four.[52] Outside Cataluña, the momentum for this project was driven by ideas and initiatives published in the anarchist press, in particular *Tribuna Libre*, which stated that the idea would aid 'the development and the combined action of the Spanish syndicalist movement'.[53]

The Tragic Week

The enthusiasm for a national federation was punctured shortly afterwards. In July 1909 conscript reservists were called up following an increase in fighting in Spanish-controlled Morocco. This move was deeply unpopular in Cataluña, where it sparked a series of public anti-war protests.[54] This was a critical juncture for SO. While its support was growing across Spain, the organisation in Cataluña was being challenged by both the strength of Lerroux's Radical Republican Party and its inability to overcome employer intransigence in the textile area of the Ter Valley.[55] When its leadership refused to sanction a general strike in Barcelona following the call-up, a committee of SO officials, anarchists and socialists took matters into their own hands, and set about organising a city-wide work stoppage on Monday 26 July.[56]

Industrial action rapidly developed into a generalised eruption of popular unrest in Barcelona, which later became known as La Semana Trágica (The Tragic Week).[57] Barricades were erected in working-class districts, dividing the city between a popular insurgency of anarchists, socialists, radical republicans, labour leaders, 'freethinkers' and educators on one side, and the army and Civil Guard on the other. Clashes between these two blocs became increasingly violent, while the middle classes and ruling elites of the city closed their businesses and withdrew to their homes. After paralysing the city's economy and clashing with the forces of order, protesters turned against the Catholic Church.[58] Between a third and a half of Barcelona's churches and convents were burned by protestors, in the most spectacular eruption of anticlericalism in Spain in almost a century. By the end of the week 104 civilians (both protesters and onlookers) had been killed, alongside two civil guards, five members of the military, one municipal policeman, one security guard and three members of the clergy.[59]

Despite what many anarchist commentators thought about it, the Tragic Week was not a revolution, nor was it a principally anarchist affair. Neither SO nor the city's anarchists instigated or directed this popular rebellion, a fact acknowledged by both movements. Indeed, Anselmo Lorenzo was inspired by what had occurred in Barcelona precisely because it had not been directed by his anarchist comrades: '"this is amazing!"'—he is reported to have exclaimed—'"A social revolution has broken out in Barcelona, initiated by an entity so ill-defined, [ill]-understood, or [ill-] recognised that it is sometimes vilified as a mob and other times hailed as The People. No-one has instigated this revolution! And no one directs it!'"[60] Likewise, the publisher Leopoldo Bonafulla was clear that 'the revolution in Catalonia did not have a leader [. . .] in reality the protest was spontaneous, a generalised expression of outrage.'[61] Yet, as in the aftermath of other 'headless' uprisings, such as that of Jerez in 1892, as repression began it was clear that blame would be shouldered by the anarchist and workers' movements. SO and *Solidaridad Obrera* were closed under martial law and high-profile anarchists and labour leaders fled the city. A number of those who stayed were accused (and acquitted) of directing the rebellion, alongside senior figures in the Radical party. In total over 2,000 people were arrested in Barcelona, of which five were executed, 59 given life sentences and 178 exiled from the city.[62]

Alongside labour militancy, 'rational', 'anti-religious', 'anarchist' education were deemed the key factor in the disturbances. Over 100 schools and educational centres were closed in Cataluña, as were many similar establishments outside the province.[63] Key individuals in alternative education were singled out for repression, most notably Francisco Ferrer, who was cast as the figurehead of revolutionary ideas in Spain. He was arrested on 31 August and charged with being the decisive influence behind the insurrection.[64] Few contemporaries genuinely believed these charges, and the prosecution barely attempted to prove them. Instead, Ferrer was attacked for being the source of seditious ideas, namely, his role in anarchist education and print, which the state regarded as equally dangerous to 'social order' as outbursts of revolutionary activity. He was an obvious scapegoat for the rebellion: a recognisable figure to anarchists and the general public, whose punishment would demonstrate the state's commitment to crushing radical ideas. In reality, Ferrer was an idiosyncratic figure, often more remote from developments within the Spanish anarchist movement (particularly after 1906) than his posthumous standing would suggest. He had supported the anticlerical violence of the Tragic Week, but did not take part in it, nor could he have possibly orchestrated it alone. Nevertheless, Ferrer's guilt for the 'crime' in spreading revolutionary ideas was evident. He was declared 'the author and chief of the rebellion' and was shot by firing squad in Montjuich Castle on 13 October.[65]

All public communications to Barcelona were either severed or censored during the Tragic Week, and afterwards martial law was in place across the country until 27 September, curtailing all anarchist publishing in Spain.[66] This made it impossible for the movement to publish commentary on the events as they unfolded. This situation improved in November, with the arrival of a number of new anarchist periodicals: *Al Paso* (Sevilla), *El Libertario* (Madrid) and *El Rebelde* (Las Palmas de Gran Canaria). Between them, these papers established the Tragic Week and its repercussions as part of the collective memory of the movement. Depictions of the event varied: it was portrayed as a 'strike', a 'brief revolutionary moment' and a reaction against 'bourgeois clerical-ism' by different authors.[67] Socialists and republicans were attacked for not assisting the 'revolutionary movement,' and consigning it to failure.[68] Anger at these groups intensified following the Republican-Socialist electoral pact in November 1909, which confirmed to anarchists their image of the socialists as non-revolutionary, bourgeois-appeasing cowards and the republicans as cynical operators seeking working-class votes.[69]

In January 1910 Bonafulla published the only extended contemporary anarchist piece of writing on the Tragic Week, *La revolución de julio*. The book was rushed through production in order to give an 'official' anarchist reaction to the events of the previous six months, leaving it underdeveloped and full of typographical errors. The account freely blends Bonafulla's eye-witnesses testimony with a fairly comprehensive survey of available evidence, including the reactions of a number of religious authorities.[70] While clearly designed to exonerate Ferrer and the wider movement of any wrongdoing during the uprising—which is unsustainable—it remains a valuable example of how publishers tried to frame the movement's reaction to the Tragic Week and its aftermath: that is, as a spontaneous, 'turbulent, angry manifestation' which was met with a 'shameful, ignoble, disastrous' reaction, 'more inquisitorial, if that is possible, than during the times when the agony of barbaric passions touched even the children of the children of the torture victims'.[71]

In contrast, few periodical papers examined the events of the Tragic Week in depth, and all refused to discuss anarchist participation in the events, in a manner similar to *El Corsario*'s reaction to terrorism in the 1890s. Instead, they focused on the repression in Barcelona and the execution of Ferrer. Contributors to *Al Paso* saw Ferrer as part of a lineage of radical thinkers who had suffered at the hands of the Catholic Church, such as Jan Hus, Giordano Bruno, Galileo Galilei and Michael Servetus.[72] Ferrer's treatment was also explicitly linked to that of Christ, including in one postcard titled *Ecce Homo* ['behold the man': the words used by Pontius Pilate when he presented a scourged Jesus Christ to the Jerusalem crowd], which displayed Ferrer's bloodied head over a shroud, surrounded by a crown of thorns.[73] Another vivid evocation of Ferrer's death was a story published in *Al Paso*, in which the author-protagonist awoke to a downpour of blood, after which Ferrer's name was spelled out in the sky by a series of moons.[74] As well as giving space for veneration and expressions of grief, this coverage of Ferrer's martyrdom was a boost to sales, as shown by the thousands of extra requests sent in for *Al Paso*'s proposed 8-page special issue on the 'unforgettable' educator, which included his portrait and texts by Kropotkin, Malato, Malatesta and Lorenzo.[75]

Ferrer became the most prominent martyr in anarchist culture to date, marked out by both his commitment to the anarchist cause and the baselessness of the charges which had condemned him. His works were regularly republished, and pamphlets and books on his martyrdom continued to be produced by the movement into the 1930s, while the martyrs of the 1890s had been largely forgotten.[76] Papers of an educationalist style, such as Samuel Toner's *Escuela Moderna*, were keen to maintain the memory of Ferrer, particularly in issues published on the anniversary of his death.[77] References to Ferrer also emerged in acts of naming.[78] Several anarchist groups adopted Ferrer's name directly—such as the 'Ferrer' group of Estepona (Málaga) and Alcoy (Alicante)—or made reference to the date of his execution, as with the '13 October' groups in Málaga and El Ferrol.[79] This latter group went on to publish *Cultura Libertaria* (El Ferrol, 1912–1913, 12 issues), a paper which declared the rational education promoted by Ferrer to be 'the true religion'.[80]

Like the repression of the 1890s, Ferrer's execution sparked a campaign of international protests against the Spanish state.[81] His name and date of execution were taken up by anarchist groups abroad, such as the '13 October' group of Havana and the 'Ferrer' group of Las Cascadas (Panamá), who helped to launch the periodical of the Panamanian Anarchist Federation, *El Único* (Cólon, 1911–1912, 14 issues) on the second anniversary of Ferrer's execution. Another 'Ferrer' group was formed by Spanish migrants in South Wales.[82] In the Netherlands, postcards of Ferrer's portrait and children's books about his life could be bought from anarchist publishers, and plays based on his life and execution became a popular feature of socialist clubs from Mexico to Beirut.[83] Beyond anarchist circles, Ferrer's status as the world's foremost radical educator was assured by his execution, as demonstrated by the Modern Schools that emerged in almost every continent from 1909 onwards.[84] This was particularly pronounced in the USA, where a long-lasting Modern School movement emerged immediately after Ferrer's execution, supported by the 'Francisco Ferrer Association,' which included the novelists Jack London and Upton Sinclair among its members.[85]

However, the construction of 'Ferrer the martyr' did not meet with uniform approval from Spanish anarchists, many of whom criticised this development as 'idolatry'.[86] To Mella, this was pure 'fetishism', a 'christianisation' of Ferrer that was the work of 'pseudo-revolutionaries' who 'could not be anarchists'.[87] Anarchists also attacked parliamentary socialists and middle-class educators who 'mourned Ferrer as a freethinker and neglected his anarchism' and were critical of the international campaigns aroused by Ferrer's execution.[88] When Belgian radicals began an international subscription to fund a statue to Ferrer—who had spent time in exile in Brussels following Mateo Morral's attack on Alfonso XIII in 1906—they were lambasted in *El Libertario*, which suggested that the money would be better spent on rational schools.[89] There was a feeling that the ideas for which Ferrer lived and died were being overlooked in the construction of his martyrdom, while his memory was appropriated for political gain.[90] Thus it appears that some sections of the movement had become deeply uncomfortable with the notion of martyrdom. Rather than return to the language and practices of the 1890s, they sought to downplay and ultimately eradicate this 'religious' behaviour and concentrate instead on organising the movement in preparation for future struggles.

Anarchist papers, such as *Al Paso* and *El Libertario*, attempted to use the repression of the Tragic Week as a means to rouse united revolutionary activity. Early in 1910 both papers published aims for a 'federation of Spanish anarchist groups and individuals', calling anarchists across Spain to form into groups, which would work in their localities to spread anarchist propaganda. *El Libertario* would act as a coordinator for these efforts, while keeping their details out of public record to avoid repression.[91] Their organisation would be much looser than trade unions, based upon shared values rather than shared labour. Although these plans came to nothing, they were resurrected a few years later with more promising results, as will be shown later in this chapter. Meanwhile, syndicalist papers were hesitant to invoke the memory of the Tragic Week, and decided that rather than 'naming streets after [Ferrer],' the most fitting tribute would be to continue his work for revolutionary syndicalism, which was overlooked by non-anarchists and anarchists alike.[92] If his death was to be remembered, it should not be in order to make Ferrer a saint—he was, after all, 'no more than putrefied material'—but as a stimulus to organisation.[93] This position is understandable, given that the Tragic Week was a disaster for SO, resulting in the closure of its paper and an end to the organisations' ambitions for national expansion. For syndicalists, the best course of action was to move on from this event as quickly as possible.

Confederación General—Confederación Nacional—Huelga General: 1910–1911

In November 1909 a new *Solidaridad Obrera* was launched in Gijón. With the Barcelona paper suppressed, this publication briefly became the principal source of syndicalist ideas in Spain. This was not a direct handover from one paper to the other—as in 1893 when *El Productor* passed over its accounts to *El Corsario*—but a spontaneous, local response to the void created by repression.[94] The paper was produced by largely the same group of publishers as *Tribuna Libre*, including Quintanilla and Sierra Álvarez, and a number of articles in the paper were directly lifted from its predecessor. *Solidaridad Obrera* (Gijón) operated as the mouthpiece of the Gijón workers' federation, which claimed the support of 1,350 workers, around 15 per cent of the city's workforce.[95] This federation was regarded as a model of local syndicalism, providing a blend of 'moral and material' activity it saw as the means to 'economic and social emancipation'.[96] All constituent societies were bound by solidarity and the payment of dues, yet they were free to declare their own strikes and to act on their own accord on matters of trade. The federation was open to all occupations and to both sexes, but they would not admit societies affiliated to the socialist or republican movements, or those that had any connection to the Church. Its central committee was made up of members of all societies, operated on a one-delegate-one-vote system, and was renewed every six months.[97] Both *Solidaridad Obrera* (Gijón) and the federation were based in the workers' centre on Calle de Casimiro Velasco, and shared many members of staff. The paper was filled with news and correspondences from local workers, which invigorated its discussions and demonstrated syndicalist theory in practice. It also informed workers of the federation's activities and administered its campaigns, such as a project for a local workers' centre, which was portrayed as a panacea for all the local workers' needs, providing a stable location in which to conduct publishing and syndical activity, house a rational school and a popular library, and would offer its rooms out for night classes, arts, theatre, courses and conferences. Although the centre was not completed until 1928, *Solidaridad Obrera* (Gijón) helped to spark enthusiasm for the idea, planning fund-raising activities, such as raffles, theatre shows, literary performances, and emphasising the 'emancipatory' quality of the work ahead.[98]

The city's socialist unions, based in the Calle Anselmo Cifuentes, claimed a similar number of affiliates to the syndicalist federation. These two organisations attacked one another using well-established insults and caricatures. Gijón's socialists portrayed the syndicalist federation as disorganised, hysterical and extreme, while *Solidaridad Obrera* attacked local socialists as authoritarian and 'political'.[99] The moderation of the socialists was seen as futile, a product of the centralised structure of the UGT and its affiliation to the PSOE. The syndicalist federation aimed to avoid these pitfalls, combining flexibility with bottom-up unity, which was regarded as the opposite of the socialists' hierarchical union structure.

Outside Cataluña, *Solidaridad Obrera* (Gijón) articulated the most well-defined argument for syndicalism prior to the creation of the CNT. Its serialisation of José Prat's *La burguesía y el proletariado* gave its readers a fortnightly discussion of syndicalist ideas and proposals: the difference between revolutionary syndicalism and 'impotent' reformist unionism; the lineage of syndicalism from the First International; syndicalism's apolitical stance; its weapons of general strike, boycotts and sabotage; and the need for increased syndicalist propaganda.[100] In earlier years, Prat had been cautious about the adoption of syndicalism within anarchism, partly as a result of his experiences in Argentina in the late 1890s, yet by 1909 he had begun to advocate in favour of a synthesis of the two positions.[101] In part this perspective was a result of Prat's Marxian analysis, which set him apart from many of his contemporaries. Marx was often resented by Spanish anarchists, who saw his arguments with

Mikhail Bakunin as the cause of the collapse of the First International and the root of parliamentary socialism.[102] Marx's emphasis on capitalism as the prime source of oppression was also seen as limited. Prat, however, employed Marx's focus on class and capitalist economics as a means to advocate syndicalism, which he saw as an inevitable response to contemporary economic relations. In Prat's words, syndicalism was 'not a theory but a deed . . . an immediate consequence of the system of salaries'.[103] This shift towards Marxian analysis was evident throughout *Solidaridad Obrera* (Gijón), to the extent that some articles discussed 'authority' not as the tripartite 'trilogy' of traditional anarchist analyses (the State, Church and Capital) but the result of the system of production alone.[104]

In addition to Prat, the paper published the works of a range of French syndicalist thinkers and activists, particularly Victor Griffuelhes, former secretary general of the CGT (1901–1909) and author of the Amiens Charter. Griffuelhes's views on syndicalism were similar to Prat's, affirming the value of direct, worker-led action and the need for syndicalists to avoid electoral politics. Yet Griffuelhes was uneasy about the relationship between syndicalism and anarchism. While anarchist ideas were influential in the CGT, the organisation refrained from calling itself 'anarchist,' stressing that anarchist ideas were only useful as a means to syndicalist ends.[105] As such, the organisation is best described as one of 'syndicated anarchists' rather than anarcho-syndicalists.[106] The influence of French revolutionary syndicalism upon Spanish movement was mixed.[107] For papers such as *Solidaridad Obrera* (Gijón), the CGT was the prime example of syndicalism in action, yet its contributors were much more openly supportive of anarchism and recognised the strong influence of anarchist principles upon the Spanish working class.[108] Thus the paper stressed that the principles of the CGT should be applauded, yet also adapted to the Spanish context, which meant reversing Griffuelhes' position by presenting syndicalism as the best means to an anarchist end.[109]

Further international inspiration, and caution, was drawn from the Argentine anarchist movement. Unlike their Spanish counterparts, Argentinian anarchists had established and maintained a national organisation since the early years of the twentieth century, the Federación Obrera Regional Argentina (FORA), which at its 1905 Congress had declared itself in favour of revolutionary, anarcho-communist (i.e. non-syndicalist) principles. Four years later, syndicalists in Argentina launched their own organisation, the Confederación Obrera Regional Argentina (CORA), as the result of a schism with the country's socialist movement.[110] Advocates for syndicalism within the anarchist movement in Spain looked to both organisations during 1909–1910, in particular *Solidaridad Obrera* (Barcelona), which soon after its return to print in early 1910 reprinted the CORA's founding statement on its front page.[111] They did not, however, seek to emulate the organisational division between Argentina's anarchist

(FORA) and syndicalist (CORA) factions, which appeared to make a single, unitary body unfeasible. Indeed, even after the CORA joined the FORA in 1914, the organisation almost immediately split into its old blocs, now identified as the FORA V (anarchists, following the principles of the 1905 Congress) and FORA IX (syndicalists, adhered to the Congress of 1915 which rejected anarcho-communism).[112]

The examples of France and Argentina had showed Spanish anarchists who favoured of a single, organised, expression of the movement that a bridge had to be found between revolutionary and unionist principles, avoiding both the dominant syndicalism of the CGT and the instability of the FORA and CORA. This view formed the basis of Spanish anarcho-syndicalism as it developed over the following decade, which at its roots held that: 'if the complete emancipation of the working class can only be achieved in anarchism, and syndicalism searches for the complete emancipation of the working class, syndicalism has to be anarchist'.[113] Anarcho-syndicalism did not solve the inherent problems of anarchist organisation, but it did appear to provide a more satisfactory way of accommodating desires for individual autonomy and collective action than previous models, which *Solidaridad Obrera* (Gijón) cast as old fashioned and limited.[114] Prominent anarchist contributors in the paper, such as Mella and Quintanilla, labelled previous anarchist practice as too 'speculative' and 'illogical,' prone to inactivity and 'puritanical' in its attitude to new ideas.[115] Several articles in the paper referenced the Gijón general strike of 1901, which had been given scant support by the FSORE and had ended in abject failure. This episode hung heavy on those seeking to remobilise the *gijonés* workforce, who called upon the readers of *Solidaridad Obrera* (Gijón) to put this past failure behind them and have faith that the coherency of syndicalism would bring victory, where older, praiseworthy but chaotic, forms of organisation had suffered noble defeat.[116] Syndicalism would be a means to break the cycle of repression and defeat; a means to 'materialise' anarchism and make it effective.[117]

SO and *Solidaridad Obrera* (Barcelona) resumed activity in early 1910. The Tragic Week and its repercussions had fortified SO's resolve for national expansion, and the organisation soon made plans for a congress which would found a confederation of syndicates across the whole of Spain. The original name for the proposed federation was the Confederación General del Trabajo, chosen in direct imitation of the French confederation.[118] The only objection to these developments came from SO's socialist minority, who saw the idea as a challenge to the UGT. Rather than a national syndicalist organisation, they sought to integrate SO within the UGT.[119] Elsewhere in Spain, reception to the idea of a national federation was mixed. Of the handful of papers in print at this time, the most detailed discussion of SO's proposals came, unsurprisingly, from *Solidaridad Obrera* (Gijón). The idea was discussed in a weekly forum named 'A General Confederation of Labour in Spain?', which demonstrated an openness common to anarchist print culture, allowing for different and competing perspectives within a single newspaper. The strongest critic of the proposed organisation was José Sánchez Duque, a Galician anarchist who had formerly been involved in the editorial of *Tiempos Nuevos* (Gijón; 1905–1906: 2 issues).[120] In 1910 Duque was living in Paris, where he had witnessed the problems of the CGT first hand. For Duque, syndicalism, as 'plagiarised' from France, was not an end in itself. Only 'conservative anarchists' could support the codification and centralisation of the 'organic' idea of worker solidarity, which would 'castrate' independence while promoting 'mandarins and governors'.[121] Duque was challenged by a number of contributors to the paper, including another émigré to Paris, José Rodríguez Romero, who regarded syndicalism as a means to address the 'lack of cohesion and necessary environment in the rest of the peninsula [i.e. outside Cataluña]'. Rodríguez Romero was tired of the ideological wrangling of self-styled revolutionaries such as Duque, asserting that 'deeds have to follow words . . . enough of the theories and let us get on with practice'.[122] The paper tried to strike a balance between these two opinions. As 'those who call themselves anarchists and accept syndicalism as a means of positive action,' they supported the idea of a national syndicalist federation but were opposed to the idea of simply imitating the CGT, seeking instead a more anarchist-influenced, federalised structure, which would ensure harmony between the principles of autonomy and organisation.[123]

The 1910 Congress

The creation of the CNT not a 'determined *moment*' but a 'constitutive *process*,' which began at the first national congress of SO, held in the Palacio de Bellas Artes in Barcelona from 30 October to 1 November 1910.[124] Although this Congress did not fully constitute the CNT—which took place a year later—it was an important step towards this point, extending the regional SO into the national Confederación General del Trabajo. Anarchists across Spain learnt about the Congress from an 8-page special edition of *Solidaridad Obrera* (Barcelona) and three issues of *Solidaridad Obrera* (Gijón), which based its coverage on the reports of Pedro Sierra Álvarez, who was present as the delegate of workers' societies in Gijón and La Felguera.[125]

Sierra Álvarez was keen to stress the national support for the Congress in his reports, which stated that of the 170 societies represented or adhered to the Congress, 76 (~45 per cent) were from outside Cataluña, located in 19 different provinces across Spain [Table 4.1].[126] All of these localities had a local correspondent for both versions of *Solidaridad Obrera*, reflecting the continued significance of print networks within the structure of the movement. During the Congress, efforts were made to include non-Catalan delegates as fairly as possible: they made up three of the six commission presidents, seven of the 25 named commission

Table 4.1 Societies and Delegates at the 1910 Congress

	Represented Societies	No. Delegates	Unrepresented Societies
Spain	**121**	**124**	51
Cataluña	*84*	*105*	*10*
Barcelona	82	103	9
Lérida			1
Tarragona	2	2	
Non-Cataluña	*37*	*19*	*41*
Andalucía	*7*	*8*	*14*
Almería			1
Cádiz	2	2	1
Córdoba	1	1	1
Granada	2	2	
Huelva			1
Málaga	1	2	4
Sevilla	1	1	6
Aragón	*6*	*3*	*1*
Zaragoza	6	3	1
Asturias	*17*	*1*	*2*
Castilla la Vieja	*1*	*1*	
Logroño	1	1	
Galicia	*1*	*1*	*10*
A Coruña			
Pontevedra	1	1	3
Islas Baleares	*1*	*1*	*1*
León	*1*	*1*	
Murcia			1
Provincias Vascongadas			1
Vizcaya			1
Valencia	*2*	*2*	*8*
Alicante	2	2	1
Valencia			7

Individual Adherences: Anselmo Lorenzo; Vicente García; Fransisco Abayá

Sources: Solidaridad Obrera (Barcelona, II), 4 November, 1910, 7–8; Xavier Cuadrat, *Socialismo y anarquismo en Cataluña (1899–1911): Los orígenes de la CNT* (Madrid: Ediciones de la Revista de Trabajo, 1976), 463–469; Antonio Bar, *La CNT en los años rojos: Del sindicalismo revolucionario al anarcosindicalismo (1910–1926)* (Madrid: Akal, 1981), 156

secretaries and 22 of the 61 discussion group members. The group delegated to write up the provisional statues of the Federation was the most geographically mixed of all, containing one representative each from Gijón, Zaragoza, Vigo, Río Alhama (Logroño), Sevilla and Tarrasa, as well as the secretary of SO, José Negre.[127]

Yet Sierra Álvarez was exaggerating when he reported to *Solidaridad Obrera* (Gijón) that 'the rest of Spain' was represented in Barcelona.[128]

214 Our Love of Organisation

Non-Catalan societies were far less likely to be directly represented at the Congress, as many societies could not afford to send a delegate.[129] Instead, they nominated an individual via *Solidaridad Obrera* (Barcelona). Most of these substitute delegates were from Barcelona, and there is little in the reports of the Congress to suggest they mentioned either the society or locality that they represented.[130] In contrast, delegates sent directly from non-Catalan societies—Sierra Álvarez (Asturias), Gil (La Cervera del Río Alhama), Ordinas (Palma de Mallorca), Plaza (Vigo), Mora and Zuferri (both Zaragoza)—spoke of issues particular to their locality, as a means to demonstrate the shared nature of the struggles of the Spanish proletariat.[131]

Many non-Catalan societies also shared delegates. Sierra Álvarez, for example, represented 17 societies from two different localities in Asturias. Over half of the non-Catalan societies had no representation at all, and simply 'adhered' to the Congress without having any input in its decisions. In contrast, around 90 per cent of Catalan societies sent a delegate, twenty-four of which sent two, and two sent four delegates each. Since each delegate only had a single vote regardless of how many societies they represented, non-Catalan societies thus had less direct influence in the Congress than their Catalan counterparts. This lack of representation from outside Cataluña was a problem for the organisers of the Congress. Direct representation had been an ideal within anarchist organisation since the FRE, as a means to avoid excessive organisational bureaucracy and hierarchy.[132] The difference between the number of non-Catalan societies claimed to support the Congress (76) and the number of non-Catalan delegates (12) exposes the limits of this ideal in practice. Another qualification of the Congress' 'national' character lies in its geographic spread. Of the 37 societies that were represented, a large concentration was from Asturias (17), a smaller cluster from Zaragoza (6), while the remainder were scattered groups across the rest of the country. Areas such as Madrid, which had a strong history of anarchist publishing, were entirely absent from this Congress, while Andalucían societies were far less prominent than they had been in both the FTRE and the FSORE. Thus the 'national' character of the Congress was more of an ambition than a reality, reflecting the patchy, unequal spread of syndicalist ideas amongst many traditional areas of anarchist support.

Of the fifteen themes on the table for discussion, the most controversial was the extension of SO into a national organisation. The socialist delegates Juan Durán and Jacinto Puig saw no reason for a new organisation, and instead called for a union between the UGT and SO. Puig warned that any new national organisation would be tarred as '*amarillo*' [yellow] by the national and international socialist movement, a statement which offended many of those in attendance.[133] In contrast, the majority of delegates were in favour of the creation of a national organisation, separate from the UGT, which would eventually 'unite' the Spanish working class into a single organisation together with its socialist counterpart.[134]

Rather than an attempt at reconciliation between parliamentary and revolutionary tactics, this unity was predicated on the UGT abandoning its connection to the PSOE and its 'politics', in effect subordinating the socialist union to the syndicalist confederation and 'capturing' its affiliates.[135] The only non-Catalan delegate to speak on this matter was Sierra Álvarez, who argued in favour of SO expansion. He pointed out that in areas outside Cataluña where the socialists were strong—such as Gijón—syndicalists were already free to join the UGT, but had formed a syndicalist federation instead. Using figures of the socialist writer Juan José Morato, Álvarez also claimed that only 43,000 of the 400,000 unionised workers in Spain were part of the UGT, as proof that the vast majority of workers did not agree with the socialist union's tactics.[136] The Congress approved national expansion by 83 to 13 votes. This moment is frequently portrayed as a turning point in the history of Spanish anarchism; a point where SO affirmed its national ambitions and, as a result, alienated the remaining socialists within the organisation.[137] While this was an important issue within the Catalan labour movement, outside this region socialist participation within syndicalist organisations was rarely countenanced, as the latter had always been associated with the anarchist movement. The more pressing concern outside Cataluña was thus not whether the organisation would be acceptable to socialists, but to anarchists.

The Congress did not adopt anarchism as its guiding ideology. Anarchism was not discussed during the Congress, except at one point when Negre asserted that SO was 'neutral' and by no means an 'exclusively anarchist' organisation.[138] Several discussions did, however, suggest the ascendency of anarchist attitudes, for example, the discussion theme 'should syndicalism be a means or an end of workers' emancipation?', which was answered by: 'syndicalism . . . should not be interpreted as an ideal but as a means of struggle . . . with the aim of assuring . . . the revolutionary expropriation of the bourgeoisie'. Despite one objection this motion was approved.[139] In this regard, the 1910 Congress was similar in tone to the creation of the FSORE, which had also refrained from explicitly proclaiming 'anarchism' while asserting broadly anarchist principles and tactics. Where the new confederation differed was in its more practical elements. The Congress was clear that affiliated societies had to pay dues and provide the new Central Committee with information regarding their members, profession and location. Both of these administrative features were lacking from the FSORE. Like the FSORE, the Congress advocated the general strike, yet rather than simply asserting it was a good idea, like its predecesor, the new confederation attempted to define a workable strategy for its implementation. Local 'general strikes' were easily put down, as witnessed earlier in the decade; what was needed was coordination, preparation and agreement at a national level, which would prevent ad-hoc 'warlike adventures' in which 'the proletariat only loses blood and wins nothing'.[140]

SO also recognised that best means to maintain a regular connection to supporters of syndicalism outside Cataluña was through a periodical. From the outset *Solidaridad Obrera* (Barcelona) provided the federation with a platform, which helped to create a climate in which syndicalism meant something to its affiliates. This was something the FSORE never achieved.[141] The value of *Solidaridad Obrera* (Barcelona) was recognised in the Congress, and plans were made to expand the paper and set up a working group to 'study the most practical means' of producing a daily version. A scheme to extend propaganda was also proposed, which called for the creation of groups charged with promoting syndicalism in public meetings and conferences across Spain, as well as editing newspapers, publishing pamphlets and distributing free *hojas* to 'the workshop, the field and the mine'.[142]

These plans could not be implemented straight away, as the new confederation had little presence outside its Catalan base. The success of the confederation thus rested on its ability to turn the proposals made at the 1910 Congress into a reality, solidifying the scattered support it received outside Cataluña into a coherent organisation. In order to do this, it had to engage with anarchist groups across Spain and demonstrate to them that syndicalism was the best means to achieve their goals, providing a cultural base of support for the organisation which was lacking in 1910.[143] This process of adding 'meat to the bones' of the confederation began in earnest in January 1911, at the same time that the organisation changed its name to the Confederación Nacional del Trabajo (CNT).[144]

Building a National Presence

The CNT's expansion required the support of the anarchist press. Yet, neither the anarchist movement outside Cataluña nor its publications were universally committed to syndicalism or the new confederation. For example, the newly-founded *Anarquía* (Zaragoza, 1911-c.1912) had doubts about the effectiveness of syndicalism as the best means to advance the revolution. The paper advised its readers to ensure that syndicates paid attention to the 'eminently revolutionary' input of anarchists, and did not become subject to the reformist influences of 'professional charlatans'.[145] This paper was edited by Joaquín Zuferri, a delegate of the Zaragoza workers' federation at the 1910 Congress, who had since turned his back on the confederation.[146] Equally skeptical was *El Látigo* (Madrid, 1911), the last periodical edited by Federico Urales and Soledad Gustavo prior to the 1920s.[147] This was an unusual publication. Alongside crude satire and gibes levelled at politicians such as Lerroux and Iglesias, the paper ran a column named 'political brushstrokes,' which consisted of short fictitious dialogues between various political groups—including anarchists—to ridicule them.[148] In *El Látigo*, syndicalism was presented as simply a new trend, or fad, within the anarchist movement, which would soon be abandoned.[149] This was quite a departure from Urales, who had been at the forefront of the movements' organisational efforts a decade earlier, yet after his disputes with Antonio Apolo in 1904–1905, discussed in the previous chapter, Urales had been ostracised—labelled an 'ex-anarchist' by some within the movement—to the point that he no longer seemed to identify as an anarchist, nor did many anarchists identify with him.[150] Unlike Urales's previous publications, *El Látigo* struggled to attract a readership and closed after just four issues.[151] Urales did not edit another publication until 1923, when he began the second epoch of *La Revista Blanca* in Barcelona.[152]

In Gijón, prospects for syndicalist support were more encouraging. United working-class action appeared to be growing in 1910, after the local anarchists, republicans and socialists joined in solidarity strikes against employer intransigence and the widespread use of lock-outs.[153] They also received support from dockers in Aviles (Asturias), Bilbao, El Ferrol, and La Coruña, where boycotts were launched against ships diverted from Gijón. This local and translocal solidarity was praised by *Solidaridad Obrera* (Gijón) as a 'beautiful movement', which cut through 'politics' as the true articulation of the Spanish working class.[154] After months of unrest and hardship in Gijón, figures in the employers' association became the target of violent attacks. On 24 June the President of the employers' circle was shot and wounded by the anarchist Marcelino Suárez, and a month later Celestino Lantero (spokesman of the association) was stabbed and died two days later.[155] These incidents were used as a reason to suppress syndicalist and anarchist groups. The homes of Quintanilla and Sierra Álvarez were searched and both were held in custody, while the editor of *Solidaridad Obrera* (Gijón), Emilio Rendueles, was arrested and charged as an accomplice in Lantero's murder.[156] Marcelino Suárez, the only one of those charged to admit any guilt, became a regular correspondent in *Solidaridad Obrera* (Gijón), providing a fortnightly column from his cell in Gijón's Modelo prison, which criticised the appalling state of the institution.[157] By the end of 1910 *Solidaridad Obrera* (Gijón) was in trouble. Rendueles was still in prison and the paper was running at a massive deficit, which it blamed on non-paying correspondents. Shortly afterwards the paper was forced to close.[158]

At the same time a new anarchist publication emerged in the city: *Acción Libertaria*, (Gijón, 1910–1911, 27 issues). Although it shared a number of contributors, *Acción Libertaria* was not a direct replacement for *Solidaridad Obrera*. It was published by the city's anarchist 'Germinal' group, which included Quintanilla and Sierra Álvarez, and had the support of notable figures in the wider movement.[159] *Acción Libertaria* sustained a print run of approximately 2,300.[160] Although this figure was modest, the paper became the most important anarchist periodical outside Cataluña in 1910–11, comparable only to *Tierra y Libertad* (Barcelona) in its standing within the movement, as demonstrated by the number of high-profile contributors to the paper and its extensive correspondence network.[161] The paper saw hope in the CNT, but it did not pretend that anything substantial had yet been achieved. Strikes in Gijón, Bilbao, Zaragoza, Barcelona, Tarrasa, Sabadell, El Ferrol and Huelva were cited by contributors as proof of growing proletarian activity across Spain, yet the paper's editors did not credit this to syndicalism: 'the wave of strikes does not answer to instigations of socialist or anarchist militants . . . the present proletarian generation defines itself above all in moments of excitation and crisis, by a certain rebellious radicalism which does not completely fit into any doctrinal model'.[162] This impression is backed by data from the government's Institute of Social Reforms, which observed that explicitly 'syndicalist' activity remained limited in Spain in 1909–1911, despite an increase in union membership and strike activity.[163] In Sevilla, for example, there was a general upsurge in worker organisation in 1910–1911, yet many of these associations were 'defensive' and concentrated on questions such as wages. 'True,' 'revolutionary' syndicates, which used offensive tactics and declared a desire to destroy capitalism, were rare.[164]

For *Acción Libertaria*, syndicalism had to establish itself in local contexts before it could harness this 'rebelliousness'.[165] It had to innovate and adapt to the new climate, not simply replace old words with new ones. It had to abandon its faith in 'old' strikes and plan coordinated revolutionary action, and accept the new tactic of sabotage as the only means to combat employer intransigence.[166] Some correspondents expressed doubts about this development, criticising the current obsession with economic theory at the expense of the 'moral and philosophical' elements of anarchist ideology.[167] Those who advocated cultural emancipation felt threatened by the current obsession with organisation, and reminded the editors of *Acción Libertaria* that the revolution meant more than a new system of production.[168] It also required the creation of a 'new morality' and intellectual action, for which print was essential.[169] Yet *Acción Libertaria* was not prepared to abandon syndicalism because some of its contributors were uneasy with the idea, and it stressed that changes had to be made from within the anarchist movement. Mella was particularly forthright in this stance, frequently criticising the lack of 'deeds' from the anarchist movement and its 'exhausted' ideology.[170] Despite all of the doubts expressed in the paper, it remained hopeful that the expansion of syndicalism was both desirable and possible. 'Syndicalism is still weak'— wrote Anselmo Lorenzo in *Acción Libertaria* in February 1911—'note well the expression . . . it is *still* weak . . . stronger than yesterday, it will be stronger tomorrow . . . bourgeois privilege is still strong . . . it was stronger yesterday, it will be weaker tomorrow'.[171]

Acción Libertaria gives a good sense of the state of the anarchist movement at the time of the CNT's creation. The paper reflected enthusiasm for syndicalism, yet it also reflected a desire for anarchism to have a more central role in syndicalist theory and practice. Tellingly, the paper scarcely mentioned the CNT, mainly because there was nothing to report. The confederation remained little more than a gesture to national organisation, which had not yet become a reality to many anarchists or the wider labour movement. The first secretary of the CNT, José Negre, was aware of these shortcomings. In his summary of the confederation's inaugural year, he admitted that 'our works have not been as brilliant as our . . . ambition,' yet he absolved the organisation of any responsibility for its inactivity, instead blaming the poor education of the Spanish worker, bourgeois repression, and a lack of money.

Nevertheless, Negre saw reasons for optimism, particularly in the growing strength of *Solidaridad Obrera*, which had increased its distribution from 4,500 to 7,000 copies in under a year.[172] Support for the CNT was especially strong in areas that had sent delegates to the 1910 Congress.[173] In Vigo, for example, a local syndicalist federation was formed and briefly published its own newspaper, and sought to expand into a regional federation.[174] Solidaridad Obrera de Galicia was constituted in March 1911, consisting of 16 societies from La Coruña, five from Vigo and a few agricultural societies, in total representing around 3,800 workers.[175] A similar process was underway in Zaragoza, marked by the publication of the local workers' federation *La Aurora Social*.[176] In the Islas Baleares, José Ordinas, representative of the Palma bricklayers' society at the 1910 Congress, credited the marked increase in worker activity in Mallorca to the 'inspiration' given by the CNT.[177] Likewise, a month after the creation of the CNT supporters of syndicalism in Sevilla began working towards a federation of societies across Andalucía, and launched an 'anarchist and syndicalist' propaganda campaign to rally support for this idea.[178] As with similar tours in the early 1900s, print played a crucial role in these events. José Sánchez Rosa, one of the key figures in the Andalucían anarchist publishing, led one of these tours, speaking at meetings where he advocated the organisation of workers into 'modern syndicates'.[179] One correspondent to *Acción Libertaria* claimed that thousands of people attended one of Sánchez Rosa's conferences in Huelva, where anarchist print was widely distributed. Although these were encouraging signs for activists in Andalucía, support for both local federations and a regional confederation remained limited.[180] New syndicalist groups also invited repression. For example, a syndicalist federation formed in Huelva shortly after Sánchez Rosa's visit, reportedly with the support of 4,000 affiliates, and called for a city-wide strike.[181] In response, the local authorities arrested the entire federal committee.[182]

Support for syndicalism also came from groups in areas that had not sent delegates to the 1910 Congress, such as Valladolid, where the local anarchist periodical *Escuela Libre* saw itself as a publication for the 'rationalist-syndicalist worker'.[183] In March 1911 the paper announced the creation of a local 'Ateneo Obrero Sindicalista', run by Federico

Forcada, editor of paper and director of the local rationalist school.[184] The centre's organisers aimed to 'spread scientific-economic culture' and combat all 'political, religious and social sophisms,' through the construction of a library of 'syndicalist propaganda'.[185] They also asserted their affiliation to the CNT, although the centre did not appear in any of the confederation's records.

Judging by these reports in the anarchist press, by the summer of 1911 syndicalism had clearly made a mark on the movement. The CNT had inspired anarchist groups across Spain to begin the task of organising locally and regionally. Yet the organisation remained elusive, and had not fully established itself beyond its base in Cataluña. It also retained a stance of 'pure syndicalism' and had not officially embraced anarchism in either its rhetoric or declared aims. If the anarchist movement outside Cataluña was to take the opportunity presented to it by the creation of the CNT, it had to consolidate anarchist ideas within the organisation's structure and outlook. The first opportunity to do so came at the I Congress of the CNT, held in Barcelona from 8–10 September 1911.

The 1911 Congress and Repression

From the outset the CNT's support was 'elastic': it waxed and waned constantly, particularly during periods of industrial unrest. Membership figures reproduced in the press were often estimates and exaggerations, and often fluctuated dramatically. It is therefore difficult to make definite points on the CNT's size and spread at this point.[186] In the most generous reading of the figures published in *Solidaridad Obrera* (Barcelona), there were around 30,000 members of the CNT in September 1911, around half of whom were from Cataluña [see Table 4.2]. Of the remainder, roughly 7,500 were from Andalucía, 2,500 from Zaragoza, 1,700 from Gijón and La Felguera (Asturias), 1,200 from Valencia region, 920 from Mallorca, 610 from Río Alhama (Logroño), 555 from Galicia, 210 from Bilbao and Baracaldo (Vizcaya) and 100 from Santander. Around half of the societies present at the 1911 Congress were from outside Cataluña, the bulk of which were from Andalucía (~48), followed by Galicia (~19), Valencia (~13), Aragón (~11), Asturias (~11), Castilla la Vieja (~3), Mallorca (~2) and Vizcaya (~2). This would show an increase of around 40 per cent in non-Catalan involvement in the CNT from the previous year, while affiliation from Catalan societies had increased by less than 15 per cent.

Problems with representation evident in the 1910 Congress remained, however. Only a third of non-Catalan societies were linked to a Congress delegate in 1911. Affiliated societies in Sevilla—one of the areas where anarchists had most readily accepted syndicalist tactics—contributed little to the proceedings and the Asturian syndicalists were unable to send a representative due to repression.[187] As in the previous year, many representatives of non-Catalan societies were stand-ins from Barcelona, most of whom were members of the CNT Central Committee.[188]

Table 4.2 Location of Societies and Delegates of CNT in September 1911

	Represented Societies	No. Delegates	Unrepresented Societies	No. Affiliates (where known)
Spain	115	126	101	29470
Cataluña	79	102	29	14233
Barcelona	74	98	28	13830
Gerona	5	4		305
Lérida			1	98
Non-Cataluña	36	24	72	15507
Andalucía	7	8	41	7654
Cádiz	1	1	7	1129
Córdoba	1	1	2	720
Huelva	1	1	6	2260
Málaga	2	3	5	1950
Sevilla	2	2	21	1595
Aragón	2	3	9	2461
Zaragoza	2	3	9	2461
Asturias			11	1705
Castilla la Vieja			2	710
Logroño			1	610
Santander			1	100
Galicia	16	2	3	555
La Coruña	15	1	2	293
Pontevedra	1	1	1	262
Islas Baleares	1	1	1	920
Provincias Vascongadas	2	2		210
Vizcaya	2	2		210
Valencia	8	8	5	1292
Alicante	2	2	4	492
Valencia	6	6	1	800

Sources: *Solidaridad Obrera* (Barcelona, II), 8 September, 1911, 1 and 15 September, 1911, 1; Xavier Cuadrat, *Socialismo y anarquismo en Cataluña (1899–1911): Los orígenes de la CNT* (Madrid: Ediciones de la Revista de Trabajo, 1976), 625–629.

Following two years of poor representation from outside Cataluña, delegates approved a motion which stated that in future years travel costs would be covered by the CNT's central fund. They also voted to hold the next Congress in Zaragoza, hoping that this would be more accessible to delegates from the rest of Spain.[189]

The overriding theme of the 1911 Congress was the CNT's organisational structure. Its leadership advocated a highly decentred system, in which local federations and regional confederations would retain most decision-making powers. These layers of autonomy would ensure that the CNT remained focused on the immediate, local concerns of workers. Activists had to 'live the life of the different pueblos,' otherwise the CNT would cease to have meaning in the lives of its members. These local and regional bodies were to be joined by parallel national unions of trade, creating a dual system of representation which would ensure autonomy within localities and solidarity across them. The national committee would guide these federal bodies, but lacked full executive control. The only national action the committee could take was the decision to call for a general strike, which would only be approved if the entire organisation was ready. Negre presented this model as a pragmatic means of ensuring the CNT did not disintegrate as readily as its predecessors.[190]

Another reoccurring theme of the Congress was membership fees. Some representatives called for high, fixed quotas, representing a desire to codify existing anarchist voluntary donation funds, which had previously been administered by periodicals. Many resisted this centralisation of practice, invoking the movement's deep distrust of union bureaucracy and fee-paying.[191] Some fees may have been necessary, just as paying for a newspaper was necessary, however anarchists stressed that systematised due-paying created union elites and an inactive membership, as demonstrated by the socialist unions of the UGT.[192] Only a week before the Congress an article by Anselmo Lorenzo in *Solidaridad Obrera* (Barcelona) stressed this point, criticising unionists who 'believe paying dues justifies . . . apathy and inertia'.[193] Following much discussion, the Congress approved of only relatively small dues. A fund for prisoners, particularly for those imprisoned whilst undertaking work for the CNT, was to be raised by a four céntimo quota from each affiliate, while the confederation itself was to be funded through a monthly fee of 1 céntimo per affiliate. Any further dues were to be agreed at a regional level.[194] Anarchist fears of bureaucratisation was also reflected in the Congress' rejection of *syndicalismo a basé multiple*: the practice of paying society officials, maintaining large strike funds and negotiating with employers, as practiced by socialist unions.[195] This was regarded by most anarchists as hierarchical and therefore bad practice, since it deviated from the model of a future classless society. 72 delegates voted in favour of a motion censuring *a basé multiple*, and only four against.[196]

The role of print was second only to the structure of the CNT in the proceedings of the Congress. Everyone present agreed that a daily syndicalist newspaper was necessary in order to sustain the confederation and attract new members. This was a 'true evolutionary and revolutionary' endeavour, which would combat the daily slander against the working class in the bourgeois press.[197] Yet the group charged with addressing this matter was pessimistic about the prospects of this publication, unless its finances could be assured in advance. It was suggested that syndicates across Spain should follow the example of SO (now known as the Confederación Regional del Trabajo de Cataluña, CRT), and collect dues for the paper. Eventually the Congress agreed on a high monthly quota of 10 céntimos per affiliate for the daily paper, to last for a period of six months. In order to sustain it in the long term, Salvador Seguí proposed that 9,000 shares in the paper should be created and sold at a value of 1 peseta each. As with the payment of dues, these moves sought to codify previously sporadic behaviour, indicating a growing shift towards a more structured, centralised movement.[198] The expansion of print was one of the few areas in which the central CNT took primacy over local activity. Plans for new regional syndicalist periodicals were rejected, as the proposed extension of *Solidaridad Obrera* would, it was claimed, provide sufficient coverage across the whole of Spain. Instead of launching local papers, Manuel Permañer of the CNT Central Committee suggested that activists should build support for the forthcoming central, national syndicalist daily.[199] Although it would take five years before the daily *Solidaridad Obrera* was fully established, this discussion represented the desire within the early CNT for a more formal structure, with Barcelona established as the official—rather than tacit—centre of anarchist activity in Spain. The fact that this was manifest during debates over the role of the press, rather than those concerning organisational structure, reveals the continuing importance of print to the movement. In 1911, local and regional federations were largely abstract ambitions outside Cataluña, while print was seen as the current, tangible mechanism for expansion and consolidation, and thus had to be regulated in a way designed to benefit the embryonic CNT.

The decisions and plans made by the newly-inaugurated CNT would have to wait to be put into effect.[200] The 1911 Congress was held during a period of intense popular unrest in Spain.[201] A call-up for troops to fight in Morocco provoked protest meetings through the summer of 1911, which were supported by republicans, socialists and the CNT. At the same time, strikes began in Bilbao (24 August), Málaga (28 August) and the Asturian coalmining area of Mieres (5 September).[202] When the CNT Congress began on 8 September, all of these strikes were escalating. Thousands joined anti-war protests in Madrid, while in Asturias around 20,000 miners came out on strike, completely halting work in the industry. In Vizcaya clashes took place between strikers and the Civil Guard, resulting in the closure of all workers' centres and the deployment of troops.[203] As the Asturian and Málaga strikes ended, city-wide strikes in solidarity with the Basque strikes took place in Zaragoza, La Coruña, El Ferrol, Vigo, Sevilla, Gijón and Oviedo. In Valencia violence between workers and local authorities caused a number of deaths, which were followed by the burning of church property. In a bid to regain control of the situation, Prime Minister José Canalejas suspended constitutional guarantees (19 September) and enacted press censorship (21 September). Within days the strike wave had petered out and the threat of a genuine, national general strike was averted.

This moment was arguably a more serious threat to the political order than the Tragic Week of 1909. It was certainly more widespread, and primarily took the form of industrial action provoked by class solidarity, which (aside from in Valencia) was not dissipated through anti-clerical violence.[204] Like the Tragic Week, however, the strikes were not directed by any political group, and were subdued relatively quickly by repression. Key figures in the republican and socialist movements were not prepared to declare themselves in favour of political revolution.[205] The republicans were generally uninterested in such methods, while the socialists were paralysed by their 'sclerotic' leadership, which sought to moderate the strikes, despite the fact that a large section of UGT membership was keen for escalation.[206] As was often the case, the socialist movement was caught between two positions: a desire from its leadership to retain respectability in line with electoral ambitions, and the desires of its membership to act decisively. In the end neither were satisfied. Their indecision meant that direct, spontaneous action was the route chosen by thousands of workers across Spain, whether they identified as anarchists or not.[207]

In contrast, the CNT clearly wanted to see revolutionary action, but lacked the means to fully instigate or direct it on a national scale. Official messages of support were sent to the workers of Bilbao and Málaga during the Congress, although there was no explicit discussion of using these incidents to provoke a national general strike.[208] Nevertheless, the CNT was accused of planning the unrest and trying to utilise it for revolutionary purposes. The basis of this accusation came from the testimony of two brothers, Miguel and José Sánchez González (the latter also known as both Miguel Villalobos Moreno and Constant Leroy) who claimed that a number of delegates and other prominent anarchists, socialists, and republicans held a secret meeting after the CNT Congress, with the aim of exploiting the unrest to provoke a revolutionary general strike.[209] These testimonies were almost certainly fabricated at the instigation of the authorities in Barcelona as a pretext to repress the CNT.[210] The meeting probably did take place, however, and the CNT did attempt to send agitators to various cities, although their role in coordinating strikes is difficult to judge. In Sevilla, for example, a general strike was called following a meeting of socialist and anarchist groups in the city, yet the decision was taken with limited direct connection to the national CNT.[211] In the opinion of *Acción Libertaria*, the CNT's direction had been 'vague and ignored,' as each strike had been a grassroots, sporadic, local affair.[212] As with many incidents of social unrest over the turn of the century, anarchists were certainly heavily involved in the strikes of 1911, and probably tried to use this moment for revolutionary ends, but they had not caused the strikes nor were they capable of directing them.

Promoting national, coordinated action was one of the principal reasons for forming the CNT, yet at this early stage the organisation was in no position to make this a reality.[213] The CNT was singled out for repression nevertheless. The organisation was made illegal days after the

1911 Congress, its leading activists were imprisoned, and *Solidaridad Obrera* (Barcelona) was suspended.[214] As during the repression of the 1890s, the paper's subscription lists were seized and used to track down important militants across the country.[215] These episodes reveal the dangers of operating through print culture. In times of repression, periodicals became incriminating objects, while the information held at publishing houses were seen by the Spanish authorities as gateways into the workings of the movement. In the following days hundreds of workers and activists were imprisoned across Spain, and by the end of September the situation looked bleak for the anarchist movement and the CNT. One weekly round-up of 'social action' from the anarchist press was replaced with a sarcastic announcement that 'nothing has happened here, nothing is happening nor will it happen . . . we live in the best of all possible worlds. RIP'.[216]

In addition to the closure of *Solidaridad Obrera*, most Catalan anarchist papers suspended publication. *Tierra y Libertad*, for example, felt it was 'impossible' to produce any issues between 13 September and 1 November.[217] Outside Cataluña, several anarchist publications were closed, including *Escuela Moderna* of Valencia, whose editor Samuel Torner was also imprisoned.[218] The Modern School run by Torner was also closed.[219] The only available contemporary anarchist coverage of the 1911 Congress came from *Acción Libertaria*, which had moved to Vigo in the summer of 1911.[220] The paper was now edited solely by Ricardo Mella, who had returned to his hometown in 1910 to take up work constructing the city's electric tram system.[221] Throughout 1911, Mella and *Acción Libertaria* hardened their stance towards syndicalism and the CNT.[222] Signs of an increasing wariness towards syndicalism were evident following the paper's relocation to Vigo, as in the article 'Union or Culture?', which suggested that worker organisation without anarchism was prone to appropriation by reactionaries and tyrants.[223] Mella's reservations about syndicalism crystallised into a critique of the CNT three weeks after the 1911 Congress. The criticism was broad: the Congress was too long, and its discussions 'offered little for analysis,' while its concentration on matters such as piece work and a minimum wage were a sign that the confederation was veering towards reformism. Finally, the organisation was attacked for having excessively regulated its structure and dues, which would undoubtedly produce a 'quiet and stationary' organisation. 'There is no point', the article concluded, 'in creating new organisations that are easily confused with old ones,' suggesting that for all the talk of the CNT's novelty, it was no more than a rehashing of the failed experiments of the past. [224]

Mella attracted criticism for this stance.[225] His views appeared increasingly estranged from wider anarchist opinion—which he derided as 'dogmatism'—and he became embroiled in public back-and-forth arguments with contributors to *Tierra y Libertad*, who saw his 'aristocratic' position as elitist and exclusionary.[226] One high-profile subscriber to *Acción Libertaria*, Antonio Soler Cuadrat from Villanueva y Geltrú, cancelled his order for the paper, labelling it a 'dungheap'.[227] Yet the dispute did not last long, as *Acción Libertaria* published only six issues in Vigo before it closed in 1911 after its finances had been ruined by non-paying correspondents. Unlike his stance on union dues, Mella clearly regarded regular payment towards a newspaper as necessary, yet it appears few of readers of his paper felt the same way. Indeed, the only subscribers who had kept up their payments and given additional support to *Acción Libertaria* as its finances buckled in mid-1911 was a federation of anarchist migrants based in Panamá, whom Mella praised in the final issue of the paper.[228] In contrast, Mella took a swipe at the Spanish movement, claiming that it had become divorced from the people and had been reduced to mere rabble-rousing and insults.[229] Like Urales before him, Mella's pre-eminence in the movement was fading, as a new generation of thinkers took greater prominence.

Maintaining Organisational Ideas: 1911–1914

After years of promoting local agitation and countless debates in periodicals and congresses, syndicalists in Spain had managed to create a national organisation which attracted a sizeable part of the anarchist movement to its cause. All of this was undone within days of the I Congress of the CNT. In the following years there was a sharp increase in organised labour in Spain, however the UGT was the main beneficiary of these developments, as the CNT remained outlawed until 1914.[230] During the 1911 Congress Negre had asserted that the CNT's decentred structure would help it weather repression, yet the immediate suspension of the organisation came far too early in the confederation's development for this belief to be put to the test.[231] The CNT had barely established itself beyond its Catalan base, and the few local syndicalist federations outside Cataluña were 'smashed' in the aftermath of the September strikes.[232] As in 1907 and 1909, the reconstruction of the organisation centred on Barcelona. By January 1913 most of the militants imprisoned in 1911 had been released, and *Solidaridad Obrera* resumed publication in the following May as the 'Organ of the Regional Federation of Labour of Cataluña', declaring itself the standard-bearer of all syndicates and syndicalists in Spain.[233] Despite these developments, organisational connections between the Catalan Federation and groups in the rest of Spain remained informal and scarce until 1915, and opinions on how best to organise the movement were far from uniform.[234] Some groups advocated a return to the drive towards national organisation that had been curtailed by repression, while others proposed alternative models and interpretations of organisation, more akin to the decentred activism championed by Mella in the recently-closed *Acción Libertaria*.

Antonio Bar has defined the years 1911–1915 as ones of ideological development, when anarchism and syndicalism were finally consolidated into the single theory of anarcho-syndicalism.[235] While this may have been true within the CNT's central leadership in Barcelona, there is little evidence of a coherent development of a 'concrete political conception' of anarcho-syndicalism in the wider movement's press.[236] Rather, this period saw a non-linear, haphazard accommodation of syndicalism within pre-existing anarchist thought and practice. Although syndicalist ideas were maintained by some anarchist papers, a sustained critique of syndicalism also developed at this time, which regarded the movement's emphasis on economic and working affairs as damaging to other aspects of anarchist ideology and practice. Several key contributors to the anarchist press suggested modifying syndicalism, or in some cases rejecting worker organisation altogether as a means to redress this balance.

Periodicals proliferated in the years after 1911, with anarchist publishing reaching a size and scope that had not been seen in almost a decade [refer to Chart 0.2]. Many of these papers were published by groups already well-established in anarchist print culture. For example, *El Porvenir del Obrero* (Mahón) reappeared in April 1912, exactly five years after the paper had closed following the arrest after its editor, Juan Mir i Mir.[237] This second epoch of *El Porvenir del Obrero* was one the longest of any anarchist periodical prior to 1915, publishing 117 issues in two spells between April 1912 and October 1915.[238] Its reappearance was greeted with enthusiasm by a number of high-profile figures in the movement, including Anselmo Lorenzo, who saw the paper's arrival as an opportunity to unite the movement after the failures of the previous September.[239] The second epoch of the paper was largely the same as the first, carrying a similar emphasis on intellectual and scientific discussion, calls for action in the sphere of education and the dangers of vice, above all alcohol consumption.[240] Mir i Mir's attention to educational matters was respected by many of his contemporaries, including the editors of *Humanidad*—the new periodical of Toner's Valencia Modern School, which had reopened in January 1912—who praised the 'cultured' perspective of *El Porvenir del Obrero* and its 'serene and elevated labour, with which they instruct the rebellions and ennoble the yearnings for vindication'.[241] The paper's standing in the movement was affirmed when Teresa Claramunt, the most prominent female anarchist in Spain, moved to Mahón and joined the editorial staff in 1913.[242]

The paper was also celebrated for its wider contributions to anarchist print culture. The group behind *El Porvenir del Obrero* launched a publishing house in 1913 named the 'Biblioteca de Divulgación,' with the aim of adding books and pamphlets to its output.[243] Its first book was *Dinamita Cerebral*, a collection of stories by well-known anarchists and writers respected by the movement, including Emile Zola, Octavio Mirbeau, Maksim Gorky and Anselmo Lorenzo.[244] Hundreds of copies of this book were sent to almost every province in Spain, and abroad to

Marseille, Panamá, Lisbon, Havana, Boston, Río de Janeiro and Abercrave (Wales).[245] It became a classic of Spanish anarchist literature, and was reprinted several times, including a 1974 edition published in Buenos Aires.[246]

The second publication of the 'Biblioteca de Divulgación' was also a success.[247] *Hacía la emancipación* was one of the last substantial works written by Anselmo Lorenzo before his death in 1914.[248] The pamphlet outlined Lorenzo's lifelong commitment to syndicalism, a tactic he portrayed as 'nothing new' but the tactic of choice for anarchists since 1870, 'when the word *syndicalism* did not exist'.[249] Even the novelty of boycotts and sabotage—tactics held as hallmarks of 'modern' syndicalism—was questioned by Lorenzo, who claimed that they had begun in ancient Egypt.[250] By 1913, many of Lorenzo's generation of activists had passed away, including Ernesto Álvarez in 1902 and Fermín Salvochea in 1907. Few of the next generation of activists and writers prominent in the 1880s and 1890s had maintained their position in the movement. Urales and Gustavo were largely absent from the anarchist press, and Mella's position as the movement's leading theorist was in decline. Yet respect for Lorenzo remained unequivocal. As one of the last veterans of the FRE still publishing original works, he was seen as the human embodiment of the link between the movement's past and present. In *Hacía la emancipación*, Lorenzo was thus endorsing syndicalism, tying it to the sacred origins of the International and the historical narrative of anarchism in Spain.

Through Lorenzo, syndicalism had been given a history, yet its future remained uncertain. *El Porvenir del Obrero* saw action in the national and local level as necessary, lest the CNT fall into the same spiral of decline as former anarchist organisations. *El Porvenir del Obrero* frequently cajoled the workers of Menorca (predominantly fieldworkers, bootmakers, and construction labourers) to form workplace unions and larger federations. It stressed that immediate, material concerns were secondary to building unity that would allow for a broader, class-based emancipatory movement.[251] This attitude was articulated most clearly during a national railworkers' strike which erupted in September 1912.[252] Despite failing to deliver any short-term gains, the strike was seen as a step forward by *El Porvenir del Obrero* because it had fostered 'a rebellious and experimental will of the workers' and spread 'terror' in the ranks of the bourgeoisie.[253] This perspective was shared by a number of other papers, which regarded the strike as an 'educational' episode for the railworkers and the proletariat in general.[254] In stressing the moral quality of this strike, *El Porvenir del Obrero* was advancing a traditional anarchist position, which saw industrial action as only the first step to a revolutionary situation. In contrast, syndicalists usually only advocated strikes as a means to advance material gains, as approved during the Congresses of the CNT. Yet *El Porvenir del Obrero* did not see the distinction between anarchist and syndicalism as a problem. One of the paper's most frequent contributors, Vicente García, was clear that 'syndicalism is not anarchism' since it only concerned workers and working affairs, while anarchism fought 'not for the emancipation of the working class but of society as a whole'. Nevertheless, García regarded syndicalism as the only viable means of bringing forth the social revolution since a purely or 'almost' anarchist revolution would be immediately crushed. The new society that would emerge following a syndicalist revolution 'would not be the Anarchy that our mind conceives,' but it would be 'sufficiently just' for anarchists to accept it.[255]

El Porvenir del Obrero looked for signs of organisational activity and syndicalist practice wherever it could. It was in touch with local groups and *ateneos* which promoted syndicalism, in areas such as Madrid, Valladolid, Sama de Langreo (Asturias), Eibar (Gipúzcoa) and Vigo.[256] These groups aimed to keep syndicalist ideas alive at a local level, mainly through the creation and distribution of propaganda, such as the pamphlet *Sindicalismo revolucionario* produced by the Ateneo Sindicalista of Madrid.[257] The Madrid *ateneo* also organised a 'monster meeting' in December 1912 to protest the continuing repression in Spain, which was attended by delegates from Vizcaya, Asturias, Andalucía, Galicia and Castilla.[258] Closer to home, the paper was excited by the creation of the Regional Federation of the Workers' Societies of the Islas Baleares in Palma de Mallorca, which aimed to secure the 'economic and social emancipation' of the workers through solidarity and education.[259] In late 1913 the paper declared itself optimistic with these recent developments: 'in every area new periodicals appear, modest, but very well orientated; congresses are celebrated; excursions are prepared and every one of us feels with new spirits, with stronger will, with activity better directed'.[260]

Nevertheless, these developments were piecemeal compared with the initial creation and spread of the CNT. *El Porvenir del Obrero* could not disguise its exasperation with the local *mahonés* workers. 18 months after its reappearance, the paper declared its disbelief that only the bootmakers and bricklayers had formed unions in Mahón, and even within these societies only a fraction of the trade was represented. Despite the paper's best efforts, the majority of the working population remained 'completely neglected and abandoned, without association, nor spirit of class'. 'This,' declared the paper, 'is not the path to emancipation'.[261] Despite the re-emergence of the Catalan CRT in early 1913, the national scope of CNT remained a distant ambition, which the paper blamed on the 'drowsiness' of workers outside Cataluña.[262] The fragmentation of the movement was highlighted during the first International Syndicalist Congress, held in Holborn Town Hall (London) from 27 September to 2 October 1913.[263] Although the CRT and groups from Menorca and La Coruña were represented at the Congress, no delegate felt confident in representing Spain as a whole.[264] The congress 'was not a great success and much time was wasted on personal recriminations and factional infighting,' and made little impression on the anarchist press outside Cataluña.[265]

In August 1913 García attempted to put a positive spin on this situation, claiming that the CNT was 'not an entity which requires a legalised regulation' to exist.[266] But he could not deny that syndicalist groups were struggling. The Galician syndicalist federation was repressed, prompting a wave of disaffection amongst the workers of Vigo, where many groups turned towards the socialist party and the UGT.[267] Previous gains in the province were reversed, and the movement became restricted to La Coruña and El Ferrol.[268] In Sevilla, mass demonstrations and strikes broke out in March 1912, as local anarchist and syndicalists attempted to repeat the united front witnessed during the general strike of the previous September. This movement lacked the support of local socialists and was put down relatively quickly. In the summer of the same year activists changed tactic, and set up a syndicalist *ateneo* with the aim of 'extending culture' and rebuilding a radical workers' movement in the city, yet this also collapsed after another attempt to launch a general strike in November. By the end of 1913 the movement in Sevilla had fractured along doctrinal lines, with more 'orthodox' anarchist groups criticising the turn to syndicalism as a 'materialist deviation'. The city's syndicalists had failed to mobilise local workers from their 'lethargy' and their plans to form an Andalucían Syndicalist Federation received support from just two other localities, Chiclana (a town of approximately 11,500 on the Bay of Cádiz) and Churriana (a district of Málaga city).[269]

Anarchist and syndicalist groups in Asturias faced similar problems.[270] Syndicalist workers' groups slowly began to re-emerge in Gijón in early 1912, based once again in the Calle Velasco Workers' Centre.[271] This was also the site of a popular library set up by the local 'Grupo Sindicalista,' with the help of donations of 300 books from local militants.[272] This period was 'extraordinarily difficult' for the erstwhile supporters of the CNT.[273] Yet, unlike their contemporaries in Sevilla, the anarchists and syndicalists of Gijón were able to launch and sustain a periodical: *El Libertario*, which ran between August 1912 and April 1913.[274] As with *El Porvenir del Obrero*, this paper had a history in anarchist print culture: it was basically a refashioning of *Acción Libertaria* by largely the same editorial staff, including Eleuterio Quintanilla and Pedro Sierra Álvarez.[275] As with its predecessor, *Acción Libertaria* (Gijón-Vigo), this new paper was given substantial financial support from groups of Spanish anarchists based in Panamá. Indeed, *El Libertario* was in part the initiative of the Panamanian Federation of Free Groups and Individuals (FAILP), which had formed along the Canal Zone in March 1911, whose periodical *El Único* had recently collapsed. In a move to re-establish their presence in the international print networks of anarchism, the FAILP contacted Quintanilla, Sierra Álvarez and Mella in the summer of 1912, and gave them 140 pesetas to launch a new periodical. It appears that the organisation's de facto head, M.D. Rodríguez, also left Panamá for Gijón at this point. While *El Libertario* did not bear much relation to *El Único*, which was vehemently anti-syndicalist, it did publish regular news of the FAILP and was sustained by its money over the following year.[276]

El Libertario marked the ascendency of Quintanilla—now in his late twenties and working more independently from his mentor Ricardo Mella—to a position of pre-eminence within the anarchist movement.[277] His confidence in the possibility of a full synthesis of anarchism and syndicalism placed him at the forefront of the intellectual developments of this period.[278] Rather than a new term for the age-old class struggle, Quintanilla saw syndicalism as a direct product of the changes in technology and production in the early twentieth century. Anarchism had to adapt to these developments and must accept the fact that the era of the International was over. Likewise, for Quintanilla, the socialist parties and centralised, national mobilisation of the Second International were soon to pass into a new stage in the evolution of socialism, defined by mass, revolutionary, apolitical syndicalism, committed to direct action and an anarchistic future.[279] Other contributors to the paper concurred. One regular correspondent, Noé Desmenjez [J. Menéndez] used his column to both celebrate the past exploits of anarchists—their 'red heroism', 'axiomatic' conviction and 'beautiful, yet innocent discourses'—and consign them to a failed past of 'fantastical exaggerations'.[280]

Quintanilla's analysis was based on his observations of the failures of parliamentary socialism in Spain. Unlike the relative successes of socialist parties in countries such as France and Germany, in Spain the PSOE remained on the margins of governmental politics, despite the election of Pablo Iglesias to the Cortes in 1910.[281] The socialist movement had, however, built up substantial support in Asturias, primarily in Oviedo and the coalmining areas of the region, where a powerful, highly-centralised socialist Miners' Federation (SOMA) was established in 1910.[282] *El Libertario* committed a great deal of space to criticising their regional rivals, particularly within the metalworking industry which was central to the economies of Gijón and La Felguera.[283] One favourite tactic of the paper was to ridicule the Oviedo-based socialist paper *La Aurora Social* [*The Social Dawn*], referring to it as *La Basura Social* [*The Social Rubbish*].[284] This argument continued over the following years through *Solidaridad*, the new publication of the *gijonés* syndicalist federation, which was presided over by Quintanilla.[285]

Alternative Models of Organisation

El Libertario closed in April 1913, after the paper was denounced for articles criticising the Church and local police.[286] A month later the paper reappeared in Madrid as *Acción Libertaria*.[287] This hand-over was similar to that of *El Productor—El Corsario* in 1893, representing a sense of unity amongst publishers to maintain periodicals in the face of repression. The paper soon established itself as the main anarchist paper published outside Cataluña, with a stable print-run of 5–6,000, and correspondents in almost every province in Spain.[288]

Acción Libertaria (Madrid) was largely the same as its *gigonés* predecessor. It had almost identical layout, the same sections and subsections, the same campaigns and many of the same contributors: Mella and Prat remained prominent voices in the paper, Desmenjez kept his regular column and Marcelino Suárez continued to report from Gijón prison. It also maintained *El Libertario*'s links to the Panamanian FAILP and continued to receive strong financial backing from this migrant community. Yet unlike *El Libertario*, and in particular Quintanilla, the new editors of *Acción Libertaria* had mixed opinions on the value of syndicalism. Like *El Porvenir del Obrero*, the paper saw strike activity as having transcendental qualities that were not confined to immediate victories or defeats. Rather, each strike was a 'milestone planted in the long path which leads to the integral emancipation of humanity'.[289] The paper affirmed that worker organisation 'was not anarchism,' but a potential precursor to its victory. Nevertheless, the paper was hesitant to use the phrase syndicalism, which it saw as 'superfluous,' as it added nothing to the tactics which had been advocated by the anarchist movement since the mid-nineteenth century.[290] The paper clearly thought that anarchists had to engage with syndicalism, yet it also maintained that they should not abandon other strategies in pursuit of homogeneity in the revolutionary movement. This position was demonstrated in the paper's serialisation of Errico Malatesta's critique 'Sobre sindicalismo' ['On Syndicalism'] which expressed fears that an over-concentration on economic goals would dilute the broader revolutionary principles of anarchism. For Malatesta, syndicalism had no inherent virtue, and the economic struggle it espoused could not solve the 'social question' alone. Readers of 'Sobre sindicalismo' were thus advised against joining 'syndicalist syndicates' and regulated national federations and were instead encouraged to form their own 'anarchist syndicates' which would take advantage of the 'fertile terrain' provided by workers' organisations.[291]

While the CNT was repressed, some anarchists appeared to take up Malatesta's advice to organise educational groups aimed at directing the movement. As in the early 1900s, many of these groups were linked to periodicals, and saw the distribution of print as central to their activity. For example, within a month of *Acción Libertaria*'s appearance a new anarchist group named 'Los Iguales' formed in Madrid. This group shared the same offices as *Acción Libertaria*, and was almost certainly comprised of many of the paper's staff.[292] The group took it upon themselves to 'completely organise the sale of the [anarchist] press in Madrid,' and suggested that they work as a distribution hub for pamphlets and *hojas* across the whole of Spain.[293] Unfortunately for 'Los Iguales,' they soon attracted the attention of the Madrid police, who pressurised local kiosks to cancel their relationship with the group.[294] Undeterred, the day before municipal elections of November 1913, 'Los Iguales' plastered anti-voting *hojas* on trees, lampposts and tram stops in Madrid. Most of the group were then arrested.[295] Tens of thousands of copies of the same *hojas* were sent across Spain to areas such as Barcelona, Gijón, San Sebastián, Sevilla, Córdoba, Elda (Alicante), Algeciras (Cádiz), Játiva (Valencia), Valladolid, Málaga and Río Tinto (Huelva), where—according to reports sent to *Acción Libertaria*—they made a great impression and contributed to the high rate of voting abstentions.[296] Two years later 'Los Iguales' briefly launched a journal-style publication, named *Los Refractarios* (Madrid 1915), which declared itself 'not completely adhered to the syndical movement' and regarded anarchism as a 'scientific-educational method applied to social questions'.[297] This paper folded after just a single issue as the group split over internal differences.[298]

Acción Libertaria and groups such as 'Los Iguales' rarely rejected syndicalism outright, but were cautious of organisational concerns eclipsing the broader message of anarchism. As a means of halting this trend, plans for more coordinated activity between anarchist groups were proposed towards the end of 1913. *Acción Libertaria* claimed this idea would provide cohesion to the movement while maintaining the specific 'characteristics, social and economic conditions' of each region of the country.[299] Unlike the CNT, this anarchist project would not be bound to workplace activity, but focused on the broader, and vaguer, goal of spreading propaganda. The results of this project were varied. Anarchist federations were formed in Valencia (September 1913), Andalucía (September 1913), Extremadura (September 1913), Cataluña (December 1913) and the two Castillas and León (July 1915), yet few of these organisations achieved anything of note.[300]

The first, and only relatively stable of these federation was the Federación de Grupos Libertarios de la Región Vasca, formed in December 1912 at a meeting between anarchist groups from the Basque towns of Baracaldo, Bilbao, San Sebastián, Eibar, Tolosa and Vitoria.[301] These groups were small cells of no more than 16 persons, which aimed to ensure that all members knew one another, thereby reducing the likelihood of infiltration by the police.[302] The Basque Federation was quick to declare itself free from written regulations, committees and dues. Its cohesion was based on a 'free pact' between groups and a shared desire to spread anarchist propaganda.[303] Unlike other anarchist federations, the group managed to maintain a periodical, *El Látigo* (Baracaldo), which became the federation's official organ in February 1913.[304] *El Látigo* devoted a great deal of space to organisational concerns. The paper's editor, Aquilino Gómez, wrote regular pieces on working conditions in the Basque region, which appeared alongside poetry dedicated to the 'magic word' of 'Union' and a reprinting of José López Montenegro's 1902 study *El Paro*

234 Our Love of Organisation

General (The General Strike).[305] Yet the paper did not wholeheartedly endorse syndicalism. A long running series titled 'Aspects of Syndicalism' from the paper's Santander correspondent, J. Ruíz, was cautious of 'syndicalist syndicalism' (echoing Malatesta), which was confined solely to 'economic terrain'. This would 'excessively materialise the question' and side-line action against the Church and State. Similarly, over-regulation of workers' groups and reliance on strike funds would 'make automatons' and reproduce the structure of bourgeois society. What was needed was 'fewer rules . . . less authority . . . less effort to capitalise quotas and more to foment education and culture between associates, creating libraries, opening schools and organising conferences stimulating art'.[306] Such statements reveal that the educational programme of the previous decade was still regarded as a central component of anarchist strategy, particularly for those who had reservations about the shift in emphasis towards syndicalism. Other correspondents were also keen to stress the need for 'combative associations' that were 'genuinely worker-led, but independent of the syndicates of trade' in order to maintain anarchist propaganda.[307]

In February 1913 *El Látigo* opened a subscription for a propaganda tour across the north of Spain, aiming to 'germinate' existing anarchist sympathies in the Basque region, Santander and Logroño.[308] Money was also raised for the tour by a raffle conducted by anarchists in Santander, offering portraits of Fermín Salvochea and Francisco Ferrer as a prize.[309] The main figures in the tour were all engaged in anarchist print culture: Aquilino Gómez, editor of *El Látigo*, Emilio Carral, a Santander-based activist, writer and former editor of *Adelante*, and José Sánchez Rosa, who had recently launched the 'Biblioteca del Obrero' in Sevilla with his wife Ana Villalobos, which became one of the most important sites of anarchist print culture until the outbreak of the Civil War in 1936.

The tour began in October 1913, after Sánchez Rosa had arrived from Madrid, where he had been speaking at a conference organised by the 'Los Iguales' group.[310] Beginning in Santander, the tour passed through towns in Cantabria, Vizcaya, Gipuzcoa, Vitoria and Logroño.[311] Printed materials formed a central aspect of the tour. A 'vast number' of *hojas*, pamphlets and periodicals were distributed, providing a base of anarchist literature in each locality.[312] In areas such as San Sebastián, new kiosks were established to ensure the continual supply of anarchist papers.[313] The main message of tour was the same as that advanced in the pages of *El Látigo*: that organisation was a useful strategy, but should not be considered as the ultimate goal. In Fuenmayor, for example, Aquilino Gómez affirmed his paper's stance to a packed crowd, declaring that syndicalism was 'the only fraternal tactic able to struggle . . . against the assault of capitalism . . . "but it has to be recognised—[Gómez] said—that syndicalism does not meet the aspirations of integral and definitive emancipation . . . nor can it hold itself as a concrete end capable of elevating consciences to the glories of the ideal'".[314] *El Látigo* was buoyant as the tour grew to a close, claiming to have inspired action and free organisation across the north of the country.

El Látigo closed soon afterwards, unable to maintain its print run of around 2,000 issues while its correspondents failed to pay for their subscriptions.[315] Yet the federation continued, and soon called for a second propaganda tour and the renewal of efforts towards a national confederation of anarchist groups. At the request of the *gigonés* anarchist group 'Divulgación,' the Basque Federation later united with those of Galicia, Asturias and Cantabria to form the Federación Anarquista de la Región Cantábrica at a meeting in Eibar in August 1914. Other than sending a delegate to the El Ferrol Peace Congress of 1915 (Constancio Romero from La Coruña), this new federation appears to have done very little and disbanded in September 1915.[316]

Few of the other anarchist federations achieved even the limited levels of success of the Basque Federation. The highpoint of activity was late 1913, when federations were declared in Valencia, Andalucía and Extremadura.[317] The Valencian Federation was able to carry out a propaganda tour in the summer of 1914. Again, Sánchez Rosa was the main attraction, this time accompanied by his daughter Paca, who 'painted the misery and labour which weighs upon the working woman with eloquent strokes' during her speeches.[318] The Andalucían Federation had less success with their proposed tour, and failed to expand beyond Sevilla and its surrounding towns.[319] Despite the traditional support for anarchism in these areas, both federations were locked in a 'permanent state of crisis' and collapsed in 1915, making only sporadic attempts to reform in the following years.[320]

Although equally unsuccessful, the Extremadura Federation was notable for its relationship with anarchist print culture. It was based in the small town of Azuaga (Badajoz, population in 1910: 14,192), which had reportedly received around 40,000 copies of *Tierra y Libertad*, almost 65,000 pamphlets and 350 books between 1910 and 1913.[321] Articles and letters from Azuaga appeared regularly in the anarchist press in this period, mainly from the correspondent Luis Zoais [Luis García Muñoz], who was also a contributor to *El Látigo*.[322] In September 1913 three anarchist groups in the town agreed to form a regional federation, and one month later launched *Luz* (co-edited by Zoais) as the group's periodical, which was a feat not managed by their Valencian and Andalucían counterparts. Although no copies of *Luz* have survived, it was reportedly printed on 'good paper' and was the 'size of *El Porvenir del Obrero*'.[323] These qualities did not save it from folding almost as soon as it appeared.[324] Likewise, the Extremduran Federation was short-lived. It briefly claimed the support of 34 groups across the region, before disappearing in January 1915.[325]

As in the early 1900s, anarchist propaganda groups formed and dispersed with regularity after the suppression of the CNT. The idea of federating anarchist propaganda groups was relatively novel, and indicative of a broader trend towards organisation across the movement. Yet the 'structure' of these federations was no firmer than that of the groups which constituted them, leaving them prone to disintegration. Although these federations largely came to nothing, the idea of a 'purely' anarchist federation across Spain did resurface at various points in the following years and was ultimately accomplished with the creation of the Federación Anarquista Ibérica (FAI) in 1927.[326]

A Plural, Indifferent Press

Between 1911 and 1915 anarchist periodicals appeared in the towns of Logroño (La Rioja), Huesca, Salamanca, Elche, Elda (both Alicante), Villena (Valencia), Llano del Beal (Murcia), Ecija (Sevilla), Castro del Rio (Córdoba), Nerva (Huelva) and Linares (Jaén) for the first time in the history of the movement. In Alcoy, Murcia and Cartagena, periodicals appeared for the first time since 1907 and in El Ferrol for the first time since 1884. These papers were indicative of a geographic expansion of the movement into areas of Spain that had almost no prior connection to the movement, comparable to that of the turn of the century [see Map 4.1].[327] For example, Béjar, (Salamanca) became the site of an active propaganda group, which proposed a propaganda tour across the provinces of Salamanca, Zamora, León, Burgos, Palencia and Avila, all

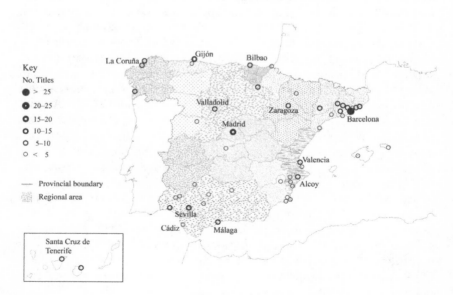

Map 4.1 Areas of Anarchist Publishing in Spain, 1907–1915.

Source: Map created by James G. Pearson.

of which had previously been completely ignored by the anarchist press. This group was headed by José María Blázquez de Pedro—a well-known figure in anarchist print culture —who had moved to the town in 1906 and acted as the town's contact for anarchist periodicals.[328]

Most of these new papers were broadly supportive of syndicalism. Both *Liberación* (Elche) and *Villena Obrera* (Villena) promoted syndicalism as a means for increased worker organisation across Alicante.[329] *El Trabajo* performed a similar role in Logroño.[330] Although none of these papers made reference to the CNT, some discussed the idea of a synthesis of anarchism and syndicalism, for example *Acción Directa* (Cartagena) was keen to stress the harmony of anarchism and worker orgxanisation, stressing that the 'economic equality' advanced by syndicalism would bring forth the 'moral' emancipation and revolutionary society advocated by anarchist philosophy.[331] A similar message appeared throughout *Acción Ferroviaria*, launched in 1913 as the organ of the rail-workers' syndicates of Huelva. This paper praised the transformative potential of syndicalism as the 'best and most beautiful' tactic for assuring the interests of the working class.[332] Support for syndicalism also came from anarchist papers independent of workers' groups, such as *Cultura Libertaria* (El Ferrol). The '13 October' group behind this publication were primarily supporters of anarchist educational programmes, regarding 'ignorance' as the main obstacle between the current society and anarchism.[333] But they were also keen to promote local workers' matters, and in February 1913 the paper published a passionate call for a reorganisation of the CNT by one of the confederation's former critics, José Suárez Duque.[334]

Through these papers, anarchist publishers and correspondents maintained the ideas of syndicalism following the repression of the CNT. However, there is sparse evidence in the press outside Cataluña that these years were spent solidifying a 'formalised' ideology of anarcho-syndicalism. Indeed, the term 'anarcho-syndicalism' did not appear at all in *Solidaridad Obrera* (Barcelona), or any anarchist periodicals of this period.[335] Syndicalism was generally regarded in a positive light, although anarchist papers were keen to stress that it was not the sole element of the struggle against authority. For some papers, such as *Acción Libertaria* (Madrid), syndicalism remained simply a tactic, distinct from the ultimate goal of anarchism, which required protection from overly zealous advocates of a 'purely' syndicalist doctrine. For others, such as *La Voz del Obrero*, (La Coruña), organisation was both the tactic and the goal. As with earlier syndicalist papers, this paper was clearly influenced by anarchism but rarely employed the term. On the ground, it appears that most members of the movement identified with both terms, often without seeing a distinction between anarchism and syndicalism, or demonstrating much interest in combining these theories.[336] Rather than revealing a need for a unitary theory of anarcho-syndicalism, this indifference suggests that anarchists in Spain were perfectly capable of supporting both ideas simultaneously, not least because to many of them they meant largely the same thing.[337]

The movement's press was also largely indifferent to two other developments in these years. The first was a brief resurrection of anarchist violence, marked by the assassination of Prime Minister José Canalejas by Manuel Pardiñas in November 1912, and the attempted assassination of King Alfonso XIII by Rafael Sancho Alegre in April 1913. Both Pardiñas and Sancho Alegre were self-declared anarchists, yet the movement's press showed little enthusiasm for their actions. For example, one commentator pointed out that Pardiñas was also a painter, and from Aragon, yet that did not mean that all Aragonese painters were terrorists.[338] Pardiñas shot himself as soon as he killed Canalejas, and was soon forgotten to the anarchist press. The death sentence handed to Sancho Alegre did briefly rouse indignation in a few papers, but he too was forgotten after his punishment was reduced to life imprisonment.[339] These attacks did not prompt any special legislation against the anarchist movement or its press, as in the 1890s, rather the reaction of both the movement and the state suggests that neither saw a direct link between individual terrorists and the wider anarchist movement.[340]

The second omission from the press is perhaps more surprising. In April 1913, a new anarchist organisation was founded in Córdoba, named the Federación Nacional de Obreros Agricultores (National Federation of Agricultural Workers: FNOA). The FNOA aimed to organise the massive rural labour force of Spain into a revolutionary body, adapting the industrial theory of syndicalism to a rural economy largely based on surplus, seasonal labour. Although it was not particularly successful, Antonio Bar has stressed the importance of this organisation, seeing it as a testing ground for the new synthesis of anarchism and syndicalism, giving anarcho-syndicalism a 'formal' character which would later be adopted by the CNT. While this may have been true within the internal discussions of the FNOA, neither the organisation nor its ideas appeared to have influenced the wider movement prior to 1916. Judging by contemporary accounts, the FNOA was initially rather small, attracting only 9,000 members in 1913.[341] Likewise, its periodical, *La Voz del Campesino*, struggled to attract a readership outside Cataluña and ran at a considerable loss.[342] Although a number of papers outside Cataluña stressed the need for greater organisation of *campesinos*, few appeared to be aware of the FNOA's existence, and when the organisation was mentioned in the press there was little to suggest that its fusion of anarchism and syndicalism was considered significant, or a model to follow.[343]

Through 1911–1915 the anarchist movement in Spain remained broadly supportive of syndicalist ideas, yet Negre's belief that the CNT would weather repression better than its predecessors was misplaced. A few papers and individuals, such as *El Libertario* (Gijón) and Quintanilla, had spent these years developing a theory of syndicalism as a new and necessary element of the class struggle. Many others saw the apparent disappearance of the CNT as an opportunity to challenge syndicalist models of organisation, attempting to redirect the movement towards more 'purely' anarchist activities. What was clear from all of these papers was that the CNT had disappeared outside Cataluña, and no tangible efforts had been made to re-establish the organisation in local or regional contexts. The prospects for the organisation looked bleak, until the outbreak of the First World War offered the movement an unexpected opportunity to reorganise.

Reformation: 1915

Two decisions made in El Ferrol (La Coruña) in the spring of 1915 laid the foundations for a reformation of the anarchist movement in Spain.[344] The first was an agreement to revive the CNT; the second approved the publication of a daily version of *Solidaridad Obrera* (Barcelona) as the movement's official mouthpiece. Together, these decisions were crucial to the dramatic expansion of the CNT which took place in the following years. Membership of the confederation rocketed from 30,000 in 1915 to almost 800,000 in 1919, making the CNT the largest anarchist organisation in world history. The organisation only surpassed such numbers twenty years later at the outbreak of the Spanish Civil War.[345] These developments were only possible because of the unprecedented economic and social upheaval brought about by the First World War. Although Spain remained neutral, the war was a transformative event for the country. Industries supplying both belligerent blocs boomed from 1914 onwards, sparking a huge shift towards urbanisation and industrial employment. Many other areas experienced economic crisis, as international markets for Spanish exports such as oil and cork collapsed. Across Spain, basic living standards were eroded as dramatic spike in inflation saw the price of food and housing soar far beyond wage increases.[346] It was this turmoil that gave the CNT a context in which it could expand into a mass movement, yet this would not have been possible had the war not also provoked a crisis within the anarchist movement, which forced it to meet in El Ferrol and agree upon direction and a strategy, forming a sense of common purpose which had been absent since the collapse of the CNT in 1911.

A War of Print

The threat of a war between European powers was discussed with increasing regularity in the anarchist press from 1911 onwards.[347] Diplomatic efforts to prevent a European war were regarded as useless by anarchist commentators, who saw working-class internationalism as the only means to prevent such a conflagration.[348] They called upon workers to launch general strikes across the continent upon the declaration of war, simultaneously guaranteeing peace and provoking a wider revolution.[349] When war broke out in August 1914 it was clear that hopes for such a response were ill-founded. Not only did social democratic parties in belligerent nations back their respective war efforts—as was predicted by anarchist commentators—so too did the French syndicalists of the CGT, despite the organisation's professed anti-militarism.[350] In contrast, the small syndicalist organisations of belligerent Germany and Italy, and neutral USA, Sweden and the Netherlands all committed to an anti-war stance in the early stages of the war.[351] Likewise, in Ireland, the 'syndicalist-inspired' Irish Transport and General Workers' Union (ITGWU) stood against the war, which helped the union to recover from its near-collapse in 1913.[352] Despite this range of syndicalist opposition to the First World War, nothing could diminish the 'shock, disillusionment and anger' provoked by the CGT's decision, both in France and among the confederation's international supporters.[353]

Many of Europe's leading anarchists also came out in support of the Entente war effort. In August 1914, Pyotr Kropotkin publically backed Belgian and French efforts to liberate themselves from 'invasion', portraying the conflict in terms of aggressors (Germany) and victims (France and Belgium), using the rhetoric employed by anarchists who supported colonial independence movements, as in *El Corsario*'s support for the Cuban insurgency in the 1890s (see Chapter 2).[354] Kropotkin was joined by fifteen leading names in European anarchism in a public declaration known as the Manifesto of the Sixteen, which stated that the only acceptable solution to the war was an Entente victory. Many anarchists in Europe and the Americas were angered by Kropotkin's stance. In March 1915 the London-based Anarchist International, which included Emma Goldman, Errico Malatesta and the Spanish exiles Vicente García and Pedro Vallina, published a counter to Kropotkin's numerous pro-Entente articles, declaring that the outbreak of war had been inevitable, and instead of Entente victory they called for peace, to be brought about by an international anarchist revolution against all 'exploiters'.[355]

Similar divisions emerged within the Spanish anarchist movement during the early years of the war.[356] The majority of the movement favoured a complete denunciation of the war, a position articulated by the two main periodicals of the movement: *Solidaridad Obrera* (Barcelona), representing the Catalan Regional Federation of Labour (CRT) and most syndicalists in the country, and *Tierra y Libertad* (Barcelona), by far the largest anarchist periodical in print. Both saw the war as an abject example of the 'love of the nation' triumphing over the 'love of Humanity [*sic*]'.[357] To these papers, there was no distinction between the belligerents. Germany, France, Britain and Russia all oppressed their own people and those of other nations. Only an immediate declaration of peace would bring a halt to the bloodshed.[358] These papers were supported by the FNOA and its organ *La Voz del Campesino* (Valls), which declared that no 'true revolutionary' could support the Entente.[359] This view was shared by papers and groups outside Cataluña, for example the syndicalist periodical *Acción Directa* (Cartagena), which ran a piece by Vicente García which attacked the 'warlike madness' of Kropotkin and Malato.[360] Numerous regional anarchist groups of Spain also came out against the war. 'Juventud en Marcha' (an anarchist group based in La Coruña) made declarations through *Tierra y Libertad* against the pro-Entente stance of Kropotkin, and called for their contemporaries in Spain to do likewise.[361] Groups from Cartagena, Vitoria and the Anarchist Federations of Cataluña and Extremadura affirmed that the war was not as a result of German aggression but a 'product of capitalism'.[362] Anti-war statements also came in from Spanish anarchist groups abroad, such as the 'Ni dogmas ni sistemas' group in Dowlais (Wales), which attacked the British image of Belgium as a 'heroine' by reminding readers of the colonial horrors in the Congo.[363] Anti-war meetings were also held by anarchist groups, most notably in Mataró (Barcelona) in October 1914.[364] This majority opinion, led by the Barcelona periodicals, corresponded to the well-established anarchist critique of war. It united individuals, groups and publications, providing a common cause which had not been evident within the movement since the repression of the CNT in 1911. The neutral status of Spain ensured these anarchists and syndicalists did not have to face the immediate threat of invasion and war, as did the CGT in France. In this 'relatively favourable context' of neutrality, anti-militarism could be maintained without facing the threat of conscription or prosecution, like their contemporaries in belligerent nations.[365]

Despite the strength of the anti-war position, a minority within the movement accepted the stance of the CGT and Kropotkin and came out in support of the Entente. Although much smaller in number, this group was not 'isolated' from the movement, as claimed by some scholars of international syndicalism.[366] The pro-Entente position centred around the three most prominent non-Catalan publications in print: the recently reformed *Acción Libertaria* (Gijón), edited by Quintanilla and Sierra Álvarez; *El Porvenir del Obrero* (Mahón); and *Cultura y Acción* (Zaragoza), the organ of the Centre of Social Studies of Zaragoza, edited by José Chueca, a long-term contributor to a number of anarchist papers and advocate of neo-Malthusian ideas.[367] Also among this minority were several individuals who had been crucial to the intellectual development of the movement since 1890, including Ricardo Mella and Federico Urales, as well as key figures in regional anarchist circles, such as the Bilbao-based publisher Aquilino Gómez. They regarded an Entente victory as both morally correct and necessary, claiming that all revolutionaries had a vested interest in seeing a German defeat, as the alternative was a nightmarish, militaristic Prussian Empire, which would crush the radical dreams of anarchists forever.[368] Urales explained his position by declaring himself a Francophile and a pragmatist. He judged the French as having 'better culture, better civilisation, better moral progress, better liberty, better justice' than their adversaries, and saw them as being 'closer' to anarchist ideas than the Germans. His conviction was so strong that he put his support for the Entente above anarchism, stating: 'if my doctrine compels me to condemn as equal those that, in the midst of barbarous war, remember that they are the most perfect animal in Nature [i.e. the Entente], to those that, in equal condition of barbarous war, do not [i.e. the German army] . . . I curse my doctrine'.[369] For *Acción Libertaria*, the war provided the opportunity for a long-overdue reflection on anarchism and syndicalism. It was a sign that the world had changed, creating a context which required studious analysis, rather than adherence to axiomatic principles. To illustrate this point, the paper stated that belief in the internationalism of the working class had proved futile and should be abandoned as a guiding principle for the movement. They foresaw a new world order emerging in the event of an Entente victory, in which new avenues could be explored where past models had failed.[370] Although the majority of the movement supported the anti-war opinion advocated by *Solidaridad Obrera* and *Tierra y Libertad*, dissidents could be found in almost every area of anarchist support, as shown by the many letters sent to the pro-Entente press from across Spain.[371]

These conflicting interpretations of the war rapidly escalated into a bitter and public war of words.[372] The neutralist majority insisted that those who supported the Entente—both internationally and in Spain—could no longer be considered anarchists, as they had 'excommunicated' themselves through their public affirmations of support for militarism.[373] They derided Kropotkin and his supporters, frequently labelled them as hypocrites, as in one letter from Vicente García to the pro-Entente *El Porvenir del Obrero*:

> this ill-fated war has transformed everything and even those spirits which we believed most serene, reflexive, the intelligences which we judged most solid, have lost their balance and lurch towards the impulse of the warlike hurricane; they are its toy, they cannot dominate it and they are going to stumble and slip. They make *a priori* affirmations, they ignore that which they have always preached: they say white today, black yesterday; they print the biggest contradictions to sustain the errors that have filled their brains. This is not serious, nor logical, nor reasonable, nor *anarchic*.[374]

The charge of hypocrisy was hard to deny, as prior to 1914 all anarchist papers and thinkers had advocated internationalism and revolution in the face of war, which was uniformly portrayed as an imperialist 'madness'.[375] These pro-Entente anarchists defended themselves by stating that the First World War was an unforeseeable conflict, which had brought into question all previous positions, even those as steadfastly held as antimilitarism and internationalism. They saw themselves realists, while their opponents were guilty of intransigence in the face of reality.[376] Supporters of the Entente were equally prepared to criticise the anarchist credentials of their adversaries.[377] Because they regarded the Entente as the morally superior, yet weaker, of the belligerents, they saw neutrality as implicit support for Germany.[378] In the summer of 1915 Urales went one step further and claimed that the 'neutralists' of *Solidaridad Obrera* had received money from German agents to produce anti-Entente propaganda, prompting an angry exchange with the editors of *Tierra y Libertad*.[379] Although strongly denied, the charge of accepting German money stuck to the CNT and *Solidaridad Obrera* throughout the war.[380]

Participants in the debate did not refrain from personal insults. The pro-Entente José Chueca labelled those who were 'attacked by Anglophobia' as idiots, blind to the fact that in 'England' [*sic*] there was 'no warlike atmosphere' as was rife in Germany.[381] On both sides, correspondents' letters which questioned editorial positions were censored and reproached as 'anti-anarchist'.[382] When debates were published they revealed the divisions that were tearing apart old friendships within the movement. *El Porvenir del Obrero* was one paper which invited and publicised a plurality of opinions on the war, without abandoning its pro-Entente editorial stance.[383] As a long-term contributor to the paper, Vicente García initially felt it important to express why his old friend, Juan Mir i Mir, was in the wrong.[384] Yet this respectful tone soon disappeared. García labelled Mir 'mad' if he thought the war would mark a new era for revolutionaries, while Mir i Mir mocked García as a '*señorito* tourist' (García had lived in exile in France and Britain for almost a decade), whose insights could be challenged by 'intelligent and studious' examination of the war.[385]

Not since the terrorism of the 1890s had such acrimony been provoked by divergences over the interpretation of anarchism, which cut across older divisions between supporters of syndicalism and its opponents. For example, Urales had previously attracted strong criticism from *El Porvenir del Obrero* for his individualist, anti-organisational attitudes.[386] Yet when the paper resumed publication in 1915 (following a year-long break enforced by Mir's ill health) it gave a platform to Urales because he shared their pro-Entente stance. Amongst the 'neutralists' were staunch syndicalists such as Negre, and groups which defined themselves as 'purely' anarchist, free from syndicalist ideas. The division was in part generational. Mella, Urales and Mir i Mir had grown out of a tradition of nineteenth-century federalist republicanism, which maintained a respect for the French revolutionary tradition.[387] These figures had been involved in the movement for much longer than many of those behind the creation of the CNT, such Negre and Angel Pestaña, and their quarrel with these figures was in part unwillingness to be eclipsed by this new generation.[388] They were also hostile to the idea of a unified 'line' within the anarchist movement, as was now being promoted by 'neutralist' majority.[389] Yet generational difference does not explain all of the conflicting positions taken during the war. The pro-Entente Quintanilla and Sierra Álvarez, for example, were equally symbolic of a new generation within the movement as their counterparts in the CNT. Although they were influenced by Mella, they had begun to develop their own distinctive outlook on the anarchist movement and its future. Likewise, on the 'neutralist' side of the debate were figures who had been involved in the movement for a long time, such as Vicente García and José Sánchez Rosa. With no obvious solution to this deep fracture running through the movement, ambitions to reform the CNT on a national level appeared to be a distant dream.

The El Ferrol Peace Congress, 1915

In early 1915 plans were made for an international peace congress in Spain. Inspired by Sebastián Faure—a French anti-war anarchist and critic of the CGT—a syndicalist group in El Ferrol announced their ambition to hold a meeting of socialists, syndicalists, anarchists and workers' organisations at their local *ateneo*.[390] The Congress was seen as an opportunity to put aside grievances and work towards a strategy to end the war as quickly as possible. Both sides of the debate in Spain showed enthusiasm for this idea. Representatives from 34 federations, groups and newspapers made their way to El Ferrol for the opening of the Congress on 29 April, and a further 133 groups adhered without sending or nominating a representative [see Table 4.3].[391] Amongst those supporting a neutral position were Angel Pestaña (representing the CRT), the Catalan and Cantabrian Anarchist Federations, dozens of workers' groups, independent anarchist groups and Tomás Herreros, editor of *Tierra y Libertad*. The pro-Entente position was represented by Pedro Sierra Álvarez of *Acción Libertaria*, Quintanilla, and Aquilino Gómez, the latter speaking for three anarchist groups from the Basque region. *El Porvenir del Obrero* had intended to send Urales as their representative, but he did not travel after he had been being wrongly informed that the Congress had been cancelled.[392]

Shortly before the Congress, the Spanish government blocked international representation from belligerent nations and attempted to ban the meeting altogether.[393] The only international delegates in attendance thus came from Portugal and Brazil, although further adherences came from France, Argentina, the Italian Unione Sindicale, and four anarchist groups based in South Wales.[394] Following the opening day of the Congress the Portuguese delegates were arrested and deported, making the remaining session an exclusively Spanish affair. Very little of substance was agreed in matters related to the war. A general strike across all nations was mooted as a means to end the conflict, as was the foundation of a new International, free from parliamentary socialists and based on exactly the

Table 4.3 Groups and Delegates at the Ferrol Peace Congress, 1915

	Represented	Representatives	Affiliated
Spain	34		**131**
National Organisations	2	M. Bajatierra; C. Romero	4
Andalucía	4	J. S. Rosa; M. Andreu; A. Pestaña; F. Miranda; E.C. Carbó*; A. Loredo*	52
Aragón	1	M. Andreu; A. Pestaña; F. Miranda; E.C. Carbó*; A. Loredo*	2
Asturias	2	P. S. Álvarez	4
Castilla la Nueva	4	A. Lozano; M. Pascual; J. Iñíguez; J. L. Bouza*	10
Castilla la Vieja	2	M. Manzano	3
Cataluña	5	M. Andreu; A. Pestaña; F. Miranda; E.C. Carbó*; A. Loredo*; J. Sánchez; T. Herreros; F. Vilaplana; I. Gari	12
Extremadura			2
Galicia	6	C. Romero; J. Nó; N. Trabaleda; M. Suárez; A. Porto	20
Islas Baleares		F. Urales**	1
Murcia	4	G. Pagán; G. Ros; M. Jiménez; M. Ferreira	4
Provincias Vascongadas	3	A. Gómez	6
Valencia	1	M. Andreu; A. Pestaña; F. Miranda; E.C. Carbó*; A. Loredo*	11
International	9		**13**
International Associations			1
France	1	E. Quintanilla	1
Italy			1
Portugal	7	C. Romero; E. Quintanilla; M. Campos; J. Nogueira; M. Nogueira; E.C. Cardoso***; S.C. Lucena***; M.J. de Souza***; A.A. Pereira***	3
UK			4
Argentina			2
Brazil	1	A.F. Vieytes	1

* Carbó, Loredo and Bouza arrested on 30 April 1915
** Federico Urales scheduled to represent *El Porvenir del Obrero* but did not travel
*** Portuguese delegates arrested and deported on night of 29 April 1915

Sources: *Tierra y Libertad* (Barcelona, IV), 12 May, 1915, 1–2; *Solidaridad Obrera* (Barcelona, III), 13 May, 1915, 1–2; *Acción Libertaria* (Gijón, II), 14 May 14, 1915, 1. See also José Luis Gutiérrez Molina, *La tiza, la tinta y la palabra: José Sánchez Rosa: Maestro y anarquista andaluz (1864–1936)* (Ubrique: Tréveris, 2005), 76–78

same principles of the First International. No practical means to achieve these goals were agreed and the Congress ended on 30 April after three further delegates were arrested.[395]

On a domestic level, the Congress did nothing to settle the debate within Spanish anarchism, which continued for the remainder of 1915. The pro-Entente delegate Gómez returned from El Ferrol embittered, and wrote to *El Porvenir del Obrero* to state that his opinions on the war had not changed: 'true pacifists' wanted a quick end to the conflict, and the best way to ensure that was to support Britain and France.[396] *Acción Libertaria* affirmed that the proposals to end the war by calling general strikes was not the product of a 'serene examination with reality' and had 'little in harmony with circumstances'.[397] In contrast, the neutralist position took heart from the Congress, which had 'saved anarchist from ridicule' brought upon it by 'traitors'.[398] In May 1915 *Tierra y Libertad* published a letter sent to Urales by the pro-Entente Charles Malato, in which Malato stated that the Congress was useless. The paper's scathing commentary labelled Malato a 'neo-nationalist' and maintained that El Ferrol had been an act of 'revolutionary importance'.[399] The debate continued to hinder new initiatives within the movement, as in Sevilla, where plans to launch a new anarchist periodical collapsed because of disagreements between neutralist and pro-Entente groups.[400]

Consolidation

The only positive result of the Congress was that it had brought together the leading anarchists and syndicalists in Spain for the first time since the CNT Congress of 1911. This was crucial for the reorganisation of the movement. In a session separate from the main Congress, Ángel Pestaña of the CRT proposed the reorganisation of the CNT and the transformation of *Solidaridad Obrera* into a daily publication. Both received unanimous support. Immediately after the Congress a commission was formed in Barcelona with the task of making the national organisation a reality, aiming to 'purify organisation, perfect it, give it orientation, unite the scattered . . . and generalise and unify propaganda'.[401] Support for these ideas extended across the whole country. In Sevilla, Congress delegate José Sánchez Rosa encouraged the local movement to action during a debate with a local socialist, advocating syndicalist tactics as the best means towards an anarchist future. Sánchez Rosa planned to follow this event with a speaking tour through Andalucía, with the aim of convincing the *campesinos* of the region to join the CNT. The tour was cut short after all of the speakers were arrested during its first event in Úbeda (Jaén).[402]

The plan for a reformed CNT was initially supported by both anti-war and pro-Entente sections of the movement. *Acción Libertaria* regarded the CNT as essential, stating that although the paper was 'above all an anarchist periodical' it was 'ready to contribute with its modest force to this labour of worker reorganisation under a frank, revolutionary inspiration'.[403] Mella, who had been critical of the CNT in 1911, now saw its reconstitution as necessary to further the principles of anarchism.[404] Despite their enthusiasm, these supporters of the Entente were accused of fostering anti-organisational sentiments and were ostracised from the movement, as both *Solidaridad Obrera* and *Tierra y Libertad* conflated support for the CNT with an anti-war stance, suggestive of a 'party line' on the subject. This was anathema to papers such as *Acción Libertaria*, who saw it as their duty to defend their principles in the face of a perceived homogenisation.[405] They accused the Barcelona papers of advising readers to cancel their subscriptions to pro-Entente papers, forcing them to close.[406] This accusation may have been true. All of the pro-Entente papers had folded by early 1916, and although the group behind *Acción Libertaria* returned to print culture with the journal *Renovación* a few months later, by August 1916 this too had closed after only four editions.[407] Individuals were also cut out from the movement's debates. Federico Urales was once again left without a platform in the anarchist press. He only returned to a position of prominence within the movement a decade later, when he embarked on a series of public arguments with the CNT through the second epoch of *La Revista Blanca*, which was launched in 1923.[408] Ricardo Mella, embittered by the apparent victory of dogmatism within Spanish anarchism, played no further role in the movement until his death in 1925.[409] Not all of the pro-Entente supporters left the movement at this time, however. Quintanilla, for example, remained one of the most respected anarchist thinkers in Spain and a prominent figure in the Asturian and national CNT.[410] He continued to develop his interpretation of syndicalism as a new tactic for revolutionaries, more suited to the contemporary world than social democracy and the older methods of the First International.[411]

The crisis provoked by the outbreak of the First World War had clearly favoured the neutral majority of the movement. It was this faction which led the reformation of the CNT in Barcelona, and ensured that the organisation would maintain a united opposition to the war in the coming years. This stance helped the organisation attract mass support from the Spanish working class, which was growing increasingly hostile to food shortages blamed on wartime conditions.[412] The CNT returned as a fragile organisation in 1915, and was heavily dependent upon its Catalan base.[413] Moves to address this imbalance took place over the coming years. In May 1916 the CNT organised a regional conference in Valencia—its first outside Cataluña—which was designed to raise awareness of the organisation to unaffiliated groups.[414] The 1919 CNT National Congress—the first since 1911—drew almost half of its affiliates from outside Cataluña. This Congress was viewed as a victory for the anarchists within the organisation, who assured that their ideology was the defining goal of the

CNT.[415] Yet fluctuations in support for syndicalism continued. In most of Spain, the reconstruction of the CNT did not take place until after the 1919 Congress, when regional federations were created in Andalucía, Levante (Valencia and Murcia), the North (Provincias Vascongadas, Cantabria and Asturias) and Galicia.[416]

A key part of the consolidation of the CNT was the expansion of *Solidaridad Obrera* into a daily publication. The proposals to expand *Solidaridad Obrera* during the 1911 Congress had come to nothing, as the paper had been immediately suspended. When the paper returned in 1913 it returned to its plans for expansion, and held conferences in favour of the idea through 1914.[417] The paper opened a voluntary subscription, sold propaganda postcards and organised a raffle of anarchist literature to raise money for the project.[418] One of their most ardent supporters of this idea was the veteran militant Anselmo Lorenzo.[419] In the last pamphlet published before his death in November 1914, Lorenzo stressed that the 'conquest' of a workers' daily was the most important task currently facing the movement.[420] Not only were anarchist and syndicalist publications dwarfed by their 'bourgeois' counterparts, they were now struggling to match the output of *El Socialista*, which had been converted into a daily in April 1913.[421]

News of the unanimous approval for Pestaña's proposal for a daily *Solidaridad Obrera* in El Ferrol prompted an acceleration of activity. Within a few months the paper had raised 9,000 pesetas from donations across Spain, and in August 1915 the paper opened up sales for shares in the new daily to its readers.[422] The first daily edition of the paper appeared in March 1916.[423] This massive increase in output severely tested the precarious financial situation of the paper, which relied on membership fees from CNT syndicates in order to stay in print.[424] It also began to run adverts for the first time in its history to cover its additional costs. The new daily paper was one of the first anarchist publications to pay its workers. This move attracted controversy, as the Barcelona printers' union accused its editors of holding back wages and called for a boycott of the paper.[425] Despite these difficulties *Solidaridad Obrera* published around 800 daily editions until 1919. Given the average print run of an anarchist paper from 1890 to 1915 was between 20 and 30 issues, this marked a huge development within anarchist print culture.

The establishment of the daily *Solidaridad Obrera* caused a decrease in the spread and heterogeneity of the anarchist press. The daily's output dwarfed that of other papers, containing as much information in a week as most other papers managed in months. *Solidaridad Obrera* became seen as the best means to participate in the movement, making the plural, fragmented print culture of the movement seemingly redundant. Anarchist groups refrained from launching new periodicals, or in some cases even abolished existing ones, as was the case of the FNOA publication *La Voz del Campesino*, which was closed in order 'to give more force and life to the daily *Solidaridad Obrera*'.[426] Between 1916 and 1917 the number of anarchist periodicals in print almost halved, from 32 to 18, the fewest number of titles in print since 1900 [see Chart 0.2]. This moment thus marks a change in the relationship between the anarchist movement and its press. Although it never lost its heterogeneity, its regional differences or its prolific, ephemeral, and diverse print culture, the movement did become increasingly identified with the CNT and its paper. Thus *Solidaridad Obrera*, the syndicalist daily, marked the ascendency of a more organised and coherent movement, and a waning in importance of the anarchist press network.

Through the anarchist press, the tactics of syndicalism had been developed and debated for almost a decade. These developments can be traced to several key moments: the creation of Solidaridad Obrera and its paper in 1907, the CNT Congresses of 1910 and 1911, and the El Ferrol Peace Congress in 1915. All were markers for the spread and consolidation of syndicalism within the anarchist movement. By 1916 syndicalism had been accepted by the majority of the anarchists in Spain, and was seen as central to the movement's self-definition and its articulation as a mass organisation. Yet this process was far from linear. Support for syndicalism had waxed and waned, while the term had meant different things to different papers and groups. At the same time, events such as the Tragic Week and the First World War affected the development of syndicalism in ways which had little to do with the merits of one ideological position over another. Nevertheless, the one constant throughout this process was the central role played by the anarchist press. The press was the prime means by which groups across Spain could engage with organisational developments in Cataluña and interact with one another. At the same time, the networks of anarchist print culture established in previous decades assisted in the creation of a national organisation, as well as a forum for dissent against the idea.

In 1910, *Solidaridad Obrera* (Gijón) declared that 'we will be victorious if we maintain our love of organisation'.[427] In many ways the paper was correct. The anarchist movement in Spain in 1916 was different to that of 1890, 1899 and 1907. It had a national organisation which would soon attract a mass following. It had established the first stable, daily anarchist paper in the history of the movement. It had also lost many of the figures which had dominated the movement over the turn of the century, replacing them with a new generation of activists, thinkers and publications. These 'victories' were overseen by the anarchist press, which had shaped and sustained the movement through this crucial period in its history.

Notes

1. Comparison made with analysis of contemporary social movements in Andy Cumbers, Paul Routledge and Corinne Nativel, 'The Entangled Geographies of Global Justice Networks,' *Progress in Human Geography* 32, 2 (2008): 190.

2. For example see *Acción Libertaria* (Gijón), 7 July, 1911, 1.
3. Joan Zambrana, 'El anarquismo organizado en los orígenes de la CNT: *Tierra y Libertad*, 1910–1919,' (2009), 1103. Published online, accessed 21 January, 2013, http://cedall.org/Documentacio/IHL/Tierra%20y%20Liber tad%201910-1919.pdf.
   For analysis of this cycle in later periods see Eduardo Romanos, 'Factionalism in Transition: A Comparison of Ruptures in the Spanish Anarchist Movement,' *Journal of Historical Sociology* 24, 3 (2011): 355–380.
4. Carl Levy, 'Social Histories of Anarchism,' *Journal for the Study of Radicalism* 4, 2 (2010): 11–12.
5. Constance Bantman, 'Internationalism without an International? Cross-Channel Anarchist Networks, 1890–1914,' *Revue belge de philology et d'histoire* 84, 4 (2006): 966.
6. George Esenwein, *Anarchist Ideology and the Working-Class Movement in Spain, 1868–1898* (Berkeley: University of California Press, 1989), 204. On later expressions of this form of anarchism see Xavier Diez, *El anarquismo individualista en España (1923–1938)* (Barcelona: Virus, 2007).
7. Esenwein, *Anarchist Ideology*, 111–112. Anarcho-communists later became more accepting of unionism, see Jason Garner, *Goals and Means: Anarchism, Syndicalism, and Internationalism in the Origins of the Federación Anarquista Ibérica* (Edinburgh: AK Press, 2016), 10–12.
8. A similar model was proposed by some collectivists for the organisation of the post-revolutionary anarchist society, see José Álvarez Junco, *La ideología política del anarquismo español (1868–1910)* (Madrid: Siglo XXI, 1991), 326–333.
9. See Chapter 3.
10. Álvarez Junco, *La ideología política*, 554–555. On fraternalism see Antonio Elorza, 'Los orígenes del asociacionismo obrero en España,' *Revista de Trabajo* 37 (1972): 125–345 and Jesús de Felipe Redondo, *Trabajadores, lenguaje y experiencia en la formación del movimiento obrero español* (Palma de Mallorca: Genueve Ediciones, 2012), 109–135.
11. For example, see Antonio Bar, *La CNT en los años rojos: Del sindicalismo revolucionario al anarcosindicalismo (1910–1926)* (Madrid: Akal, 1981).
12. Marcel van der Linden, 'Second Thoughts on Revolutionary Syndicalism,' *Labour History Review* 63, 2 (1998): 182–196.
13. Marcel van der Linden and Wayne Thorpe, 'The Rise and Fall of Revolutionary Syndicalism,' in *Revolutionary Syndicalism: An International Perspective*, ed. Marcel van der Linden and Wayne Thorpe (Aldershot: Scolar Press, 1990), 1–2.
14. David Berry, *A History of the French Anarchist Movement, 1917–1945* (London: Greenwood Press, 2002), 18.
15. Bantman, 'Internationalism,' 974–975. See the various case studies in Steven Hirsch and Lucien van der Walt, eds., *Anarchism and Syndicalism in the Colonial and Postcolonial World, 1870–1940: The Praxis of National Liberation, Internationalism and Social Revolution* (Leiden-Boston: Brill, 2010).
16. Barbara Mitchell, 'French Syndicalism: An Experiment in Practical Anarchism,' in Linden and Thorpe, *Revolutionary Syndicalism*, 33–34; Berry, *French Anarchist Movement*, 18; Wayne Thorpe, 'Uneasy Family: Revolutionary Syndicalism in Europe from the *Charte d'Amiens* to World War I,' in *New Perspectives on Anarchism, Labour and Syndicalism: The Individual, the National and the Transnational*, ed. David Berry and Constance Bantman (Newcastle-upon-Tyne: Cambridge Scholars Publishing, 2010), 16–23.

17. Malatesta's comments were applauded by *Tierra y Libertad* (Barcelona), see Pere Gabriel, 'Sindicalismo y huelga: Sindicalismo revolucionario francés e italiano: Su introducción en España,' *Ayer* 4 (1991): 39.

18. *The International Anarchist Congress Held at the Plancius Hall, Amsterdam on August 26th–31st, 1907* (London: Freedom, 1907), 8–9 and 15–22. See also Bantman, 'Internationalism,' 968–969; Zambrana, 'El anarquismo organizado,' 1066–1067 and Garner, *Goals and Means*, 52–55.

19. Gabriel, 'Sindicalismo y huelga,' 33–36. On Pouget see Constance Bantman, 'The Militant Go-between: Emile Pouget's Transnational Propaganda (1880–1914),' *Labour History Review* 74, 3 (2009): 274–287.

20. Joaquín Romero Maura, *La rosa de fuego: Republicanos y anarquistas: La política de los obreros barceloneses entre el desastre colonial y la Semana Trágica* (Barcelona: Ediciones Grijalbo, 1975), 463–464.

21. Bar, *La CNT*, 26–28. A list of the early societies affiliated to SO is published in *Solidaridad Obrera* (Barcelona), 26 October, 1907, 2. See also Joan Zambrana, 'El movimiento obrero catalán en el periódico *Solidaridad Obrera* (1907–1919),' (2012). Published online, accessed 11 December, 2012, www.cedall.org/Documentacio/IHL/MovObreroCat%20Solidaridad%20 Obrera%201907%201919.pdf.

22. *Solidaridad Obrera* (Barcelona), 26 October, 1907, 2.

23. Bar, *La CNT*, 31–32. The paper was also reportedly funded by Francisco Ferrer, although this claim was never verified, see Francisco Madrid Santos, *Solidaridad Obrera y el periodismo de raíz ácrata* (Badalona: Ediciones Solidaridad Obrera, 2007), 86–88.

24. Joan Connelly Ullman, *The Tragic Week: A Study of Anticlericalism in Spain* (Cambridge: Harvard University Press, 1968), 112–116; Bar, *La CNT*, 30.

25. Gabriel, 'Sindicalismo y huelga,' 34–37. See also Ángeles González Fernández, *Utopía y realidad: Anarquismo, anarcosindicalismo y organizaciones obreras: Sevilla, 1900–1936* (Sevilla: Diputación Provincial de Sevilla, 1996), 124.

26. *Humanidad Libre* (Jumilla, II), 27 January, 1907, 2–3; *Humanidad* (Toledo), 1 October, 1908, 2.

27. *Humanidad Libre* (Jumilla, II), 27 January, 1907, 2; *Humanidad* (Toledo), 1 October, 1908, 1.

28. *La Voz del Obrero del Mar: Trabajadores del mar: ¡Altera!* (Cádiz), 18 June, 1907, 1–2; *La Voz del Obrero del Mar* (Cádiz, II), 30 November, 1907, 4 and 4 November, 1908, 4. See also Santiago Castillo, *Historia de la UGT: Un sindicalismo consciente, 1873–1914* (Madrid: Siglo XXI, 2008), 185–186.

29. *La Voz del Obrero del Mar* (Cádiz, II), 30 September, 1908, 3; 4 November, 1908, 2; 31 December, 1908, 3. See Juan José Castillo, *El sindicalismo amarillo en España: Aportación al estudio del catolicismo social español (1912–1923)* (Madrid: Editorial Cuadernos para el Diálogo, 1977).

30. The next anarchist papers published in the city were *Bandera Libre* (c.1919–1921, c. 7 issues) and *Rebelión* (c. 15 November 1919–21 February 1920, 13 issues), see Francisco Madrid Santos, 'La prensa anarquista y anarcosindicalista en España desde la I Internacional hasta el fin de la Guerra Civil,' (PhD thesis, Barcelona: Universidad Central de Barcelona, 1988–89), 221, n.1223.

31. As well as the papers discussed above see *Liberación* (Madrid), an individualist-anarchist paper and *Verdad* (Sevilla), which played down the potential of worker organisation and instead advised to its readers 'to pick up the book,' in 31 July, 1908, 4.

32. *La Acción* (La Coruña), 11 November, 1908, 2.

33. *La Acción* (La Coruña), 15 December, 1908, 2.
34. See *La Acción* (La Coruña), 30 November, 1908, 4 and 15 December, 1908, 4. The paper made 10.85 pesetas and 8.40 pesetas from sales in La Coruña of issues 1 and 2 respectively; this would suggest sales of between 215–315 and 160–250, depending on whether packets of 30 (1 peseta) or individual papers (5 céntimos) were bought.
35. *La Acción* (La Coruña), 11 November, 1908, 4 and 15 December, 1908, 4.
36. Ángeles Barrio Alonso, *Anarquismo y anarcosindicalismo en Asturias, 1890–1936* (Madrid: Siglo XXI, 1988), 60–63.
37. Antón Fernández Álvarez, *Ricardo Mella o el anarquismo humanista* (Barcelona: Anthropos, 1990), 79. See also Ángeles Barrio Alonso, 'Cultura del trabajo y organización obrera en Gijón en el cambio de siglo,' *Historia Contemporánea* 5 (1991): 48–49.
38. *Tribuna Libre* (Gijón), Quintanilla: 30 April, 1909, 1; 5 June, 1909, 2; 19 June, 1909, 2–3; 3 July, 1909, 3; 17 July, 1909, 3; Sierra Álvarez: 30 April, 1909, 1; 22 May, 1909, 1 See also the columna 'Donativos recibidos a favor de este periódico,' 10 April, 1909–17 July, 1909, all 4.
39. *Tribuna Libre* (Gijón), 8 May, 1909, 1.
40. Full details of the Federation's societies given in *Tribuna Libre* (Gijón), 5 June, 1909, 4; 19 June, 1909, 4; August 1909, 4. See also Barrio Alonso, *Anarquismo en Asturias*, 63–64.
41. *Tribuna Libre* (Gijón), 3 July, 1909, 2.
42. *Tribuna Libre* (Gijón), 10 April, 1909, 2; 8 May, 1909, 4; 5 June, 1909, 3. Sabotage had been adopted by the CGT as an official tactic in 1897. Its main advocate was Pouget, who claimed that the tactic was a development of British union militancy; see Bantman, 'Emilé Pouget,' 282. Anselmo Lorenzo, *Hacía la emancipación: Tática de avance obrero en la lucha por el ideal* (Mahón: El Porvenir del Obrero, 1914), 109–111 states that the phrase 'boycott' derived from Charles Boycott, an English land agent in Ireland who was ostracised through a campaign led by the Irish Land League. An alternative history of the term was given in *El Látigo* (Baracaldo), 17 May, 1913, 2, which dates the tactic to seventh-century Scotland.
43. *Tribuna Libre* (Gijón), 8 May, 1909, 2–3.
44. *Tribuna Libre* (Gijón), 30 April, 1909, 3 and 8 May, 1909, 2.
45. *Tribuna Libre* (Gijón), 8 May, 1909, 1 and 3.
46. *Tribuna Libre* (Gijón), 3 July, 1909, 4.
47. *¡Despertad!* (Madrid), May, 1909, 1–2.
48. *La Protesta* (La Línea de la Concepción), 19 December, 1901, 2. A critique of the loose use of the term 'general strike' can be found in *Acción Libertaria* (Gijón), 3 February, 1911, 2. See also Chris Grocott, Gareth Stockey and Jo Grady, 'Anarchism in the UK('s Most Famous Fortress): Comradeship and Cupidity in Gibraltar and Neighbouring Spain, 1890–1902,' *Labour History* 56, 4 (2015): 391.
49. *Nueva Aurora* (Málaga), 16 June, 1909, 1.
50. A comparable assessment of changes to the anarchist 'vocabulary' during the Franco dictatorship can be found in Eduardo Romanos, 'Emotions, Moral Batteries and High-Risk Activism: Understanding the Emotional Practices of the Spanish Anarchists under Franco's Dictatorship,' *Contemporary European History* 23, 4 (2014): 563.
51. Barrio Alonso, *Anarquismo en Asturias*, 63.
52. Xavier Cuadrat, *Socialismo y anarquismo en Cataluña (1899–1911): Los orígenes de la CNT* (Madrid: Ediciones de la Revista de Trabajo, 1976), 350–351.
53. *Tribuna Libre* (Gijón), 19 June, 1909, 4.

54. Angel Smith, *Anarchism, Revolution and Reaction: Catalan Labour and the Crisis of the Spanish State, 1898–1923* (New York: Berghahn, 2007), 175.
55. See Maura, *La rosa de fuego*, 465–466.
56. Ullman, *The Tragic Week*, 142–163; José Álvarez Junco, 'Maneras de hacer historia: los antecedentes de la Semana Trágica,' *Zona Abierta* 31 (1984): 43–92.
57. There are numerous studies of this event. Ullman, *The Tragic Week*, 167–282 provides perhaps the most comprehensive account of the day-by-day developments. See also Maura, *La rosa de fuego*, 509–542; Cuadrat, *Socialismo y anarquismo*, 382–392; Antoni Dalmau, *Siete días de furia: Barcelona y la Semana Trágica (Julio de 1909)* (Barcelona: Ediciones Destino, 2009), 97–105.
58. Smith, *Anarchism, Revolution and Reaction*, 176–180.
59. Ullman, *The Tragic Week*, 285–287; Maura, *La rosa de fuego*, 516; Dalmau, *Siete días de furia*, 107–111.
60. Cited in James A. Baer, *Anarchist Immigrants in Spain and Argentina* (Chicago: University of Illinois Press, 2015), 72.
61. Leopoldo Bonafulla, *La revolución de julio: Barcelona 1909* (Barcelona: Toribio Taberner, 1910), 115.
62. Ullman, *The Tragic Week*, 283–284, 292; Smith, *Anarchism, Revolution and Reaction*, 181.
63. For example, the Free School in Mahón run by Mir i Mir (editor of *El Porvenir del Obrero*) was closed, see *El Porvenir del Obrero* (Mahón, II), 13 February, 1913, 4.
64. Juan Avilés Farré, *Francisco Ferrer y Guardia: Pedagogo, anarquista y mártir* (Madrid: Marcial Pons, 2006), 221–232. See also the near-contemporary account in William Archer, *The Life, Trial and Death of Francisco Ferrer* (London: Chapman and Hall, 1911), 171–253, and his translation of the official report on 257–324.
65. Ullman, *The Tragic Week*, 298–304; Smith, *Anarchism, Revolution and Reaction*, 181–182; Avilés Farré, *Francisco Ferrer*, 232–243.
66. See Ullman, *The Tragic Week*, 195. Official censorship of national papers was in place from Tuesday 27 July, see *El País* (Madrid), 27 July, 1909, 1. *Al Paso*'s editors were also imprisoned following the Tragic Week, see *Al Paso* (Sevilla, II), 4 November, 1909, 4 and González Fernández, *Utopía y realidad*, 126.
67. *Al Paso* (Sevilla, II), 31 December, 1909, 1 and 14 January, 1910, 1; *El Libertario* (Madrid), 27 November, 1909, 1.
68. *El Libertario* (Madrid), 22 December, 1909, 1. On 22 July the national socialist leadership agreed to declare general strike across Spain on 2 August in support of the Barcelona strike, see Cuadrat, *Socialismo y anarquismo*, 376. After the event anarchist commentators claimed that the 'effeminate' socialists knew this would never take place, see *El Libertario* (Madrid), 27 November, 1909, 1.
69. *Acción Libertaria* (Gijón), 30 December, 1909, 1 and 6 January, 1910, 1. See also Cuadrat, *Socialismo y anarquismo*, 404–406.
70. Some of these observations are taken from the introduction to an English translation of Bonafulla's work, undertaken by Slava Faybysh. My thanks to Slava for sharing the manuscript of this translation.
71. Bonafulla, *La revolución*, 37–38.
72. *Al Paso* (Sevilla, II), 4 November, 1909, 1 and 2–3. See also *Rebelión* (Sevilla), 25 February, 1910, 1.
73. This image drew sharp criticism from Ricardo Mella in *Acción Libertaria* (Gijón), 13 January, 1911, 1. The postcard can be viewed at 'Verdadera

efigie de Francisco Ferrer sacrificado en los fosas de Montjuich,' Cartoliste, accessed 5 April, 2018, https://cartoliste.ficedl.info/article299.html?lang=fr.

74. *Al Paso* (Sevilla, II), 16 December, 1909, 3.
75. *Al Paso* (Sevilla, II), 16 December, 1909, 4 and 31 December, 1909, 4.
76. Ignacio Soriano and Francisco Madrid Santos, 'Antología documental del anarquismo español VI.I: Bibliografía del anarquismo en España, 1868–1939, Enriquecida con notas y comentarios,' (5th edition, 2012), 87, 106, 156, 169–171, 174–175, 177, 203, 233, 277, 292, 297. Published online, accessed 12 December, 2012, http://cedall.org/Documentacio/Castella/cedall203410103.htm.
77. See *La Enseñanza Moderna* (Valladolid), 10 October, 1910, 1–12; *Escuela Moderna* (Valencia), 13 October, 1910, 1–8.
78. *Acción Libertaria* (Gijón), 2 December, 1910, 4.
79. *El Libertario* (Madrid), 27 November, 1909, 2; *Acción Libertaria* (Gijón), 25 November, 1910, 4 and 23 December, 1910, 4.
80. *Cultura Libertaria* (El Ferrol), 3 December, 1912, 1.
81. Daniel Laqua, 'Freethinkers, Anarchists and Francisco Ferrer: The Making of a Transnational Solidarity Campaign,' *European Review of History* 21, 4 (2014): 467–484; Pol Dalmau, *Press, Politics and National Identities in Catalonia: The Transformation of La Vanguardia, 1881–1931* (Brighton: Sussex Academic Press, 2017), 152–154.
82. *La Voz del Obrero* (La Coruña), 30 October, 1913, 2; *Acción Libertaria* (Gijón), 2 December, 1910, 4; *Acción Libertaria* (Vigo), 6 September, 1911, 4 and 13 September, 1911, 4.
83. Anna Ribera and Alejandro de la Torre, 'Memoria libertaria: Usos del calendario militante del anarquismo hispanoamericano,' *Historias* 75 (2010): 116–118; Ilham Khuri-Makdisi, *The Eastern Mediterranean and the Making of Global Radicalism: 1860–1914* (Berkeley: University of California Press, 2010), 21; Cristoph de Spiegeleer, '"The Blood of Martyrs Is the Seed of Progress": The Role of Martyrdom in Socialist Death Culture in Belgium and the Netherlands, 1880–1940,' *Mortality* 19, 2 (2014): 194–195.
84. See Paul Avrich, *The Modern School Movement: Anarchism and Education in the United States* (Princeton: Princeton University Press, 1980), 33; Avilés Farré, *Francisco Ferrer*, 276.
85. *Escuela Moderna* (Valencia), 10 September, 1910, 2.
86. See *El Libertario* (Gijón), 12 October, 1912, 1.
87. See for example *Acción Libertaria* (Gijón), 6 January, 1911, 1.
88. Spiegeleer, '"The Blood of Martyrs",' 199.
89. *El Libertario* (Madrid), 27 November, 1909, 2; 12 December, 1909, 1. In contrast, *Escuela Moderna* (Valencia), supported the project, see 4 February, 1911, 3–4. A statue to Ferrer was erected in Brussels in 1914 but was pulled down by the invading German army. The statue was later re-erected on the Franklin Rooseveltlaan, where it remains.
90. *Solidaridad Obrera* (Gijón), 25 December, 1909, 2 and 15 October, 1910, 1; *El Látigo* (Baracaldo), 16 November, 1912, 4; *Acción Libertaria* (Gijón), 13 January, 1911, 4.
91. *El Libertario* (Madrid), 10 January, 1910, 1; *Al Paso* (Sevilla, II), 14 January, 1910, 3 and *El Libertario* (Madrid), 20 February, 1910, 1. See also Zambrana, 'El anarquismo organizado,' 1070–1071.
92. *Solidaridad Obrera* (Gijón), 15 October, 1910, 1.
93. *Al Paso* (Sevilla, II), 4 November, 1909, 4; *El Porvenir del Obrero* (Mahón, II), 28 September, 1912, 1 and 5 October, 1912, 1.
94. Madrid Santos, *Solidaridad Obrera*, 89–91.
95. *Solidaridad Obrera* (Gijón), 11 December, 1909, 3. Using figures of 10,000 workers in Gijón, see Barrio Alonso, *Anarquismo en Asturias*, 67.

96. See Bar, *La CNT*, 332.
97. *Solidaridad Obrera* (Gijón), 2 April, 1910, 3–4.
98. *Solidaridad Obrera* (Gijón), 26 November, 1910, 3–4 and 24 December, 1910, 3. Pamela Beth Radcliff, *From Mobilization to Civil War: The Politics of Polarization in the Spanish City of Gijón, 1900–1937* (Cambridge: Cambridge University Press, 1996), 177.
99. Radcliff, *From Mobilization to Civil War*, 173–175.
100. José Prat, *La burguesía y el proletariado: Conferencia leída en el centro Joventut Republicana de Lérida el 16 de enero de 1909* (Barcelona: Salud y Fuerza, 1909), 1–29.
101. See Baer, *Anarchist Immigrants*, 55. I would point to Prat's later work as a counter to Baer's claim that Prat 'opposed syndicalism.'
102. For example see *La Protesta* (La Línea de la Concepción), 1 February, 1902, 3–4.
103. *Solidaridad Obrera* (Gijón), 11 December, 1909, 1.
104. *Solidaridad Obrera* (Gijón), 11 December, 1909, 1. Some articles in the paper appeared as (unattributed) summaries of Marx's works, for example see *Solidaridad Obrera* (Gijón), 5 February, 1910, 1, which presents a near-identical argument to the chapter 'The Industrial Reserve Army,' in *Das Kapital*, Vol. 1.
105. Mitchell, 'French Syndicalism,' 25–26 and 32–33.
106. See Garner, *Goals and Means*, 48–52. Examples of articles by V. Griffuelhes in *Solidaridad Obrera* (Gijón), 14 May, 1910, 2; 28 May, 1910, 1; 11 June, 1910, 1–2; 25 June, 1910, 1–2; 9 July, 1910, 2; 24 December, 1910, 2.
107. Gabriel, 'Sindicalismo y huelga,' 44–45.
108. *Solidaridad Obrera* (Gijón), 25 June, 1910, 2 and 3 September, 1910, 2.
109. *Solidaridad Obrera* (Gijón), 5 March, 1910, 2 and 6 August, 1910, 1–2.
110. Baer, *Anarchist Immigrants*, 56–57.
111. Baer, *Anarchist Immigrants*, 77.
112. Baer, *Anarchist Immigrants*, 87–92.
113. Bar, *La CNT*, 304, 332. See also Garner, *Goals and Means*, 53–60.
114. *Solidaridad Obrera* (Gijón), 5 March, 1910, 2.
115. *Solidaridad Obrera* (Gijón), 25 November, 1909, 3–4; 19 March, 1910, 1–2; 16 April, 1910, 2.
116. *Solidaridad Obrera* (Gijón), 9 June, 1909, 4; 11 December, 1909, 1; 25 December, 1909, 2.
117. Bar, *La CNT*, 331.
118. *Solidaridad Obrera* (Gijón), 5 January, 1910, 3.
119. Bar, *La CNT*, 153–155; Smith, *Anarchism, Revolution and Reaction*, 195–198.
120. Madrid Santos, 'La prensa anarquista,' 155, n.813; Ramón Álvarez, *Eleuterio Quintanilla: (Vida y obra del maestro): Contribución a la historia del sindicalismo revolucionario en Asturias* (México, DF: Editores Mexicanos Unidos, 1973), 23.
121. *Solidaridad Obrera* (Gijón), 16 April, 1910, 2 and 26 November, 1910, 2.
122. *Solidaridad Obrera* (Gijón), 25 June, 1910, 2.
123. *Solidaridad Obrera* (Gijón), 25 June, 1910, 2–3. See Thorpe, 'Uneasy Family,' 23–42, for other differences between other syndicalist movements and the French CGT.
124. Cuadrat, *Socialismo y anarquismo*, 545. Emphasis in original.
125. *Solidaridad Obrera* (Barcelona, II), 4 November, 1910, 1–8; *Solidaridad Obrera* (Gijón), 12 November, 1910–10 December, 1910, all 1–2. Many *ginonés* societies would also have liked Quintanilla to attend, yet 'diverse reasons' prevented him from doing so. See *Solidaridad Obrera* (Gijón), 30 September, 1910, 4 and 15 October, 1910, 3.

126. The number of societies used is an amalgamation of those listed in *Solidaridad Obrera* (Barcelona, II), 4 November, 1910, 1–8; Cuadrat, *Socialismo y anarquismo*, 463–469; Bar, *La CNT*, 156; including the corrections made by Cuadrat and adherences made during the Congress.
127. *Solidaridad Obrera* (Barcelona, II), 4 November, 1910, 6.
128. *Solidaridad Obrera* (Gijón), 12 November, 1910, 1. See also map in Manuel Tuñón de Lara, *El movimiento obrero en la historia de España* (Barcelona: Editorial Laia, 1977), 536.
129. Cuadrat, *Socialismo y anarquismo*, 470.
130. Barcelona-based substitute delegates: José Negre [representing societies in La Línea (Cádiz) and Loja (Granada)]; Antonio Salud [representing the Algeciras (Cádiz) workers' centre]; Rafael Avila [representing the La Coruña sawyers' society], and Joaquín Bueso [representing Sevilla's Arte de Imprintir society]. One exception: Esteve formed part of a discussion group dedicated to the question of rural organisation, due to his role as representative of the workers' centre of Bujalance, an agro-town in Córdoba province.
131. *Solidaridad Obrera* (Barcelona, II), 4 November, 1910, 6–7.
132. For example see *Solidaridad Obrera* (Barcelona, II), 15 September, 1911, 1; *El Porvenir del Obrero* (Mahón, II), 10 August, 1912, 4.
133. Cuadrat, *Socialismo y anarquismo*, 475.
134. Antonio Bar, 'The CNT: The Glory and Tragedy of Spanish Anarchosyndicalism,' Linden and Thorpe, *Revolutionary Syndicalism*, 121–122.
135. This matter was discussed in more depth in the 1911 Congress, see Bar, *La CNT*, 283–284.
136. *Solidaridad Obrera* (Gijón), 12 November, 1910, 1–2. The figures used by Álvarez for UGT membership were slightly higher than the official number at the most recent UGT Congress (June 1910), which was 40,984, see Tuñón de Lara, *El movimiento obrero*, 485 and Castillo, *Historia de la UGT*, 158.
137. Cuadrat, *Socialismo y anarquismo*, 483–486.
138. *Solidaridad Obrera* (Barcelona), 4 November, 1910, 3.
139. *Solidaridad Obrera* (Gijón), 26 November, 1910, 1–2. See also Garner, *Goals and Means*, 61–62.
140. *Solidaridad Obrera* (Gijón), 26 November, 1910, 2.
141. The FSORE did manage to publish its own *Boletín* three years after its creation, but by this point enthusiasm for the Federation had waned substantially. See Madrid Santos, 'La prensa anarquista,' 169–171.
142. *Solidaridad Obrera* (Gijón), 26 November, 1910, 1.
143. See Smith, *Anarchism, Revolution and Reaction*, 200–201.
144. Garner, *Goals and Means*, 62.
145. *Anarquía* (Zaragoza), 9 March, 1911, 3.
146. *Acción Libertaria* (Gijón), 17 March, 1911, 3–4.
147. Madrid Santos, 'La prensa anarquista,' 149, n.773 and 536–537.
148. For example, see *El Látigo* (Madrid), 18 February, 1911, 13–14; 25 February, 1911, 8–9; 4 March, 1911, 2–3.
149. *El Látigo* (Madrid), 4 March, 1911, 4 and 11 March, 1911, 5.
150. Rumours that Urales was standing as a deputy for the Cortes circulated in the anarchist press in 1910, see *Al Paso* (Sevilla, II), 24 December, 1909, 1–2 and *El Libertario* (Madrid), 10 January, 1910, 3–4. Both of these articles make reference to Urales's past high standing in the movement and his subsequent fall from grace.
151. See notices in *El Látigo* (Madrid), 11 March, 1911, 4 and 11.
152. Urales did attempt to publish a new paper in 1913, but the project failed, see *El Porvenir del Obrero* (Mahón, II), 19 June, 1913, 4 and Madrid, 'La prensa anarquista,' 977.

153. *Solidaridad Obrera* (Gijón), 8 January, 1910, 1 and 16 April, 1910, 1. See also Barrio Alonso, *Anarquismo en Asturias*, 69–75 and Radcliff, *From Mobilization to Civil War*, 174–175 and 262–266.
154. *Solidaridad Obrera* (Gijón), 30 April, 1910, 1–2.
155. *Solidaridad Obrera* (Gijón), 15 January, 1909, 3.
156. *Solidaridad Obrera* (Gijón), 16 September, 1910, 1 and 2; Álvarez, *Eleuterio Quintanilla*, 56–65.
157. *Solidaridad Obrera* (Gijón), 15 October, 1910, 2; 12 November, 1910, 2; 26 November, 1910, 2–3; 10 December, 1910, 2; 24 December, 1910, 1. See also Barrio Alonso, *Anarquismo en Asturias*, 98–100.
158. *Solidaridad Obrera: 2° suplemento al número 32* (Gijón), 4 March, 1911, 1–2 and *Solidaridad Obrera: 3er suplemento al número 32* (Gijón), 18 April, 1911, 1–2; *Acción Libertaria* (Gijón), 13 January, 1911, 4.
159. *Solidaridad Obrera* (Gijón), 23 June, 1910, 2 and 16 September, 1910, 4.
160. *Acción Libertaria* (Gijón), 17 June, 1911, 4.
161. *Tierra y Libertad* (Barcelona, IV), 3 December, 1911, 2.
162. *Acción Libertaria* (Gijón), 9 December, 1910, 1.
163. Bar, *La CNT*, 232–233.
164. González Fernández, *Utopía y realidad*, 139–140.
165. *Acción Libertaria* (Gijón), 13 January, 1911, 3.
166. *Acción Libertaria* (Gijón), 3 February, 1911, 2; see also 20 January, 1911, 2.
167. *Acción Libertaria* (Gijón), c.March, 1911 [title page with date missing], 4.
168. *Acción Libertaria* (Gijón), 17 March, 1911, 1–2.
169. *Acción Libertaria* (Vigo), 13 September, 1911, 1.
170. *Acción Libertaria* (Gijón), 27 January, 1911, 1.
171. *Acción Libertaria* (Gijón), 3 February, 1911, 1.
172. *Solidaridad Obrera* (Barcelona, II), 15 September, 1911, 2. The largest anarchist paper of the time, *Tierra y Libertad* (Barcelona), claimed a distribution of around 11,000. See *Tierra y Libertad* (Barcelona, IV), 7 June, 1911, 3–4.
173. Bar, *La CNT*, 231–235.
174. *Acción Libertaria* (Gijón), 13 January, 1911, 3 and 4.
175. Óscar Freán Hernández, *El movimiento libertario en Galicia, 1910–1936* (Sada: Ediciós do Castro, 2006), 14–16.
176. Madrid Santos, 'La prensa anarquista,' 181.
177. *Solidaridad Obrera* (Barcelona, II), 15 September, 1911, 4.
178. *Acción Libertaria* (Gijón), 9 December, 1910, 4; González Fernández, *Utopía y realidad*, 136.
179. *Acción Libertaria* (Gijón), 23 December, 1910, 3. See also José Luis Gutiérrez Molina, *La tiza, la tinta y la palabra: José Sánchez Rosa: Maestro y anarquista andaluz (1864–1936)* (Ubrique: Tréveris, 2005), 67.
180. González Fernández, *Utopía y realidad*, 140–141.
181. *Acción Libertaria* (Gijón), 2 December, 1910, 3 and 30 December, 1910, 4.
182. *Escuela Libre* (Valladolid), 15 March, 1911, 4; *Acción Libertaria* (Gijón), 21 April, 1911, 4.
183. *Escuela Libre* (Valladolid), 15 February, 1911, 1 and 1 March, 1911, 2–3.
184. *Escuela Libre* (Valencia), 13 August, 1910, 2; *Acción Libertaria* (Gijón), 2 December, 1910, 3–4. On the workers' movement in Valladolid in this period see Guillermo Ángel Pérez Sánchez, *Ser trabajador: Vida y respuesta obrera (Valladolid, 1875–1931)* (Valladolid: Universidad de Valladolid, 1996), 365–368.
185. *Escuela Libre* (Valladolid), 1 March, 1911, 2.
186. Bar, *La CNT*, 230–233.
187. González Fernández, *Utopía y realidad*, 141, n.89; Angeles Barrio Alonso, 'El anarquismo asturiano entre el sindicalismo y la política, 1890–1920,' *Ayer* 45, 1 (2002): 164.

188. José Negre (representing societies in Puerto Real, Baracaldo and Vigo), Tomás Herreros (representing the general trades' society of Bilbao) and Manuel Permañer (representing the 15 societies of the La Coruña workers' federation). For the CNT committee members, see Bar, *La CNT*, 233.
189. *Solidaridad Obrera* (Barcelona, II), 15 September, 1911, 2–3.
190. *Solidaridad Obrera* (Barcelona, II), 15 September, 1911, 1–3.
191. See letter by Lorenzo to Congress, in *Solidaridad Obrera* (Barcelona, II), 15 September, 1911, 1.
192. *Acción Libertaria* (Gijón), 3 February, 1911, 1.
193. *Solidaridad Obrera* (Barcelona, II), 8 September, 1911, 3.
194. *Solidaridad Obrera* (Barcelona, II), 15 September, 1911, 1–2.
195. Smith, *Anarchism, Revolution and Reaction*, 108.
196. *Solidaridad Obrera* (Barcelona, II), 15 September, 1913.
197. *Solidaridad Obrera* (Barcelona, II), 15 September, 1911, 2.
198. Vicente García suggested a similar idea in June 1911 to *Tierra y Libertad* (Barcelona), which was also considering expansion into a daily print-run, see *Tierra y Libertad* (Barcelona, IV), 7 June, 1911, 3–4 and Madrid Santos, 'La prensa anarquista,' 188, n.1018.
199. *Solidaridad Obrera* (Barcelona, II), 15 September, 1911, 2.
200. Garner, *Goals and Means*, 62–65.
201. Cuadrat, *Socialismo y anarquismo*, 538–577.
202. Barrio Alonso, *Anarquismo en Asturias*, 114–115.
203. *El Látigo* (Baracaldo), 20 September, 1913, 2–3.
204. Ullman, *The Tragic Week*, 322.
205. *Solidaridad Obrera* (Barcelona, II), 15 September, 1911, 3; *Acción Libertaria* (Vigo), 3 November, 1911, 1–2.
206. Cuadrat, *Socialismo y anarquismo*, 562.
207. Cuadrat, *Socialismo y anarquismo*, 577.
208. *Solidaridad Obrera* (Barcelona, II), 15 September, 1911, 4.
209. Bar, *La CNT*, 306–307.
210. Cuadrat, *Socialismo y anarquismo*, 552–556 and 567–571. For a later attack on Villalobos Moreno on his role in the repression of 1911 see *El Porvenir del Obrero* (Mahón, II), 22 May, 1913, 4 and 29 May, 1913, 3.
211. González Fernández, *Utopía y realidad*, 156–158.
212. *Acción Libertaria* (Vigo), 6 September, 1911, 1 and 6 October, 1911, 1. See also *El Libertario* (Gijón), 19 October, 1911, 1–2.
213. Smith, *Anarchism, Revolution and Reaction*, 203–206.
214. *Tierra y Libertad* (Barcelona, IV), 11 November, 1911, 1. On the bleak situation in Barcelona nine months later see *El Porvenir del Obrero* (Mahón, II), 1 June, 1912, 3.
215. *Acción Libertaria* (Vigo), 6 October, 1911, 3.
216. *Acción Libertaria* (Vigo), 27 September, 1911, 3. The reference here to Pangloss's phrase in Voltaire's *Candide* was deliberate, and can be found throughout many anarchist papers in this period.
217. *Tierra y Libertad* (Barcelona, IV), 11 November, 1911, 1.
218. *Acción Libertaria* (Vigo), 27 September, 1911, 2.
219. Cuadrat, *Socialismo y anarquismo*, 573; Luis Miguel Lázaro Lorente, *La Escuela Moderna de Valencia* (Valencia: Generalitat Valenciana, 1989), 298–304.
220. Alonso, *Anarquismo en Asturias*, 88–89, n.10; Madrid Santos, 'La prensa anarquista,' 191.
221. Fernández Álvarez, *Ricardo Mella*, 82.
222. *Acción Libertaria* (Gijón), 5 May, 1911, 2 and 30 June, 1911, 2.
223. *Acción Libertaria* (Vigo), 13 September, 1911, 2.
224. *Acción Libertaria* (Vigo), 27 September, 1911, 1–2.

225. *Acción Libertaria* (Gijón), 5 May, 1911, 1–2 and 12 May, 1911, 1.
226. *Tierra y Libertad* (Barcelona, IV), 28 December, 1910, 3.
227. *Acción Libertaria* (Gijón), 7 July, 1911, 4 and *Acción Libertaria* (Vigo), 6 September, 1911, 2. On Soler see Miguel Íñiguez, *Esbozo de una enciclopedia histórica del anarquismo español* (Madrid: Fundación de Estudios Libertarios Anselmo Lorenzo, 2001), 578.
228. *Acción Libertaria* (Vigo), 17 November, 1911, 1. See the section 'Interiordades: Correspondencia administrativa,' in *Acción Libertaria* (Gijón/Vigo), 18 November, 1910–17 November, 1911 for money sent to the paper from Panamá via *Tierra y Libertad*. See also Kirwin R. Shaffer, 'Panama Red: Anarchist Politics and Transnational Networks in the Panama Canal Zone, 1904–1913,' in *In Defiance of Boundaries: Anarchism in Latin American History*, ed. Geoffroy de Laforcade and Kirwin R. Shaffer (Gainesville: University Press of Florida, 2015), 64–67.
229. *Acción Libertaria* (Vigo), 17 November, 1911, 1.
230. See figures in Castillo, *Historia de la UGT*, 158–161. See also Smith, *Anarchism, Revolution and Reaction*, 217–218.
231. *Cultura Libertaria* (El Ferrol), 1 February, 1913, 3.
232. Bar, *La CNT*, 357.
233. *El Porvenir del Obrero* (Mahón, II), 19 October, 1912, 4; *El Libertario* (Gijón), 22 March, 1913, 1; *Solidaridad Obrera* (Barcelona, III), 1 May, 1913, 1.
234. Bar, *La CNT*, 308–314.
235. Bar, *La CNT*, 321.
236. Bar, *La CNT*, 304. On the developments in Barcelona see Smith, *Anarchism, Revolution and Reaction*, 206–218.
237. Josep Portella Coll, 'Juan Mir i Mir: Obra anarquista 1898–1915,' *Revista de Menorca* 27 (1988): 238–240.
238. Numbers 297–384 published April–December 1912, after which point Mir fell ill. Numbers 385–413 published between March and October 1915. See *Acción Libertaria* (Madrid), 12 December, 1913, 3 and *El Porvenir del Obrero* (Mahón, II), 11 March, 1915, 1.
239. *El Porvenir del Obrero* (Mahón, II), 6 April, 1912, 1. See also 13 April, 1912, 1 and 15 July, 1912, 4.
240. Examples of the paper's attacks on alcohol include: *El Porvenir del Obrero* (Mahón), 8 June, 1912, 2; 5 June, 1913, 2; 9 October, 1913, 2. See also *La Voz del Obrero* (La Coruña), 12 October, 1913, 3–4 and *El Trabajo* (Logroño), 1 June, 1914, 3.
241. *Humanidad* (Valencia), 30 August, 1912, 144; *El Porvenir del Obrero* (Mahón, II), 7 September, 1912, 4.
242. *El Porvenir del Obrero* (Mahón, II), 19 June, 1913, 4; 11 September, 1913, 4; 18 September, 1913, 4. Articles by or about T. Claramunt in *El Porvenir del Obrero* (Mahón, II), 9 October, 1913, 1; 25 September, 1913, 2; 16 October, 1913, 2; 13 November, 1913, 2–3. See also Portella Coll, 'Juan Mir i Mir,' 240.
243. *El Porvenir del Obrero* (Mahón, II), 20 February, 1913, 1; *El Libertario* (Gijón), 1 March, 1913, 3–4. During the paper's first epoch a 'Biblioteca de El Porvenir del Obrero' was also set up, which continued to sell pamphlets after 1912, see *El Porvenir del Obrero* (Mahón, II), 6 April, 1912, 4 and Soriano and Madrid Santos, 'Antología documental,' 384.
244. *El Látigo* (Baracaldo), 8 March, 1913, 4.
245. See 'Correspondencia,' in *El Porvenir del Obrero* (Mahón, II), 6 March, 1913–4 December, 1913, 4.
246. In 1982 the collection was refashioned by Lily Litvak into *El cuento anarquista*. See Lily Litvak, 'Estudio preliminar,' in *El Cuento Anarquista*

(1880–1911): Antología, ed. Lily Litvak (Madrid: Fundación de Estudios Libertarios Anselmo Lorenzo, 2003), 7–60.

247. *El Porvenir del Obrero* (Mahón, II), 29 May, 1913, 1 and 7 August, 1913, 1. For distribution see 'Correspondencia,' in *El Porvenir del Obrero* (Mahón, II), 12 June, 1913–4 December, 1913, 4.

248. *Acción Libertaria* (Madrid), 15 August, 1913, 4; *El Látigo* (Baracaldo), 30 August, 1913, 3–4.

249. Lorenzo, *Hacía la emancipación*, 7–9. Emphasis in original.

250. Lorenzo, *Hacía la emancipación*, 120.

251. *El Porvenir del Obrero* (Mahón, II), 25 May, 1912, 2–3; 6 April, 1912, 4; 19 October, 1912, 3; 23 November, 1912, 4; 6 March, 1913, 1.

252. Tuñón de Lara, *El movimiento obrero*, 514; Castillo, *Historia de la UGT*, 162.

253. *El Porvenir del Obrero* (Mahón, II), 28 September, 1912, 1; 19 October, 1912, 2–3; 26 October, 1912, 1.

254. *El Libertario* (Gijón), 5 October, 1912, 1–2 and 9 November, 1912, 2–3; *El Látigo* (Baracaldo), 5 October, 1912, 1; *La Voz del Obrero* (La Coruña), 11 October, 1912, 1, 3 and 3–4. A more scathing analysis of the 'fiasco' of the strike can be found in *El Libertario* (Gijón), 19 October, 1912, 2–3.

255. *El Porvenir del Obrero* (Mahón, II), 14 August, 1913, 2.

256. *El Porvenir del Obrero* (Mahón, II), 9 November, 1912, 4; 16 November, 1912, 4; 5 June, 1913, 4; 14 August, 1913, 4; 25 September, 1913, 4. See also *Acción Libertaria* (Madrid), 3 October, 1913, 3.

257. *El Porvenir del Obrero* (Mahón, II), 30 January, 1912, 4; *Liberación* (Elche), 30 November, 1912, 4. The Ateneo Sindicalista of Madrid also published a manifesto following the 1912 rail strike, see *El Libertario* (Gijón), 12 October, 1912, 4.

258. *El Libertario* (Gijón), 23 November, 1912, 4; 30 November, 1912, 3; 14 December, 1912, 4; 28 December, 1912, 3. See also *El Porvenir del Obrero* (Mahón, II), 12 December, 1912, 3; *Cultura Libertaria* (El Ferrol), 3 December, 1912, 3 and 15 December, 1912, 2; *El Látigo* (Baracaldo), 16 November, 1912, 4; 30 November, 1912, 4; 14 December, 1912, 4; 1 February, 1913, 1. Reports on meeting: *El Libertario* (Gijón), 11 January, 1913, 3; *Cultura Libertaria* (El Ferrol), 16 January, 1913, 2. See also *Acción Libertaria* (Madrid), 6 June, 1913, 4 and 22 August, 1913, 4.

259. *El Porvenir del Obrero* (Mahón, II), 17 July, 1913, 4 and 31 July, 1913, 4; *Acción Libertaria* (Madrid), 11 July, 1913, 4.

260. *El Porvenir del Obrero* (Mahón, II), 23 October, 1913, 1.

261. *El Porvenir del Obrero* (Mahón, II), 4 December, 1913, 1.

262. *El Porvenir del Obrero* (Mahón, II), 27 March, 1913, 1 and 3 April, 1913, 4.

263. On the build up to the Congress, its stated aims and organisational notes see *El Porvenir del Obrero* (Mahón, II), 13 February, 1913, 1; 3 April, 1913, 2; 4 September, 1913, 1.

264. See *El Porvenir del Obrero* (Mahón, II), 18 September, 1913, 1 and 30 October, 1913, 2; *La Voz del Obrero* (La Coruña), 12 October, 1913, 3; 30 October, 1913, 1–2 and 2–3; 2 December, 1913, 2. See also Bar, *La CNT*, 311–313.

265. Garner, *Goals and Means*, 65–69, 68.

266. *El Porvenir del Obrero* (Mahón, II), 28 August, 1913, 4.

267. *El Libertario* (Gijón), 14 December, 1912, 3. See also *Acción Libertaria* (Madrid), 29 August, 1913, 3–4.

268. Freán Hernández, *El movimiento libertario*, 15–16. See also *Acción Libertaria* (Madrid), 5 September, 1913, 4 and 12 September, 1913, 4.

269. González Fernández, *Utopía y realidad*, 160–166; Gutiérrez Molina, *José Sánchez Rosa*, 72–73.
270. Barrio Alonso, *Anarquismo en Asturias*, 117–121.
271. *El Libertario* (Gijón), 10 August, 1912, 4 and 5 October, 1912, 4; *El Látigo* (Baracaldo), 30 November, 1912, 4.
272. *El Libertario* (Gijón), 21 September, 1912, 3.
273. Barrio Alonso, *Anarquismo en Asturias*, 127.
274. A handful of short-lived titles were launched in Sevilla in this period, no copies of which have survived: *El Hombre Libre* (c. March 1911); *Regeneración Obrera* (Ecija, c.November–December 1912) and *La Voz del Trabajo* (c.February 1913).
275. *El Libertario* (Gijón), 10 August, 1912, 4; *El Porvenir del Obrero* (Mahón, II), 17 August, 1912, 4.
276. See Shaffer, 'Panama Red,' 64–67.
277. Barrio Alonso, *Anarquismo en Asturias*, 120–121.
278. *El Libertario* (Gijón), 9 November, 1912, 1–2 and 16 November, 1912, 1.
279. *El Libertario* (Gijón), 10 August, 1912, 2; 17 August, 1912, 3 and 4; 22 February, 1913, 2–3. See also *El Látigo* (Baracaldo), 12 June, 1913, 2 and *Acción Libertaria* (Madrid), 26 September, 1913, 1; Barrio Alonso, *Anarquismo en Asturias*, 121–122.
280. *El Libertario* (Gijón), 18 January, 1913, 1. This article was strongly criticsed in *El Porvenir del Obrero* (Mahón, II), 20 February, 1913, 2.
281. Barrio Alonso, *Anarquismo en Asturias*, 122. See also *El Libertario* (Gijón), 30 November, 1912, 2.
282. See Adrian Schubert, *The Road to Revolution in Spain: The Coal Miners of Asturias, 1860–1934* (Chicago: University of Illinois Press, 1987), 108–114.
283. *El Libertario* (Gijón), 31 August, 1912, 3 and 4; 7 September, 1912, 4; 14 September, 1912, 4; 21 September, 1912, 2; 5 October, 1912, 4; 21 December, 1912, 3 and 4; 15 February, 1913, 2; 15 March, 1912, 2. See also *Acción Libertaria* (Madrid), 30 May, 1913, 4; *Solidaridad* (Gijón), 16 May, 1914, 4. Critiques of SOMA: *Acción Libertaria* (Madrid), 26 September, 1913, 3 and 3 October, 1913, 3. See also Barrio Alonso, *Anarquismo en Asturias*, 123–128 and Schubert, *The Road to Revolution*, 115.
284. *El Libertario* (Gijón), 10 August, 1913, 2 and 29 March, 1913, 3; *El Libertario* (Gijón), 5 April, 1913, 2. See also *El Látigo* (Baracaldo), 26 July, 1913, 3.
285. *Solidaridad* (Gijón), 16 May, 1914, 3. See also Barrio Alonso, *Anarquismo en Asturias*, 130–135.
286. *El Porvenir del Obrero* (Mahón, II), 1 May, 1913, 3 and 7 May, 1913, 4. See also *Acción Libertaria* (Madrid), 23 May, 1913, 2.
287. *El Porvenir del Obrero* (Mahón, II), 5 June, 1913, 4; *El Látigo* (Baracaldo), 14 June, 1913, 4; *Acción Libertaria* (Madrid), 23 May, 1913, 1.
288. *Acción Libertaria* (Madrid), 3 October, 1913, 4 and 19 December, 1913, 4.
289. *Acción Libertaria* (Madrid), 8 August, 1913, 1.
290. *Acción Libertaria* (Madrid), 15 August, 1913, 1 and 22 August, 1913, 1.
291. *Acción Libertaria* (Madrid), 10 October, 1913, 2 and 17 October, 1913, 2. See also Garner, *Goals and Means*, 52–55 and Carl Levy, 'The Rooted Cosmopolitan: Errico Malatesta: Syndicalism, Transnationalism and the International Labour Movement,' in Berry and Bantman, *New Perspectives on Anarchism*, 68–71.
292. *Acción Libertaria* (Madrid), 19 December, 1913, 4. Neither the new editorial group of *Acción Libertaria* nor 'Los Iguales' published their names.
293. *Acción Libertaria* (Madrid), 11 July, 1913, 4; 19 December, 1913, 4; *Tierra y Libertad* (Barcelona, IV), 30 July, 1913, 1; *La Voz del Obrero* (La Coruña), no date c.December 1913, 4.

294. *Acción Libertaria* (Madrid), 18 July, 1913, 1; 26 September, 1913, 2; 10 October, 1913, 3; 26 September, 1913, 4; 10 October, 1913, 4; 17 October, 1913, 4.
295. *Acción Libertaria* (Madrid), 14 November, 1913, 1.
296. *Acción Libertaria* (Madrid), 14 November, 1913, 4; 28 November, 1913, 1; 12 December, 1913, 4; 21 November, 1913, 3.
297. *Los Refractarios* (Madrid), 1 September, 1915, 1 and 12–13.
298. Madrid Santos, 'La prensa anarquista,' 198.
299. *Acción Libertaria* (Madrid), 12 September, 1913, 1.
300. Zambrana, 'El anarquismo organizado,' 1073–1103.
301. *El Látigo* (Baracaldo), 14 December, 1912, 1.
302. *El Látigo* (Baracaldo), 28 December, 1912, 1.
303. *El Látigo* (Baracaldo), 14 December, 1912, 1 and 21 February, 1913, 1.
304. Alfredo Velasco Núñez, *El hilo negro vasco: Anarquismo y anarcosindicalismo en el País Vasco (1870–1936)* (Bilbao: Martxoak, 2009), 70–77.
305. *El Látigo* (Baracaldo), 7 September, 1912, 3–4; 21 September, 1912, 3–4; 5 October, 1912, 2–3; 28 December, 1912, 2; 26 April, 1913, 3; 31 May, 1913, 2; 14 June, 1913, 2; 12 July, 1913, 2; 26 July, 1913, 2; 30 August, 1913, 3.
306. *El Látigo* (Baracaldo), 14 December, 1912, 1. See also 12 April, 1913, 3 and 26 April, 1913, 3.
307. *El Látigo* (Baracaldo), 30 November, 1912, 4.
308. *El Látigo* (Baracaldo), 1 February, 1913, 4. Subscription detailed in 1 February, 1913–30 August, 1913, 4. See also *El Látigo* (Baracaldo), 20 September, 1912, 1; *Acción Libertaria* (Madrid), 14 November, 1913, 3–4 and 21 November, 1913, 3.
309. *El Látigo* (Baracaldo), 30 August, 1913, 4 and 6 December, 1913, 4.
310. *El Látigo* (Baracaldo), 20 September, 1912, 1; *Acción Libertaria* (Madrid), 10 October, 1913, 3.
311. *Acción Libertaria* (Madrid), 15 August, 1913, 4. On his way home from the tour Sánchez Rosa also gave a speech in Valladolid, see *Acción Libertaria* (Madrid), 28 November, 1913, 3; *La Voz del Obrero* (La Coruña), 2 December, 1913, 3–4.
312. *Acción Libertaria* (Madrid), 10 October, 1913, 4. See also Ángel Herrerín López, 'Anarchist Sociability in Spain: In Times of Violence and Clandestinity,' *Bulletin for Spanish and Portuguese Historical Studies* 38, 1 (2013): 168.
313. *Acción Libertaria* (Madrid), 17 October, 1913, 3.
314. *Acción Libertaria* (Madrid), 21 November, 1913, 3.
315. *El Látigo* (Baracaldo), 1 February, 1913, 4; 30 August, 1913, 4; 16 January, 1914, 1–2. See also balances printed in 14 December, 1912, 3–4 and 16 January, 1914, 4.
316. Zambrana, 'El anarquismo organizado,' 1077–1080.
317. *Acción Libertaria* (Madrid), 18 July, 1913, 4; 22 August, 1913, 3. See also *Cultura Libertaria* (El Ferrol), 16 January, 1913, 4.
318. *Tierra y Libertad* (Barcelona, IV), 5 August, 1914, 3.
319. Zambrana, 'El anarquismo organizado,' 1089–1097.
320. *Tierra y Libertad* (Barcelona, IV), 23 December, 1914, 4. See also González Fernández, *Utopía y realidad*, 236–240.
321. Madrid Santos, 'La prensa anarquista,' 198.
322. *El Látigo* (Baracaldo), 12 July, 1913, 1–2 and 26 July, 1913, 1–2. See also Zoais' contributions to *Cultura Libertaria* (El Ferrol), 1 February, 1913, 1 and *Los Refractarios* (Madrid), 1 September, 1915, 5. Zoais later moved to Valladolid, where he edited *Ideal* (Valladolid, c.05/1916). See Soriano and Madrid Santos, 'Antología documental,' 368–369 for a list of Zoais' pamphlets.

323. *Acción Libertaria* (Madrid), 5 September, 1913, 4 and 17 October, 1913, 3.
324. *Acción Libertaria* (Madrid), 12 December, 1913, 3.
325. Zambrana, 'El anarquismo organizado,' 1097–1100.
326. Madrid Santos, 'La prensa anarquista,' 186–187. On the FAI see Garner, *Goals and Means*, 213–246.
327. For example, see propaganda group in La Carolina (Jaén) in *Acción Libertaria* (Madrid), 5 September, 1913, 4.
328. *Acción Libertaria* (Madrid), 3 October, 1913, 4. See also Íñiguez, *Esbozo de una enciclopedia*, 578.
329. *Villena Obrera* (Villena), 5 January, 1913, 4.
330. *El Trabajo* (Logroño), 1 June, 1914, 1–2.
331. *Acción Directa* (Cartagena), 28 February, 1914, 3.
332. *Acción Ferroviaria* (Huelva), 5 July, 1913, 1.
333. *Cultura Libertaria* (El Ferrol), 15 December, 1912, 4 and 2 January, 1913, 1.
334. *Cultura Libertaria* (El Ferrol), 1 February, 1913, 3. Duque went on to become an important figure in the Galician CNT, see Íñiguez, *Esbozo de una enciclopedia*, 585.
335. Garner, *Goals and Means*, 63–64.
336. González Fernández, *Utopía y realidad*, 240–241.
337. For example, see the distinction made by *Liberación* between 'anarchist' and 'syndicalist' papers while advising readers subscribe to both, *Liberación* (Elche), 1 September, 1912, 4.
338. *El Porvenir del Obrero* (Mahón, II), 12 December, 1912, 3. See also *El Libertario* (Gijón), 23 November, 1912, 2–3.
339. *Acción Libertaria* (Madrid), 18 July, 1913, 1–2.
340. See for example *Acción Libertaria* (Madrid), 5 September, 1913, 1–2.
341. Bar, *La CNT*, 316–338.
342. See *La Voz del Campesino* (Sans), 30 May, 1914, 4; Madrid Santos, 'La prensa anarquista,' 184–185.
343. See short reports on founding of FNOA in *El Porvenir del Obrero* (Mahón, II), 29 May, 1913, 4 and *Acción Libertaria* (Madrid), 28 November, 1913, 4.
344. An earlier version of this section has been published as James Michael Yeoman, 'The Spanish Anarchist Movement at the Outbreak of the First World War: A Crisis of Ideological Neutrality,' in *Shaping Neutrality Throughout the First World War*, ed. José Leonardo Ruíz Sánchez, Inmaculada Cordero Olivero and Carolina García Sanz (Sevilla: Universidad de Sevilla, 2015), 83–101.
345. The explosion in membership of the CNT came between 1918–1919, when membership rose by almost 90 per cent. Bar, *La CNT*, 338–339 and 490–492.
346. González Fernández, *Utopía y realidad*, 179–181 and 193–201. Francisco J. Romero Salvadó, *Spain, 1914–1918: Between War and Revolution* (London: Routledge, 1999), 31 and 44–45.
347. *El Libertario* (Gijón), 9 November, 1912, 3; *El Porvenir del Obrero* (Mahón, II), 2 January, 1913, 4; *Acción Libertaria* (Madrid), 20 June, 1913, 2–3.
348. For example, see *El Porvenir del Obrero* (Mahón, II), 11 September, 1913, 3 and 2 October, 1913, 1.
349. Wayne Thorpe, 'The European Syndicalists and War, 1914–1918,' *Contemporary European History* 10, 1 (2001): 12.
350. *Tierra y Libertad* (Barcelona, IV), 20 January, 1915, 2 and 14 April, 1915, 2–3. See also Ralph Darlington, 'Revolutionary Syndicalist Opposition to the First World War: A Comparative Reassessment,' *Revue belge de philology d'histoire* 84, 4 (2006): 983–984 and 900–993.
351. Wayne Thorpe, 'El Ferrol, Rio de Janeiro, Zimmerwald and Beyond: Syndicalist Internationalism, 1914–1918,' *Revue belge de philology d'histoire* 84,

4 (2006): 1007–1009. On the German FVdG see Wayne Thorpe, 'Keeping the Faith: The German Syndicalists in the First World War,' *Central European History* 33, 2 (2000): 195–216. On the Italian (USI) see Charles L. Bertrand, 'Italian Revolutionary Syndicalism and the Crisis of Intervention: August–December 1914,' *Canadian Journal of History/Annales Canadiennes d'Histoire* 10, 3 (1975): 349–368. On the US IWW see Melvyn Dubofsky, 'The Rise and Fall of Revolutionary Syndicalism in the United States,' in Linden and Thorpe, *Revolutionary Syndicalism*, 203–220 and Darlington, 'Revolutionary Syndicalist Opposition,' 997–1000; on Dutch syndicalists see Marcel van der Linden, 'The Many Faces of Dutch Revolutionary Trade Unionism,' in Linden and Thorpe, *Revolutionary Syndicalism*, 49–50.

352. Darlington, 'Revolutionary Syndicalist Opposition,' 987–990.

353. Berry, *French Anarchist Movement*, 21–22; Constance Bantman and David Berry, 'The French Anarchist Movement and the First World War,' in *Anarchism 1914–18: Internationalism, Anti-Militarism and War*, ed. Matthew Adams and Ruth Kinna (Manchester: Manchester University Press, 2017), 155–174.

354. Letter from Kropotkin to Gustav Steffan, published in *El Porvenir del Obrero* (Mahón, II), 11 March, 1915, 1–2.

355. *El Porvenir del Obrero* (Mahón, II), 1 April, 1915, 1. See also Peter Ryley, '*The Manifesto of the Sixteen*: Kropotkin's Rejection of Anti-Militarism and His Critique of the Politics of Peace,' in Adams and Kinna, *Anarchism 1914–18*, 49–68 and Matthew Adams, 'Anarchism and the First World War,' in *The Palgrave Handbook of Anarchism*, ed. Carl Levy and Matthew Adams (Cham: Palgrave Macmillan, 2018), 389–407. See also *Tierra y Libertad* (Barcelona, IV), 30 December, 1914, 1.

356. The argument provoked by the war belies the claim by Wayne Thorpe and Ralph Darlington that the Spanish movement offered a 'clear and . . . consistent response' to the conflict, see Thorpe, 'The European Syndicalists,' 10; Darlington, 'Revolutionary Syndicalist Opposition,' 985.

357. *Solidaridad Obrera* (Barcelona, III), 8 October, 1914, 1–2 and 5 November, 1914, 1; *Tierra y Libertad* (Barcelona, IV), 14 October, 1914, 1 and 6 January, 1915, 1.

358. *Tierra y Libertad* (Barcelona), 20 January, 1915, 1–2; 27 January, 1915, 1–2; 10 February, 1915, 2.

359. *La Voz del Campesino* (Valls), 15 December, 1914, 1; *Reivindicación* (Sabadell), 27 August, 1915, 1.

360. *Acción Directa* (Cartagena), 4 December, 1914, 1–2.

361. *Tierra y Libertad* (Barcelona), 16 December, 1914, 4.

362. *Tierra y Libertad* (Barcelona), 13 January, 1915, 4; 20 January, 1915, 3–4; 20 January, 1915, 4. See also formation of 'Pro-Peace' anarchist group in Zaragoza, 24 February, 1915, 4 and Zambrana, 'El anarquismo organizado,' 1099.

363. *Tierra y Libertad* (Barcelona, IV), 10 March, 1915, 3.

364. *Tierra y Libertad* (Barcelona, IV), 30 December, 1914, 4 and 17 March, 1915, 3–4. Joan Zambrana, 'La asamblea de sociedades obreras—Mataró—18/10/1914: Una repuesta unitaria del movimiento obrero ante la crisis de trabajo en los inicios de la I Guerra mundial,' (2010), 1–17. Published online, accessed 12 March, 2012, http://cedall.org/Documentacio/IHL/LA%20ASAMBLEA%20DE%20MATARO%20DEL%2018.pdf.

365. Darlington, 'Revolutionary Syndicalist Opposition,' 985. See also Berry, *French Anarchist Movement*, 21–22.

366. See Thorpe, 'The European Syndicalists,' 10 and Darlington, 'Revolutionary Syndicalist Opposition,' 986.

367. Barrio Alonso, *Anarquismo en Asturias*, 148–151; Madrid Santos, 'La prensa anarquista,' 181 and 190; Richard Cleminson, *Anarchism, Science and Sex: Eugenics in Eastern Spain, 1900–1937* (Oxford: Peter Lang, 2000), 141–157.
368. *El Porvenir del Obrero* (Mahón, II), 8 April, 1915, 1.
369. *El Porvenir del Obrero* (Mahón, II), 15 April, 1915, 2.
370. Barrio Alonso, *Anarquismo en Asturias*, 148–162.
371. See for example: *Acción Libertaria* (Gijón, II), 13 August, 1915, 2–3. Also discussed in González Fernández, *Utopía y realidad*, 234 and Gutiérrez Molina, *José Sánchez Rosa*, 78. Support for *El Porvenir del Obrero* (Mahón, II), 15 June, 1915, 1; 12 August, 1915, 2–3; 2 September, 1915, 2.
372. On the various positions in wider Spanish society at the outbreak of the war see Romero Salvadó, *Spain, 1914–1918*, 5–22.
373. *Tierra y Libertad* (Barcelona, IV), 14 April, 1915, 1.
374. *El Porvenir del Obrero* (Mahón, II), 13 May, 1915, 3. Emphasis added. See also *Tierra y Libertad* (Barcelona), 12 May, 1915, 3.
375. *El Porvenir del Obrero* (Mahón, II), 21 September, 1912, 1; *El Libertario* (Gijón), 10 August, 1912, 1 and 14 December, 1912, 1.
376. *Renovación* (Gijón), May, 1916, 1–2.
377. *El Porvenir del Obrero* (Mahón, II), 22 April, 1915, 3; see also García's response in 20 May, 1915, 2.
378. *Acción Libertaria* (Gijón, II), 13 August, 1915, 2–3.
379. *El Porvenir del Obrero* (Mahón, II), 17 June, 1915, 3; 8 July, 1915, 1; 15 July, 1915, 1; 5 August, 1915, 1. *Tierra y Libertad* (Barcelona, IV), 30 June, 1915, 3. *Acción Libertaria* did not believe Urales' accusations, and said that he had 'left the field of anarchism,' see 30 July, 1915, 3.
380. Bar, *La CNT*, 343.
381. *El Porvenir del Obrero* (Mahón, II), 20 May, 1915, 1 and 5 August, 1915, 3–4.
382. *Tierra y Libertad* (Barcelona, IV), 13 January, 1915, 4.
383. *El Porvenir del Obrero* (Mahón, II), 5 August, 1915, 2–3.
384. *Acción Directa* (Cartagena), 4 December, 1914, 1–2.
385. *El Porvenir del Obrero* (Mahón, II), 13 May, 1915, 3 and 29 April, 1915, 4.
386. *El Porvenir del Obrero* (Mahón, II), 9 October, 1913, 2; 16 October, 1913, 3; 5 November, 1913, 3–4.
387. Fernández Álvarez, *Ricardo Mella*, 65–66; Federico Urales, *La evolución de la filosofía en España*, ed. Rafael Pérez de la Dehesa (Barcelona: Editorial Laia, 1977), 28–29; Portella Coll, 'Mir i Mir,' 118–123.
388. *Tierra y Libertad* (Barcelona, IV), 14 April, 1915, 3. See also Bar, 'The Glory and Tragedy,' 123.
389. Barrio Alonso, *Anarquismo en Asturias*, 100–105.
390. *Tierra y Libertad* (Barcelona, IV), 3 March, 1915, 1.
391. Information on Congress compiled from reports in *Tierra y Libertad* (Barcelona, IV), 12 May, 1915, 1–2; *Solidaridad Obrera* (Barcelona, III), 13 May, 1915, 1–2; *Acción Libertaria* (Gijón, II), 14 May, 1915, 1. See also Garner, *Goals and Means*, 71–75; Molina, *José Sánchez Rosa*, 76–78 and Thorpe, 'Syndicalist Internationalism,' 1010–1013.
392. *El Porvenir del Obrero* (Mahón, II), 15 April, 1915, 1 and 13 May, 1915, 1.
393. Gutiérrez Molina, *José Sánchez Rosa*, 77.
394. Quintanilla spoke for the French Syndicalist Youth, and was referred to as 'Aurelio Quintanilha' in the accounts of *Solidaridad Obrera, Tierra y Libertad* and *Acción Libertaria*. The reason for this is unclear.
395. Gutiérrez Molina, *José Sánchez Rosa*, 78.
396. *El Porvenir del Obrero* (Mahón, II), 8 July, 1915, 2–3.
397. *Acción Libertaria* (Gijón, II), 21 May, 1915, 1.
398. *Solidaridad Obrera* (Barcelona, III), 3 June, 1915, 1–2.

399. *Tierra y Libertad* (Barcelona, IV), 19 May, 1915, 1–2.
400. González Fernández, *Utopía y realidad*, 242–243.
401. *Solidaridad Obrera* (Barcelona, III), 3 June, 1915, 1.
402. Gutiérrez Molina, *José Sánchez Rosa*, 78–80.
403. *Acción Libertaria* (Gijón, II), 21 May, 1915, 1.
404. Barrio Alonso, *Anarquismo en Asturias*, 156.
405. *Acción Libertaria* (Gijón, II), 6 August, 1915, 3.
406. *Acción Libertaria* (Gijón, II), 20 August, 1915, 1.
407. *El Porvenir del Obrero* (Mahón, II), last issue 14 October, 1915; *Cultura y Acción* (Zaragoza), last issue c.November, 1915 [see Madrid Santos, 'La prensa anarquista,' 557]; *Acción Libertaria* (Gijón, II), last issue 14 January, 1916; *Renovación* (Gijón), last issue August, 1916.
408. Teresa Abelló Güell and Enric Olivé Serret, 'El conflicto entre la CNT y la familia Urales-Montseny en 1928: La lucha por el mantenimiento del anarquismo puro,' *Estudios de Historia Social* 32–33 (1985): 317–332.
409. Fernández Álvarez, *Ricardo Mella*, 62.
410. Álvarez, *Eleuterio Quintanilla*, 186–189.
411. *Renovación* (Gijón), June, 1916, 9–12.
412. Romero Salvadó, *Spain, 1914–1918*, 22–31; Garner, *Goals and Means*, 75–81; Smith, *Anarchism, Revolution and Reaction*, 225–258.
413. *Renovación* (Gijón), June, 1916, 31.
414. See Joan Zambrana, 'La CNT y la Asamblea de Valencia (Mayo 1916): Un estudio sobre la CNT y el proceso aglutinado de un bloque sindical y social contra la crisis de subsistencias y la represión del movimiento obrero español,' (2014). Published online, accessed 8 June, 2014, www.cedall.org/Doc umentacio/IHL/LA%20CNT%20Y%20LA%20ASAMBLEA%20DE%20 VALENCIA.pdf.
415. Bar, *La CNT*, 479–555 (data from 492).
416. Pere Gabriel, 'Propagandistas confederales entre el sindicato y el anarquismo: La construcción Barcelonesa de la CNT en Cataluña, Aragón, País Valenciano y Baleares,' *Ayer* 45, 1 (2002): 105–145; Freán Hernández, *El movimiento libertario*, 18.
417. *Solidaridad Obrera* (Barcelona, III), 11 December, 1913, 1. *Tierra y Libertad* doubted that this idea would be a success, due to the 'indifference' of the Spanish working class, see *Tierra y Libertad* (Barcelona, IV), 14 January, 1914, 2.
418. *Solidaridad Obrera* (Barcelona, III), 8 January, 1914, 2; 5 November, 1914, 4; 3 June, 1915, 4.
419. *Solidaridad Obrera* (Barcelona, III), 1 January, 1914, 2 and 8 January, 1914, 1.
420. Anselmo Lorenzo, *El trabajador libre: Impulso a la creación del diario obrero sindicalista* (Barcelona: Solidaridad Obrera, 1914), 2.
421. *El Socialista* (Madrid), 1 April, 1913, 1.
422. *Solidaridad Obrera* (Barcelona, III), 12 August, 1915, 4.
423. No copies of *Solidaridad Obrera* exist between number 99 (8 August, 1915) and number 211 (25 May, 1916). See *Tierra y Libertad* (Barcelona, IV), 1 March, 1916, 1 for notice of publication.
424. Madrid Santos, 'La prensa anarquista,' 202.
425. Bar, *La CNT*, 343–346; Madrid Santos, *Solidaridad Obrera*, 103–104.
426. Madrid Santos, 'La prensa anarquista,' 184; Bar, *La CNT*, 337.
427. Paraphrase from 'Juzgando la situación,' in *Solidaridad Obrera* (Gijón), 14 May, 1910, 1. Full quote: 'We will be victorious at any time if we maintain our consciousness and our love of organisation'.

Bibliography

Archives

AFPI: Archivo Fundación Pablo Iglesias. Online.
BNE: Biblioteca Nacional de España. Madrid.
BPC: Biblioteca Provincial de Cádiz. Cádiz.
BVA: Biblioteca Virtual de Andalucía. Online.
CDHS: Ateneu Enciclopèdic Popular—Centre de Documentació Històrica i Social. Barcelona.
CED: cedall.org. Online.
HMM: Hemeroteca Municipal de Madrid. Madrid.
IISG: Internationaal Instituut voor Sociale Geschiedenis. Amsterdam.
LOC: Library of Congress: Digital Collections. Online.
US: University of Sheffield Library. Sheffield.

Primary Sources

Anarchist Press

¡Despertad!. Madrid, 1909. IISG.
¡Justicia!. Gijón, 1911. IISG.
Acción Directa. Cartagena, 1914. IISG.
Acción Ferroviaria. Huelva, 1913. IISG.
Acción Libertaria. Gijón/Vigo, 1910–1911. HMM and IISG.
Acción Libertaria. Gijón, II Epoch, 1915–1916. IISG.
Acción Libertaria. Madrid, 1913. IISG.
Al Paso. Sevilla, II, Epoch, 1909–1910. IISG.
Anarquía. Zaragoza, 1911–1912. BNE.
Cultura Libertaria. El Ferrol, 1912–1913. IISG.
El Látigo. Madrid, 1911. BNE and IISG.
El Látigo. Baracaldo, 1912–1914. IISG.
El Libertario. Madrid, 1909–1910. IISG.
El Libertario. Gijón, 1912–1913. HMM and IISG.
El Porvenir del Obrero. Mahón, II Epoch, 1912–1915. BNE, HMM and IISG.
El Trabajo. Logroño, 1914. HMM.
Escuela Libre. Valladolid, 1911. IISG.
Escuela Moderna. Valencia, 1910–1911. IISG.
Humanidad. Toledo, 1907–1908. IISG.
Humanidad. Valencia, 1912. IISG.
Humanidad Libre. Jumilla, II Epoch, 1907. IISG.
La Acción. La Coruña, 1908. IISG.
La Enseñanza Moderna. Valladolid, 1910. IISG.
La Protesta. Valladolid/Sabadell/La Línea de la Concepción, 1899–1902. BVA and IISG.
La Voz del Campesino. Sans/Valls, 1913–1916. IISG.
La Voz del Obrero. La Coruña, 1910–1917. IISG.
La Voz del Obrero del Mar. Cádiz, II Epoch, 1907–1908. BPC and IISG.

Liberación. Madrid, 1908. HMM.

Liberación. Elche, 1912. IISG.

Los Refractarios. Madrid, 1915. IISG.

Nueva Aurora. Málaga, 1909. IISG.

Rebelión. Sevilla, 1910. IISG.

Reivindicación. Sabadell, 1915. IISG.

Renovación. Gijón, 1916. IISG.

Solidaridad. Gijón, 1914. IISG.

Solidaridad Obrera. Barcelona, 1907–1909. CED and IISG.

Solidaridad Obrera. Barcelona, II Epoch, 1910–1911. CED and IISG.

Solidaridad Obrera. Barcelona, III-IV Epoch, 1913–1919. CED and IISG.

Solidaridad Obrera. Gijón, 1909–1910. IISG.

Tierra y Libertad. Barcelona, IV Epoch, 1910–1919. CED and IISG.

Tribuna Libre. Gijón, 1909. IISG.

Verdad. Sevilla, 1908. IISG.

Villena Obrera. Villena, 1912–1913. IISG.

Supplements and Almanacs to Periodicals

La Voz del Obrero del Mar: Trabajadores del mar: ¡Altera!. Cádiz, 18 June, 1907. BPC.

Solidaridad Obrera: 2º suplemento al número 32. Gijón, 4 March, 1911. IISG.

Solidaridad Obrera: 3ᵉʳ suplemento al número 32. Gijón, 18 April, 1911. IISG.

Other Press

El País. Madrid, 1887–1921. BNE.

El Socialista. Madrid, 1886–1939. AFPI.

Memoirs, Books and Pamphlets by Contemporary Authors

Archer, William. *The Life, Trial and Death of Francisco Ferrer*. London: Chapman and Hall, 1911. US.

Bonafulla, Leopoldo. *La revolución de julio: Barcelona 1909*. Barcelona: Toribio Taberner, 1910. IISG.

The International Anarchist Congress Held at the Plancius Hall, Amsterdam on August 26th–31st, 1907. London: Freedom, 1907. LOC.

Lorenzo, Anselmo. *El trabajador libre: Impulso a la creación del diario obrero sindicalista*. Barcelona: Solidaridad Obrera, 1914. CDHS.

Lorenzo, Anselmo. *Hacía la emancipación: Tática de avance obrero en la lucha por el ideal*. Mahón: El Porvenir del Obrero, 1914. BNE.

Prat, José. *La burguesía y el proletariado: Conferencia leída en el centro Joventut Republicana de Lérida el 16 de enero de 1909*. Barcelona: Salud y Fuerza, 1909. Serialised in *Solidaridad Obrera* (Gijón), 13 November, 1909–6 August, 1910.

Urales, Federico. *La evolución de la filosofía en España*, edited by Rafael Pérez de la Dehesa. Barcelona: Editorial Laia, 1977. IISG.

Secondary Sources

Abelló Güell, Teresa, and Enric Olivé Serret. 'El conflicto entre la CNT y la familia Urales-Montseny en 1928: La lucha por el mantenimiento del anarquismo puro.' *Estudios de Historia Social* 32–33 (1985): 317–332.

Adams, Matthew. 'Anarchism and the First World War.' In *The Palgrave Handbook of Anarchism*, edited by Carl Levy and Matthew Adams, 389–407. Cham: Palgrave Macmillan, 2018.

Adams, Matthew, and Ruth Kinna, eds. *Anarchism 1914–18: Internationalism, Anti-Militarism and War.* Manchester: Manchester University Press, 2017.

Álvarez, Ramón. *Eleuterio Quintanilla: (Vida y obra del maestro): Contribución a la historia del sindicalismo revolucionario en Asturias.* México DF: Editores Mexicanos Unidos, 1973.

Álvarez Junco, José. 'Maneras de hacer historia: los antecedentes de la Semana Trágica.' *Zona Abierta* 31 (1984): 43–92.

Avilés Farré, Juan. *Francisco Ferrer y Guardia: Pedagogo, anarquista y mártir.* Madrid: Marcial Pons, 2006.

Avrich, Paul. *The Modern School Movement: Anarchism and Education in the United States.* Princeton: Princeton University Press, 1980.

Baer, James A. *Anarchist Immigrants in Spain and Argentina.* Chicago: University of Illinois Press, 2015.

Bantman, Constance. 'Internationalism without an International? Cross-Channel Anarchist Networks, 1890–1914.' *Revue belge de philology et d'histoire* 84, 4 (2006): 961–981.

Bantman, Constance. 'The Militant Go-Between: Emile Pouget's Transnational Propaganda (1880–1914).' *Labour History Review* 74, 3 (2009): 274–287.

Bantman, Constance, and David Berry. 'The French Anarchist Movement and the First World War.' In Adams and Kinna, *Anarchism 1914–18*, 155–174.

Bar, Antonio. *La CNT en los años rojos: Del sindicalismo revolucionario al anarcosindicalismo (1910–1926).* Madrid: Akal, 1981.

Bar, Antonio. 'The CNT: The Glory and Tragedy of Spanish Anarchosyndicalism.' Linden and Thorpe, *Revolutionary Syndicalism*, 119–138.

Barrio Alonso, Ángeles. *Anarquismo y anarcosindicalismo en Asturias, 1890–1936.* Madrid: Siglo XXI, 1988.

Barrio Alonso, Ángeles. 'Cultura del trabajo y organización obrera en Gijón en el cambio de siglo.' *Historia Contemporánea* 5 (1991): 27–51.

Barrio Alonso, Ángeles. 'El anarquismo asturiano entre el sindicalismo y la política, 1890–1920.' *Ayer* 45, 1 (2002): 147–170.

Berry, David. *A History of the French Anarchist Movement, 1917–1945.* London: Greenwood Press, 2002.

Berry, David, and Constance Bantman, eds. *New Perspectives on Anarchism, Labour and Syndicalism: The Individual, the National and the Transnational.* Newcastle-upon-Tyne: Cambridge Scholars Publishing, 2010.

Bertrand, Charles L. 'Italian Revolutionary Syndicalism and the Crisis of Intervention: August-December 1914.' *Canadian Journal of History/Annales Canadiennes d'Histoire* 10, 3 (1975): 349–368.

Castillo, Juan José. *El sindicalismo amarillo en España: Aportación al estudio del catolicismo social español (1912–1923).* Madrid: Editorial Cuadernos para el Diálogo, 1977.

Castillo, Santiago. *Historia de la UGT: Un sindicalismo consciente, 1873–1914*. Madrid: Siglo XXI, 2008.

Cleminson, Richard. *Anarchism, Science and Sex: Eugenics in Eastern Spain, 1900–1937*. Oxford: Peter Lang, 2000.

Cuadrat, Xavier. *Socialismo y anarquismo en Cataluña (1899–1911): Los orígenes de la CNT*. Madrid: Ediciones de la Revista de Trabajo, 1976.

Cumbers, Andy, Paul Routledge, and Corinne Nativel. 'The Entangled Geographies of Global Justice Networks.' *Progress in Human Geography* 32, 2 (2008): 183–201.

Dalmau, Antoni. *Siete días de furia: Barcelona y la Semana Trágica (Julio de 1909)*. Barcelona: Ediciones Destino, 2009.

Dalmau, Pol. *Press, Politics and National Identities in Catalonia: The Transformation of La Vanguardia, 1881–1931*. Brighton: Sussex Academic Press, 2017.

Darlington, Ralph. 'Revolutionary Syndicalist Opposition to the First World War: A Comparative Reassessment.' *Revue belge de philology d'histoire* 84, 4 (2006): 983–1003.

Diez, Xavier. *El anarquismo individualista en España (1923–1938)*. Barcelona: Virus, 2007.

Dubofsky, Melvyn. 'The Rise and Fall of Revolutionary Syndicalism in the United States.' In Linden and Thorpe, *Revolutionary Syndicalism*, 203–220.

Elorza, Antonio. 'Los orígenes del asociacionismo obrero en España.' *Revista de Trabajo* 37 (1972): 125–345.

Esenwein, George. *Anarchist Ideology and the Working-Class Movement in Spain, 1868–1898*. Berkeley, CA: University of California Press, 1989.

Felipe Redondo, Jesús de. *Trabajadores, lenguaje y experiencia en la formación del movimiento obrero español*. Palma de Mallorca: Genueve Ediciones, 2012.

Fernández Álvarez, Antón. *Ricardo Mella o el anarquismo humanista*. Barcelona: Anthropos, 1990.

Freán Hernández, Óscar. *El movimiento libertario en Galicia, 1910–1936*. Sada: Ediciós do Castro, 2006.

Gabriel, Pere. 'Sindicalismo y huelga: Sindicalismo revolucionario francés e italiano: Su introducción en España.' *Ayer* 4 (1991): 15–45.

Gabriel, Pere. 'Propagandistas confederales entre el sindicato y el anarquismo: La construcción Barcelonesa de la CNT en Cataluña, Aragón, País Valenciano y Baleares.' *Ayer* 45, 1 (2002): 105–145.

Garner, Jason. *Goals and Means: Anarchism, Syndicalism, and Internationalism in the Origins of the Federación Anarquista Ibérica*. Edinburgh: AK Press, 2016.

González Fernández, Ángeles. *Utopía y realidad: Anarquismo, anarcosindicalismo y organizaciones obreras: Sevilla, 1900–1936*. Sevilla: Diputación Provincial de Sevilla, 1996.

Grocott, Chris, Gareth Stockey, and Jo Grady. 'Anarchism in the UK('s Most Famous Fortress): Comradeship and Cupidity in Gibraltar and Neighbouring Spain, 1890–1902.' *Labour History* 56, 4 (2015): 385–406.

Gutiérrez Molina, José Luis. *La tiza, la tinta y la palabra: José Sánchez Rosa: Maestro y anarquista andaluz (1864–1936)*. Ubrique: Tréveris, 2005.

Herrerín López, Ángel. 'Anarchist Sociability in Spain: In Times of Violence and Clandestinity.' *Bulletin for Spanish and Portuguese Historical Studies* 38, 1 (2013): 155–174.

Hirsch, Steven, and Lucien van der Walt, eds. *Anarchism and Syndicalism in the Colonial and Postcolonial World, 1870–1940: The Praxis of National Liberation, Internationalism and Social Revolution*. Leiden-Boston: Brill, 2010.

Íñiguez, Miguel. *Esbozo de una enciclopedia histórica del anarquismo español*. Madrid: Fundación de Estudios Libertarios Anselmo Lorenzo, 2001.

Khuri-Makdisi, Ilham. *The Eastern Mediterranean and the Making of Global Radicalism: 1860–1914*. Berkeley: University of California Press, 2010.

Laqua, Daniel. 'Freethinkers, Anarchists and Francisco Ferrer: The Making of a Transnational Solidarity Campaign.' *European Review of History* 21, 4 (2014): 467–484.

Lázaro Lorente, Luis Miguel. *La Escuela Moderna de Valencia*. Valencia: Generalitat Valenciana, 1989.

Levy, Carl. 'Social Histories of Anarchism.' *Journal for the Study of Radicalism* 4, 2 (2010): 1–44.

Levy, Carl. 'The Rooted Cosmopolitan: Errico Malatesta: Syndicalism, Transnationalism and the International Labour Movement.' In Berry and Bantman, *New Perspectives on Anarchism*, 61–79.

Linden, Marcel van der. 'Second Thoughts on Revolutionary Syndicalism.' *Labour History Review* 63, 2 (1998): 182–196.

Linden, Marcel van der. 'The Many Faces of Dutch Revolutionary Trade Unionism.' In Linden and Thorpe, *Revolutionary Syndicalism*, 45–57.

Linden, Marcel van der, and Wayne Thorpe, eds. *Revolutionary Syndicalism: An International Perspective*. Aldershot: Scolar Press, 1990.

Linden, Marcel van der, and Wayne Thorpe. 'The Rise and Fall of Revolutionary Syndicalism.' In van der Linden and Thorpe, *Revolutionary Syndicalism*, 1–24.

Litvak, Lily. 'Estudio preliminar.' In *El Cuento Anarquista (1880–1911): Antología*, edited by Lily Litvak, 7–60. Madrid: Fundación de Estudios Libertarios Anselmo Lorenzo, 2003.

Madrid Santos, Francisco. 'La prensa anarquista y anarcosindicalista en España desde la I Internacional hasta el fin de la Guerra Civil.' PhD thesis, Barcelona: Universidad Central de Barcelona, 1988–1989. Published online, accessed 12 May, 2012. http://cedall.org/Documentacio/Castella/cedall203410101.htm.

Madrid Santos, Francisco. *Solidaridad Obrera y el periodismo de raíz ácrata*. Badalona: Ediciones Solidaridad Obrera, 2007.

Mitchell, Barbara. 'French Syndicalism: An Experiment in Practical Anarchism.' In Linden and Thorpe, *Revolutionary Syndicalism*, 25–42.

Pérez Sánchez, Guillermo Ángel. *Ser trabajador: Vida y respuesta obrera (Valladolid, 1875–1931)*. Valladolid: Universidad de Valladolid, 1996.

Portella Coll, Josep. 'Juan Mir i Mir: Obra anarquista 1898–1915.' *Revista de Menorca* 27 (1988): 101–244.

Radcliff, Pamela Beth. *From Mobilization to Civil War: The Politics of Polarization in the Spanish City of Gijón, 1900–1937*. Cambridge: Cambridge University Press, 1996.

Ribera, Anna, and Alejandro de la Torre. 'Memoria libertaria: Usos del calendario militante del anarquismo hispanoamericano.' *Historias* 75 (2010): 105–124.

Romanos, Eduardo. 'Factionalism in Transition: A Comparison of Ruptures in the Spanish Anarchist Movement.' *Journal of Historical Sociology* 24, 3 (2011): 355–380.

Romanos, Eduardo. 'Emotions, Moral Batteries and High-Risk Activism: Understanding the Emotional Practices of the Spanish Anarchists under Franco's Dictatorship.' *Contemporary European History* 23, 4 (2014): 545–564.

Romero Maura, Joaquín. *La rosa de fuego: Republicanos y anarquistas: La política de los obreros barceloneses entre el desastre colonial y la Semana Trágica.* Barcelona: Ediciones Grijalbo, 1975.

Romero Salvadó, Francisco J. *Spain, 1914–1918: Between War and Revolution.* London: Routledge, 1999.

Ryley, Peter. '*The Manifesto of the Sixteen:* Kropotkin's Rejection of Anti-Militarism and His Critique of the Politics of Peace.' In Adams and Kinna, *Anarchism 1914–18*, 49–68.

Schubert, Adrian. *The Road to Revolution in Spain: The Coal Miners of Asturias, 1860–1934.* Chicago: University of Illinois Press, 1987.

Shaffer, Kirwin R. 'Tropical Libertarians: Anarchist Movements and Networks in the Caribbean, Southern United States and Mexico, 1890s–1920s.' In *Anarchism and Syndicalism in the Colonial and Postcolonial World, 1870–1940: The Praxis of National Liberation, Internationalism and Social Revolution,* edited by Steven Hirsch and Lucien van der Walt, 273–320. Leiden-Boston: Brill, 2010.

Shaffer, Kirwin R. 'Panama Red: Anarchist Politics and Transnational Networks in the Panama Canal Zone, 1904–1913.' In *In Defiance of Boundaries: Anarchism in Latin American History,* edited by Geoffroy de Laforcade and Kirwin R. Shaffer, 57–80. Gainesville: University Press of Florida, 2015.

Smith, Angel. *Anarchism, Revolution and Reaction: Catalan Labour and the Crisis of the Spanish State, 1898–1923.* New York: Berghahn, 2007.

Soriano, Ignacio, and Francisco Madrid Santos. 'Antología documental del anarquismo español VI.I: Bibliografía del anarquismo en España, 1868–1939, Enriquecida con notas y comentarios.' 5th edition, 2012. Published online, accessed 12 December, 2012. http://cedall.org/Documentacio/Castella/cedall 203410103.htm.

Spiegeleer, Cristoph de. '"The Blood of Martyrs Is the Seed of Progress": The Role of Martyrdom in Socialist Death Culture in Belgium and the Netherlands, 1880–1940.' *Mortality* 19, 2 (2014): 184–205.

Thorpe, Wayne. 'Keeping the Faith: The German Syndicalists in the First World War.' *Central European History* 33, 2 (2000): 195–216.

Thorpe, Wayne. 'The European Syndicalists and War, 1914–1918.' *Contemporary European History* 10, 1 (2001): 1–24.

Thorpe, Wayne. 'El Ferrol, Rio de Janeiro, Zimmerwald and Beyond: Syndicalist Internationalism, 1914–1918.' *Revue belge de philology d'histoire* 84, 4 (2006): 1005–1023.

Thorpe, Wayne. 'Uneasy Family: Revolutionary Syndicalism in Europe from the *Charte d'Amiens* to World War I.' In Berry and Bantman, *New Perspectives on Anarchism,* 16–42. Newcastle-upon-Tyne: Cambridge Scholars Publishing, 2010.

Tuñón de Lara, Manuel. *El movimiento obrero en la historia de España.* Barcelona: Editorial Laia, 1977.

Ullman, Joan Connelly. *The Tragic Week: A Study of Anticlericalism in Spain.* Cambridge: Harvard University Press, 1968.

Velasco Núñez, Alfredo. *El hilo negro vasco: Anarquismo y anarcosindicalismo en el País Vasco (1870–1936).* Bilbao: Martxoak, 2009.

Yeoman, James Michael. 'The Spanish Anarchist Movement at the Outbreak of the First World War: A Crisis of Ideological Neutrality.' In *Shaping Neutrality Throughout the First World War*, edited by José Leonardo Ruíz Sánchez, Inmaculada Cordero Olivero and Carolina García Sanz, 83–101. Sevilla: Universidad de Sevilla, 2015.

Zambrana, Joan. 'El anarquismo organizado en los orígenes de la CNT: *Tierra y Libertad*, 1910–1919.' 2009. Published online, accessed 21 January, 2013. http://cedall.org/Documentacio/IHL/Tierra%20y%20Libertad%201910-1919.pdf.

Zambrana, Joan. 'La asamblea de sociedades obreras-Mataró-18/10/1914: Una repuesta unitaria del movimiento obrero ante la crisis de trabajo en los inicios de la I Guerra mundial.' 2010. Published online, accessed 12 March, 2012. http://cedall.org/Documentacio/IHL/LA%20ASAMBLEA%20DE%20MATARO%20DEL%2018.pdf.

Zambrana, Joan. 'El movimiento obrero catalán en el periódico *Solidaridad Obrera*, (1907–1919).' 2012. Published online, accessed 11 December, 2012. www.cedall.org/Documentacio/IHL/MovObreroCat%20Solidaridad%20Obrera%201907%201919.pdf.

Zambrana, Joan. 'La CNT y la Asamblea de Valencia (Mayo 1916): Un estudio sobre la CNT y el proceso aglutinado de un bloque sindical y social contra la crisis de subsistencias y la represión del movimiento obrero español.' 2014. Published online, accessed 8 June, 2014. www.cedall.org/Documentacio/IHL/LA%20CNT%20Y%20LA%20ASAMBLEA%20DE%20VALENCIA.pdf.

Website Content

Cartoliste. 'Verdadera efigie de Francisco Ferrer sacrificado en los fosas de Montjuich.' Accessed 5 April, 2018. https://cartoliste.ficedl.info/article299.html?lang=fr.

Conclusion

The formation of a mass anarchist organisation in Spain looked unlikely in 1890, when the movement was in disarray, and even more so in 1896, when anarchism faced severe repression. Anarchism not only survived through this period, it then expanded at a scale and speed which was unprecedented in its history, largely in the absence of a national organisation or a recognised leadership. Instead, it relied upon the fragile, contested, informal structures created by publishing groups and distributors. The plural, heterodox word of local anarchist publishing never disappeared from the movement, but it was superseded, and never again had the significance it had held in the years between 1890 and 1915. After this point, anarchists in Spain were not only part of a movement, but also an organisation; as well as a local periodical, they now had a paper. The consolidation of these two institutions cemented Barcelona's position as the focal point of the movement. Whereas in 1890–1915 the city had been the tacit centre of anarchism in Spain, it was now its undisputed headquarters. Despite numerous disputes, difficulties and suppression, the CNT and *Solidaridad Obrera* remained the prime markers of anarchist identity in Spain until the Civil War of 1936–1939.

In 1915 Spain was the only country in the world where anarchism had a mass following and a national organisation of substantial support, which it would maintain until 1939. For some scholars, it is only after the consolidation of the CNT that anarchism in Spain becomes worthy of serious discussion, as before this point it was just like any other anarchist movement: violent, irrational, fragmented and difficult to examine.[1] Yet the strength of anarchism in Spain had much older and much deeper roots than the statutes and programmes of the CNT. The cultural foundations of anarchism in Spain stretched back to the 1860s, and developed significantly over the turn of the century. The strong anarchist tradition in Spain was thus crucial in shaping the CNT's development as a decentred, flexible, porous and popular organisation. Print played a crucial role in this development. It gave the movement its words, its ideas, its martyrs, heroes and villains, its news, and its campaigns. It also gave anarchism a structure. The networks of producers, distributors and readers of print sustained the movement, providing a framework in which the grassroots could communicate and collaborate with one another. Although this system broke down on numerous occasions it was also remarkably durable, and succeeded—where anarchist movements in other countries failed—in making anarchism compatible with mass support by ingraining the movement's ideas and practices within the cultural fabric of communities across Spain. This reservoir of support was maintained during future periods of repression, most notably during the dictatorship of Primo de Rivera (1923–1930), allowing the movement to spring back to life during the Second Republic. Even decades of fierce repression under the rule of Francisco Franco did not fully quell the movement, which reappeared after the dictator's death in 1975. Although its support soon faded, the initial post-Franco resurgence of anarchism in Spain gave hope to many within the movement that a return to the strength it had in the early twentieth century was possible.[2]

Rather than a linear story of increasing homogenisation, anarchism in Spain from 1890 to 1915 was marked by repeated cycles of greater or lesser accommodation between the many elements of anarchist theory and practice. From 1890 to 1915 the anarchist movement in Spain experimented with three strategies for bringing forth the revolution. At first, some turned to violence, seeking to spark an immediate, revolutionary reaction from the working class. Their interpretation of anarchist theory led them to see the state as the source of violent oppression, which could only be overcome by an equally violent response. Others rejected this strategy as morally unacceptable, and correctly predicted the immense damage that it would do to the movement. These differences accentuated existing divisions, exposing the fragility of the plural, fissiparous nature of anarchism, and hastened its collapse in the 1890s. As the movement reformed after the 'disaster' of 1898, it turned away from violence and adopted a gradualist strategy of education. Cultural practices flourished, expanding and implementing anarchist theory in areas which had hitherto been neglected. Once again, however, differences emerged about the correct application of theory, and by 1904 a string of setbacks provoked serious divisions over strategy. Finally, the movement turned towards syndicalism, seen by many a new means of organising the working class while remaining true to anarchist principles of individual autonomy. Despite external pressures and internal disputes over the validity of this strategy, syndicalism was eventually accommodated, becoming the tactic of choice for the majority of anarchists in Spain. The resulting movement was far from uniform. Anarchism remained a nebulous, malleable ideology, and the movement continued to hold many seemingly contradictory ambitions and identities.

Although the specific development of anarchism in Spain was unique, it bears comparison with many other movements in history. Anarchism is not the only ideology to have advocated decentralised, local action above hierarchy and bureaucracy. It was by no means the only movement to advocate violence, education, or organisation as political strategies. The success of anarchism in Spain may appear out of time in the context of the early twentieth century, appearing alongside the growth of social democracy, communism and fascism, all of which looked towards the state, to some degree, as the means of bringing political and social change. If we look at the way in which anarchism was culturally constructed, however, we can find numerous similarities with these contemporary movements, as well as with those of previous and subsequent eras. The notion that a movement can form through collaborative media is now common amongst scholars of contemporary social and political movements, such as those which emerged during the Arab Spring of 2010–2011.[3] The 'horizontalist connectivity' of these movements is sometimes presented as a new phenomenon, produced by globalisation and facilitated by new forms of social media.[4] This study has demonstrated that a similar process was evident in the formation of the anarchist movement in Spain, through much older—yet equally 'social'—forms of media, namely books, pamphlets, broadsides and, above all, periodicals. Attention to media helps to explain how these processes take place, the meaning of discourse and ideology, and the ways in which the construction and transmission of ideas affect their realisation in practice.

Focusing on media also highlights the ways in which bottom-up movements operate across boundaries within and between nations. In Spain, the anarchist press provided a forum in which local struggles were used to articulate universal truths. Print networks also made translocal action possible, creating and managing networks of exchange, which gave a practical significance to ideas such as solidarity, unity, and organisation. Outside Cataluña, this system was often the only means by which disparate groups of anarchists could participate in the movement. A reliance on the structures created within and between publishing groups and the movement also created informal hierarchies and elites. The press also reveals the ebbs, flows and shifting geographies of anarchist support. The presence of anarchist publishing in an area marked it out within the movement, giving local activists an opportunity to share their thoughts and experiences across the whole of the country. Press correspondents ensured that areas of support remained in contact with one another, sustaining a multidirectional flow of information between the producers and readers of print. Anarchist support was strengthened and maintained by these bonds, and weakened when they broke down.

The formation of the anarchist movement in Spain was an on-going, dynamic process.[5] Assumptions about what anarchism was, based on behaviour, or a fastidious reading on anarchist theory, do little to explain what the movement meant to its grassroots support. This investigation has sought to avoid presumptions about what anarchism was, or question why it was so prevalent in Spain. Instead, it has sought to understand how anarchism developed in Spain, in the words of those who belonged to the movement.

Anarchist periodicals represent the site where the movement came together, where ideology developed and where the boundaries of good anarchist practice were established. They give us a sense of what anarchism meant, and how this meaning developed over time. In many cases this has produced a confused, imprecise depiction of anarchism, which is appropriate for an ideology which professed to loathe dogma and regulation. For a researcher, anarchism can seem a bewildering collection of thoughts, experiences, emotions, traditions and practices; just as it would to a contemporary reader of the anarchist press. The task has been to reflect this plurality, and explain how it coalesced and operated as a movement.

This study has focused on print as a means to explore the anarchist experience from 1890–1915. It has engaged with ideology, discourse and practice, in regards to their construction and transmission in the periodical press. It has shown the convergences and contradictions within the movement, the successes, missteps and contingencies which shaped the development of anarchism in Spain. Above all, it has shown that being an anarchist from 1890–1915 meant engaging with print. Print reflected the experience of the anarchist movement in Spain and, in doing so, fundamentally shaped its formation.

Notes

1. Julián Casanova, 'Terror and Violence: The Dark Face of Spanish Anarchism,' *International Labour and Working-Class History* 67 (2005): 80.
2. Ángel Herrerín López, *La CNT durante el franquismo: Clandestinidad y exilio (1939–1975)* (Madrid: Siglo XXI, 2004); Maggie Torres, *Anarchism and Political Change in Spain: Schism, Polarisation and Reconstruction of the Confederación Nacional del Trabajo, 1939–1979* (Brighton: Sussex Academic Press, 2019).
3. Gilad Lotan, Erhardt Graeff, Mike Ananny, Devin Gaffney, Ian Pearce and Danah Boyd, 'The Revolutions Were Tweeted: Information Flows during the 2011 Tunisian and Egyptian Revolutions,' *International Journal of Communication* 5 (2011): 1375–1405; Paolo Gerbaudo, *Tweets and the Streets: Social Media and Contemporary Activism* (London: Pluto, 2012).
4. Habibul Haque Khondker, 'The Role of the New Media in the Arab Spring,' *Globilizations* 8, 5 (2011): 675–679.
5. Richard Cleminson, *Anarchism, Science and Sex: Eugenics in Eastern Spain, 1900–1937* (Oxford: Peter Lang, 2000), 255.

Bibliography

Secondary Sources

Casanova, Julián. 'Terror and Violence: The Dark Face of Spanish Anarchism.' *International Labour and Working-Class History* 67 (2005): 79–99.
Cleminson, Richard. *Anarchism, Science and Sex: Eugenics in Eastern Spain, 1900–1937.* Oxford: Peter Lang, 2000.

Gerbaudo, Paolo. *Tweets and the Streets: Social Media and Contemporary Activism*. London: Pluto, 2012.

Haque Khondker, Habibul. 'The Role of the New Media in the Arab Spring.' *Globalizations* 8, 5 (2011): 675–679.

Herrerín López, Ángel. *La CNT durante el franquismo: Clandestinidad y exilio (1939–1975)*. Madrid: Siglo XXI, 2004.

Lotan, Gilad, Erhardt Graeff, Mike Ananny, Devin Gaffney, Ian Pearce, and Danah Boyd. 'The Revolutions Were Tweeted: Information Flows During the 2011 Tunisian and Egyptian Revolutions.' *International Journal of Communication* 5 (2011): 1375–1405.

Torres, Maggie. *Anarchism and Political Change in Spain: Schism, Polarisation and Reconstruction of the Confederación Nacional del Trabajo, 1939–1979*. Brighton: Sussex Academic Press, 2019.

Index

Sánchez Duque, José 212, 237
Sánchez Rosa, José 23, 72, 144, 155, 219, 234–235, 244–246
Santander (city and province) 10, 120, 136–137, 144–145, 150, 220, **221**, 233–234
schooling 121, 131–136, 151–162; free, integral, modern 131–134, 151–155, 162, 207, 225; gender and 132–133, 152–153, 154–155; local schools 155–162; *see also* Escuela Moderna; literacy
Second Spanish Republic 13, 162, 275
Sevilla (city) 23–24, 77, 167–168, 218–219, 246; and anarchist print *11, 45, 80, 149,* 234–235, *236;* and education 160; strikes in 123, 158, 223–224, 230; support from 212–214, 220
Sevilla (province) **10,** 21, 147, 150, **213, 221**
Sierra Álvarez, Pedro 202, 208, 212–217, 230; and the First World War 241–244, **245**
Silva Leal, Manuel (pseud. el Lebrijano) 72, 74–76; *see also* martyrdom, Jerez martyrs
socialism 2–4, 7, 125–126, 135–136, 200, 209–210, 231
socialist education 121, 135–136, 150
socialist press 9, 42, 231; *see also El Socialista* (Madrid)
Sola, Francisco 156, 166; *see also* Cuba; teachers; *Tierra y Libertad* (Madrid)
Solidaridad Obrera (Barcelona) 48, 199–202, 210–214, 219–220, 226, 237; daily edition 15, 27, 216, 222–223, 239, 246–249; and the First World War 240–243; repression 205, 224–225
Solidaridad Obrera (Gijon) 43–44, 208–212, 212–214, 217, 249
Solidaridad Obrera Workers' Federation, Galicia 203, 219
Solidaridad Obrera Workers' Federation, Gijón 202–203, 208–209, 230–231
solidarity campaigns 25–26, 42, 47–48, 82, 92, 95, 101
South Wales (Dowlais and Abercrave) 17–18, *45,* 207, 227–228, 241, 244
Spanish Civil War 13, 156, 162, 234, 239, 275

state, the 16–18, 98–100, 125–126, 133, 137–141, 157, 199, 205, 210, 234, 275–276; attacks on 3, 66–67, 128, 207; *see also* nefarious trilogy
state of war 63, 82, 158–159; *see also* repression
strikes 9, 41, 93–94, 102, 145, 167, 203, 208–209, 218, 228, 232; 1890–1891 Cádiz 67–68; 1901 Gijón 123, 211; 1901 Sevilla 24, 123; 1902 Andalucía 158–159; 1902 Barcelona 163; 1903 Cádiz 163–164 (*see also* Alcalá del Valle uprising); 1909–1911 (throughout) 204–206; 1909 Barcelona 204–206 (*see also* Tragic Week); 1910 Gijón 217; 1910 Huelva 219; 1911 September strike wave 13, 223–226; 1912 Railworkers 228; 1912 Sevilla 230; during the First Republic 3–4; in response to First World War 240, 244–246; strike-breakers (*esquiroles*) 201–202; strike relief and funds 47, 160, 222, 234
subscribers 4, 18, 42–44, 49–52, 89, 138, 146, 156, 222, 235, 247–248; remittances 18, 51, 226, 230–231; to rival papers 130, 160; subscription lists 77, 85, 94–95, 225
Suplemento a la Revista Blanca 48, 122–126, 129–130, 134, 140–141, 147–148, 153, 157; campaigns against repression 97, 123; conversion to *Tierra y Libertad* 165–166; launch 97, 123; print run 51–52
syndicalism 22–23, 26–27, 126, 198–200, 208–212, 226–229, 240, 246, 275; anarcho-syndicalism 2, 5, 211, 215, 227, 237–239; debates over 49–50, 208–212, 216–220, 225–226, 232–235, 243; international 17–18, 200–201, 240–241, 244; as a 'new' idea 203, 231, 242, 247; and socialism 214–215; spread in Spain 201–204, 208, 214–223, 229–230, 237–239, 249

Taboada, Enrique 156, 177n171, 183n300
Tárrida del Marmól, Fernando 17, 99, 140
teachers 24, 91, 97, 134, 156–158

AK PRESS is small, in terms of staff and resources, but we also manage to be one of the world's most productive anarchist publishing houses. We publish close to twenty books every year, and distribute thousands of other titles published by like-minded independent presses and projects from around the globe. We're entirely worker run and democratically managed. We operate without a corporate structure—no boss, no managers, no bullshit.

The **FRIENDS OF AK PRESS** program is a way you can directly contribute to the continued existence of AK Press, and ensure that we're able to keep publishing books like this one! Friends pay $25 a month directly into our publishing account ($30 for Canada, $35 for international), and receive a copy of every book AK Press publishes for the duration of their membership! Friends also receive a discount on anything they order from our website or buy at a table: 50% on AK titles, and 30% on everything else. We have a Friends of AK ebook program as well: $15 a month gets you an electronic copy of every book we publish for the duration of your membership. *You can even sponsor a very discounted membership for someone in prison.*

Email **friendsofak@akpress.org** for more info, or visit the website: **https://www.akpress.org/friends.html**.

There are always great book projects in the works—so sign up now to become a Friend of AK Press, and let the presses roll!